**WITHDRAWN
NDSU**

THE TAJ MAHAL GARDEN

From a native artist's painting on elephant-tusk ivory, in author's collection.

> "Anemones and Seas-of-Gold,
> And newblown lilies of the river,
> And those sweet flow'rets that unfold
> Their buds in Camadera's quiver."
> (Moore: Lalla Rookh ... Light of the Harem.)

The history of Shah Jahan and his Mumtaz-i-Mahal is evidence that True Romance exists among Garden-lovers everywhere. This, from where heather purples the moors of Annie Laurie's home, thru the Sunny Italy of Romeo and Juliet, out to the Land of Lalla Rookh, who had "passed all her life in the Gardens of Delhi."

The garden idea apparently dominated the Grand Mogul's mind. When Mumtaz-i-Mahal, in 1629, died at Burhanpur in childbed of her eighth child, the Shah refused to be consoled. Her body was moved to the Agra Garden. There, afterward, the Taj was built. Oriental love of perfume-laden garden flowers is crystallized into an inscription at the Taj:—"May this grave ever be fragrant."

Shah Jahan seems to have found consolation in building his garden tomb. On this desk is an estimate of its cost:—More than 30,000,000 rupees. ($10,000,000). This, where writer paid his coolies the fixed 4-cent daily wage. Shah Jahan's workers were mostly slaves from that Great Mogul's conquests.

The Taj Garden motif was carried indoors. The Taj's white marbles are inlaid in flower designs with precious stones. The garden apparently was designed by some forgotten Italian landscape-artist. The architect of the building ("the world's most beautiful"), was Austin of Bordeaux. His Gallic imagination is credited with these pleasing indoor inlays of flowers. The cypresses repeatedly are replaced when they obstruct view of the Taj.

COPYRIGHT 1955
BY
C. M. GOETHE

PRINTED IN THE UNITED STATES OF AMERICA
BY
THE KEYSTONE PRESS
SACRAMENTO, CALIFORNIA

Garden Philospher

BY

C. M. GOETHE

Author of Elfin Forest; Seeking to Serve; What's In a Name; Geogardening; Sierran Cabin From Skyscraper; War Profits and Better Babies; Pomegranate Blossom; Where Queen and Pope Failed; New Wine From Old Bottles; Luther Wong, Coolie; Gambling for Dulces; A Playground Hard by a Temple of Hate; Children of Loneliness; Immigration Into New France; Peons Need Not Apply; Filipino Immigration Viewed As a Peril; Russia's Future and Ours; Guano; Extinction of the Inca Highcastes; Eugenics in Postage Stamps; Sunworshipping Conservation; Gretchen of Hildesheim, (a story of the *Kleingartenvertrieb*); Bird Music for the Blind; Czechoslovakia Caught in a Nutcracker; Overpopulation in Java; Dr. Jan Mjoen's Windern Laboratorium; Eugenic Aspects of Famine in Hindustan; Translation France's *Code de la Famille;* Eugenist at CroMagnon; Eugenic Aspects of Life in the Sahara; Albuquerque—And After; 45% College Women Do Not Marry; Is Population Pessimism Justified?; Eugenical Studies in Korea; Eugenical Aspects of Iceland's Conquest of Illiteracy; Europe's Mistress system; Finland's Heterogeneity.

VI

SB
453
G62

THIS LITTLE BOOK
LOVINGLY IS DEDICATED
TO THE MEMORY
OF GRANDFATHER MATTHIAS, MARTYR,—
OF GRANDFATHER PIERRE, EXILE,—
OF FATHER, BOOMERANG-LAND'S NATURE LOVER,—
OF MOTHER, TEACHER AS TO GOD-IN-NATURE,—

AND

OF MY SWEETHEART,
GARDEN-PHILOSOPHER EXTRAORDINARY,
WHO KNEW ALSO THE GARDENS OF THE SKY, AND
WHO ENVISIONED THE URGENT NEED OF REDUCING
BIOLOGICAL, AS WELL AS ASTRONOMICAL ILLITERACY.

VIII

God Almighty first Planted a Garden. And indeed, it is the Greatest Refreshment to the Spirit of Man; without which Buildings and *Pallaces* are but Grosse Handy-works.

(Francis Bacon, Essay XLVI, "Of Gardens")

―――o―――

Even the Gentle Carpenter of Nazareth did not find our Garden flowers beneath His notice when He sought for examples for His parable:—

"Consider the lilies of the field, how they grow; they toil not, neither do they spin. And yet I say unto you: That even Solomon, in all his glory was not arrayed like one of these."

―――o―――

"Underlying our inquiries, (as to God, or Nature or Man), is a first philosophy. It seeks to ascertain the principles of knowledge, and the causes of things." (Voltaire)

―――o―――

"When Jesus had spoken these words, He went forth with His disciples over the brook Cedron, WHERE THERE WAS A GARDEN." (John XVIII:1)

―――o―――

"A place called Gethsemane." Matthew XXVI:36)

CONTENTS

	Page
1. History	1-44
2. Paleobotany	45-82
3. Food	83-112
4. Reproduction	113-138
5. Insects	139-154
6. Birds	155-180
7. Humans	181-204
8. Color and Scent	205-214
9. Cooperation	215-218
10. Selection, Survival	219-258
11. Camouflage	259-266
12. The Niche	267-278
13. Names, Geogardening	279-286
14. "Hewers of Wood, Drawers of Water"	287-290
15. The Garden's Eugenical Thoughts	291-300
16. God-in-Nature	301-320

X

FOREWORD

At the very beginning, a record of humility.

The word "Philosopher" in this title is used with its primitive meaning. May it be remembered that, in ancient Athens, there grew up the "Sophists", selfstyled "Wise Men", (Greek *sophos*—wise). Socrates commenced asking these Sophists embarrassing questions. He knew said Sophists (like some public letterwriters of today's Hindustan), were grafters. Socrates, therefore, disclaimed being any "reservoir of wisdom". No Sophist, he was only one who humbly had *"phileo"* (love) of *"sophia"* (wisdom). He was a mere Searcher for the Truth....

And so, you Gentle Reader, you and I do not claim to be bursting with wisdom, do we? We are mere "lovers of wisdom", PHILOSOPHERS IN THE ANCIENT SENSE. As we spade a bed, and turn up a scarab larva—or set out seedlings from a flat, full of joy anticipating the coming harvest —or clip sweet peas with Shylock-like avarice to force more blooms,—or look in amazement on a beefly's mimicry of the honey-maker,—or watch a purplethroat forage the tritomas' nectar-laden trumpets,—or an Anna's hummingbird's "wedding dance" with all the mystery of sex, (Mother Nature's crowning invention)—we, you and I, possess *phileo* or love for the *sophia* or wisdom of these thousand books—the flowers, the shrubs, the trees, the insects, the birds of our garden. We are, are we not, just simply Lovers of that elusive but charming WISDOM?

XII

PROLOGUE

New moon, First Quarter, Full Moon, Last Quarter—and that Luna fades to a fingernail-pareing Crescent. So with Life. One may be spared into the Last Quarter, into the Four Score Years. If, during those decades one, an ardent gardener, has been owner of a string of ranches, (wherein survival depended upon alertness to new mutations of plant breeders, also upon ever watching for improvements in his own livestock)—If those decades also included being under every flag, (except perhaps a half dozen), where one has enjoyed contacts which perhaps carry also a duty to record impressions, one feels an urge to reduce them to "between covers".

The wanderings under those many flags brought glimpses. Thus came talks with the plant breeders of Holland, Denmark, France, Germany. They yielded "look-sees" at gardens of Chinese mandarins. (There one sensed a symbolism at which an Occidental boor could only guess)—at the dwarf gardens of Japanese intellectuals—(and of their flower arrangement indoors, always a source of delight—and of wonder.)... Came, also talks with Abbotts of Buddhist monasteries. (Once, when stricken in the jungle, there was a convalescence which brought a lengthened opportunity to learn with deep admiration how these gifted men have watched—century after century,—for mutations.) ... Days with orchid professionals in the deep jungle,—(as eager to gain a "stake" as any goldseeker on California's Mother Lode or in the Klondike.) ... With keeneyed breeders of peonies in China as masterful in organizing the unceasing hunt for *sauvage* mutations as a Caravan King in Palestine or Anatolia in managing his strings of camels fanning out all over the Back of Beyond. Likewise watching the instinctive Motherlove of a woman finding expression in tending a couple of pots of geraniums in the slums of Strassburg. (Papa Dachert had good selective material for his Jardins Ungemach tenants.) ... Also similarly pathetic tins containing miniature cacti and succulents in windows where, in Midnight Sun Land, Norway's North Cape looks out toward Spitzbergen.

Carefully notebooked conversation with such a wide range of garden philosophers must have yielded some golden nuggets among much gravel. These have been treasured during those many years. This book is an attempt to melt them down into a form that may prove worth the reader's passing attention.

XIV

A YARN ABOUT BALUCHISTAN, NEAR WHERE GARDEN-ART ORIGINATED

If he lives long enuf, a philosophizing gardener learns something about Time's disappointments. He therefore treasures the brightly humorous incidents that, fortunately, are contrasted against the drab bits of Life's mosaic. Perhaps a recording of one may be forgiven:—

It happened in San Francisco,* the week United Nations was born. Writer had been asked to a little St. Francis Hotel meeting. This, because of something he had done in the Far East after the Russo-Japanese War. But, as Kipling would say, "THAT is another story." The meeting finished, this author was emerging from the elevator into the hotel lobby. A book, along with a fountain pen, was thrust into his face. "I just MUST have your autograph! And from what country are YOU a delegate?" The speaker was a nervous, sharp-nosed woman, in, say, the 40's.

The sudden attack left one momentarily nonplussed. Then to one's rescue came one's sense of humor. "I? Why, I'm from Baluchistan." She was perplexed, "Baluchistan? Baluchistan?? Have I that country on my list? Where IS Baluchistan" "OH! come now. Surely you Americans are not THAT ignorant of geography! Out our way, we add 'STAN' to any tribal name. Arabi-stan is the Arab's region. I think you call it 'Arabia!' Turke-stan is Turks' Land. Kurdi-stan belongs to the Kurds,—Afgani-stan, to the Afgans. Baluchi-stan is the Fatherland of us Baluchis!"

Despite a sternly-suppressed smile, she must have caught the eye's twinkle. "Give me back my book and pen. You're spoofing me" ... THAT autograph hound trotted off for another victim.

Above story from Gardening's birthplace is risked relating here because, beneath whatever humor-value it may have, it safely can be used as the locus of a bit of history, whereof the concept of CO-OPERATION, (taught by certain garden flowers), may be worth reflection:—There once was a young Oriental. We are quite safe in calling him the Emir of Baluchistan. His boyhood had been saddened by that environment where Cooperation plummets to zero, i.e. the *harem*. As a wee laddie, he had suffered from plottings and intrigue that gravitate to that unfortunate child destined by all that is holy to be the next ruler. Sent to Europe to be educated, he was thrilled at Occidental progress. He later, because of his father's assassination, was recalled. A fatiguing camel trip over burning desert sands to his capital made him yearn for an automobile. The day after arrival he

---

* Today's is a very different San Francisco from writer's boyhood. Then, steampowered street cars ran on Market Street beyond Woodward's Gardens. Mission Dolores then centered a decaying village of adobes. Here was heard more Spanish than English. Mexican longhorn herds grazed on the hills behind the Mission. The Embarcadaro's streets then still buzzed with Comstock Lode stock deals' news. We boys then could go crabbing from Presidio Wharf. In sight were Fort Scott's guns, guarding the Golden Gate. It now is said to be covered by that Bridge's ramp.

announced reforms he had decided upon while jolting along those camel-trails' hot, dusty miles. Came ministers' scowls, mutterings. That initial conference over, the British Resident, his father's trusted friend, whispered: "Immediately assume camouflage as an insane *mullah**. Don ribboned rags and skedaddle." That night young Emir crossed the Border to safety. Ruler for less than one day, he thereafter lived, died in exile. . . .

You, too, may question whether the entire world, to which the United Nations tries to teach Cooperation is not somewhat like Kipling's Asia. If, at that task, you feel baffled, turn to your garden dandelions, daisies, sunflowers, asters, chrysanthemums. From these composites, Mother Nature almost shouts: "The Cooperators shall inherit the earth."

Current history, (including United Nations' happenings), comes over radio, also television, hourly. This, along with world series' innings, football scores. May it not be profitable to turn back History's pages? There is something to be gained, is there not, in contemplating the gardens of the England of Elizabeth I as well as Elizabeth II? Is there not forgotten wisdom in those of the days of Marcus Aurelius, of Socrates? Also, are not lessons preserved in Miocene, Eocene, even Cretaceous, Jurassic, Carboniferous floras? After all, was it not from those ancient plants our garden floras originated?

HOW TO INCREASE COOPERATION IS A DOMINANT PROBLEM INTRIGUING THE GARDEN-PHILOSOPHER

Perhaps it will help us puzzle out why sunflowers and Michaelmas daisies evolved. Perhaps reflection upon folkways expressed in gardening in Cuba, in Cape Colony, in Ceylon, in China, in Czechoslovakia, in Canada or in Crete, all these may help us understand why overseas's folks accept our help—then proceed to hate us cordially for being able to give it to them. If we can clean up the mess at the United Nations— even by trying to gain light from sympathetically studying the gardenings of many lands, and of various countries, may not we, ourselves, perhaps be able to form those sounder judgments which, some day, continually will lessen the numbers of International Wars, of Civil Wars. This just as successfully as Man abolished those Personal Wars he dubbed "Duels"?

---

* See also Kipling's Daniel Dravat in "The Man Who Would Be King."

> Even Horace, alarmed at Rome's decay, turned to the gardens of the sea for a parable: *"Et genus et virtus, nisi cum re villior ALGA est."* (Noble descent and worth, unless united with wealth, are esteemed no more than seaweed-manure.)

ITALY

San Gimanango's Towers, also City Walls, illustrate the cramping of centuries that made for their garden regimentation.

After our half-century's search, under almost every flag, for facts about the Philosophy of Gardening, We-2 still were puzzled. We recalled, however, the admonition of our philosophy professor:
"Philosophy's problems never will be solved."

Marshalling our collected data, we wondered whether gardening, as we of the Northwest European group* view same, is not part of the democratic process. Northwest European gardening is at least as much by the John Smiths as by the Percy Fauntleroys. The history of Northwest European Gardening, of even its Garden-Philosophy, may be telescoped into a few recent centuries. It is perhaps, as concentrated **GARDENS:—** as the golfing education of Mrs. Jones, wife of a **DEMOCRATIC,** certain Country Club member. The Pro had com- **AUTOCRATIC** pleted her first lesson the previous day. Now he met her coming out of the clubhouse. With her was another woman. He greeted her encouragingly:—"Good to see you so persistent. That is the way to learn,—lesson after lesson!" To this she indignantly replied "Lesson? Why I learned yesterday. Mrs. Brown, my friend, came to learn today."

Mrs. Jones, however, HAD learned a big lesson. One might question her one-day golf education. She, however, had found out how to

---

* This includes U.S.A., Canada, Australia, New Zealand, Nordic South Africa as well as the Baltic Nations, the Netherlands, and France.

telescope a lot of time into 24 hours. So, within the next few paragraphs we will recklessly, and with, perhaps, equally poor judgment, attempt likewise to telescope some items about the history of Gardening, hence of Garden Philosophy. This will include Northwest European as well as Oriental. . . .

FERTILE JAVA RICE PADDY

Did irrigation originate in Babylon or Egypt? Spain learned from the Moors Oriental gardening skills. Above rice paddy, Java, produces 5 crops every 2 years.

Crossing the Pyrenees, one may take the road of Andorra's smugglers. Or, he may climb into Italy thru French Alps' passes, their glaciers rosepink with alpenglow. On entering Spain, likewise Italy, one becomes conscious of another kind of gardening. Seldom does one see the tall pink hollyhocks, contrasted with blue delphiniums as at Stratford-on-Avon. He finds no plantings wayward as a wanderlusting Viking off Greenland's icy shores. There is little raggedy-taggedy like the aster drift at Kew. There is no urge to work for uncontrolled mass color, almost as wild as Scotland's purple moors. Instead one finds in Spain,—also in Italy,—stern regimentation. There also is far less color than is usual northward, as in the mottling of Holland's gardens. Instead one finds severely-restricted, clipped cypresses. One encounters even jail-like, pebbled paths. One finds more potted plants, altho the Mediterranean has far more sunshine than Edinburg, even London.

REGIMENTATION IN GARDENING

The Italian garden gives one of Covered Wagon descent a feeling of imprisonment. It is something like the experience We-2 had in visiting the home of our clansman, J. W. von Goethe in Frankfurt/a/M. Leaving Goethehaus, we crossed the Roemer. (This is where the fountains used to spout wine when the matter of a new Elector had been settled). We ventured into one of the narrow streets off the Roemer's square. It was so narrow that, by stretching out his arms, writer could touch with fingertips, the walls of the houses on either side. Doing this, behind was a voice with an unforgettable Texan drawl. Turning around, one saw he was a 6 foot 4 inch blueeyed rider from the Pecos ranges. He ejaculated:—"Say, Pardner, do you suppose humans live in these buildings?" Then he continued:—"Out in The Panhandle, when some squatter moves in within 10 miles, we jess reckon the air is getting polluted and we move on to new pastures."

The same regimentation that crowded homes within walls to survive an attack from another city-state, also sent towers skyward to be alert against feuds of family against family. All this restriction still is reflected in Italian gardening's regimentation. . . .

ASSYRIAN ROYAL PALACE AT NINEVEH
(Restored by Hayard)

Babylon's Hanging Gardens excited the admiration of Greek visitors. Nebuchadnezzar constructed same to satisfy a whim of his wife's Amytis. Tired of the monotony of the Babylonian plains, she longed for her native Media's mountains. These unique "gardens" apparently were built on the model of the pyramidal tower-temples. Stages were erected one upon another. The successive terraces, (which

BABYLON'S HANGING GARDENS

rose to a considerable height above Babylon), were covered and beautified with rare plants. This gave the appearance of a small verdure clad mountain. The gardens were irrigated by means of hydraulic devices which elevated and distributed Euphrates' water over the terraces.

Hormuzd Rassam's excavations, (circa 1880), made in the ruins of Babylon, indicated the so-called "Babel Mound", with ruined hydraulic works of great extent, reservoirs, stone-lined aqueducts. As these are the remains of the celebrated Gardens of Nebuchadnezzar....

CROCODILE-HEADED GOD

Lioness-headed Sekmet was the Egyptian Mars. Sobek, the crocodile-headed God of ancient Egypt was, however, the Water God. He presided over irrigated gardens and fields.

Of Egypt's gardens, we have glimpses in their cultivation of the lotus. Its blossoming, out of the black, (and often stinking) muck, seems to have inspired Eastern poets from the Nile to the Yangstekiang, and from B.C. 1950 to A.D. 1950. Most of the papyri on gardening probably were lost forever when Caesar's legions burned the precious Alexandrian library....

On Upper Nile one spring, We-2 were on Egyptology studies. All signs of curiosity-seeking tourists had melted with the oncoming summer heat. Only one other European was within miles. Let us call him "Stewart Pasha." He WAS a Pasha by royal Egyptian decree, a Scot by birth. He apparently was interested in quite a slice of Africa, including Uganda and Kenya, "the Sudan of Kipling's Fuzzywuzzys".

History 5

Now Africa is impressively big. Kenya Protectorate, for example, is larger than France. It stretches from its coastal fringe's mangrove-swamps across semidesert scrub, then parklike country with scattered baobab to Mt. Kenya's glaciers. Much of Kenya has so little rainfall, its only use is low-grade pasture.

Stewart Pasha's main concern, however, was Anglo-Egyptian Sudan. It was being developed to make English looms independent of our Dixieland. It, like Kenya, had, for centuries been a land of constant civil war between desert tribes. Even then there was overpopulation in proportion to food supply. Then had come the pithhelmeted blue-eyed, pink-cheeked British engineers. There Oxford and Cambridge men were making grow, where once even one blade of grass yellowed, many stems of long-staple cotton.

One fullmoon Stewart Pasha and We-2 sat under the gingerbread palms. Our only companions were two 4-foot greenstone statues of Sekmet, now forever silent lioness-headed Goddess of the Pharoahs. It was full moon. The shadows were as clear cut as if made by an en-

Photo: Courtesy New Zealand World War I History.

VILLAGE PUMP, PALESTINE
No water faucets here!

graver. The Negro drums were booming for the allnight dance. Stewart Pasha tapped one Sekmet statue impatiently with his cane. "I am here to serve. I ask myself: Why? This exile is awful. You-2 are the only Caucasians within many miles. British brains make possible, with irrigation, sanitation, and enforcement of peace, livings for 30,000,000 more." He repeated Kipling:—"Fuzzy-Wuzzy, with your 'ayrick 'ead of 'air, you big black boundin' beggar, you bruk a British square." Then he said, "When will the armed force of these 30,000,000 be cast into the scales against us?"

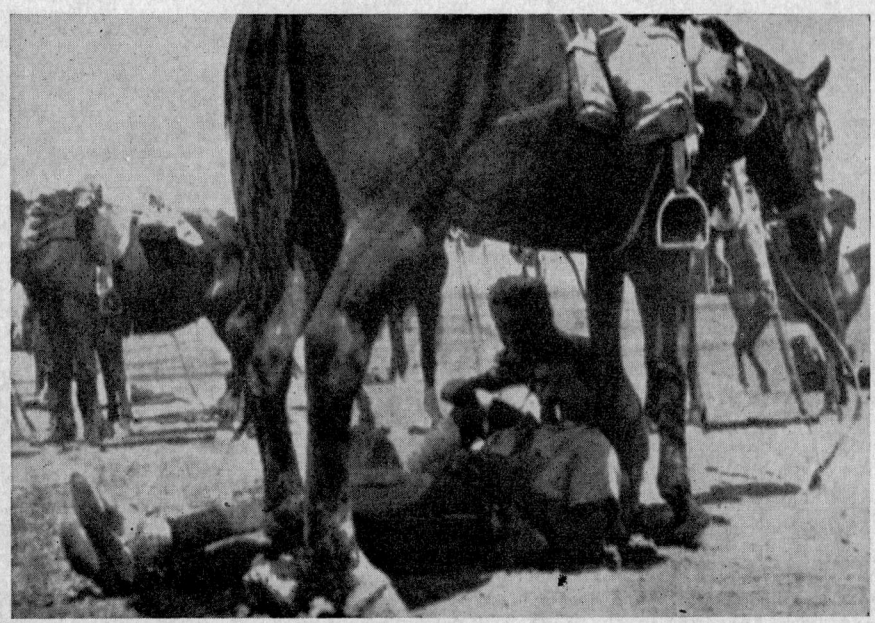

Photo: Courtesy New Zealand World War I History.

SHADE-LOVING ANZACS
Anzacs soon adopted one folkway of the "Shade-loving Moors."

There's a bower of roses by Bendemeer's stream,
And the nightingale sings round it all the day long,
In the time of my childhood 'twas like a sweet dream,
To sit in the roses and hear the bird's song.
(The Veiled Prophet of Kharassan)

Whether there was gardening, as we know it, in Ancient Egypt is problematical. If there was, there also came the beginning of garden philosophy. Some of Egypt's philosophic remnants preserved to our day are remarkable. The advice of one official to his departing son is almost as protectively canny as Polonius' in Shakespeare's Hamlet.

MOSLEM GARDENS

As to Moslem gardens, 'twas truly thrilling, exploring North

Africa's camel trails before France's brilliant army engineers netted it with military highways. Late one winter, We-2 were guests of a Sheik. It was at a little oasis on the "Trail Toward Timbuctu". Our host, an elderly man, resented said engineers' operations, then already commencing. Writer reminded him their artesian wells had expanded some oases' areas. He grumbled:—"We were better off when, as grass became exhausted, we moved our herds from place to place." Then, slapping his leg, he said:—"Our young men's muscles become flabby. No longer can they endure".

What interested Us-2, as garden devotees, was the way this patriarch showed us hospitality. His tablecloth was a long narrow Oriental rug. Its center had an earthenware bowl. In it were some oleander blooms.* Was all this a relic of original gardening:—Wildflowers in an earthenware bowl on an Oriental rug? This Sheik's rug design was distinctly floral....

As to garden philosophy, a rug in our own home also has a floral design, with, at one end, a cartouche. Neither the dealer from whom we purchased it, nor anyone else we questioned, could translate its motto. This, despite persistent trials. Finally, on one of our Mediterranean trips, writer purchased an Arab dictionary. This to familiarize him with that alphabet. He then carefully copied the inscription. Still no one could explain its meaning.

One unforgettable fullmoon week we were up-Nile. Thru 3 consecutive midnights we heard the all-night-long negro drum beatings. Our companion, Stewart Pasha, said:—"Those drums are beating from South-of-Cairo thru to The Cape." On that expedition we found next day a roadside artisan. He was sawing women's combs out of an elephant-ivory tusk. This had been bought from a northbound camel caravan. I asked him:—"Can you read this cartouche?" He replied:—"Yes, but it is not in Arabic. It is in Syriac. It is a Koran text:—'He has the greatest wealth who is CONTENT with that which Allah has bestowed upon him'." What philosophy captured in that gardening form rug!

ORIENTAL RUG MOTIFS Altho we Occidentals have developed gardening marvellously, must we not suspect said art had some origin in the Orient? The long use of blossoms and of leaves is evident in antique rugs of the Shiah Mohammedans. (The orthodox Sunni seem always to have held strictly to geometrical designs. These sternly puritanical Moslems apparently had little enjoyment of the beauty of flowers. One wonders if the rugs that Marco Polo praised were Sunnite or Shiah.)

---
* Oleanders grow along North African water courses much as do tamarisks in Palestine, willows in North America.

Conventionalized designs of iris, tulips, narcissi, anemones, lotus, as well as of butterflies are seen in writer's collection of rugs. Certain it is that the Grand Moguls, (who appreciated color in rubies, emeralds, turquoise, lapis lazuli, topazes), also loved color in their floral-design carpets. (May here be repeated a reminder "ANARKALI" that such colorful gems were used to give natural color to the flowers in the marble-inlay at Taj Mahal.) ... Anyone who has lived in Moslem lands cannot help being impressed with the deep love of flowers. It shows in their names of girl babies. From Morocco to the Punjab often one finds one named "Anarkali" (Pomegranate Blossom.) ...

Buddhist temples from Ceylon, across Burma and China, to Japan usually have gardens. These vary with their respective life zones. Emphasis is on trees and shrubs—less on herbaceous plants. Discussions with Buddhist priests as at the Temple of the Tooth at Kandy, also in Burma, China, Japan seem to indicate that plant-breeding, thru instinctive selection, has been continuous over many centuries. Might not folk, (credited with such inventions as the compass, gunpowder, papermaking), also be expected to persistently improve strains from peonies to peaches?

Almost side-by-side with Kandy's Temple-of-the Tooth is one of the world's most interesting gardens. It is the Botanical Garden and Agricultural Experiment Station of Peridenya. When We-2 were there, interesting experiments were being conducted to improve rubber-latex, also the extracts of citronella. Latter then were used to perfume the gaudy cheap soaps, usually dyed pink or green.

Another fascinating garden at the turn of this century was Royal Dutch Botanical Garden at Buitenzong, Java. One here could leisurely study such trees as the nutmeg, with its bright orange-colored seed-net, source of mace. Their single specimen of the "deadly" upas tree was shrub-sized. Writer managed however to crawl under it, just to prove that such action did not result in the fabled instant death.*

Green, from Morocco to Hindustan, from Anatolia to Somaliland, also to the Sahara, is always the Prophet's sacred color. An American, accustomed to summer rains from the Atlantic to the Rockies, can hardly sense Moslem reverence for sprouting vegetation's greenery. Once We-2 had been on the desert southeast from Damascus. We had en route, endured a depressing sandstorm. We had taken shelter in an illiterate native's hut. Outside, our poor camels moaned, trying to get their noses in a foothigh wall's lee. Some stones thereof bore Roman inscriptions that the Gallic legion once had been there. Next day we

---

* Read, however, Mr. Lovering's "The Tree that Hates" (Nature Magazine 1954). It describes experiences, (commencing with von Humboldt) of the tropical manchineel, cousin of our Christmas poinsettias. Ranging from Venezuela across the Caribbean, it is another example of how Everglades National Park is becoming a great University in Tropical Biology.

continued over a sand-blasted terrain toward Damascus. Out of this dreariness we suddenly came to the escarpment rim. Below lay centuries-old Damascus, an oasis of spring-fresh apricot foliage. Our servants knelt in adoration of the holy green. Our Christian Nordic hearts beat in unison. It was a rare spiritual experience.

Photo: Courtesy French Embassy.

ANGOR-WAT'S DOMES LOOM DEFIANTLY AGAINST A STORM

Oriental mystics who claim Aryan ancestry tell one Eastern architecture is based upon Nordic memory of the snow-shedding conifers of their Scandinavian Broodland. (See page 23) Why not re-read herein a book by writer's friend, the late Grant Madison's "Passing of the Great Race", Fourth Edition, pp. 67 to 70 on the Nordic Invaders of Hindustan about 1600 B.C. (p. 258). It is interesting to note that above book passed into several editions. His "Conquest of a Continent" he told this author "had been adroitly prevented a public, however, by U.S.A.'s unseen censorship."

For years thereafter we were to see much more of Moslem worship of the Prophet's color. On camel caravan routes we were to meet Mohammedans wearing the green turbans. Of these they were ostentatiously proud as evidence that they recently had kissed Mecca's holy Kaaba. . . . Coming out of Khyber Pass, we watched Afghans. Beards of elderly men were henna stained. Occasionally one, dyed green, evidenced it had crossed the burning sands to the Holy of Holies. In Somaliland We-2 found negroes trading ivory palm nuts. These later would appear as button material on the coats of Germans, also Americans. We found these diminutive Somalis, (the Japanese of East Africa), with kinky wool stained vermillion or canary. Here again several that had crossed the Straits to Arabia making pilgrimage to the Holy Shrine. They also were entitled to dye their hair, not plebian red or yellow, but the verdant shade sacred to Mohammed.

Spain's recent Civil War's outbreak brought regret to Us-2. We had arrived at University of Salamanca. This, to try to uncover possible data about Salamanca-Hebrew intellectuals' remarkable contributions to world culture. Arab civilization's main service seems to have been preservation of ancient Greek learning. This, those Hebrews bridged from the then-decadent Arab scholarship to Italy's Renaissance. Repeatedly we had revelled in the gardens of Moorish Spain, as will hereinafter be noted.

It was from the garden owners of Islam that we learned the delicacy of garden-gifts. When an Egyptian gentleman shows welcome by sending you a basket of his garden's pomegranates—an Algerian sheik a dish of his golden brown Deglet Noors—a Damascene citizen a bowl of sunripened apricots from the prized tree in his patio,—or a Moor a net of those sugary oranges we call Mediterranean Sweets, you have the thrill of Mohammedan welcome. . . .

OUR PATIO GARDENING IS ROOTED IN MOSLEM LANDS

As in modern Mexico, patio gardening is characteristic. The Mexican vogue is an inheritance from Moorish Spain. The Moors in turn developed this gardening technique from Anatolia.

Persian gardening had a profound influence on that of Hindustan, particularly in the Grand Moguls' Northwest. Chinese method also filtered thru into, not only Hindustan, but to Ceylon. In the Land of "Sinbad the Sailor and Fitbad the Tailor", they will tell you the Persian's nomads, while drifting from meager pasture to meager pasture, loved their wild tulips and narcissi. Hence an earthenware pot con-

History

taining not-too-much of precious water, would keep fresh a handful of these blooms at the center of an Oriental rug. This, spread on the sand floor inside the sheik's tent, was the tablecloth at which he dispensed the hospitality required by the Prophet.

COMORANTS TRAINED TO FISH

Such birds are evidence of Chinese patience ("No can-do, muchee-do, bime-by can do"). This same patience over the centuries has given mankind much from better peaches to improved peonies.

TEMPLE SEAL FOX-GOD'S

Inari, Goddess of Fecundity, supposedly was feminine. Later it acquired masculine whiskers as in this temple-seal.

When, a half century ago, We-2 were first in Japan we were told Inari was a kind of fecundity goddess. The fate of the rice yield depended upon her. Her servant was the Fox. Usually the images in the temples were not of the goddess but of her messenger Reynard. Fox-respect seems world wide. Note our English surnames: Fox, Todd, also Toddhunter, in the north of England . . . Scotch Lowrie, South England Reynolds, (based on French Reynard). Fuchs in German is common for a wise or foxy man.

When We-2 were sleuthing the classic peony of China to its *sauvage* beginnings, we neared the Siberian border of Manchuria. This trip, delayed until autumn, prevented our finding it flowering wild. We met, however, an American who had been exploring the Coast

of Siberia. At some 450 miles north of Vladivostok, wild peonies—
white, pink, magenta—were found in impressive color masses. This
explorer remarked they reminded him of the color-sheets of California
poppies. These *"sauvage"* peonies were mostly single. Some, however,
even among these wild ones, showed tendencies toward "doubling."

Occidental gardeners owe a deep debt of gratitude to that master
Geogardener Baron Phillip Franz von Siebold (1796-1866). He is
credited with the introduction of peonies, aralias, chrysanthemums,
scores of other interesting and beautiful plants with which our gardens today are adorned. He wrote many books, in Latin, in German,
on the zoology, botany, language, and bibliography of Japan. Like
Kaempfer, a century and a half before him, he judged, and rightly,
that the Dutch East India service was the royal road to a knowledge
of the then mysterious empire of Japan. Appointed leader of a scientific mission, he landed at Nagasaki, August 1823 (He died 1866.)
By force of character, by urbanity of manner, by skill as a physician,
he obtained an extraordinary hold over the usually-suspicious natives.

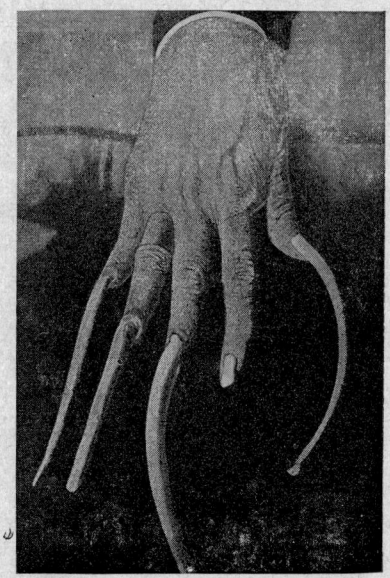

CHINESE MOTHERHOOD'S FINGERNAILS

That the sole function of the wife of the wealthy Chinese was motherhood
was demonstrated by their pride in the growth of fingernails. This was evidence
that they never soiled their hands in housework. The high development of their
gardening, one is told in China, is partly the result of planned for contentment
for the really-imprisoned wife and her females.

When our family, three generations ago, began to be interested
in China, little girls' footbinding was a deeply fixed folkway. A maid-

History

en's desirability for marriage was gauged by this deformation. For such wives (and concubines), the garden was THE place to spend pleasantly their secluded existence. Chinese men entertained their friends in an outer garden. The Chinese garden's main purpose, however, was r e l i g i o u s. Taoism stressed appreciation of Nature. Chinese planned their gardens to be quiet, restful.

CHINESE GARDEN PHILOSOPHY

Gardens in China usually are walled. The inside of same generally is painted red. Paths of hammered gravel or broken tile are laid out in curved pattern. This, because Chinese believe evil spirits can move only in straight lines. That is why gates have curved tops. Arbors of lattice work and paper provide protection from wind and sun. When possible, as also in Japan, the garden will have a running stream. Running water is symbol of purity. The garden also often contains a quiet pool. This to suggest reflection, contemplation. The pool usually has goldfish. Chinese centuries of breeding here again have produced desired types. (See illustration page 186)

THE QUEUE, A BADGE OF SLAVERY

Most unhappy to be in overpopulated China would be the gay modern Lothario who complained "Two's company—Three's a Board-of-Directors!" This photograph was taken before Sun Yat Sen's Rebellion. Note the queues down men's backs. Later, in overthrowing the Manchu dynasty, Sun Yat Sen reminded the somnolent Chinese the queue was originally the badge of Chinese slavery to the Manchu conquerors. So long had they worn this means of quick-arrest (used also by California police in Gold Rush Days) that aged men were bitter when mobs of freedom-intoxicated enthusiasts roamed Chinese streets with shears, clipping all conservatives' queues.

The lotus plant, representative of the soul, also has its place in said pool. As in all Chinese art, there is seen a symbol in this plant that grows out of the black muck. "The dry dead plant is the Past." which cannot be brought back. The open flower represents the possibilities of human endeavor. Chinese gardens often have the pine and the peach, both symbols of immortality. There almost always is a clump of bamboo, symbolic of the scholar. As explained by one student of Chinese folkways, bamboo is useful, as the Chinese feel the scholar should be in society. It is divided in segments, as the scholar should divide his time. It is polished, as is a learned person. It is flexible, can bear weight, yet spring back as a wise man should when adversity is past.*

CHINESE WIFE'S BOUND FOOT
"A maiden's desirability for marriage was gauged by this deformation."

The daring Cantonese, who flocked to California at the beginning of the Gold Rush were followed by those imported to help build across the Sierras the Central Pacific Railroad, (the "Dutch Flat Swindle" as its earliest stockholders came to dub it.) In those days it was cheaper to ship laundry by clipper ship to Canton than attempt to have it done in the mines. Thus, to those of us born in the last decades of the Gold Rush, Chinese houseboys were our beloved servants. These patient ones taught us children "pidgin" English, such as "no can do ... muchee do ... bime-by can do"—the Celestial version of "If at first you don't succeed try, try again."† These trusted servants of yesteryear all were garden lovers. Before each Chinese New Year they unfailingly brought us an indoor garden—the fragrant, sacred narcissus in

---

* The reader interested in the Chinese gardens of antiquity may care to reread Dr. H. H. Hart's "A Garden of Peonies" (Stanford University Press). It contains garden verse as early as the Wei Dynasty. One remarkable one is composed by T'sao Chih. (A.D. 192-232).
† The unwearying patience of the Chinese is shown in their training of comorants to do their fishing. The Occidentals, tho skilled in falconry, never attempted this. (See Page 11)

its bowl of pebbles and water. How we would watch to see if a bloom by Chinese New Year predicted a year of good luck!

Once in Singapore we were guests of a Chinese gentleman. The detailed story from tin mine coolies to powerful bankers of his family's 5 generations this author elsewhere has written. His garden was landscaped English manor-park style. Thus, a unique result. Instead of the greens of English oaks and lindens, were the purples, scarlets, burnt-orange, golds, pinks of tropical trees whose flowers are at branch tips.

On the veranda of his home, this Chinese Solomon repeated his family story, beginning with greatgreatgrandfather Bing. Though a coolie, he was what eugenists would classify as "highpower". China's venerable civilization has worked eugenically over centuries. The Chinese never had heard of chromosomes, of I.Q.s, of human genetics. Greatgreatgrandpere Bing was, nevertheless, result of centuries of natural selection. Physically strong, mentally alert, commendably ambitious, the first immigrating Bing soon rose from shovelman in the Malaysian tin mines to "No. 1 Boy," or a labor contractor. To reach this, he had commenced saving microscopic sums of his low earnings. He ate the absolutely efficiency-minimum of rice, avoided tin mines' vices, opium smoking, fantan gambling, "China gin". He soon commenced lending a little money at 10% to 20% monthly to addicts among his fellow coolies. He was on his way to becoming a banker.

Thus this multimillionaire descendant of coolie Bing made of his garden entrance a symbol of the two philosophies that dominated his life. One was his reverence for his ancestors. The other, his profound appreciation of the American ideal, (transplanted to his native Kwantung by Dr. Sun Yat Sen), of democracy displacing the Manchus absolute despotism. . . .

"Oh Thou beauteous Dawn Goddess
Clad in thy robes of saffron."

VEDIC "HYMN TO THE DAWN" When, in late September, the air is filled with microscopic dust particles, the "robes of saffron" of the Dawn Goddess gleam with rare color. We-2 loved Landscapist McLaren. This, because of his vision in converting the forbidding San Francisco sanddunes of our early childhood into Golden Gate Park. We invited him, therefore, to plan our garden. He then recalled how We-2, there to start for Hindustan's playgrounds at Baligata, had gone up in The Deodars. We herein had been told that, climbing from the hot Bengal plain up into the snowy Himalayas, we could get glimpses into the souls of various types inhabiting "The Hills".

This prediction proved to be most canny. We saw weakling Bengalis on the swampy plains. At Silliguhri, on Ganges' bank, a Brahmin, eager to convince an Occidental as to the superiority of Hindu philosophy, invited us to join him at his 3 a.m. devotions. Thus We-3 awaited the first glimmer, above the willows, of the coming of the Dawn Goddess. He then sang that ancient Vedic "Hymn to the Dawn Goddess." Since then We-2 used to arise to go also before dawn into our Garden. There we likewise paid homage to the eternal Dawn Goddess:—She "who uncovers all hideous things and all the hateful darkness." She who "makes plain our trails and all of our paths". We thus enjoyed the blackgreen of our garden's tall Deodars against the diffused saffron of the dust-laden Dawn-sky, just as years before, we had, en route to those Hills, to which Kipling wrote "one returns to die."

In such a magic hour, we sometimes reminded each other of our Deodar's pagoda shape. This matter of conifer-shape adjustment to snow-weight stress is fascinating. Note pointed top of the silver firs, as at Fallen Leaf Lake, (page 23) also of Sitka Spruce. Remember a Brahman once said to us "The Hindu temple is a forest frozen into architecture." Then compare Sabine's pine, of the snowless California Upper Sonoran Life Zone. It does not need a snow-shedding form. Thus Mother Nature ever teaches us adjustment to environment. Arizona's Petrified Forest Araucanias bear mute testimony to this. THE MORAL OF ALL THIS IS:—THE HEREDITY OF CONIFER SHOWS IN BOTH TREE-FORM AND NEEDLE-EFFICIENCY. Compare a yellowpine needle with a maple leaf.

NIKKO'S RED LACQUER BRIDGE

Halfway between Nikko Station and the Lacquer Bridge, we were amazed to find some ancient cryptomerias recently felled. (See page 21.)

History 17

ONE OF MIKADO'S
TWO CRESTS

Any wonder we urban dwellers prize our little gardens—even a window-box? No Scotch clan but had its bonnetpiece—a sprig of heather, a thistle, or some rowanberries. So, too, one finds flowers across Eurasia as royal crests. England's rose, France's *fleur-de-lys*. This royal use of the flower-symbol appears in Japan as 2 crests. One is *kiri-no-mon*, Paullownia flower-above-leaf. The other is the *Kiku-no-mon*, the chrysanthemum. Misuse of either the latter was signal to any of the 2-sworded *Samuri* to proceed with instant beheading. (See page 25.)

CHERRY FESTIVAL JAPAN

The first Mikado, Jimmu Tenno, descended from the Gods Themselves. He ruled about B.C. 660. His, therefore, allegedly is the world's oldest dynasty. No one was on hand, however, to kodak his movements. We sense, nevertheless, he was a true Oriental despot. This, long before Caesar gazed across the English Channel at Dover's white chalk cliffs and named that island "Albion."

Gardening in Japan can also point, with proverbial pride, to a long ancestry. American garden-philosopher contrasts Occidental and Oriental appreciation of gardening. The outpouring of Japanese crowds to enjoy the cherry blossoms can hardly be duplicated in U.S.A., except at baseball's World Series or at a football match.

Must we not be patient however. Our Garden Clubs ARE expanding their membership. Gladioli shows, rose shows, even Saintpaulia shows ARE slowly educating us. It makes one wistful. One recalls that, in Madrid, We-2 often heard the loyal song of the Madridlanos:

"First Madrid, then Heaven,
But, even in Heaven,
A little window
To look back on Madrid."

Would we could glimpse U.S.A. in A.D. 2954 after ten centuries of garden-clubs' devotion!

WATER TORII AT MIYAJIMA—JAPAN
It is at Japan's temples, one observes deep affection for gardening. Sometimes the sentiment centers on a single cycad or ginko . . . sometimes on a camphor laurel or pine. This simplification parallels their home life. Overnight guests in old Japan, We-2 were charmed at the one iris plus one kakemono in our bedchamber.

    Mankind, perhaps, owes more than it concedes to the priests of Buddhist temples across Southeastern Asia. The Abbott of Temple of the Tooth in Kandy during our stay there impressed Us-2 with his learning in such matters. We had come to have glimpses of the intellectual treasures accumulated in the libraries of these Buddhist Temples. Out in the jungles, the binding of the books would simply be a piece of teak. This would be plain, or, if the resources permitted, lacquered. In the wealthier libraries, such as that at the Temple of the Tooth, they were inlaid with precious stones. These included topazes, emeralds, turquois, lapis lazuli, even rubies.

TEMPLE GARDENS

    These Temples not only were rich in Buddhist literature etched upon palm leaf segments and threaded on these book covers . . . they also had gardens worth Occidental study. One found at such Temples in Japan the finest specimens of camphor laurel, ginko, cryptomeria. It was in ancient China, however, that there seemed to be the beginnings of plant-breeding thru SELECTION. There they seemed to have commenced with a perhaps rather bitter wild peach, without much pulp surrounding the seed. By careful budding and grafting, they continually improved this important fruit—important because it's the

History

Chinese symbol of immortality. The strategy of budding/or grafting of the Chinese Buddhist priests apparently had not penetrated into South Hindustan.*

* For anecdote describing American Know How applied to budding mangos earning a contribution of Rupees 180,000, see Eugenics Pamphlet No. 50. (At most U.S.A. libraries.)

PATIO-GARDENING, (JAPANESE STYLE)

When, a half century ago, we-2 were first in Japan we were told Inari was a kind of fecundity goddess. The fate of the rice yield depended upon her. Her servant was the Fox. Usually the images in the temples were not of the goddess but of her messenger Reynard. Fox respect seems world wide. Note our English surnames: Fox, Todd, also Toddhunter, in the north of England . . . Scotch Lowrie, South England Reynolds, (based on French Renard). Fuchs in German is common for a wise or foxy man. (See "Foxy God" page 20.)

Japanese gardening highlights are (1) Cherry blossoming time; (2) autumn color; (3) chrysanthemum bloom. That latter season is important is evidenced by the Chrysanthemum being the Imperial Crest. There are, however, also minor joys: Iris, Wisteria, Lotus,

JAPANESE GARDENS Peony, Azalea flowerings. Some gardens that are famous all over Japan. One is Uwajima's wisteria garden. It is the goal of thousands. One wonders, however, how much of attraction there is in the garden, how much in the adjacent 88 Holy Places. Iris enthusiasts should not miss the Horikiri. Its blooms are at their best in June. Japanese also will make a long pilgrimage afoot, as to the teahouse at Awata no Goten, near Kyoto. As they sip their tea they enjoy the wonderful azalea blooms. These are the cause of a kiosk being located there.

FOXY GOD OF ABUNDANT RICECROPS

Going, at the century's turn to visit the charming garden of a Japanese host, he suggested our rickshaws pause. This, at a stand under a big camphor laurel which stocked dolls. Note in above picture the Fox doll. He is the messenger of Irani, Goddess of rice fertility. Notice said illustration also shows 2 gigantic figures of the same Fox-God. Also, almost half of the lower row to the right holds that sensitively big-eared member of Japanese mythology. Likewise in the right background, a couple of figures of the corpulent, good natured Lucky God of the Full Tummy.

Is not use of dolls in children's education fascinating? This, particularly, when one studies the part they play among primitive people. We long had noticed North Germany's tendency to utilize blonde dolls. These represented the dominant Teutonic caste. This as against brunette dolls picturing the "Schwabs," a more primitive type. The name "Slav" indicated Eastern or Russian origin, meant those so designated once were literally "slaves".

Japanese landscape gardening includes dwarfed trees, tiny bridges over artificial lakelets, stone lanterns, moss carpets, man-made islets, also hillocks. Much in both Chinese and in Japanese art is symbolic. We-2 used to take the Lake Bewa Canal excursion, then to Nanzenji Temple. Its garden, to us Occidentals, is in the very severe *Chanoyu* style. Some sneer at it as "just sand, stones, scraggly bushes." Your

History

Japanese artlover, however, explains that it represents how a tiger mother teaches her kittens to ford a stream. Such incidents make one wonder whether the Orientals gain something from their gardens to which we Occidentals are blind.

In Japan we find elaborate praise when a garden approaches perfection. That at Kanazawa Castle is Kenrokuen, the 6-fold garden. It exemplifies the 6 requirements, among which are running water, charm at view and the semblance of respected antiquity. . . .

JAPANESE GARDEN WITH MINIATURE ARCHED BRIDGE

Religious devotion in our Occident may take the form of trying to engrave the Lord's Prayer on a pinhead. In Japan there is a tendency to also admire dwarfing. A large garden will have a miniature bridge over an elongated pond, (to imitate a river). On one's dining table may be a Satsuma bowl, with a bit of lawn, imitated with a patch of moss,—a tiny tea house, a thumbnail-sized stone lantern, and a diminutive pine. The latter often will illustrate what Lafcadio Hearne dubbed "the charm of the irregular."

After having inspected some attractive gardens of the Japanese temples, also Japanese noblemen's homes in and around Tokio, we entrained for Nikko. Its shrine has the world-famous Red Lacquer Bridge, also the Mountainous Lake Chuzenji hinterland. The highway from Nikko railroad station to said bridge was lined with venerable cryptomerias. These trees, to Us-2, were attractive because of their cousinship with the sequoias of our native California.

TELEGRAPH POLE "BEAUTY"

Halfway between station and bridge we were amazed to find a space where these trees had evidently recently been felled. They had been allowed to topple over to either right or left of the highway. We asked the reason therefor from No. 1 Boy of our rickshaw coolies. He pointed to a castle to the right, then to a telegraph line to the left. He said:—"Old Baron, he die. Young Master, he crazy about Quick-talk. He have old trees chopped down so he can see beautiful Quick-talk." We were not able to probe for truth of his statement. It was evident, however, any inhabitant of that castle, with the trees removed, could admire the doubtful "beauty" of the new telegraph line....

WISTERIA-LOTUS-IRIS COMPLEX

It was a rare garden-philosophy experience to have visited Japan after the Russo-Japanese war. At that time still resident there were not a few of the Occidental educators invited to live in Japan to teach Western techniques. These became expert Orientalists. They learned how some Occidental garden gems cost martyrdom in the Orient. The Siebold efforts were an example.

SOME OCCIDENTAL GARDEN GEMS COST ORIENTAL MARTYRDOM

The court astronomer, Takahashi, presented him with a map of Japan. It was high treason to give this to a foreigner. The affair leaked out. Takahashi was cast into a dungeon where he died. Siebold's servants were arrested, tortured. Siebold had to appear on his knees before the Governor of Nagasaki. He adroitly saved, however, his chief treasures including the map. He was, nevertheless banished in 1830.

A flowerless garden may sound contradictory. Many Japanese gardens, however, are flowerless. The Japanese landscape-artist aims

History 23

to produce some famous natural scene. In some, flowers may, may not appear.* When they do, they generally are grouped, removed after bloom. Impressive horticultural triumphs are achieved by dwarfing. A pine tree, or a maple, perhaps 60 years old may be a foot high.

Japanese landscape-gardening is a fine art. (It dates back 500 years). Since then its devotees have established canons. There is a whole vocabulary for garden lanterns, water-basins, screen fences, large stones.

Such gardens symbolize abstract ideas, such as peace, or old age. One student of 5 Japanese gardening described how certain Buddhist abbot garden suggests such symbolization:—"This garden consists almost entirely of irregular stones. Its sentiment depends on a Buddhist legend: The monk Daita, ascending a hillock, collecting stones. He preached to them about Buddha. The truths worked a miracle. The lifeless stones bowed reverently. The Saint consecrated them as the 'Nodding Stones'.". . .

* A Japanese *hakoniwa* is a landscape-garden compressed into a single dish. It still can have paths, bridges, mountains, stone lanterns, dwarf plants.

SILVER FIRS, FALLEN LEAF LAKE, CALIF.

Observe the cone-shaped silver firs. This circumpolar form, our Brahman friends insisted, was reproduced in Hindu temples. Note, too, that the snowshedding conifers of the Northern Hemisphere have replaced those of the less-efficient type now fossil in Petrified Forest National Monument. (See Domes, page 9.)

"L'Alhambra! l'Alhambra! palais que les genies
   Ont dore comme un reve et rempli d'harmonies;
   Forteresse aux creneaux festonnes et croulans,
   Ou l'on entend la nuit de magiques syllabes
   Quand la lune, a travers les mille arceaux arabes,
   Seme les murs de trefles blancs." (Victor Hugo)

The Alhambra, with the Garden of the Generaliffe, is perhaps the most familiar example to Americans of Moslem gardening art. Washington Irving's classic, "The Alhambra" has peopled it with the ghosts of Boadbil, of Alhamar, of Prince Ahmed al Kamel, Pilgrim of Love, of Don Munio Sandio de Hinojosa and the Grand Master of Alcantara.

Mohammed I selected the Alhambra as his residence, began his buildings on a modest scale. He was originator of the motto *"Wala ghaliba ill' Allahta 'ald"* (There is no Conqueror but the Most High God). This is conspicuous, along with Charles V's "plus ultra" among Alhambra inscriptions. Yusuf I, (1333-54), commanded greater resources than his predecessors. He built the superb Court of the Myrtles. The king there sat in state, holding councils and receiving embassies. Mohammed V, (1354-91) had the glory of building the finest parts of the whole structure, including the Court of the Myrtles, the Cuarto de Machuca to the N.W., where part of the royal family spent the summer, and the sumptuous Court of the Lions, the winter-residence of the court, with the royal harem.

The Garden of the Generalife, with its terraces, grottoes, waterworks, clipped hedges is a most interesting survival of the Moorish period. The Patio de los Cipreses has an arcade of 1584 with a pond shaded by venerable, gigantic cypresses. Under the 600-years-old Cipres de la Sultana is placed the imaginary tryst between Boadbil's wife and Hamet the Abencerrage. The Camino de las Cascades, a well-preserved flight of Moorish steps with runlets for water on the top of its balustrades, ascends to the upper part of the garden.

THE ALHAMBRA GARDEN

Evacuating French troops, 1812, decided to blow up Alhambra "fortress". Several towers were destroyed. The main part was saved by a Spanish soldier. He secretly cut the fuse....

"Within the infant rind of this small flower
Poison hath residence, and med'cine power:
For this, being smelt, with that part cheers each part:
Being tasted, slays all senses with the heart."

There is something almost Shinto about the stern regimentation of Italian gardening. One does not find quite such creations as a garden mostly of pebbles with only a couple of dwarf pines, relying on one's knowledge of the miraculous Bowing Stones. One does not quite expect

the instinctive smile of greeting from Nipponese peasant on a bamboo-
lined trail, knowing that smile is based upon the right of
ITALIAN the two-sworded samuri to promptly behead a slave who
GARDENS fails to give the greeting smile. A Nordic DOES have,
however, a feeling, in certain Italian gardens, of being
cramped. Comes, a haunting reminder of the skill of the Borgias in the
use of poisonous herbs in eliminating those who displease....

STONE PINES, APPIAN WAY

Stone pines on Appian Way near Rome. The nuts of these pines are agreeable food, resembling those of California's Sabine Pines, long next acorns in the "Digger" Indian diet. Stone pines are common in the Eastern Mediterranean gardens. We-2 found the nuts used in the everpresent *pilau* of fattail mutton, rice, raisins and pinenuts in Anatolia, Palestine, and French-mandated Gran Leban.

One wishes there might have been more data about many phases of life in classic Greece. We know only too little about how Greek philosophers taught in gardens. We do know that there were groves at Eleusis and Delphi. We have Plato's account of his disciples who followed his footsteps in the portico. We also have items on the Hanging Gardens of Babylon. The love of the moderns, both Greek and Italian, of arbor life undoubtedly is
PHILOSOPHERS IN a folkway rooted in antiquity. Who can
GOLDEN-AGE ATHENS' forget the dancing of the Tarantella un-
GARDENS der arbors at Amalfi or Sorrento? Also,
there seems to be much in common with
patio life in Spain and the two garden courts (one for men guests, the other for women) of Chinese homes of the wealthy. The climate of the

Mediterranean is conducive to outdoor life. This we are commencing to grasp in the wider use of California gardens with such innovations as barbecue conveniences. . . .

MILLET'S "THE GLEANERS", LOUVRE
We-2 would go daily to the Louvre, to study just one masterpiece. Millet's "The Gleaners" is the type of painting worth such concentrated study. Pay your Louvre admission, contemplate such a painting, then for meditation outdoors, go into the Garden of the Tuilleries.

Few gardening, indeed few gardening-philosophy experiences, burned deeper into memory than those in France. It was the good fortune of Us-2 to meet several brilliantly-successful hybridizers. One of these concentrated on pansy-breeding. Is not rather significant the contrasting French and German pansy folknames? Our English is based on France's *la pensee or* "thought-flower". The German *stiefmutterchen*, or "little stepmother" reminds us how the Nordics (witness Hans Christian Anderson, also Grimm) revel in children's fairy tales. The "stepmother" is the top petal. The next two are her own daughters. The lower two (lower in every way) are the children of the first wife. They are despised Cinderellas.

This Pansy breeder became interested in our tales of worldwide botanizing. He insisted he would accompany us to where he still collected and studied the highly variable wild pansy, (Viola tricolor), of the Dordogne. In a fortnight's botanizing in hillcountry of Mont-Dore and, another year at Besse en Chandesse, we found every pansy color variant from the whites, thru the yellows, and the reds to the purples.

FRENCH GARDENS

History

The Tuilleries Gardens sometimes offer striking pansy shows. On the Seine's right bank, it adjoins the historic Palace, the site bought in 1518 by Francis I. It originally was a tile works, whence the name. Catherine de Medici, 1564, began erecting the buildings. The garden, (56 acres between the Palace and the Place de la Concorde), was laid out by Le Notre.

We-2, in Paris, repeatedly over much of a half century, used daily to go to The Louvre. Here we concentrated each day's admission fee upon study of just one masterpiece. The range was from Leonardo da Vinci's Mona Lisa to the Raphaels, Murillios, Grecos, Valasquez, thru Rembrandts, Van Dycks, Rubens, Millets, Corots, Davids. Before entering, again on leaving the Louvre, we would take seats in the Tuilleries gardens, surrounded by the colorful flower beds. We thus became better acquainted with that matchless aggregation of paintings, shrewdly selected over the years by discriminating French critics. Enjoyment of their coloration was increased by the flowers' bright hues about us.

The mild climate of Brittany affords gardens as luxurious as those of Ireland's West Coast, or of the Coastal Plain of California.

GARDEN OF PREMIER CLEMENCEAU, BRITTANY

"Brittany's mild climate affords gardens as luxurious as California's coastal plain" . . . How much of Clemenceau's unyielding determination to gain victory was rooted in his garden-philosophy? At above garden, "The Tiger" as this Premier of France affectionately was called during World War I, was planting a tree. A neighbor sneered "You are too old for that job." He replied, "Nevertheless, I am an octogenarian who plants trees!" Could a eugenist ask more canny philosophy?

TULIP POLDER, HOLLAND
Holland leads the world in certain branches of gardening. These include the so-called "Dutch bulbs", also hothouse tomatoes, grapes, peaches.

To Holland one must go to study certain phases of the best in gardening. Most *polders* are small. To overcome restricted acreage, high quality becomes the aim. Hence hothouse tomatoes, peaches. An old Californian has seen cowboys on the cattle ranges take 20 lb. boxes and fill them with the garden's ripe peaches. Then a row would squat on the ground along the ranch house's picket fence to compete as to who could first eat all his box contained. Imagine the contrast of a French pension's special Sunday dinner:—The table holds a box of a dozen Holland hothouse peaches. Each is wrapped in cotton. One peach is dessert as a special Sunday treat.

HOLLAND'S GARDENS

A good way to study Holland gardening is by an all day canalboat trip. Ours cost us five cents each. The canal lay thru the bulb-growing district. Most canalmen speak English or German. As they stop to trade knickknacks with farmers' wives, they also have absorbed much folkknowledge. A California rancher, from virginland where plows cut the turf first in all history, is amazed at the yields the Dutch coax from their soil. This, too, on land cropped for perhaps a millenium. Holland long has avoided the flats or tenements, hence most cottages are a one-family affair with private garden. Windmill landscapes were much more common at century's turn. Names of villas are significant: *"Lust and rust"* (pleasure and rest) ... *"Wel Tevreden"*, (well content) ... *"Vreudge by Vrede"* (Joy with Peace) ... The dykes remind a Californian of his own levees.

Such a garden inspection via canal boat yields byproducts in

History

unforgettable mental pictures. At one windmill where we stopped came the clatter, on the brick face of the dyke, of many children's wooden shoes. They stopped at a hand pump for a drink. One laddie was too short to reach the spout. His elder sister removed one wooden shoe, filled it with water, gave him his drink!

The tulip comes to us from Persia's mountains. Indeed both our English words "tulip" and "turban" are derived from Persian *"dulband,"* for "turban". It was so-called from the shape of the flower. This, just as our English plant folknames arise from characteristics such as "honey-suckle," "black-berry", "haw-thorne," "pink," "peanut," "cotton-wood", "poplar" (from the tree of The Populace, everybody planted it.)

Conrad Gesner brought the tulip from Turkey to Augsburg in 1559. Haarlem, in Holland, long has been a principal seat of the production of tulip bulbs for the European and American markets. During the seventeenth century the value of tulip bulbs became inflated to as high as 4,600 florins. Thus arose the yarn about the hungry returned sailor. Waiting for his pay, he munched on onions. They were the shipowner's 4,600-florin tulip bulbs! During the 1600s there was wild speculation in tulips in Holland, much as yesteryear gambling in Wall Street stocks, or in grain. . . .

KAISERSTRASE IN MAINZ
Kaiserstrase in Mainz is an example of rigid formal gardening and street forestry. As soon as spring weather permits, flower beds become colorful almost overnight. Here is an example of sternly regimented uniformity with a sense of order. It is in marked contrast with certain effects in Japan which display what Lafcadio Hearn called "the Aesthetic Value of the Irregular".

The skill evident above is paralleled in vegetable gardening in what the Germans call *"Kleingartenvertrieb"*. Of these plots for factory hands, writer has written elsewhere.

This bit of gardening at Dinkelsbuhl carries testimony as to the cheer from flower-color. The depression in Germany after World War I was unbelievably profound. One who was not actually on the ground could hardly grasp the depths into which the Germans had fallen. The reaction from the propaganda of such groups as the Flottenverin was painfully deep. We-2 were told at places like Dinkelsbuhl, Ochsenfurth, Feuchwangen, Rothenburg-ob-der-Tauber that the authorities distributed free bright colored paints for the facades of houses that long had been deteriorating. The effect of these contrasting bright pinks and yellows and blues with an occasional white and even a red or a violet was indeed morale-building. Simultaneous with this was the encouragement of the revival of window boxes. Gardening in Germany requires a much greater outlay of labor for just a bit of gardening of floral brightness. The effect of window boxes of red geranium story after story on the old medieval houses was most evident.

PRACTICAL GARDEN-COLOR PSYCHOLOGY

Less known to Americans, perhaps, than Britain's, Holland's or France's gardens are Germany's. The Fatherland's gardening, however, compares favorably with the best. At one castle where We-2 were guests, not only the gardens, but every room's vases showed taste. We were there in summer when the phlox, in many contrasting shades, were at its best. At another castle to which we had been invited, a bed below our apartment window was, the evening we arrived, a glory of blue and gold blooms. At breakfast, the gardeners, in those

GERMAN GARDENS days of long sunshine, already had dug up ageratum and dwarf marigold. They had replaced them (probably from a potted reserve) with a blending of phlox from rose-pink to magenta. One could hardly believe one's eyes.

The Germans also make pleasing garden use of bits of water. One often may have a pair of white swans. Sometimes, in contrast, are West Australian black swans. In German, French gardens one frequently

History

finds dwarf apples or pears. Really bushes, they carefully are branched against south-exposure stone walls. Their fruit often is deliciously flavored. Such solar heat utilization is worldwide. We-2 found potatoes maturing at 16,000 feet in similarly protected sun-exposured plots in the Peruvian Andes.

In certain plantings, Germany has long led the world. The Schwartzwald Forestry School was model for Japan's reforestation of Korea after occupation. At the century's turn We-2 became absorbed in winning public opinion for Governor Pinchot's new National Forests plan. Korea, also North China, were included at his suggestion in our Far Eastern trip. This to obtain firsthand evidence of total deforestation. In mountain valleys, we found rivers meandering, snakelike, between containing mountain ranges. The flat lands were filled with soil from the hills, washed down to bedrock. Japanese forestation engineers, Schwartzwald-trained, superintended coolies blasting holes. These were filled with soil, also fertilizer to reestablish forests.

We-2 earlier had noted fruit trees, nut trees, "sawdust trees" lining a German highway paralleling a railroad. Apple tree No. 614 was leased to Heinrich Meyer; Nos. 615 to 619 to Joseph Pfaffenberger.

Stern German police saw roadside crops of apples and nuts never were molested. "Sawdust" trees, birches, aspens, poplars, were not numbered. A German officer explained same had been planted against 3 coming wars: In 1915, France and Russia were to be overrun. In 1925, Germany's great war fleet, (out of shipyards from Bay of Biscay to Behring Sea) would end British seapower. In 1935, the Americas, Hudson Bay to Tierra del Fuego, would become Pan-German colonies. Germany, in these 3 wars, would have to fight encirclement. Aspen- or birch-sawdust held, indeed, no nourishment. 60% sawdust bread, however, would bolster morale in the last desperate weeks before victory! Such use of sawdust, also of moss, was not unknown in Medieval European famines.

We-2 determined to reproduce certain elements of Germany's roadside forestation in California. We invited Sacramentans, who could consolidate public opinion, to our Sutter's Fort Park home. Heated differences arose between palm- and elm- enthusiasts. After two hours' debate, no one questioned expense. A delegation to the County Supervisors was selected. The Legislature already had enacted our County Forestry Board Act. The Supervisors agreed to legislate, would not appropriate, would appoint anyone foolish enough to spend time, their own money. Writer was Sacramento County Forestry Board's first President. One Supervisor demanded chaingang holedigging. The Sheriff, however, said "No jailbirds to powder-blast Folsom Boulevard's hardpan." Our first planting, under such restrictions, was not a brilliant success. Later installations also were in better soil. The fine H Street sycamore avenue is an example. Eventually, from such beginnings, roadside forestry was welded to the State Highway System.

>MacIver: "Sandy, would we were lads again."
>Sandy: "Aye, in those days we traveled half fare!"

Kant found his garden at Konigsburg all sufficient. He allegedly never, in all his life, wandered beyond a half dozen miles' walk from home. Kant could hardly be classed as a "Forgotten Man", as Bible Toter Jedediah Smith was in 1900. Have not most of us forgotten however Kant's father was a Scot? Also have we not forgotten he was so much a victim of Government censorship that, from 1792 to his death, in 1804 he was permitted, no teaching, no publication.

IMMANUEL KANT

Does it not intrigue the garden lover, however, that, from the date he commenced as tutor at the University of his native Koningsberg,— this when he was 22—he found his garden all sufficient as recreation from his arduous studies in mathematics and philosophy.

He was a rebel. He was irritated because of the extravagant jargon of the Wolffian system of philosophy then dominant in Germany. He admired the Great English philosophers Locke and Hume. He fought the ponderous intellectuals of his native land. He often was tired to extreme discouragement. Then he found refuge in his garden. From that writer's garden walls came light that illuminated all lands!

Part of Kant's struggle was for Simplicity. In current slang he tried to take Philosophy to Grass Root Folk. He abhorred what the plantation negroes used to admiringly call "dem big words". Kant's efforts herein, indeed, recall George Ade's Fable in Slang of:

>"The Preacher who flew His Kite but not
>Because He wished to Do So."

It will be remembered that this parson had tried "to expound in a clear straight forward manner, omitting Foreign Quotations." ... "No one told him after service he was a Pansy". Thereupon he repeated certain "familiar lines of the great Icelandic Poet Ikon Navrojk." This was followed by "Quarolius' disputation of the Persian Theologian Ramtazuk." After this he quoted from "some Celebrated Poet of Ecuador or Tasmania or some other Seaport Town."

Witty George Ade satirized various human frailties. He understood how Kant's attack at the German philosophers of his day, could bring censorship.

History

HINDU TEMPLE, BENARES

Kant lived in the "Aryan" Broodland. Our Brahmin friends told us Hindu temple architecture reproduced in stone the motif of closely-ranked conifers of the snow-shedding type of the forests of their "Aryan" ancestors. (See this tree form in Fallen Leaf Lake reflection photo on Page 23.)

Few bits, worldwide, of window gardening can compete with the artistry of Hans Sachs' House, Nuremberg. Once when We-2 were there, the two ample arched windows at their base glowed with pots of red geraniums, contrasting with healthy green foliage. From the second story's oriel window gracefully dropped red, also orange nasturtiums. One window had a trailing fuchsia, whose wealth of bloom provoked admiration of canny gardening. Here was "Green Thumb". Here was "Know How". One remembered that "Fuchsia" is FUCHS-IA, recalled the courage of Dr. Fuchs, who indeed had the skill of his fox-y name. High up in the Mansard area were contrasted lavender and purple petunias. All these bits of color against the tobacco brown half-timbering and its stucco. The architect of bygone days may have, and again may not have, planned for light and shadow. Anyhow the effect was gripping on even an American-born boy whose early childhood had its daily Grimms' fairy tale.

HANS SACHS' HAUS

All this is setting for drama—for Power based on the skillful use of the Dramatic. No one of our century sensed this more clearly than —shall we say that human enigma—Hitler—or shall we say "The Men Around Hitler"—who after all were but the "Men Around the Kaiser" —in other words, the Pan Germans. At this writing, it is difficult for even one who repeatedly was overseas when History was being made,

1910-1940, at a highly accelerated rate, to estimate how much Soviet imperialism is but the result of Pan Germanic dreaming?

IN ANY EVENT, GARDENING COLOR MEANS THE DRAMATIC AND ALL THAT THAT IMPLIES!...

Nordics' careful housekeeping is, at times, painfully evident in Holland, Denmark, Sweden. This almost fanatical cleanliness and love of order is evident in many ways. This, from the jurisprudence of both Britain and of early Rome's Nordic Senators to Nordic Europe's window Boxes. A pleasing manifestation of this tendency was Gothenburg's careful gardening shown **SCANDINAVIAN** in circular garden boxes surrounding its trolley **GARDENING** poles.

We had gone to Gothenburg much troubled. We had had considerable juvenile crime in our native Sacramento. Writer used to have such boys assigned to his guardianship. Further data came from our Fairhaven work. (This, an unmarried mothers' home our family founded). Still more case material was from our Sacramento Orphanage Farm gardening and nature study classes. We thus accumulated stacks of notes. These indicated alcoholism was one important contributing factor causing poverty. For its reduction We-2 were working. Deeply devoted to Protestantism's ecumenical movement, we knew many believed in Prohibition. Our Mediterranean underworld's sociological studies had convinced us most of U.S.A. profiteering therein was by ungrateful aliens given citizenship. We, however, were loath to believe that correction could come by law. A Swedish guest in our home, discussing above, said:—"Go to Gothenburg, study its *Bolag*."

That *Bolag* experience WAS illuminating. Hotel accommodations secured, contact was made with that marvel of efficiency, that reservoir of encyclopedic wisdom, the hotel porter. I told him I wanted a drink of *brannvin*. Where was a *bolag* On-Station? To my amazement he said:—"I don't know!" This from one who supposedly knows everything. Then, jingling some coins enticingly, I sought a bellboy. At that On-Station question, he just stared. (Imagine that from an American bellhop!) Out on the street however was a sailor. "Sure, he knew".

We entered an On-Station. A very pretty young waitress approached, asked "Coffee, tea or chocolate?" I said:—"No, *brannvin*." With intelligence and charm, she tried to talk us out of it. Finding me stubborn, she pointed to a rear door. We entered the *Brannvin* Room. Another waitress, of exceedingly mature years, there took our order. She explained, before we could have the alcoholic stimulant, we first must order a meal. This was prepared with tortoise-like lack of speed. We had time to contemplate the walls' contrast pictures. Afront us, side by side, in convincing colors, were illustrations of a healthy liver contrasted with an alcoholic's diseased organ. Dante's Inferno hardly could have made a sensitive man shudder more deeply. On the wall to the left were similar stomach contrasts. Other walls were similarly ornamented with anatomical frightfulness.

We ate our meal. She then served the *brannvin*. The sailor tossed off his glass, also mine. Signaling the waitress, I said "Now another *brannvin*." She said sarcastically:—"You must be a stranger. A second glass only after another meal. And no duplicate orders. You walk to the next station for it." It was a half mile away. Above *Bolag* scheme assertedly had been worked out by a board of physicians, sociologists, social service workers, churchmen. The meal before the drink the half-mile walk between two drinks was planned strategy. WE HAD LANDED AT GOTHENBURG WITH TROUBLED HEARTS AS TO WISE ALCOHOLISM CONTROL. IMAGINE OUR DELIGHT WHEN GREETED BY THESE BEAUTIFUL BOX-GARDENS ON HOMES, AT BUSINESS HOUSES, EVEN ON STEEL TROLLEY MASTS!

It remained for the highly intelligent and always resourceful Icelanders to utilize hot springs warmth to ripen grapes grown indoors. These Vikings were the first to create parliamentary government (1,000 years ago). Iceland also was the first nation to a c h i e v e 100% literacy. They eugenically r e f u s e d marriage licenses to those of low I.Q.

VOLCANIC HEAT RIPENS GRAPES

Our Icelandic host was proud of his Arctic circle "crops". These included turnips, swedes, beets. Most wonderful of all, grapes! With our tiny Iceland ponies, our trip from Rejkiavik to Thingvillier gave glimpses of the lives of these very remarkable folk. Roadside cottages often lacked chimneys. We asked "Why?" The answer was a smile and "Wait and see!" Our host's own dwelling was our luncheon objective. In this chimneyless but comfortably warm home, we were served freshly-pulled turnips. After luncheon, we were shown the "garden". It was indoors—a hothouse. This, as well as the dwelling, was heated from a hot spring. The pilgrimage of Us-2, students of Eugenics, to Iceland was to study a folk who intelligently could ripen grapes north of the Arctic Circle, could invent a lasting form of democracy, could gain the distinction of being the first nation to achieve 100% literacy.

One of the most impressive ceremonies of our generation is already almost forgotten. It was Iceland's 1931 celebration of the world's 1st Parliament's 1,000th anniversary. It was at inland Thingvillier. Britain's ranking statesman remarked "Ours on the Thames is called 'Mother of Parliaments'. It truly is the model for those of our Dominions, our Crown Colonies. On it was patterned America's Congress, 48 state legislatures. We salute Iceland's Thingvillier, birthplace of the Grandmother of Parliaments". It truly is where was first seen a Parley-ment—a meeting for frank democratic discussion. . . .

ARCTIC CIRCLE GARDENS

THATCHED COTTAGE, STRATFORD-ON-AVON

Somerset, also Devon, also have tasteful gardens at the thatched roof cottages.

History

PORT SUNLIGHT (BEFORE)
Of all "Before and Afters" was any more appealing than those of that successful Garden City, England's Port Sunlight? (See page 39)

BRITISH GARDENS

A bit of garden philosophy might be illustrated by a Kentish experience. An iris enthusiast who has won prizes over the years had remarked "The man who gardens does not gamble." This came to mind when We-2 visited Canterbury. The magnet, of course, was the Cathedral. There was, however, another urge. We felt we could, as Kolb said to Dill, "Kill two birds mit vun rock". There was the temptation to write gambling history on postcards and mail to sandwich-consuming folks at home under the "Sandwich" postmark. The Earl of Sandwich, inveterate gambler, never gardened.

The story they tell about the Earl is that he would be at the gaming table hour after hour. When hungry he would order a slice of ham between the halves of a split bun. Thus the name of his earldom came to permanency as the designation of a dishless dish of ever growing popularity at American lunch counters.

In marked contrast with the dissolute Earl's wasted hours at the Sandwich "pubs" gaming table was the loving care invested in these window boxes over Stour River. The South of England's milder climate (compared with Yorkshire's) gives opportunity for more colorful gardening than in the North. Kent grows hops like California. Somerset and Devon have tasteful gardens at the thatched-room cottages. Out Penzance way, one finds an environment permitting fuchsia growing like Ireland's West Coast or California's Monterey peninsula. And where better gardeners than those canny Scots?

Of all "Before and Afters" was any more appealing than those of that successful garden city, England's Port Sunlight?

WINDOW GARDENS, CANTERBURY

"One urge to visit Canterbury was to mail friends postcards postmarked Sandwich from nearby Sandwich with its legend of the gambling Earl of Sandwich."

Into British gardening has been injected the spirit of their Viking forbears: Angles, Saxons, Danes, Normans. Thus Albion's gardens radiate much we prize. This, from the bulbous beauties, natives of South Africa, to many shrubs from the Himalayas even Yunnan.

> Up wi' the flowers o' Scotland,
> The emblems o' the free,
> Their guardians for a thousand years,
> Their guardians still we'll be.
> A foe had better brave the deil
> Within his reeky cell,
> Than our thistle's purple bonnet,
> Or bonny heather bell.
> (Hogg—The Flowers of Scotland)

History

PORT SUNLIGHT GARDEN CITY. (AFTER) (See page 37)

Is this not significant: the farsighted British industrialists at the century's turn worked toward improvement of housing? Also garden patrons dubbed their efforts, "GARDEN CITIES". These humanitarians knew the tonic value of flowers in the sunlight!

Another problem in Garden Philosophy is: Whence came Aztec love of flower cultivation? Is it Asiatic, and from a generalized ancestor, common also to the Japanese? Was it absorbed from the Mayans? (This, just as the Germanni, the Ostrogoths, the Lombards, the Allemanni, conquering by military force, themselves then willingly were conquered by the Latin civilization of the defeated)

AZTEC GARDENS In marked contrast with Aztec (Mayan) love of gardening, one finds no appreciation of flowers among the descendants of Incas.* This, tho they revel in color of garments. Xochimilco's name roots in the Aztec *xochitl*, (or flower). Apparently some warlike tribe, whose ancestors may have crossed the Bering Sea on the ice, cut their bloody way down to this land of delights. There they built an Amerind Venice. Their *chinampas* or Floating Gardens at that time actually floated. They were made by weaving sticks into a raft. (The peons to this day still weave a *petate*,

---

*After this author's field studies of Aztec, also Inca remains in Peru, he is intrigued by certain differences. Both Amerind and Mexican love of flower or feather color. Peruvian highlanders dress continues same a persistance of old folkways. Incan law required dressing in the village costume (of yesteryear German traachten). Here was quickly-visible identification. Congress long was blocked, by Hyphenate plotting, from enacting any registration of aliens act as "insulting".

or mat, of rushes which, stretched on an earth floor, forms their only bed). Upon these wood-woven rafts was piled the rich lake-muck. Such soil, with abundant moisture plus a tropical sun, meant floral wealth. These garden-rafts could support human habitations. In fact, one senses the redskins' protective strategy paralleled that of the prehistoric Swiss lakedwellers....

Gradually bird-dispersed, water-borne, also wind-carried tree seeds sprouted on the *chinampas*. These, more and more, became anchored as roots penetrated the lake bottom. ... To have known Xochimilco's "floating gardens" in the opening decade of our century was to have enjoyed one of the world's greatest geogardening thrills. Today they are tourist-spoiled. There one once met smiling Carmens, each with coiffure brightened with a red poppy. In place of these flower girls, now are whining beggars. These cry: *"Diez centavos, senor, y vaya Usted con Dios!"*

XOCHIMILCO'S COLORFUL "FLOATING" GARDENS

"Xochimilco's name roots in the Aztec *xochitl*, flower." Apparently some warlike tribe, whose ancestors may have crossed the Bering Sea on the ice, cut their bloody way down to this land of delights.

COLONIAL MANSION IN MISSISSIPPI

In these fine gardens of aristocratic Dixie Land, one discovers some of the most-discriminating gardening taste (and garden-philosophy) to be encountered world wide.

The story of the naming of the gardenia would not fit a Mid-Victorian novel—(the kind retailed, before it occurred in book form, in instalments in a Ladies' Weekly). It could not truthfully have the ending "and then they were married and lived forever happily thereafter." Do not think, gentle reader, above belittles the mid-Victorian. That era was one of excellent morals. Also it had the merit of never having contained a brace of World Wars. It had no super-super Hollywood. It had no submarines, no B-29s—no cobalt-jacketed H-bombs, no Soviet spies high in government—no tele-vision, not even one tele-phone!

COLONIAL AMERICAN GARDENS

In the days when Dr. Garden's Juliet begged Linneaus to name that genus after this brilliant young Charlestown physician—only to be later jilted for her pains—the gardens of America already were famous worldwide for their domestication of American plants.

This advance by the Colonial intellectuals was to influence gardening westward for 3,000 miles. Seeds tied in handkerchief corners traveled via Covered Wagon from St. Joseph, Missouri to Pinchemtight, You-be-damned, Whiskeytown, Delirium-Tremens, Shirttail, Pair-o-dice. Thus arrived locust trees, cypresses. The Chinese brought the Tree-of-Heaven for their Joss-houses. . . .

"Vell! Led us begin bei der Beginnings"
(Kolb to Dill)

Attempting to assemble one's bits of Garden Philosophy, one perhaps may well follow above from yesteryear's vaudeville. This, even if Kolb also did question "Vere ignorance vas blisters, vas it vise to be foolish?"

"BEI DER BEGINNINGS"

Does not one who tries to probe to beginnings come to the question as to whence came the plants whose flowers adorn his garden? Once he starts this investigation, he is entering upon what can easily become a life-long hobby. Such hobbies are essential to happiness if a calculating commercial world issues a Retirement ukase. Fortunate is the child who has been guided hobbywise. This, especially if he has a home museum and has acquired, by exchange with other school children, fossil plants.

Should a complete garden not include reminders of the Paleobotanical era? If one wants always to have, not only the ordinary gardening joys, but the thrills of its Why and its Whence, is not a "museum" reservation as essential as a compost heap, a toolhouse, a cold frame? "Museum", of course, is literally a place wherein to "muse". Much of any garden-philosopher's thinking will be with trowel or shears in hand or foot on spade. There do come, however, days when rain-downpour keeps one under a roof. Then one can profitably, (and lovingly), finger plant records preserved in indestructible strata.

If there be in the gardener's household, or in the neighborhood even one child interested in pressing wildflowers, collecting specimens of woods, of nuts, of seeds—such a "home museum" becomes more than a mere garden adjunct to parallel the gardener's library. It can become the means of awakening in said child, in even an adolescent, his life-long interest. To same this writer can testify out of an exceedingly rich boyhood.

When one contemplates the evolution of plants from the primitives, such as the early fossil algae, he is impressed with the clarity of Victor Hugo's reasoning:—"My religion is PROGRESS." ...

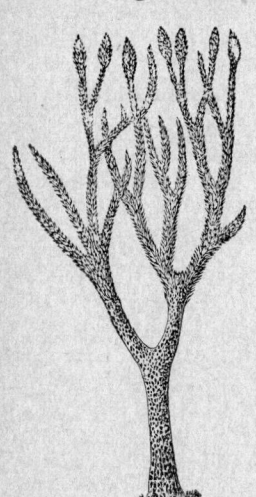

COAL AGE PLANT

Lepidodendron. "When we come to Coal Age Plants, the story unfolds much more clearly with abundant lepidodendron and sigillaria."

Should not a home museum, also a garden patch, however small, be the birthright of every child? This author's boyhood museum began with pressing flowers and leaves for a kiddie herbarium ... an attic row of bottles with various seeds grown in his own garden ... spore prints of his garden fungi ... cones and bits of bark, also neatly whittled twigs from garden trees. Cigarboxes contained pinned, garden-netted insects according to families. (Mother patiently handled the cyanide killing-bottle). Then on hillcountry holidays these collections expanded. Also there were mineral specimens from creekbed, quarry and especially from Dad's goldmining. Followed, thru Agassiz Association, exchanges with schoolboys across U.S.A. Here was education as sugarcoated as geography via the postage stamp album. All this kept an energetic lad busy and away from certain happenings of a neighborhood gang that were hardly character-building.

T'ao Ch'ien, in Dr. Hart's "Garden of Peonies," loved his chrysanthemums, lamented his garden's choking weeds, is dated a half century before Roman Empire's end. The chrysanthemum long has held its grip upon Oriental affections. One Emperor of Japan permitted a certain ancient institution to also continue to use his chrysanthemum crest, symbol of the world's oldest dynasty. In writer's garden some 45,000 'mum blooms this month show season's height. The Orient's flower of flowers competes for favor with England's rose, even in California.

The Chin dynasty, however, was only a millenium and a half ago. To contemplate the beginnings of what developed into our garden plants, must we not turn back many pages of geological record?*

Some geologists say the first recognizable plants are from the Great Lakes' ironbeds. They are Proterozoic bacteria, also algae, both microscopic. They apparently had ability to extract iron from water, just as other algae today extract, deposit lime. These primitive plants lived long, long ago. Their Huronian Period of the Algonkian was perhaps one thousand million years ago. It is not easy to picture the time that elapsed between these first plants and that when T'ao Ch'ien worried about weeds displacing his chrysanthemums. Suppose T'ao Ch'ien, with each step a one-yard stride, was encircling our Earth at its Equator. After 24-world-rounds, he would have taken approximately as many 1-yard steps as the years from the first known plants to T'ao Ch'ien's backbreaking weeding. Similar yardstrides, T'ao Ch'ien to President Eisenhower, would fall far short of a half-mile! . . .

Of Cambrian, Ordivician, even Silurian plants, little is known. Writer, in New York, discovered some that are fossil there. Later, while collecting in British Columbia, he found what have been classified as algae. Up there is a Cambrian locality rich in **CAMBRIAN,** animal species, such as Trilobites. Tantalizingly little, **ORDIVICIAN,** however, is known about these primitive plants. This, **SILURIAN,** tho' their descendants are, quite unnoticed, in our **DEVONIAN** gardens of today.
PLANTS In the New York State Museum at Albany is a group any inquisitive gardener would enjoy. It is a replica of the oldest known fossil forest of seed ferns. They grew in the Devonian. This some geologists estimate to have been perhaps 500,000,000 years ago. They resemble somewhat the modern treefern forests thru which this author traveled in Java, Jamaica, also Australia. The Devonian was the Age of Fishes. The lung fishes, also the scorpions already were flourishing. In Devonian oceans were many sharks. This was the era of the landmasses geologists call Laurentia, also Appalachia. Latter is now mostly covered by the Atlantic Ocean. With such a venerable ancestry, the gardening philosopher studies the Albany Museum's group with respect, with almost awe.

There was seedmaking back in the Devonian with its seed-ferns. Here Nature, ever restless for something, if not bigger, at least better, developed the tiny plant inside the seed cover. This together with food for those dangerous days of infancy.

---

* As to reducing U.S.A.'s Geological Illiteracy, be it remembered World War I was reported to have shown 25% of certain draftees could neither read nor write. . . . Also, King John could not SIGN the Magna Charta. He merely SEALED it.

Paleobotany 45

Our garden ferns today, however, are spore-bearers. Somehow the seedferns seem to have ended in EXTINCTION. Mother Nature, it is true, WAS groping toward seedmaking in those Devonian seedferns. Somehow they just "didn't click." They were displaced by more primitive sporebearers which have persisted to those in our gardens today.

There also is DISPLACEMENT toward EXTINCTION among humans today. Witness the New Englanders of the type of Longfellow, Emerson, Thoreau. The unnecessary Civil War drained Massachusetts and Maine, just as much as it did Virginia and South Carolina, of precious idealistic stocks. Displacement came with factory-hand immigrants from low-wage areas overseas. . . .

LEPIDODENDRON
Some of these "fishscale trees" were 60 feet high. They had root systems ample to support them in their swamps.

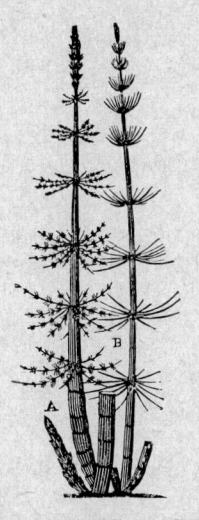

COAL MEASURES MARESTAIL
A Calamite. "Coal Measures had giant marestails. . . . One Tokio dinner table decoration was a Satsuma bowl with several dwarfed marestail."

When we come to the Carboniferous, or Coal Age plants, the story unfolds much more clearly. Here we have abundant plants such as Lepidodendron, Sigillaria, Calamites, as well as the interesting Mazan Creek and other ferns. In the collection of 10,000 scientific objects writer gave Sacramento city schools were specimens from Coal Measures' giant trees, like marestails. Later these flowerless trees met competition with much more efficient flowering plants. Marestail, also called "scouring brush"* thereupon became relegated to comparative obscurity. Writer finds them, however, still growing in damp spots on his river ranches.

COAL AGE PLANTS

After Russo-Japanese war, We-2 went to Japan to try breaking down Child Labor by introducing the then-new American supervised playground. At one Tokio dinner, our host's table decoration was a centerpiece of several dwarfed scouring rushes. Instead of an American home's elaborate floral centerpiece was this charming simplicity: The old Satsuma bowl, filled with earth, had grown, under patient Japanese gardening, this appealing decoration. We later learned it was much more difficult to reduce a 2-foot marestail to table size than to dwarf pine.

Above was a case of "Japanese Know How". They today recognize their need also of our "American Know How"† in rebuilding wartorn Japan. Did you read "Private Point Four in Japan"? (Reader's Digest 6/53.)

Passing in our gardens' home museum, from the Paleozoic to the Mesozoic, fossil material naturally is much more abundant, much less tantalizing. We commence to see far more clearly whence came at least some of our beloved garden plants. Most of them still are more "horse-and-buggy" than "airplane" types. Family resemblances are, however, more and more apparent. Indeed, toward the end of the Mesozoic, (in the Cretaceous) we commence to anticipate the earliest plants that produce flowers. In the Jurassic, the cycads, (distant relatives of the palms), were numerous. Now also we find conifers. Some are not unlike the Norfolk Island pine or the monkey-puzzle tree of today's gardens. Here, too, are primitive sequoias, also the ginko we call "maidenhair tree". (The Chinese call it the "ducks-foot-leaf tree.")

JURA-TRIAS VEGETATION

---

* Our California species still seem to have considerable silica. This probably gave them their mediaeval usefulness as "scouring rushes." This, before the Industrial Revolution gave housewives inexpensive brushes.

† The "American Know How" did not just happen. It is the product of 10 years of history's fiercest selection. Those coming to James River in 1606, to Plymouth Rock in 1620, courageously faced annual mortality rates as high as 50%. This meant that, 2 people last New Year's knew that, before next New Year's one might be dead. Peopling Saxon America required 10 Pioneering generations. On the Frontier, the weakling, physically or mentally, just died. He did not live long enough to father many children.

Paleobotany

In the Triassic ferns, also cycads abound. The latter still persist in the Orient, are favorite plants with the Buddhist monks. They grow regularly in temple gardens in Japan. In the Triassic also came Araucarioxylon, of the "petrified forests" of Arizona. Most fascinating is the displacement and eventual extinction of these earliest of cone-bearers by our modern ones. Our gardens today contain pines, cedars, firs, sequoias, yews. Occasionally there is a Cryptomeria from Japan. Note that these are efficiently needled, hence shed snow weight. Other qualifications for a North-Hemisphere niche are (a) elasticity, (useful in heavy snows), (b) tree-shape. It would be difficult to mathematically devise a better snowshedder than some of the Alaskan and Canadian spruce or even Sierran firs. We pass from the Jura-Trias to the Cretaceous.

PAINTED DESERT, ARIZONA DINOSAUR TRACKS

The Jurassic, age of the palm-like cycads in today's Japanese temple gardens (also some in U.S.A.) was the age of Dinosaurs. Near where this was kodaked, writer found fossil tree trunks of primitive conifers. These were not unlike the monkey-puzzle trees of our gardens. These conifers, (non snow-shedders), now are extinct in our snow forests.

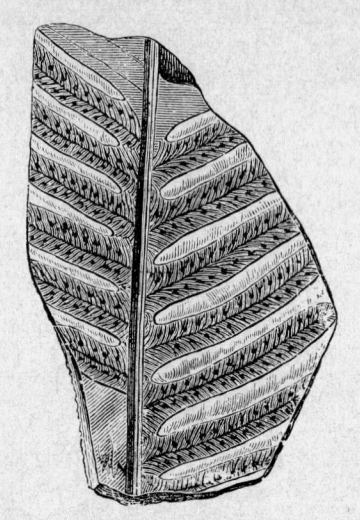

JURATRIAS FERN

Neuropteris linefolia, a Juratrias fern, (after Le Conte). In this author's boyhood, specimens of gold bearing quartz from his father's mines attracted, in exchange, fossil ferns from Illinois also Pennsylvania schoolboys. One wishes the old Agassiz Association could be revived.

"PETRIFIED FOREST", PAINTED DESERT, ARIZONA (TRIASSIC)

New Zealand has a conifer called "celery-leaved pine". Its leaves DO resemble a tiny bunch of celery. Many of today's Southern Hemisphere conebearers are of similarly archaic types. Lacking severe competition, they can persist there. Similar primitive "pines once covered much of our Northern Hemisphere. Indeed, botanists call one Petrified Forest tree: "Araucarioxylon arizonicum" (Arizona's Araucariwooded, see above). The Araucarians are an Indian tribe in Chile. The Araucarias are Down-Under conifers of ancient type. Why did these pines become extinct up North? Perhaps because their foliage, like the "celery leaf", was less fitted to shedding snow than our needle-leaved pine branches. When they broke under snow-weight, they could not produce pinenuts.

Is there not a parallel in humans? Are our lives, also, not constantly dominated by what the German biologists call *zeilstrebigkeit*—the urge toward evolution upwards? Have we not therefore continual moral responsibility to unceasingly combat whatever hinders Nature in that trend? One such is U.S.A.'s powerfully organized Commercialized Vice.

Paleobotany

The Cretaceous' fossil leaves fascinate anyone who is intrigued by the How and the Why. The Cretaceous is placed by some geologists as 100,000,000 years ago. Writer's own collection of Cretaceous fossil leaves include willow, sycamore, magnolia (different leaf from that of our garden or Gulf States' species), sequoia leaves and cones, gingko. One gingko was found as far back as the Cretaceous. Other conifers are yew-like, also cedar-like. He has supplemented these by studies in many museums in U.S.A. and overseas.

CRETACEOUS TREES

LEAFLESS METASEQUOIA AT A CHINESE TEMPLE
In Central China, Dr. Ralph Cheney, brilliant paleobotanist, found Metasequoia a deciduous redwood. It has been dubbed a "Living Fossil".*

---
* Read "Living Fossil: Metasequoia" in Pacific Discovery (10/48). It has illustrations of Oregon's fossil metasequoia twigs, (such as in this author's collection), also a map showing former redwood distribution from Turkey, across Switzerland, also Spitzbergen, and Greenland, Pennsylvania, Kansas, Oregon, British Columbia, Alaska, to Japan and Manchuria. . . . See also Save the Redwoods League's illustrated dime pamphlet "Redwoods of the Past". Enjoy sitting in your garden under its sequoia and philosophizing about the antiquity of plants. For a full discussion of Metasequoia see Dr. Cheney's "Revision of Fossil Sequoia", etc. Transactions of American Philosophical Society New Series, Vol. 40, Part 3, 1950.

The gardening philosopher finds it most absorbing that the beloved trees of his garden can boast of such ancient lineage. There also are other stimuli to speculation. Note, for example, the genera of various Cretaceous floras. Compare these with modern habitats, of similar ones. An acacia once was *sauvage* in Maryland. Having spent some time in the Greenland-Spitzbergen-Iceland triangle, writer finds himself absorbed in speculating about the Greenland floras. His own interest is deepest in the sequoias of Greenland. He ponders, however, about finding, among the old missionary hymn's "Greenland's icy mountains," fossil dogwood, persimmon, walnut, oak, tuliptree, eucalyptus. Even cinnamon is fossil in Greenland and, believe it or not, a fossil breadfruit! Anyone who has feasted on breadfruit in the South Seas and who also knows the knife-sharp cold of Greenland is content to admit Old Timer may have some right to complain:—"The climate IS changing."

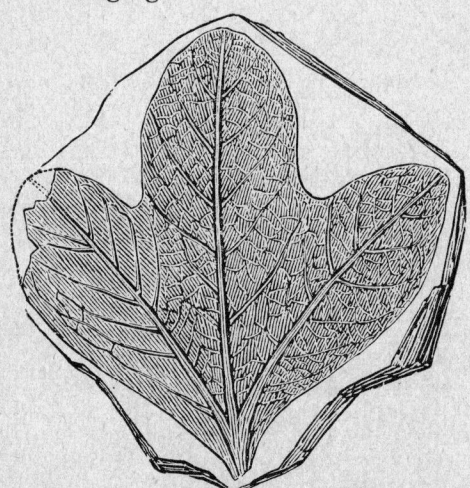

VENERABLE SASSAFRAS
Sassafrasaraliopsis.

(AFTER LE CONTE). There were no humans in the Cretaceous to enjoy sassafras. We are upstart newcomers. In our gardens we become humble in contemplating p l a n t s that have changed but little, (as, for example, willow leaf form) in 100,000,000 years. And Java Man is dated by some only 1,000,000 years ago!

All this is almost as alluring as the remarkable array of trees in the auriferous gravels of California's Tertiary lava-capped rivers. Does not all this make one ponder about EXTINCTION, even HUMAN-TYPES' EXTINCTION?...

If one finds fascinating the interaction of earlier forces that could produce aforesaid breadfruit in Greenland, how much more absorbing are the floras of the Tertiary? Here the species more nearly resemble those of today. The Tertiary also gives us a much broadened history of those remarkable Angiosperms. These then moved with accelerated motion to people the Earth by displacing the c y c a d s, the marestails. Almost, like Minerva of California's Great Seal, these apparently sprung into life fully matured. They become the ancestors of nearly all the plants that make our gardens lovely, and our life more enjoyable. Cin-

AVOCADOS, RICEPAPER TREE, EBONY, ALL NOW FOSSIL IN CALIFORNIA'S LAVA-CAPPED GOLDBELT RIVERS

Paleobotany

namon is an example. Modern cinnamon, such as is powdered on apple dowdy, grows wild in Ceylon, also Indo China. The genus, now extinct, was fossil in at least 19 states.*

Not as often nowadays, (as when there was drift mining in the Tertiary river beds at Iowa Hill, Gold Run, Yankee Jim's, Red Dog, and You Bet), are fossil leaves uncovered. The writer has found them near Timbuctu, upriver from Marysville. We are learning to be more alert as to these ancient leaves, for they tell of a California with a very different climate. In it two species of magnolias bloomed. The streams, however, even then ground quartz into white sand, with the heavy gold particles settling to the very bottom. Trees now found only in China once grew in California's Gold Belt. The nugget-transporting gravels were in a river flowing in the shade of ricepaper trees, ginkos, ebonies, persimmons, avocados. In the auriferous gravels were found seven species of figs, four of walnut, 2 of avocado, thirteen kinds of oaks, 2 liquidambers. On this desk is material about fossils of the genus Citrus. Today wild oranges, lemons, grapefruit are confined to what botanists call the Indo-Malaysia region. The data before the writer indicate citrus trees once flourished in a jungle extending from Georgia to Texas.

One little known flora is that found at Elephants Head. Writer has also collected fossil leaves in the Monterey formation of Lower Carmel Valley. A third favorite locale is Eugene, Oregon.

* Alabama, Arkansas, Colorado, Delaware, Kansas, Louisiana, Mississippi, Massachusetts, Maryland, New Mexico, New York, New Jersey, Oregon, South Carolina, Tennessee, Utah, Vermont, Wyoming, Washington.

SUNKEN ROAD IN FOSSIL LEAF BED
This photograph is of a "sunken road". The soft rhyolite has eroded until only the horses ears and driver's head appear to one on the side. This lava flowed in a Tertiary riverbed. Its lower strata contain fossil leaves. This, when a different climate, (and elevation), gave California a flora that included magnolias, ebonies, ricepaper trees, persimmons, avocados.

MODERN HIGHWAY IN TERTIARY RIVER BED
The trans-Sierran highway at Gold Run is, for a short distance, in the bed of an ancient, (and goldbearing) Tertiary river. The wall, from auto to skyline trees, is river channel material. Fossil leaves therein have been found.

In Manchuria We-2 met an unusual European botanist. To hide his identity may we call him "Dr. Jensen?" He told of what he dubbed his "Great Imperial Forest." He had come from Denmark, via New York to Manchukuo. He studied the paleobotanical collections in New York and Washington. Then he botanized thru the North Carolina, Arkansas, Louisiana hardwoods. He had brief visits to several Trans-Mississippi paleobotanically-interesting localities. Finally S e a t t l e, Japan, Korea, Manchukuo. He insisted his "Great Imperial Forest" once stretched from Virginia's oaks, Louisiana's magnolias, pecans, Michigan's black walnuts, across to Oregon, Washington, over the now-submerged Alaska-Siberian landbridge to present-day Manchuria's walnuts, Japan's gingkos. He told of Dixie fossils—many cinnamons, a score of figs, magnolias, acacias, gingkos, sweetgums, myrtles, cypresses, walnuts. Hickories then stretched across the Dakotas, Wyoming, Montana, Canada, thru Alaska.

DR. JENSEN'S "GREAT IMPERIAL FOREST"

Under gold-weighted Tertiary California river lavacaps he found a series of oaks. Different from today's California oaks, these re-

Paleobotany 53

sembled those of today's South sweetgum belt. Louisiana's Tensaw Swamp trees was recalled by a fossil magnolia leaf (M. californica). These gravels had ebonies, figs, liquidambers, myrtles, even cousins of poison ivy. He split Eugene, Oregon's white shales, for black-brown leaf impressions.

The Doctor's "Great Imperial Forest" gradually dwindled, like a glacier's slow melting. He later took Us-2 on a dugout along a walnut-lined river to see a present day remnant thereof. Natives gathered wild silkworm cocoons. The fibre, spun by Japanese weavers, made a coarse element contrasting artistically with mulberry-eating silkworm's delicate threads. He reminded us California's tanbark oaks' botanical name, Pasania, was Latinized Malay. Gingkos, fossil in Oregon's white shales, once from Kansas to Alaska, persist to shade Buddhist temple drums. In Arizona, where suhuaro now fights with thousands of sharpened needles, fossil hickory nuts. These alongside Cochise Man's artifacts, also with extinct wild horse, camel, mammoth, giant bison bones. Tensaw Swamp hardwoods, daily falling, as this is written, beneath axe and saw, are of the last remnant of Dr. Jensen's "Imperial Forest."

One interesting member of the present Oregon forest is the Douglas Tree. It is a tree which, in 1791, Sir Archibald Menzies discovered when he explored the wild shores of Vancouver Island. The tree had no name and he evidently gave it none. Not until the ardent botanical explorer, David Douglas, rediscovered the tree which now bears his name, was this unique conifer really examined and made known. In 1827 it was taken to England where it became a much-admired ornamental evergreen.

From the beginning, Douglas' tree puzzled the botanists. It had so many conflicting characteristics that scientists were at a loss as to where to classify it among the conifers. Eventually it was discovered that there were only three species in the world. Two were in Western North America, one in Japan. The tree was Japan-Latinized "False Hemlock with Yew-like Needles," (PseudoTSUGA taxifolia). It was neither a yew nor a hemlock. Neither was it a spruce nor a fir. It maintained, however, some of the characteristics of all four.* . . .

Dad, as an adolescent, "grew too fast." His parents sent him from Melbourne to the family plantation. His aunt called her headman: "Give this lad a boomerang. Take him with 3 blackfellows into the Never-Never for 2 years. Bring him back a man." Dad's boomerang thus became his sole means of obtaining his food. Dad brought on his whaler to San Francisco a half dozen boomerangs. Sunday, his sons could play with them. Each had its story. One had disabled a wallaby, another had brought down a fat "teddybear". A third felled many a

---
* From "The Living Museum" (1253.)

cockatoo. At times, cockatoo-soup was the only food. Dad refused grubs, snakes. We begged yarns about "gwannas," . . . father-kangaroo disembowling a hound with one hoof-stroke. Dad could imitate *cucaburras*, had seen lyrebird's wedding dance. Other boys' fathers could yarn about "fish that got away." OURS told "Down-Under" ones, where crows were birds-of-paradise. This competitive spirit of boys was shrewdly used. Neighborhood lads might proclaim: "My Dad's got 2 Sunday suits," or "Mine's got a saddle with Mexican-silver dollars". None could claim a 6-boomerangs' Father that had found a platypus, had eaten an emu-egg omelette....

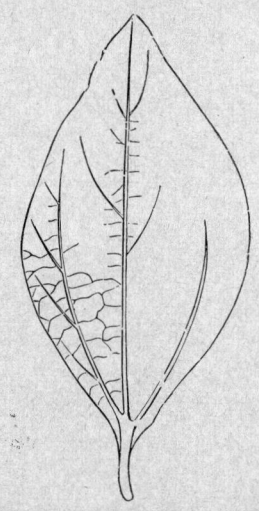

BOOMERANG FATHER

MISSISSIPPI CINNAMON (TERTIARY)
Cinnamonium Mississippieuse. (After Le Conte.) This author found modern cinnamon in Ceylon. Some seems also to come from Indo China jungles. Once cinnamons grew wild in South Carolina and Oregon,—in Vermont, Mississippi.

Mother started Nature Study with our ABC's. Each made his own butterfly net:—Mosquito netting sewn to a wire twisted around a sawn-off broom handle. We mounted our garden butterflies, beetles, bugs, with museum care. She taught us herbarium-making. Gravel from a nearly Tertiary riverbed was bought. Mother cracked pebbles: "This gray with white speck is andesite lava, from a sputtering volcano." "This pink is "rhyolite lava". "This green is amphibolite schist. This mottled rock is granite." All were labeled. Joys of joys, one day a quartz pebble, when cracked, showed a speck of free gold. We had a negro-like joy in "big words". Others struggled with 3-letter "cat", "dog", "pig". We boastfully dazzled with "basalt", "dolomite", "chalcopyrite", "serpentine"! Writer still treasures his fossil plants. Ought not every child have a home museum? Fossils are none too numerous in

Paleobotany

California. The Golden State, however, is rich in natural history "specimens" which furnish good exchange material from areas rich in fossils.* . . .

Almost any garden contains a fairly complete series of plants illustrating the evolution of, let us say, the composites from such organisms as the slime molds. Some debate as to whether latter are vegetable or animal. . . .

---

* As with friends helping when collecting postage stamps, a boy with miner friends could hope for exchange material. One of Dad's mining engineer friends sent from Montana a whole cigarbox of pyromorphite (the green phosphate of lead). Here was something attractive for one's Agassiz Association exchange list. A Pennsylvania boy wrote "I'll swap a bit of coal my father mined. It has what my teacher says is a sigillaria scar." What a thrill to unwrap that package when the mailcarrier left it with a welcome postmark!

Should not every child know the fun of studying garden fungi? Our lawn repeatedly has fairy rings. Of all our story telling to neighborhood kiddies, did anything bring more sparkle to the eyes than Grimm or Hans Christian Anderson retold with a fairy ring actually afront us? The quick child-mind sees the butterfly-winged elves dancing. In addition to our neighborhood kiddies' nature study class, (held in our garden with abundant living material to be scouted by them), We-2 had our own "Garden School." Over several decades, we budgeted units of a year each to various fields of biology. One year was devoted to studying our garden fungi. Spore prints and microscope work indoors,—in the garden was an amazing range of species. Most exciting was the discovery, then observation, of the bird's nest fungi. This also became a favorite, year after year, of the neighborhood kiddies' nature study class. There were repeatedly exciting finds:—"Inkcaps, Earthstars, Judas' Ears, Stinkhorns, (with their attracted flies), dainty little Morels, attractively-dimunitive Mycenas. Also interesting but dangerous were Death Cups. All this, it developed, was to become the basis for later worldwide study of the fungi. It lead us to many lands.

FUNGI FUN

The mycologist who does his work conscientiously in his own garden becomes qualified for the unexpected in world travel. One example was our pilgrimage to the battlefield of Morgarten. Here was a struggle that belongs to us almost as much as to the Swiss. In 1315 they, outnumbered 10 to 1, defeated their oppressors. We were able to picture this battle for liberty on the actual terrain where the courageous Swiss fought for freedom. We also there found several, to us, new species of fungi. About these we had learned in our garden year budgeted for its mushrooms and their allies. . . .

In Alsace, we knew certain species, new to us, could be found in the wonderful Vosges forests. At Strassburg's tourist office we made inquiries. The manager, an ardent mycologist, scratched his head:—"I know where you can collect what you want. To a true mycologist, they are worth a trip from California. I, however, ask myself:—Do I dare?" After further reflection, he wrote an address on a card. "Hire an automobile. Give the driver this." That driver whistled, looked at us rather searchingly, shook his head. Then he said in French:—"Well, it's none of my business. All my job is, take them there, get my fee." ... Puzzled, we nevertheless embarked.

High up in the Vosges, we motored some miles beyond a little village to an inn, deep in the forest. The landlady questioned us searchingly:—"Why came you here?" We told her. Still doubtful, "Are you members of our cult?" "We do not know what you mean, but that taxi driver acted strangely." "Who gave you our address?" Her face then brightened with an intelligent smile. "You have come to a nudist colony. True, here are very fine fungi as that Strassburg *Herr* said. He comes up here to collect. You may have his room on your promise the shade of the window looking out on the meadow will not be touched." We promised, enjoyed some of the finest collecting thrills possible for a mycologist. These joys could never have come to Us-2, had we not budgeted that year to our garden fungi.* ...

On one Indian summer day after the first October rains, for some unexplained reason, there is crowded into a space 7x4 yards in our garden, a mass of mushrooms. By counting them in one parallelogram, I estimated there are more than 2,100 units. This example of overpopulation is what stimulates garden philosophizing and thinking about world problems. From a journey by junk upriver, then overland by sedan chair, a friend knowing my interest in Eugenics sent me a photo of a father and 3 children. Since photo was taken, an epidemic struck their village. 2 out of the 3 children died. The nearest doctor, more than 100 miles away, could not begin to serve his painfully overpopulated area. Blundering American idealists now insist in the case of Hindustan's expectancy of life, as in Sweden. Would not such action enormously increase human misery? Nature automatically reduces overpopulation by pestilence, famine, by war. Left mortally wounded in battle, death comes soon. Is that not better than the long drawnout torture of starvation? Should we not give Hindustan first birth control before modern sanitation? Are not our own glaring mistakes in Puerto Rico a warning herein?

---

* As to a $225,000,000 industry, IN ONE YEAR, based on lowly plants, read Mr. Joseph Bernstein's "Natures Own Chemical Warfare." (Natural History, March, 1954.)

Because, the Breath of Flowers, is farre
Sweeter in the Aire, (where it comes and
Goes, like the Warbling of Musick) then
in the hand, therefore nothing is more
fit for that delight, than to know, what
be the Flowers, and Plants, that doe
best perfume the Aire. Roses Damask &
Red, are fast Flowers of their Smels;
So that; you may walke by a whole Row of
them, and finde Nothing of their Sweet-
nesse; Yea though it be, in a Mornings
Dew. Bayes likewise yeeld no Smell, as
they grow. Rosemary little; Nor Sweet-
Marioram. That, which aboue all Others,
yeelds the Sweetest Smell in the Aire, is
the Violet; Specially the White-double-
Violet, which comes twice a Yeare; About
the middle of Aprill, and about Bartholo-
mew-tide. Next to that is, the Muske-
Rose. Then the Strawberry-Leaues dying,
which (yeeld) a most Excellent Cordiall
Smell. Then the Flower of the Vines; It
is a little dust, like the dust of a Bent,
which growes vpon the Cluster, in the
First coming forth. Then Sweet Briar.
Then Wall-Flowers, which are very Delight-
full, to be set vnder a Parler, or Lower
Chamber Window. Then Pinks, (and Gilly-
Flowers,) specially the Matted Pinck, and
Cloue Gilly-flower. Then the Flowers of
the Lime Tree. Then the Honny-Suckles,
so they be somewhat a farre off.

     (Bacon's Essays)

"The term "National Park" ought to be like what the word sterling is to silver. It ought to indicate outstanding merit."   (Louis C. Campton)

While considering our garden plants' fossilized origins, one might be reminded of the remarkable educational material free in our National Parks and National Monuments. They are a veritable chain of marvelously well planned outdoor museums. These, incidentally, illustrate all the forces that culminated in producing our garden plants. Vulcanism, (which, along with glaciation, has been a potent factor in soil-making also in plant migration, also extinction, likewise evolution, of species), has unexcelled *al fresco* laboratories in Lassen N. P., Hawaii N. P., Crater N. P., Yellowstone N. P... What better places than Yosemite N. P., Sequoia N. P., Kings Canyon N. P., to study soilgrinding glaciation? Did that ice reduce the Great Sequoia Forest once stretching from Siberia and Alaska across Kansas, Pennsylvania to Greenland, Spitzbergen, Switzerland. (Only a few "Sylvan Islands" like the scattered Sierra Big Trees and the Coast Redwoods* remain.) A hundred examples could be cited as to how you can increase enjoyment of your garden if you make pilgrimages until you have visited ALL the National Parks. While several parks have smaller paleobotanical items, the best outdoor museum as to fossil trees in Petrified Forest National Monument....

USE NATIONAL PARKS FOR PALEOBOTANY

He who would philosophize about gardening will be rewarded with gems, if he goes a-mining in Kipling's "Plain Tales from the Hills." He may be enlightened, for example, about the Language of Flowers, in "Beyond the Pale". Its story is of Amir Nath's Gully, of the man Trejago, of Biesa, child widow, who was "good to look upon," of her "both hands cut off at the wrists."

"Next morning, as he was driving to office, an old woman threw a packet into his dog-cart. In the packet was half a broken glass-bangle, one flower of the blood-red *dhak,* a pinch of *bhusa* or cattle-food, and eleven cardamoms. That packet was a letter—not a clumsy, compromising letter, but an innocent unintelligible lover's epistle.

LANGUAGE OF FLOWERS

"Trejago knew far too much about these things, as I have said. No Englishman should be able to translate object-letters. But Trejago spread all the trifles on the lid of his

---

* So deeply convinced is this writer as to the educational value of the Coast Sequoias that he purchased for California State Park system the Mary Glide Goethe Memorial Grove bordering the Roosevelt elk meadow near Orick. . . . Later he donated the Bible Toter Jedediah Smith Grove. (This since has been expanded by the State Park Board to include some 10,000 acres of Coast Redwoods a "Jedediah Smith State Park") This author now is purchasing for State Park conservation a third grove. It is to honor Dr. Newton Drury and his brother, Mr. Aubrey Drury who have devoted much of their best years to Save-the-Redwoods League.

office-box and began to puzzle them out. The flower of the *dhak* means diversely 'desire,' 'come,' 'write,' or 'danger,' according to the other items "A broken glass-bangle stands for a Hindu widow all India over; because, when her husband dies, a woman's bracelets are broken on her wrists. Trejago saw the meaning of the things with it. One cardamon means 'jealousy'; but when any article is duplicated in an object-letter, it loses its symbolic meaning and stands merely for one of a number indicating time, or if incense, curds, or saffron be sent also, place. The message ran then—'A widow—*dhak* flower and *bhusa,*—at eleven o'clock.' The pinch of *bhusa* enlightened Trejago. He saw—this kind of letter leaves much to instinctive knowledge—that the *bhusa* referred to the big heap of cattle-food over which he had fallen in Amir Nath's Gully, and that the message must come from the person behind the grating; she being a widow. So the message ran then—'A widow, in the Gully in which is the heap of *bhusa,* desires you to come at eleven o'clock'."

GOD OF THE GODS

Ammon Ra was Egypt's God of the Gods. Is it not significant he often is pictured with the lotus?

Perhaps, after philosophizing, you, too, gentle Reader may feel the urge to try to help. It was above story of Hindu widow-tabus that helped send Us-2, (once U.S.A.'s supervised playground's campaign was safely launched), to do our bit, however feeble, attempting to carry that movement to unhappy Hindustan. That land still cruelly penalizes widowhood, even tho the British Raj had ended the *suttee*.

———o———

The boutonniere influence can emphasize flower-language. It sometimes even becomes historic. Once, at the Court dinner, a King of France appeared with a potato flower in his buttonhole.* The fawning courtiers were puzzled. When all were seated, he said:—"We are to have this evening a soup of what you'all consider a poisonous plant.

POTATO'S PURPLE BLOOM POSTPONES FRENCH REVOLUTION

If it be poisonous, let us all die now, instead of at the mob's hands." His guests knew the ominous murmurings of the hungry against excessive taxation, while Court luxury was ostentatious. The King continued:—"The potato's flower resembles the deadly nightshade's. Because of this, people suppose the New World's potato should be grown only for ornament. One of my subjects, the chemist Parmentier, has convinced me, from his own eating potato tubers, that it is not poisonous, is highly nutritious. That man has wisdom beyond most of you here tonight. His ear is close to the ground. He grasps we are on the edge of bloody revolution, preventable by food. Many potatoes are grown as garden flowers throughout France. We shall save the "eyes" for a muchly expanded new crop. The rest shall be eaten. You will have some tonight in 'Potage Parmentier'."

The King was shrewd. Next day the courtiers were wearing potato-bloom boutonnieres. Within a week, shopkeepers were bidding for single buttonhole flowers. That winter the potato saved the Dynasty. Next year France blossomed with potatoes from the English Channel to the Pyrenees, from the spout of the Brittany Teapot to Mont Blanc.

The fleur-de-lis, France's royal Coat of Arms, thus was not to be displaced. The potato flower remained as significant as the thistles of Scotland, Ireland's shamrock, the cornflower that represents German outwitting of Napoleon, the *edelweiss* of the Alps, Canada's maple leaf, Australia's warata, the lotus of the ancient Egyptians, still persisting in Buddhist folktales, or Japan's chrysanthemum.†

---

* In Barbados the negro women manufacture buttonhole bouquets of flying fish scales dyed different colors to resemble their common garden flowers.

† Townsfolk resort in thousands to the florists' gardens of Dango-zaka to see the November chrysanthemum shows. The flowers are trained over trelliswork to represent historical and mythological scenes, ships, dragons, other curious objects.

Paleobotany 61

When Queen Mary's lady-in-waiting is trying to keep Warden Paulet from opening the jewel box he has found, the jailer exclaims "A crown, ornamented with the lilies of France."

One corner of the garden might be devoted to the favorites of yesteryear. This, particularly if the garden owner has reached retirement age. Its roses might include la Marque, la France, (or its descendant, Madam Testout), also Jacquemenot. There might even be room for one of the rather unpleasantly-smelling yellow roses so popular in California in Gold Rush days.

OLD FAVORITES

The use of garden greens can be healthful. A beloved physician of California's Gold Rush came to Sacramento from Louisiana. He often wrote a prescription:—"1 green pepper daily." This doctor admitted he did not know whence came the benefits. This, before men knew anything about vitamins. . . .

The affection of men for flowers, both garden and *sauvage*, is shown by their use throughout history.

One flower, which for a while unaccountably yielded place in flower fashions to the sedum, is the peony. Its grip on the affections now seems, nevertheless, to be strong. One finds it in old New England graveyards. Peonies are in high esteem from China to Arabia. The Orientals know how to breed peonies from the best stocks. In the Near East one repeatedly hears a folksaying:—"You cannot make an Arab steed out of a donkey by cropping its ears." And in Japan, Kanazawa, on the shores of the Mutsura Inlet, is chiefly noted for its Hakkei,—a characteristically Japanese view from a small height just outside the village. Close to the ferry, at the foot of a wooded hill called Nojimayama is a celebrated peony garden. It attracts many visitors during the season of flowering. Some of the plants are said to be over 300 years old. . . .

In Japan, We-2 occasionally joined Japanese friends for a foot pilgrimage to some rural teahouse. The object might be to enjoy a waterfall, a view of Fujiyama, a garden of dwarfed plants, perhaps a venerable wisteria. One of latter was so old its trunk reminded us of a giant anaconda We-2 saw in a South American jungle. This particular wisteria experience stimulated our purchasing a *multijaga*, for pendant spring blooms before foliage buds opened. Planted at the foot of the great elm base, it was visible from our great hall. With the years the wisteria grew enormously. Came the day when its increased weight crashed down one of the elm's finest branches. Same was essential to said hall picture.

TEA HOUSE OF THE WISTERIA

At first shocked, later saw compensation in that mutilated limb, as a perpetual sermon as to improper immigrant screening. During Truman's administration, under a very adroit Displaced Persons' screen, hordes of East European immigrants were rushed on American ships to U.S.A. On this desk is a story of one immigrant, guilty of income tax fraud. His income originally was based on commercialized vice. He became the owner of a skyscraper, also of a valuable hotel. By that clipping's side is another of an aged widow's weakling son. He stole her life savings, lost them in gambling at a vice center. One study made of commercialized vice origins showed almost complete absence of oldtime American-stock names. Such lack of screening gave us Displaced Person Klaus Fuchs. He betrayed our atomic bomb secrets to Russia. Contrast Russia's methods and ours. This month the Rosenberg traitors have been executed for betraying military secrets, only after 9 Supreme Court appeals. Rioting East Berlin workers who "confessed" are shot, not after 2 years, with 9 Supreme Court appeals but within a few hours. . . .

CAMEL CARAVAN, TRAIL TOWARD TIMBUCTU
To the right of our photograph, a little above the camel colt, can be seen the shadow of an attempt at the nearer of two retaining walls. The *"wadi,"* or arroyo, is, at times, pipe for those rare but copious desert cloudbursts. Beyond the left, this *wadi* was lined, both sides, with blooming oleanders. Despite drought, also heat, the desert's biota, from Bedouin and their camels to oleanders and date-palms, succeed in reproducing. Only among our Occidental highpowers is the natural birthrate excessively reversed.

Another of the oldfashioned flowers whose return to favor seems perennial is the oleander. In countries with a kindly winter as California's they are an outdoor desirable. Who could ever forget Lake Como at the height of oleander bloom? One wonders, on seeing tubbed oleanders in occasional European castles, whether they are not another inheritance from the Crusades.

Among writer's boyhood Home Museum's seed bottles was a long one with seed pods from our garden's single oleander. Mother wound a thread several times around one pod to prevent splitting. The other discharged the parachuted seeds. Some years later writer was taught to estimate the number of seeds produced that season by that one bush. It exceeded 3,000! Here was an early overpopulation lesson.

OLEANDERS MAKE DESERT COLOR

In future years We-2 were to enjoy wild oleander blooms. The plants lined the *wadys* carrying the North African rock deserts' drainage. Same sinks later into Saharan sands, which resemble the "sinks" of our Nevada desert.

In Guatemala one sees a yellow oleander "cousin", i.e. Allamanda. The *Indios* there call attention to the color as the same as on the hair of an "Alvarado" mask of their ceremonial. One philosophizes about the persistence of the "Fair God" folktale and remembers Lew Wallace's novel of that name. Was there a pre-Columbian Nordic?

Zeri Hayford, typical colonial Nordic pioneer, was noted for great physical strength and endurance. He stood 6 feet 7½ inches in his stockings. He had cleared a full acre of primeval forest timber in a day. Growth was dense and large. They had 8 children....

U.S.A. is apparently rich in fertility and abundance of its land resources. A recent 2-year Senate study of the nation's health disclosed, however, that, of more than 14,000,000 men examined for the draft, only 2,000,000 were fully up to standard. A supplementary study indicates some 12% were mentally unfit for military duty.

Writer's friend, the late Lothrop Stoddard, (Harvard Ph.D.) wrote of another colonial family. In his "The Revolt Against Civilization", he declared that U.S.A. needs more families like that old Puritan, strain. "At their head, Jonathan Edwards. In 1900, his descendants numbering, 1,394. Of these 1,295 were college graduates. 13 were presidents of our greatest colleges; 65 college professors. Besides above many principals of other important educational institutions. 60 were physicians, many eminent. More than 100 were clergymen, missionaries, or theological professors. 75 were army or navy officers. 60 were prominent authors. 33 American States and several foreign countries have profited by the beneficent influences of their eminent activity. 30 were judges, 80 held public office, one was U.S.A. vice-president. 3 were U. S. senators. Several were governors, others members of Congress, framers of State constitutions, mayors of cities, ministers to foreign courts. One was president, Pacific Mail Steamship Company. 15 railroads, many banks, insurance companies, large industrial enterprises have been indebted to their management. Almost, if not every department of social progress, and of the public weal has felt the impulse of this healthy and long-lived family. IT IS NOT KNOWN THAT ANY ONE OF THEM WAS EVER CONVICTED OF CRIME."

Dr. Stoddard's "Revolt" is a 1923 book of rare prophecy. It should be reread in these days of Communist infiltration, especially into Latin "republics" between Texas and Panama. Incidentally, Dr. Stoddard once told undersigned he was compelled to cease such writing! Has there not been, for some years an unseen censorship in U.S.A. as efficient as any behind either the Iron or the Bamboo Curtain?

WILD ARTICHOKES

It was in a nomad camp We-2, while botanizing, found our first artichokes. The inhabitants of these thriftily patched camelshair tents resented the presence of Outlanders. Their suspicions were seconded by their dogs, (note one to the extreme left.) Their canines are as savage as those of Greek shepherds, or of Lapp owners of reindeer.

Above pictures the nomadic stage before the gardening stage. Much of that transition must have been possible, must it not, because of the eugenically high-powered intellects, such as those who invented the use of fire. In the foreground is the muchly patched ragged camels hair tent of a Bedouin. His camels and his family can only persist as long as there is grass for pasture. Once that is exhausted he must move on. Note behind in the skyline the date garden partially enclosed in an adobe fence at the right. Once mankind was able to grow food and also cook it, gardening could commence.

"Eat no fig until it wears a
beggars coat." (Arab folksaying)

Some garden plants yield blooms that are food. The clove is the clove tree's unexpanded bud. French confectioners stock candied acacia flowers, also violets.

The fig is another edible flower. Fig milk was used, as in King Tut's tomb, by painters to fix colors long before oil painting was invented. California's Smyrna fig industry parallels Maeterlinck's

EDIBLE FLOWERS

philosophy:—Bee-keeper's success depends upon observing the Law-of-the-Hive. California could raise, successfully, black Mission figs. It could not, however produce sugary white Smyrnas. American pioneer resourcefulness sent a Fresno fig grower to Anatolia. He there discovered sugary Smyrnas were based on pollenization of a certain wasp.

The fig has been an object of cultivation since Biblical days. We-2 could never forget reading the Sermon on the Mount after we had hiked to the little hillock on which it was first preached. Around us was much camel thorn, the chaparral from which the twigs for the Crown of Thorns was obtained. It was here where the Gentle Carpenter of Nazareth used the fig in a eugenic parable:—"Do men gather . . . figs of thistles?" Perhaps another translator would have said: "Artichokes instead of thistles."

One example of a truly edible flower or at least its bud is said artichoke. We-2 found same growing wild in the rock desert facing sanddunes of the Sahara proper. It is a country inhabited largely by nomadic Berbers with their herds of goats and/or camels. They stew the wild artichokes. After all, they are not bad eating if one is hungry enough.

The zenith of artichoke cookery is reached at Paris. This, even after you have feasted on artichokes and fresh fish at that tiny seaside inn in the southern Peloponnesus, have enjoyed stuffed artichokes a la Montenegro. (That nation had a royal house whose tall princess was won in marriage by the undersized King of Italy. He cannily remarked his runtishness was the DYSGENIC product of Europe's royal marriage system of interbreeding.)

ARTICHOKES, ALSO MILK THISTLES

The flowers most widely eaten are apparently those of the Compositae's thistle tribe. In Sicily, and Calabria, where overpopulation is painful, a macaroni dinner is as much of a peasant or a sulphur-miner family treat as is our Thanksgiving turkey. With such a humble dinner, We-2 once were served boiled milk-thistle flower scales as a green vegetable. They really have almost as much edible pulp as that of the wild artichoke of North Africa's rock desert. In Japan it is fashionable to serve a dainty salad of chrysanthemum petals. We never had this experience, tho in the South Seas we found quite palatable a salad, eaten quite innocently, of raw flying fish flakes flavored with fresh cocoanut milk.

Honey locust flowers are used by negro children as candy for a sweet omelette. The words of the original "Dixie Land" read:—

> 'Dey am cornmeal cakes an' honey-locust batter,
> Makes yo' fat or a little fatter'.

FLOWERS IN THE MARKET OF SAIGON

Southeast Asia (Indo China, Burma, Malaysia) is an orchid lover's paradise. Above photograph's lower righthand corner, a dozen lotus flowers. The Buddhists poetically remind one the lotus rises from the roots in the stinking mud below skyward, to beauty of bloom.

(Note the coolie to the left is barefooted. This means exposure to parasites like hookworm. Once we project Occidental medical science into the lives of these backward peoples, their death rate drops markedly. Meantime the primitive birth-rate, "a-baby-a-year", continues. Out of this grows increasingly painful population pressure . . ., finally, war. Will not a hungry man, like this barefooted coolie prefer, if necessary, sudden battlefield death to slow starvation death? In war there also is always the possibility of looting those weaker.)

A Californian, used to fresh flowers throughout the home, also thrice daily fresh fruit from his own garden, is deeply impressed by Northern Europe's widespread efforts toward window-box gardening. Perhaps, as in Read's lines, because "they" also "twinkle their mute praises" of brightness in Heaven.

WINDOW-BOX GARDENS To Desert lovers, almost pathetic seemed the window garden of a cottage at Norway's North Cape. The Iceland poppies of other visits had not yet dared unroll their carpets of orange and of canary yellow mottled with white. At the window, which later would

Paleobotany 67

look toward the Midnight Sun, were a dozen pots of succulents and cacti, mute reminders, in late winter, of brightness sure to come.

One of the garden's never-ceasing spiritual dividends is fellowship with the birds who are the gardener's guests. To entertain them so that they look forward eagerly to a return visit requires careful planning*.

In Switzerland's Bernese Oberland is Adelboden. The milk chocolate made in that little town one cannot buy anywhere else. It is like eating Emmenthaler where it is made on these high mountain pastures. At the century's turn, one could travel to Adelboden only by horsedrawn diligence. This little center is snowbound in winter, has then an industry of jewelry making. When We-2 arrived we became interested in Adelboden's beautiful window boxes. The flowers were said to have been raised indoors, to be placed when the snow was gone. Our other interest was the dwellings behind these window gardens. They were made of timber. Some dated back to the 1770's. They had weathered a beautiful brown, just as unpainted Cape Cod houses silver. Each home had a text from the Bible, as:—"I raise my eyes to the mountains, whence cometh my strength." There also was the date when the bridegroom built the house for his bride. Below it was the name of Adelboden's head carpenter at that time. One house was labeled:—"I, Alois Ulrich, bachelor, built this house for myself, in 1782, without any help from the Adelboden *hauptzimmermann*.

SWISS CHALET WINDOW GARDENS

Was it not rather significant said chalet, even years later, had no window box gardens? Isolation seemed to persist as a blight. There was still no room for the softening influence of flowers. . . .

A Japanese peasant's dwelling roof sometimes is overgrown with iris or the red rice-paddy lilies. Some say that the bulbs are planted, that the Gods will be pleased and will therefore avert pestilence. This rice-paddy "lily" is really an amaryllis. One of the most colorful sights of the old Japan was the green of the growing rice blocked into squares by the lines of blooming paddy lilies. Such gardening in roof-thatch is worldwide. In gale-swept Norway, roofs were weighted with sod. These often are one color-mass of wild pansies. In Normandy, also Brittany, roofs often are bright with the glaucous-green of stonecrops. . . .

THATCHED ROOF GARDENS

In the good old days when, at Lahore, the Governor's carriage was camel-drawn, We-2 watched, from a vantage point, the humans densely packed in the street leading to Kashmir Gate. My Sweetheart (who often had gone with me to Holland polders to select "Dutch bulbs" for our garden) remarked of the varicolored turbans: "How

---
* See item on garden-planning, city planning, statewide planning, nation planning. (See page 68.)

like tulips bobbing in the wind"? Today is not yet mid-February. One of those 3-day March northers has been ambitious and has raced to California weeks ahead of his appointed time. Under his gusts, (which come with machine-gun like regularity), the white tazettas, the yellow Emperors—yes even the stout-stemmed Tibetan saxifrages are, indeed, bobbing in the wind like the turbans of Anarkali Bazaar.

Often thereafter we repeated that as we watched Lahore's jammed foot-traffic. This approaching the Mosque of Wazir Kahn. There are beautiful and ancient gardens in the old capital of the Grand Moguls, such as Shah Jahan's Shalimar Gardens (since 1637) and Gulabi Bach, the rose garden of 1655. Anar Kali Garden was built to surround the tomb of Anarkali (Pomegranate Blossom), favorite above all the ladies of the Grand Mogul's harem. Her garden tomb is inscribed with the 99 beautiful names of Allah. In these gardens are some of the world's most beautifully colored tile work. This is the land of Zamzamah, that great green-bronze cannon whose name, the natives tell, means "the Lion's Roar". They invariably add the folksaying:— "Who holds Zamzamah holds the Punjab." . . .

> They know the time to go!
> The fairy clocks strike their inaudible hour
> In field and woodland, and each punctual flower
> Bows at the signal an obedient head
> And hastes to bed. (Susan Coolidge—Time to Go.)

One byproduct of gardening, as seen by the garden-philosopher, is the very practical educational value of garden planning. The successful garden is one that ever must be planned anew. This author's friend, the late Carl Purdy, (who did so much to educate gardeners worldwide as to appreciate California's native lillales, such as our mariposas) once wrote in our home's guest book:—

> "That garden with which the gardener is satisfied
> is a garden which should be sold."

Is not one of gardening's greatest joys the ever-necessary planning? What can equal the midwinter thrill of evenings pouring over next season's seed catalogues? As a rancher who grows seeds, this author knows the planning (necessary for

GARDEN PLANNING, CITY PLANNING, NATION PLANNING, WORLD PLANNING

even survival) by the seedmen. Then, too, there is the gardener's creative joy of ever improving his beds.

Out of this, over many years, this author can testify its worth in providing city planning. The Sacramento Woman's Council, (a coalition of many women's clubs) financed the coming, to

California's capital, at this century's turn of one well informed in what then was a new movement, city planning. Writer's friend, the late Dr. J. Horace Macfarland, had pioneered therein in Pennsylvania. He had written to Us-2 that someone out on Pacific Coast should take leadership in inaugurating the movement out West. My Sweetheart was devoted to the opportunities for civic service in Women's Clubs.* We both were untiring in our own garden planning.

This author's first adventure into Botany was as a wee bairn more than three-fourths century ago. Mother, with characteristic French thrift, had planted some prolific squash seed—to insure a young professor's family plenty of this nutritious food. Its flowers, in mother's absence one day, were diligently gathered by her firstborn for a present for her. The incident is mentioned as evidence the tendency to observe nature begins not many months after a child begins to toddle.

Hence may there be recorded here the hope that both the Sacramento-American Rivers Parkways project, also the parallel and vaster one, the Mississippi River Parkways, can be translated from dreams into actualities. Will not such strings of parks, linked by attractive river scenery, constitute perpetual outdoor Nature Study School for the kiddies, also kiddies "grown up"....

PLANNING FOR SUCCESSION OF BLOOM It is November. Since July there has been an unbroken succession of summer chrysanthemums. In August, September, October, however, they have competed for our affections with phlox, asters, French also African marigolds, goldenrod, Rudbeckias, even bougainvillea. Now, however, any day Jack Frost's infecting fingers will spread dismay among zinnias, ageratum, roses.† (In a part of Akasaka called Aoyama, is situated the palace occupied for many years by the Crown Prince. It is not open to the public; but the elite of Tokyo society is invited there once yearly to a garden party given in November, on the occasion of what is perhaps the most wonderful chrysanthemum show in the world.)

One may attempt a small orchid house, (as some Californians do even in a 5-room bungalow garden). There then is stimulated philoso-

---
* Our family, over 3 generations, had Hindustan connections. We-2, after our successful privately starting present Sacramento Playgrounds, carried "American Supervised Play" to the Orient. Our Calcutta c.nter still survives. This brought my Sweetheart's adventure with the Begum of Bhopal. Latter addressed an All-Indian Women's meeting. My Beloved and our Calcutta hostess were the only 2 not in purdah. . . . The Begum brought from her World Tour a magnificently-jeweled case. It held a red hair from the Prophet's beard. She said:—"Occidentals offer us nothing. The one exception: I attended, in Denver, a Women's Clubs' National Federation. U.S.A. Men are hopeless. Improving American living conditions is by organized womanhood!" This Maharanee's estimate impressed me profoundly. Much success We-2 had in translating our ideals into actualities came thru the Begum's deductions.

---
† "America's Vast New Leisure Class" condensed from "Business Week:" The Department of Commerce figure for the expenditure in 1952 on flowers, seeds and potted plants was $836,000,000—within hailing distance of the biggest paid-admission recreation, the movies. The outdoor-power-tool business has already developed a $200,000,000-a-year volume in mowers, tractors, saws, clippers and other equipment. . . . And leisure has been democratized. (Business Week 9/53 . . . Reader's Digest.)

phizing as to the epiphytes. Whether these be one's home grown orchids, in the jungle, an epiphytic cactus or a brilliant red air plant, the thinking observer is intrigued by their survival with a minimum of food. Many depend upon such nourishment as rainwater or the Cloud Forest's fog drips down the tree trunk whereon they grow. The wealth of Cloud Forest orchids and other airplants can be illustrated by this anecdote: When writer was birding in Venezuela, he met a Venezuelan official's nephew. This young man criticized us thusly:—"You Americans measure everything by the Dollar, and that, not always with the best judgment." He recently had danced with a young New York debutante. He asked permission to call. Before doing so, he diplomatically dispatched some 17 orchids to the girl's aunt. That lady greeted him with:—"You are extravagant! Those orchids in New York would cost $850." He whispered to writer later:—"I gave a peon a half dollar to gather them in the Cloud Forest." ...

ORCHIDS

Unforgettable is a certain Malaysia home. In its walled compound, surrounding our host's bungalow was a garden of tropical trees. He estimated that, at our visit, more than 10,000 orchids were in bloom. These were mostly epiphytic upon said trees.

In Salvador, We-2 used to enjoy before-breakfast strolls in a charming bungalow section. In its well kept gardens the dominant color note was orchids. Sometimes a simple bungalow would have literally hundreds of them.

This author has experimented with an aucuba. Because of its attractive leaves the kiddies, with active imaginations, appropriately name it "golddust plant". Writer has kept, for many months, an aucuba twig, (with 4 leaves and a terminal bud) in a bottle in his sleeping porch shade. The bud does not show much growth. The leaves, however, remain healthy, do not wilt. There also IS a fascinating growth of roots from both joints of that twig now below water.

This ability to exist, to even grow upon a minimum may be of profound importance in our solving the problems of survival between Occidentals and Orientals.

> CONSIDER the lilies of the field:—
> They toil not, neither do they spin.
> Yet Solomon, in all his glory, was not
> Arrayed like one of these. (Matthew VI-28)

A previous chapter recalled flowering plants (including the rushes, sedges, grasses, palms) came into being in the Cretaceous. The Gentle Carpenter of Nazareth bade us CONSIDER the lilies of

Paleobotany 71

the field. Just as the English, (who never had seen an apricot), translated that fruit-name as "apple", so there is uncertainty among botanists as to Palestine's "lilies". Opinions range from
HOLY LAND tulips to anemones, ranunculus, cyclamen. All are as
"LILIES" bulb-based as is our lily.* One of life's deepest spiritual experiences for Us-2 was the journey from Jerusalem, past Nablus, also the Well of the Woman of Samaria, to Nazareth. This was long ago. The only obtainable lodgings reeked with camel-stink. From our window, across the narrow street, a young apprentice was in a carpenter shop. On his floor, such scrap and shavings that once brought forth an artisan's criticism of an artist. Latter asked "What do you think of my masterpiece of The Christ?" "Well, never saw a carpentershop floor that clean of shavings!"

Our trip next day to the Sea of Galilee included leaving the highroad for a walk to a hillock. On it, that Carpenter of the Long Ago preached, in His Sermon on the Mount:—"CONSIDER the lilies." It was not "Look at the lilies!" Our trail that spring morning lay thru wild gardens. They were crimson and golden with tulips, ranunculus and anemones. The Divine admonition was to CONSIDER, to reflect, (dare it be added, to philosophize?). We Occidentals are absorbed in gardening. Our plant breeders, with modern genetics' research, give us ever novel marvels. May it not be worth while, nevertheless, in philosophizing about Gardening, occasionally to recall some bits of the "backward" Orient's flower lore . . . ?

Anagallis arvensi is a primrose. Its folk name is "poorman's weatherglass." Its flowers are vermillion, a color seldom seen in blossoms. These flowers of this 4-angle-stemmed plant close at approach of bad weather. There is a blue variety, just as some blue Lappula, also blue Forget-me-nots have pink flowers. Anagallis is an unobtrusive
"weed". To it, however, our garden does not refuse
WEATHER- hospitality. The flowers are so small that, laying them
PREDICTION side by side, they are six to one's thumb nail. The
FLOWERS plant itself is finger-high.

It is one of the so-called "weather-vane flowers". Like the daisy, also the eschscholtzia, it reacts to overcast skies which may bring rain. Another of these weather-predicting plants is Calendula. With a range from canary-yellow to orange it offers pleasing color contrasts at Christmas. This result can be obtained by planning to planting in August. Seed boxes are not necessary. It is almost weed-like in hardihood.

---

* As to Girls names, Mr. Elsdon C. Smith's "The Story of Our Names" estimates the relative U.S.A. popularity. Rose is 22nd (660,000), Rosalie 94, (114,000) Rosemary 60th (249,000) Violet 76th (195.000), Lilly-ian 23rd (650,000), Margaret 6th, (Marguerite) (1,485,000), Florence 20th (750,000). Fashions changed. In the last century, Daffodil, Dahlia, Orchid were favored. (In considering, in probing for understanding of what Mother Nature may be trying to tell us with her flowers, let us also not forget Hindustan's folksaying:—"The Sahibs have not ALL the wisdom.")

WILD CALENDULA WHICH WAS A BUTTONAIRE AT PIANO DEI GRECCI EASTER MASS

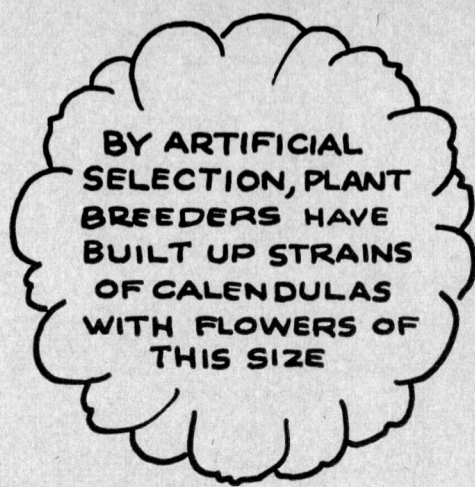

BY ARTIFICIAL SELECTION, PLANT BREEDERS HAVE BUILT UP STRAINS OF CALENDULAS WITH FLOWERS OF THIS SIZE

CALENDULA

The example of the fish form outlined with the automobile would be apparent to any teenager. They could not be expected, however, to be quite as absorbed as is an octogenarian as to human hybridization. Anyone, however, who has carried on worldwide studies therein grasps what is constantly occurring in the garden as to such ordinary plants as calendulas.

Our Sicilian gardener of yesteryear, Guiseppe, was contemptuous of "them things wot is weeds in my country". The insignificant wild calendula may deserve his contempt. On the other hand, considering one's duty as a city planning pioneer, one plants for brilliant outdoor color effect at Christmas. Hence the facade beds afront the home, also the big center bed in full view of the Boulevard have thousands of calendulas in contrasting orange and gold. This Christmas mass color effect is only obtainable because of supergiant blooms. WE BUY OUR SEED STOCK FRESH EVERY YEAR FROM A HOLLYWOOD BREEDER. We dare not utilize any seed saved from the previous year. This, because we have no control over bee-pollenization. Along with honey-gathering, the bees do a remarkably thorough job of hybridizing thru pollen from neighborhood strains with small blooms. In a single year, the strain begins to run out.

As for marigolds, poppies, hollyhocks, and valorous sunflowers, we shall never have a garden without them, both for their own sake, and for the sake of old-fashioned folks, who used to love them.
(Henry Ward Beecher—Star Papers)

When we are in Britain to trace back the origin of daisy's name, we grasp how World Wars I and II really were eugenically as needless as U.S.A.'s War of 1861-65. Just as we lost the flower of Virginia and the Carolinas and of New England, so Britain lost another irreplaceable "pool of genes" in the Oxford and Cambridge men of that "1st 100,000." We further dealt Germany, and, incidentally, all mankind, a third loss when we annihilated the 5,000 scientists concentrated at Puenemuende. "Daisy" indeed, or day's eye in the Anglo Saxon was *daeges eago*, (not very far from German *tages-augen*). On the moors of this writer's ancestors' Yorkshire, the little plant is "bairnswort", indica-

DAY'S-EYE'S MECHANISM

tive of children's love of it. The ray flowers close at night, do so even on cloudy days. . . .

Heroic poems always have persisted, century after century. As to our first trip to Finland, We-2 often remarked that its most lasting impression was the Kalavala. Note, too, Sagas, particularly the Icelandic ones. Students of Greek thumb the Iliad and the Odessy to tatters. Is there anything grander than the Vedic hymns which our Nordic blood brethren gave to all mankind forever? Mornings, this student of garden philosophy greets the break of day singing reverently a stanza from the Vedic "Hymn to the Dawn."

There is also another epic unfolding constantly in the garden. It is the Epic of the Sunflower. It is the Epic of Evolution. Tremendously accelerated by cross-fertilization, it finds its climax today in the cooperation and the work-specialization of ray flowers and of disc flowers in said sunflower. Is there not something symbolic in its inflorescence being the image of the Sun God? . . .

California gardens, with oranges, lemons, limes, figs, pomegranates (*Anarkali* of the Arabs)—even bougainvillea and gardenias— lack the winter white of snow. They do have, however, a kind of "green snow." It is not a bacteria-colored snow like red-snow and also green snow. It is however a rather satisfactory equivalent. It falls in mid-April. The nearest approach to snow we have in our Sacramento gardens is the noiseless fluttering down of ten thousand matured elm blossoms. This comes just before the leaf-buds open. They have furnished a banquet to the housefinches newly arrived from Cuernevaca, even Tasco.

Ever since We-2 were at Oxford, we have had garden border sections in Nepeta. A colorful mint cousin is none too common in American gardens. The plants are covered with the tiny blue-purple blossoms. Its nectar-offering seems attractive to both bees and butterflies. Near Balliol College, Oxford, stands Martyr's Memorial to once long forgotten martyrs—Cranmer, Latimer and Ridley. They were burned, 1555-6 in front of Balliol College. (Jedediah Smith was America's prime Forgotten Man. He jolted into being the movement destined to making California our flag's 31st star, also U.S.A. a transcontinental power. This happened in a crisis even now fully known to only a few historians. Lewis and Clark reported "impossible" when our Government hoped to militarily take Oregon Territory. "Great American Desert" then was a white blotch on map. Our Government knew nothing of the Sierra Nevadas. It supposed Sacramento River flowed westward from near Great Salt Lake. None who attempted to explore that Desert returned.)

MARTYRS

Smith, nicknamed "Bible Toter", was of remarkable moral worth, physically powerful, mentally alert. He headed a picked party of 23. All, except this leader, were lost in the two redskin massacres. Smith, staggering to Wyoming Rendezvous, gasped:—"I found a great California valley. Room for 100,000 farmsteads. Send military expedition (Fremont was sent) to blaze trail, then start Covered Wagons rolling."

Smith was a forgotten man until writer's Sweetheart, 40 years ago, while we were on university historical research, found reference to a "Bible Toter". We started probings,—finally covered much of his trail from Ohio headwaters to San Gabriel Mission, thence to *Rio de los Americanos de Jedediah Smith* (now American River, between Sacramento and North Sacramento).

THE TOPPLERSCHLOSSEN, ROTHENBURG OB DER TAUBER
This medieval town owes not a little of its charm to the skillful accenting of its incomparable architects to skillful gardening, both terrestial and window boxes.

California has the world's biggest trees. They are something about which to boast. The rest of the world, including Florida, also Australia, is just green with envy. You all know that little orphan girl who said "Goodbye, God, we're going to California." Her uncle corrected her to "Good, By God, we're going to California!" It's a threadbare joke but at least it was not recorded in the joke book of Ptah, that somebody found under one of Egypt's pyramids. This we know, because the Pharaohs never heard of California.

SMALLEST, ALSO LARGEST OF FLOWERS

Now we have something else about which to boast. In addition to world topping sequoias and California climate, we have the smallest flowering plant in existence. It is known only to botanists and by one of their jawbreaking names. It is Pilostyles. "The entire plant, 'in blossom or in fruit'," wrote Riverside Junior College's Dr. E. C. Jaeger, "is the size of a pin head." Pilostyles is parasitic on the desert's indigo bush. We two have never found it in our annual desert botanizing. Curiously, it is a cousin of Java's Rafflesia. This, the world's largest flower, has blooms up to three feet across.

Paris' Cemetery of Pere-Lachaise is a kind of garden, cemetery and pantheon combined. It was named for Lachaise, (Jesuit Confessor of Louis XIV), who owned the site for his countryseat. Thus cities grow! One could buy a *"Concession a perpetuite"*, for the smallest sized burial for $200. Pere-Lachaise Cemetery contains the tombs of many renowned Frenchmen:—David, Carot, Daubinge, Lafontaine, Daudet, Moliere, Duc de Mornay, Balzac, Delacroix.

This writer never heard the late Luther Burbank state he ever had been overseas. It is probable he never visited the cemetery of Pere-Lachaise. Being, however, an omnivorous reader, Mr. Burbank was familiar with the floral pieces that decorate French graves also *a perpetuite*. They are in the form of flowers but are of beads. Some are black. Some are white. Most, however, are of a ghastly purple.

It was this thrifty habit of the French that prompted the most characteristically Burbankarian message writer ever received from his father's friend. When the world's leading plantbreeder learned We-2 were planning to visit Dad's native New South Wales, he wrote in effect:—"Won't you extend your expedition to Western Australia? I'm disgusted with these French grave flowers of beads." (We had often visited Pere-Lachaise in our studies of French history and our dipleasure coincided with his). Mr. Burbank continued:—"Our native California immortelles are pearly grey. West Australia's are as colorful as birds-of-paradise. They have big flowers in magenta, also golden scarlet and orange." What a gift my Santa Rosa gardener could make to the Land of Lafayette and Pasteur! Unfortunately our Down Under trip did not cover Western Australia.

Passing from Flowers to that Seed necessary for Reproduction, may it not be profitable to recall memory pictures of foods from just one family of flowering plants, the Graminae. Botanically speaking, the grasses, which yield so much food production, belong to the flower-

ing plants. The world, because of these, can support a much larger
population than in the hunting days. As We-2, at
GRASSES HAVE the Cave of Solutre, France, gazed upon the bones
FLOWERS of perhaps 100,000 wild horses, we grasped that
very few inhabitants per acre could be supported
when men lived largely by hunting with weapons laboriously chipped
out of stone.

In the far North, a kilted Scot munches his oatcake. A few hundred miles to his East, in Finland, a one-room log cabin is at the north limit of rye-culture. Its rafters are strung across with gigantic bracelets. Dozens and dozens of *roggebrod*, a whole year's supply of bread, and from a FLOWERING plant, rye!

Then, too, take maize or Indian corn. The meal you enjoyed in the Guatemala highlands—an earthenware bowl of steaming iguana stew eaten with tortillas for spoons. (Some of these Indios never buy metal ones.)

Again, in China, a rice-grower's family, husband and wife—up to the knees in the paddy-water planting the rice they never can afford to eat—for it must be sold to buy the cheaper millet. Both rice and millet are, again FLOWERING PLANTS.

中華諺語說得 *A CHINESE PROVERB SAYS:*

"THE DAUGHTER OF A CRAB DOES NOT GIVE BIRTH TO A BIRD." Garden-loving Confucius never of course heard of a gene or of a chromosome. He, nevertheless, out of what we call "common sense" (and which seems none too common) philosophized eugenically.

The radio recently described the school nitwit. "Do you know what a vegetarian is?" "Sure, a horse doctor". "No, that's a veterinarian." "Why I thought that was a feller who used to be a soldier!"

We are more or less vegetarians, tho we also do depend upon the veterinarian. A great increase in population became possible when
shift was made from hunting, via nomadism, to
VEGETARIANS agriculture's beginnings. Would not many of us
starve today were it not for just five flowering
plants of the grass family? Think of the millions in whose diet wheat, barley, oats, rye, or rice constitute an essential part of the daily ration. Botanically speaking, the grasses, which thus yield so much food production, DO belong to the Flowering Plants. Because of these, the world can support a much larger population than in said hunting days.

Farming is but gardening on a more or less larger area. The

largest farms are in nations where the culture is more youthful,—Argentine, Australia or our own Texas. The cosmopolite observes, when moving from such new lands to older civilizations, that the meat consumption lowers. There is a tendency toward absolute vegetarianism. Britain, with her Dominions as supply source, and U.S.A. probably consume the most beef, mutton per capita.

This author is owner of a string of California farms producing a wide variety of foodstuffs, wheat, rice, alfalfa (for his dairy cows and for the metropolitan dairies' market), asparagus, tomatoes (for the canneries), sugar beets, vegetable seeds. Trying to trace back his first interest in all above he testifies he concludes it began in the backyard garden where as a wee laddie he was taught, in a practical way, to raise his family's own flowers and vegetables.

Test of a Cook

Ability to use herbs and spices intelligently and judiciously is the supreme test of a cook. He who masters their subtle charms is a wizard.

Professional cooks regard the six primary herbs as mint, thyme, sage, marjoram, rosemary, and basil. In the Indies it is believed that those who surround their domiciles with basil will be eternally blessed· in old-time dairies milk was circled by marjoram to keep it sweet; in ancient Rome mint was used not only in cookery but by patricians who scrubbed their tables with it before dining; rosemary has been called "the dew of the sea" one of the oldest of proverbs avers that "he that would live for aye must eat sage in May"; while thyme has been applauded by poets and philosophers for centuries.

Sacramento Union Editorial—8/6, '53

FOOD FIRST, FLOWERS FOLLOWED

Gardens started with the vegetable patch. Food first, flowers followed. Even at the century's turn we found Ho Tel, the God of the Full Tummy, the favorite of the Seven Gods of Good Luck.

> "He held a basket,
> Full of all sweet herbs
> That searching eye could cull,
> Wild thyme, and valley-lilies,
> Whiter still
> Than Leda's love,
> And cresses from the rill.
> (Keats—Endymion)

No garden is truly complete without a herb plot. Always it has marjoram, sage, mint, finnochi. (If you have never tasted Orveito's finnochi-flavored honey, you have lived in vain.) There also grows some horseradish. When boiled tongue or corn beef comes with horseradish to the table, memories are stimulated of the Horseradish Crime:—On one of writer's Sacramento river ranches, horseradish grew *sauvage*. Probably an escape. It persisted in a triangle between the levee and highway of an acreage too small to cultivate. One day came an elderly fisherman. He saw opportunity for making a living if a horse-radish peddler's route could produce income between fishing seasons. How the bandit got his life savings—But, that is another story. . . .

The primitive use of wild herbs nature evolved into the herb garden. The use of herbs has become a fine art. . . .

The Boulevardier, whose nose was so red that a tomato looked anemic in contrast, was an expert upon the **HERB GARDENS** *"specialitie"* use of herbs in various department capitals of France and even Switzerland. He knew, for example, the delicate flavor of herbs worked into a certain

Alpine blue cheese. Perhaps there is no place in the world in which the flavoring of herbs have been so intelligently developed as in France.

The pension at Batanabao, Cuba, sponge fishery was a revelation in the use of certain herbs as flavoring in their unique preparation of fish dishes. All thru Mexico, and Guatemala one finds a bit of home garden even where the bed indoors may be only a *petate* (a mat of *tules*, a kind of bulrush) on an earthen floor. Such a garden will have a corner for a few red poppies for the family debutante's hair adornment. It will have corn also those peculiar beans our prospectors call "Arizona Strawberries", but above all, CHILI PEPPERS! A few strings of this home-garden-grown delight are sure to be hanging to dry at the door.

If you join the peon family at mealtime, you may enjoy *chile con carne*. (Note it is NOT *carne con chili*.) The jerked beef is far less important in that stew than the chili. You may have instead *chili verde con queso*, which is our stuffed green peppers with a ceiling of cheese. You may have chicken with chili. (We-2 used to get it on the Juarez-Mexico City diner for 15c gold per meal.) You may have fried beans with chili. Your *enchilada* (which is theoretically an en-SALAD-a), is a tortilla or pancake of maize flour with garden products, tomatoes (which grow wild south of the Rio Grande), olives, cheese and onions and chile.

The fence of said garden will be erect-growing cactus, otherwise *ocotillo* which is the barbwire plant. Mother Nature always was "first at the Patent Office". The peon's garden is a must. Peon cooks can concoct dishes with flavors that would make author's friend, The Boulevardier, green with envy.*

* In Hindustan, when this author, owner himself of a string of ranches, was studying agricultural conditions in the Central Provinces, he was told that it was possible to work some of the zebus only 1 day in a week. This, because of under-nourishment. Such undernourishment may have been exhaustion of minerals. (See "Plundered Planet" reading 1/26/54.) Herbs sometimes supply these.

REINDEER PAW SNOW FOR REINDEER-MOSS

Between food gained thru hunting and agriculture was the nomad stage. Here flowering plants (mostly grasses) were converted into food by grazing mammals.

TAMIL PICKER IN TEAGARDEN

The garden philosopher's study of the use of herbs in cookery could be extended, with ever-increasing intellectual delight, into the use of parts of plants for beverages. This, both alcoholic and non-alcoholic.

This author believes in total abstinence toward Reduction of Poverty. He has been fascinated, however, to observe how general is the use of fermented drinks. On the road into Tibet, *tsamba* was native beer. (See page 88.) The Japanese apparently have made *sake* from rice since time immemorial. The Aztecs apparently made *pulque, mescal,* and *tequila.* Under the Pharoahs, beer was made.

The yarns We-2 collected about tea-drinking, also coffee-drinking seem almost to deserve someday a book, if only for their humor and their glimpses of why men behave sometimes as they do.

This writer, with due humility, confesses paucity of beverages wisdom. As to tea-gardens, he elsewhere has described how he could climb an iceclad New Zealand peak on tea, because he never had used it. As to tea in Japan:—We-2 were guests in a Nipponese home. Dinner served on floor,—no tables, no chairs. The geisha girls brought walnut-sized bowls, filled them with hot tea. They contained only a few sips, were continually filled. Writer being MOST stimulated, remarked across table to his sweetheart, "Guess I've missed a lot in life not drinking tea." "Tea?" she questioned with a look of horror, "Don't you know that's hot *sake?*"

Paleobotany

CAMEL-DUNG CULTURE, SAHARA DESERT
Note the handles inserted crosswise in the 2 "Rockefellers". When this author made his camel trips on the Sahara that was the common word for junked coal oil cans. The invention of fertilizer-use, like that of fire-making and of practically all other inventions enriching human life, came because of a comparatively narrow layer of those of high I.Q. Is it not highly probable, that all thru the Bronze Age, even thru the Neolithic, there was a slowly increasing number of thousands of somewhat superior intellectuals. In the perhaps one million years since Pithecanthropus munched mangosteens in Java's jungles, such progress was less than the marvelously accelerated advance; since 1900, due to research in genetics, human genetics, and eugenics. Not the least of these was the rediscovery of the forgotten Mendel's Law.

"Slum and beans, slum and beans,
Slum and beans, slum and beans,
Hoo-ver-ize on the size of the pies.
We have the mac-ca-ro-ni by the ton,
But we need real chow to swat the Hun.
Slum and beans, slum and beans,
Slum and beans, slum and beans,
We sure are tired of you.
Come feed us steaks for we hun-ga-ry,
Ham an' eggs we are call-ing you."
(World War I Trench Song)

Man always has been selective as to food. What illustrates this better than above World War I's trench song? Most Caucasians prefer a balanced diet of meat, cereals, vegetables. For dessert, fruits including berries are welcomed by most of us. Huckleberries and blueberries make a welcome addition. Do you remember the huckleberry yarn about the drummer in a country restaurant back of Wilkes Barre? He told the waitress:—"I'll have one of those huckleberry pies!" She replied "Them ain't huckelberry pies ... Shoo! Them's custard pies."

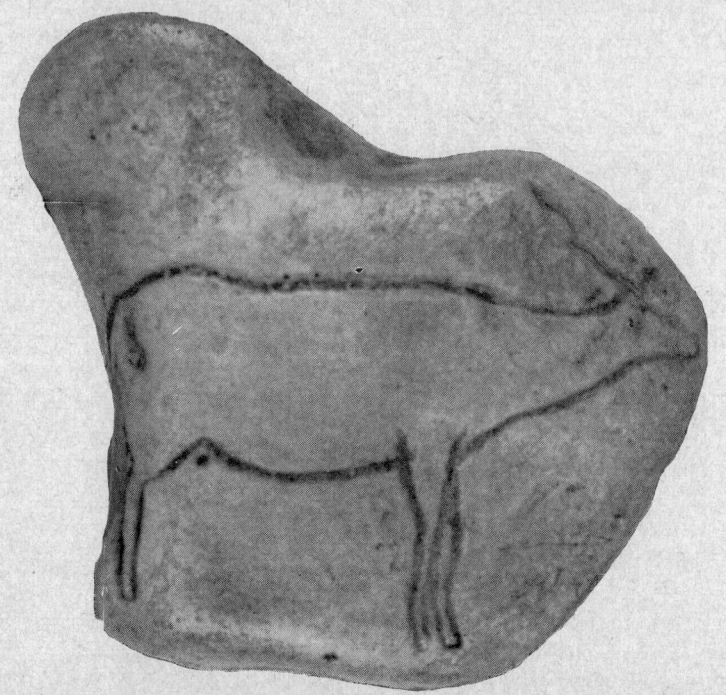

REINDEER MOTHER
One of the first human attempts at engraving was given your editor by a French anthropologist. Said scientist and We-2 were making field studies at the type locality at Cro Magnon. This savant explained it represented a reindeer with foal and was a fecundity charm. Comparison of the fauna of France today, with that known from such engravings and from fossils, shows vast changes. Today the large mammals are mostly a few *sanglier*, (wild boar), and a few little deer the Germans call *"rehbok"*. Once France had elephants, rhinoceros, lions, wild horses, bison, and, with advances southward of an Ice Age, reindeer and the woolly mammoth.

(Note: For a reproduction of the first painting of reindeer crossing a ford. Some date it circa B.C. 20,000, see Eugenics Pamphlet No. 85, page 32. Files are in most U.S.A. libraries.)

Once We-2 had a tundraberry experience. We were due at a summer home in Lapland. Arriving, our hosts had not yet appeared. The windows were still winterboarded. It being **THE BERRY GARDEN** almost dark, we asked for shelter at a nearby Lapp tent of reindeer hides. Came an explosive "no". I went to our car, took out a can of coffee for him to see. Immediately he melted. We were fairly comfortable, with plenty of reindeer blankets, thru that cold night. On frozen tundra even in

Food 83

midsummer permafrost is near the surface. The evening meal was reindeer-blood pancakes smeared with tundraberries*. We could not stomach the bloodcakes. By breakfast, however, eating some reindeer blood but with a very large proportion of tundraberries we managed to get thru. Even a second can of coffee could not induce that obstinate Lapp to cook us a bit of reindeer venison. Their folkway of food-use-for-survival demanded liquid blood must be consumed first before meat could be eaten. Lapland holds interest for eugenists because of the Norwegian-X-Lapp crosses. These were objects of hybridization research by writer's friend, the late Dr. Jan Mjoen. His research was prompted by high incidence of tuberculosis among these hybrids. Dr. Mjoen told writer he suspected one cause was inheritance of the extensive lung area of the Norwegian with unbalance because of inheritance of the small heart of the Lapp mother.

---
* The wild plants are so prolific, one's fingers can comb them into a basket. A supply is thus quickly obtained.

LAPP AND HIS REINDEER

Probably no berry garden, worldwide, yields a more acceptable crop than the wild tundra berries of Lapland. These are highly nutritious. They have an agreeable flavor. So much so they help down reindeer blood cakes, otherwise objectionable to many.

Are not those who emotionally prate about breaking down all race barriers responsible for some lifelong cruelties inflicted when children are born of disharmonious human breeding? To study same, writer was glad to be guest of Eurasian Mr. Duke-of-Kent, (name fictitious). His bungalow was in the tiger-infested, wild-elephant jungle at the Himalayas' base. He spoke freely of the contempt of Caucasians, Asiatics as to Eurasians.

Writer's worldwide studies of these unfortunates extended from Chinese Treaty Ports' orphanage to Caribbean mulattoes. A Japanese teenager swore that, when 21, he would kill his Caucasian father, his Japanese mother. Is he not an impressive example of human hybridization's injustice? Most of these illegitimates come from unions of shiftless men with lowgrade girls. Examples are the "Squaw Men" of U.S.A. Frontier. Curiously these frequently exhibit exaggerated egos. The children often are of low I.Q.

As to above, a friend's letter contrasts Pullman travel comfort in lieu of motoring across U.S.A. to a researchists' conference. This stimulates memories of why sleeping cars are called "Pullmans". Yesteryear's yarn was:—Pullman secured some early sleeping car patents. Carnegie had bought the others. To end killing competition, Carnegie suggested merger. Pullman responded:—"But what would you call the cars?" The canny Scot, thinking of pennies, not glory, promptly retorted:—"Why, of course, 'Pullmans'." Merger followed. (Perhaps the canny Caledonian knew money power also would bring fame in Carnegie libraries everywhere.)

Once, when We-2 were in the Holy Land, the biblical researchists at Jerusalem's American Colony hostel reminded us most Palestine places were of doubtful authenticity. They were organized largely with an eye to profiteering of pilgrims. Some few were beyond question. These included (a) the Synagogue at Capernaum, (b) the hill where the Sermon on the Mount was preached, (c) Jacob's well near Nabus, (d) the plain where David slew Goliath.

These learned critics offered to direct our Arab-speaking chauffeur as to where he could halt us on the scene of above historic duel. They further said, "you may have the good fortune to see a shepherd boy there. If so, watch him direct his flock with slingstones placed to right or left. Offer him a few coppers for his sling. He can easily make another by knifing some wool from a sheep's back." This photograph is of the sling thus obtained. Is it not a reminder that, as with David, "God plus one are a majority?" All the above recalls a struggle many years ago before a certain state legislature. A bill had been introduced aimed to increase commercialized vice profits. Its sponsors boasted they had a half million dollar war chest. This was supposedly enough to purchase passage. The church folks had only $6,000 . . . and their prayers. The bill failed of passage. Like the stone in David's sling, God plus one are a majority.

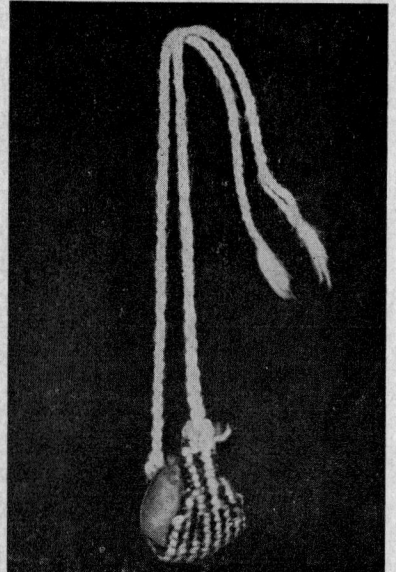

SHEPHERD'S SLING, PALESTINE

Food

Science Studies Curl Problem In Tomatoes
7/30

Can we have a curly top resistant tomato, and eat it, too? University of California scientists are at work on that problem reports Torrey Lyons, farm advisor, Sacramento County.

Curly top is a virus disease spread by leafhoppers. This year the hatch of hoppers was very great, causing the loss of a large portion of the tomato crop in San Joaquin Valley. Fortunately damage to our local tomatoes was not great. This is especially fortunate for our market tomato growers, as they have been receiving excellent prices.

Certain wild tomato species found in Peru are curly top resistant. But they are small and have to be bred back with California species for commercial size During the back crossing process they also lose the wild tomato size but also the resistance. The problem now is to get the commercial size and retain resistance.

Scientists on the Davis and Berkeley campuses of the College of Agriculture are working on that project which is all the more urgent as most of our tomato crop in the southern San Joaquin Valley was lost this year due to the curly top virus.

Entomologists in Berkeley are raising thousands of beet leafhoppers. Although there are some 2400 species of leafhoppers in North America, only one species carries the virus to tomatoes, sugar beets, watermelons, cantaloupes, peppers, spinach and other crops. The insects are shipped to Davis where they are used for testing the curly top resistance of the thousands of plants developed during the course of this tomato breeding program.

WILD TOMATO SOLVES CURLY TOP

American Know How is evident in the resourcefulness of our researchists in working back to *sauvage* and resistant stocks as in this clipping. This was also true of one lima bean disease. Is it not fascinating that the Forest Genetics Institute is developing, as a side product, disease-resistant trees. This is quite different from Founder Eddy's first concept, i.e. to speed lumber-growth.

"One cannot carve a statue from ROTTEN wood."
(Confucius)

WILD TOMATOES, GUATEMALA

The lives of those who contribute to human progress often show tragic suffering from those biologically illiterate. Columbus' voyages resulted in the addition to our diet of potato, also sweet potato, tomato, certain beans, squash, peanuts. Yet he languished in a foul dungeon because he insisted that, in his New World, "oysters grew on trees" (mangroves) and "men blew smoke thru nostrils" (tobacco). So, the morons of the F r e n c h Revolution guillotined Lavoisier, creator of the Agricultural Experiment Station. And today the Soviets "liquidated" Vavilov, our greatest geneticist, because he experimented with wheat from capitalistic areas!

Botanizing along the Cordilleras, from Central America to Peru's Andes, wild tomato is occasionally found. Some writer collected were no larger than a man's fingernail. Our photographed *ladino* left hand has a cluster. Each tomato thereof was considerably smaller than a grape.

Originally called "Loveapple," tomato at first only was grown for ornament. Its flower resembles those of its Solanaceae cousins, henbane, belladonna, nightshade, all sources of dan-
WILD TOMATO gerous poisons. It therefore once was avoided as food. Writer's own youth saw respected physicians advising avoiding eating tomato. Tomato juice, at World War II's outbreak, was at all Paris' so-called "American Bars". On this writer's rich Sacramento river bottom ranches, a single acre yields enormous crops. The canning of this once supposedly-poisonous fruit now employs thousands.

Expansion of tomato raising, tomato canning, is based upon ever-continuing improvement of the tiny wild tomato. Such results come by ARTIFICIAL SELECTION. Man has herein taken Mother Nature's NATURAL SELECTION, converted it into said ARTIFICIAL SELECTION. Thusly has been utilized, toward a fuller life for mankind, a natural trend, just as radio has enormously reduced loss of life in sinking ships.

Food 87

THE CORN GOD
Deification of a flowering plant of the grass family (maize).

When one makes staggered spring plantings of corn, one remembers the part that this important flowering plant played in the life of redskin and pioneer. This writer once was at an Arizona pueblo. A young squaw stirred dried corn kernels in a "Rockefeller", (coal-oil can) over a fire. She seemed to be mixing therein ashes from a desert wood campfire. Asked what she was doing, she said: "Make 'um hominy."

REDSKINS DISCOVERED HOMINY
At another time, at a New Mexico pueblo, We-2 climbed up ladders to an upper story. The writer, as president of World Recreation Survey, had volunteered to make studies of Amerind use of play in education. In the triangular fireplace a pot was cooking. We asked the black-haired young housewife if we might peek. It was a mess of beans and corn. She volunteered this information: — "Him succotash. We make long time ago before Paleface come." It was a curious parallel to the experience of above Arizona pueblo. Some years later, we were making

a flight from Texas over that same pueblo. The stewardess brought us a plate lunch with a dab of succotash. How remarkably the culture that resulted from centuries of Indian gardening has been projected into our own Caucasian culture!...

TSAMBA IS A TIBETAN BEVERAGE. THESE DRINK IT
Men seem early to have learned how to brew alcoholic beverages. These from the fermented mead of Viking tumblers, also the *'tsamba* of Tibet to the *leche di tigre* of the American Tibet, also the *pulque*, the *mescal*, the *tequilla* of the Aztecs. Some products of gardening bring misery to the intemperate. (See page 80.)

FRENCH FUNGI
One type of fungi is highly prized by discriminating French chefs:—The truffle is harvested by hogs.

Raising corn in one's garden so as to have it on the table 20 minutes off the stalk is as much a thrill as pink omelette a la Grenadine at

Food

La Rue's in Paris. It's fun, too, to grow one's own beans for a real home succotash.

SUCCOTASH
As to above succotash story:—At Meinkoping Pueblo, writer collected some Amerind, (American-Indian) corncobs. We-2 had made field studies of maize from Mexico thru to Peru. We had done some excavation in Inca Land. (Writer remembers unearthing a blue macaw-feather decoration. A jar with some corncobs had been found there.) The Incas of course knew about neither Darwinian selection, nor of Darwin's cousin, Sir Francis Galton's writings on eugenics.

We crossed Arizona's Painted Desert for those Hopi corncobs. This, to see if the Amerinds had grasp of what had brought Henry Wallace far more fame than U.S.A.'s Presidency. Returning from collecting said cobs down on The Wash, we saw above named squaw. Asked, as above, what she was cooking, she, stirring it, said, "Hominy!" Then she exclaimed:—"What-for Paleface always talk so big? Injun make hominy long, long, long time before Paleface come to Meinkoping."

Photo: Courtesy French Embassy, N. Y.

ANGOR WAT "GROCERY STORE"
"Vente du Mais au marche"
(Selling corn at the market)
Cambodia, Indo China

This illustration of the "corn" market in Indo China recalls recent research as to the origin of maize. The Mayan Myth is of the Fair God who taught the redskins its use. Some botanists have held it is a hybrid of an unknown crossed with *"teocintl"*. Writer collected latter while botanizing on Mexico's West Coast. Now comes suggestion that some popcorn shows relationship with a wild Oriental "corn".

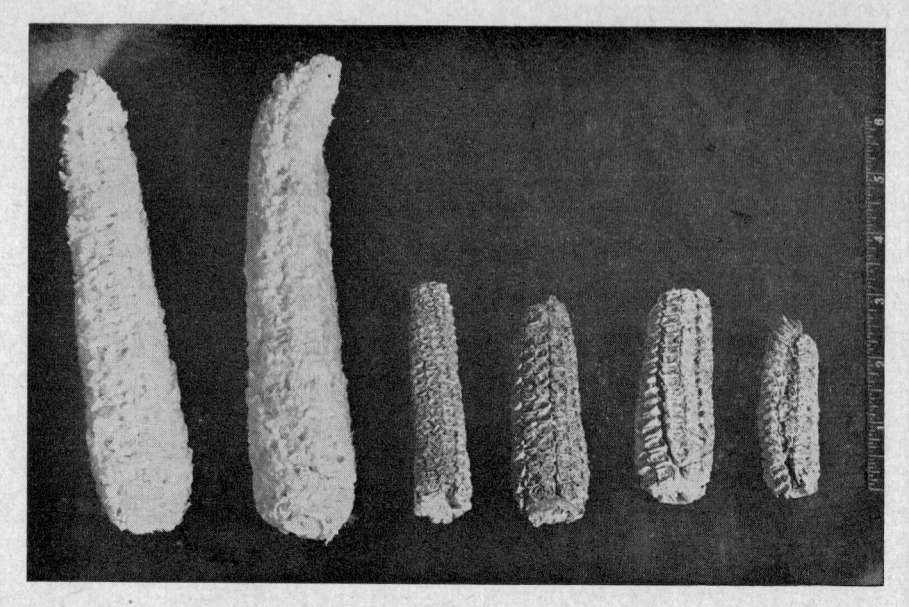

CORNCOBS, MEINKOPING, PUEBLO, ARIZONA

The short cobs to the right are from the Redskin corn gardens. The long ones to the left are from writer's home garden.

We-2 always enjoyed these flashes of primitive philosophy from Meinkoping to Morocco and to Maori Land. Sometimes they tend to shrink the Caucasian hatband just a little. Nevertheless, did "American Know How" just happen? Is it not the product of 10 generations of history's fiercest selection? Those coming to James River in 1606, to Plymouth Rock in 1620, courageously faced annual mortality rates as high as 50%. This meant that, 2 people last New Year's knew that, before next New Year's one might be dead. On the Frontier, the weakling, physically or mentally, just died. He did not live long enough to father many children.

"They are so rich, they eat white bread every day."
(Yesteryear's Swedish folksaying.)

Servant-gossip thus contrasts peasant's coarse, sawdust-like "blackbread" with the rich import-merchant's white bread. There is, of this, a Chinese equivalent. We-2 found, in certain paddy areas, growers dared not eat the rice they produced. It was sold to buy this cheaper millet. The margin bought some urgents:—loincloth, an opium pill for a few hours of forgetting.

As to pumpernickel vs. white bread, millet vs. rice, that all based

Food 91

on "fruit" in the botanical sense. The spectacled highbrows label our
flowers with names that make one want to
RICH ENUF TO EAT carry his jaw in a sling:—Geranium, Glad-
WHITE BREAD DAILY iolus, Bougainvillea. They further confuse
us simple gardeners by insisting that
"fruit" includes ALL seeds. This, whether peach, watermelon, the
beans that prdouce Boston's wisdom, even wheat, rice, or the contemptible, insignificant millet.

FRUITS
The display of fruits in native markets, like above in Morocco, often is most colorful.

PINE HYBRIDS, FOREST GENETICS INSTITUTE, PLACERVILLE. CALIF.
Genetics now is being applied to tree-breeding. Plantings of Pine Hybrids at Forest Genetics Institute, Placerville, California. Here the principles of genetics which are all-important in improving garden needs also are utilized toward (a) more rapid production of lumber (b) isolating insect—also fungi—resisters.

The gardening philosopher therefore passes from Flowers to Fruit. As this is written in the garden, one July morning before sunrise. There is a wealth of color. Pink oleanders recall the *wadys* crossed by the camel trail toward Timbuctu. The border has creamy Korean chrysanthemums. Hummingbirds already are at the redhot pokers. The air is delightful with perfume. It awakens tropical jungle's memories, gardenias, frangipani. Natural attar-of-roses comes the rose gardens. Phlox offers its incense. The night breeze's expiring gusts waft honeysuckle recalling the old plantation song Mammy sang: "Skeeters am a buzzin' in de honey-suckle vine."

We now have no more "skeeters," malaria, darkies' night calling in the yellow-fever epidemics, "Bring out yo' Dead."

The Flowers do offer color, perfume. Both, however, the Botany Professor reminds one are mere incidents in the making of the seeds he calls "Fruit". He proceeds to end our enjoyment of tint, of perfume by recalling that Food, even for carnivores, is based upon seeds (fruit). He further ding-dongs:—"Overpopulation and consequent competition for Food is THE cause of War." Then we stroll over to the Vegetable Garden, with its peas, beans, chard, beets, celery, corn-in-the-silk, to the berry patch, the orchard. Just now it is yielding golden apricots, blushing peaches. He munches a big Blenheim, (Prunus armeniaca) to show an apricot seed is smooth, then a Hale's Early (Prunus persica) to demonstrate that ITS seed is corrugated. Both, however, are simply pulp-blanketed seeds. They exist only that the hungry shall eat, that thusly some seeds gain transportation. He points to a California jay cleansing his bill on an osage orange branch. This feathered alarm clock has been pilfering in the berry patch. He likes the pulp, but is as clean as a cat about removing blackberry seeds glued to his bill.

Then this Fountainhead of Wisdom, (who knows all about algae and fungi, about microbiology and seeds that are fruits), observes the very reason we now control malaria and yellow fever became also the reason the Backward Folks' deathrate declines, while their primitive birthrate continues. Thus overpopulation is accelerated.

Most defectives breed like rabbits. One moron, son of a narcotic addict father and sib to 4 illegitimates by 3 different fathers, murdered, in a drunken rage his 9th child. In contrast, the majority of those of creative minds have 2, 1, even no children. 3 are the exception. If all live, above moron, at the 9-rate, will have 729 greatgrandchildren. The highpower, at even the 3 rate, will have only 27. Is it any wonder scientists say our national intelligence is lowered each decade? With more than half the world lacking population control, yet demanding U.S.A. feed them, may we, for survival, be forced to create A LEAGUE OF LOW BIRTHRATE NATIONS?

Food

BIDWELL'S BAR "MOTHER" ORANGE TREE

The "Mother" Orange Tree at Bidwell's Bar disputes with one in Southern California the title of being the pioneer in the Golden State's industry of growing golden oranges. It is as seen in photo, appropriately monumented. In Gold Rush Days, oranges were an expensive luxury.*

---
* The story of belles at an Illinoistown ball competing for an orange clove is detailed in the author's "Sierran Cabin . . . From Skyscraper."

"For the Maine Garden, I do not Deny, but there should be some Faire Alleys, ranged on both sides, with Fruit Trees; And some Pretty Tufts of Fruit Trees, and Arbours with Seats, set in some Decent Order." (Bacon's Essays).

CITRON, PEACH, POMEGRANATE. (CHINA'S "ABUNDANCES") No more significant present can be sent from one Chinese to another than one from "The Three Abundances." If it be possible to send all three, fruits, citron, pomegranate and peach, that indeed is Felicity! In writer's boyhood we had the only heavily-bearing citron tree in Sacramento. At the appropriate time, we had constant inquiry from Chinese merchants from Chinatown for this fruit of very great significance. We had quite a trade because the big fruits were prized for gifts.

The "apple" of Palestine is the apricot. Its specific names, Prunus armenica, locates its beginnings. When you eat apricots, why not give your imagination full play? Dream of diamond-brilliant desert stars looking down on Oriental intrigue, of burnoosed sheiks on prancing Arabians, of camel caravans, their sheepskins bursting with sun-dried apricots, of black-eyes watching you from latticed windows, of fierce eunuchs guarding harem doorways. The apricot indeed has entree to the most exclusive harems. It there ranks in favor with ruddy pomegranates, with the prized golden-brown *deglet noor*.

If one, for days, has cameled the trail of the Damascus Hinterland, filling eyes, ears, nostrils, mouth and lungs with razor-sharp sand, when one would give one's left hand for a bath,—When one's disagreeable oont, oont, oont, has tried persistently with that cavernous, dribbling mouth at the end of his hairy slide-trombone neck to nibble one's ear or one's elbow,—When one's eyes are weary of desert glares, one's hipbones are ready to come through your saddle-skin,— When, then all of a sudden, one comes to The Rim, and, beyond and below, one sees the green leaved oasis of apricot trees that is Damascus —Then, and only then, will one know why green is sacred to Allah!

The Persians claim to have been the world's first gardeners. These Moslems invented, (along with the Arabic numbers that give one a headache as one figures income tax), the indoor bouquet. It was first used, not in a house, but in a tent. It appeared, not on a table with Thanksgiving turkey-and-cranberry, but by hookah-sucking, hennabearded Moslems. These, squatted around a ground-carpet, had the first bouquet of tulips. In a bowl, they were midway between a dish of fattailed mutton and a basket of dates. There the turbaned mixed pleasure with intrigue.

After botanizing in the Holy Land one can testify that one's insight into Scripture history is remarkably improved, even in the Holy Land, by "learning to read a trailside like a book."

Until World War I, the Moslems boasted no Christian flag would displace the Turkish crescent-and-star standard "until the water of the Nile ran in the streets of Jerusalem". General Allenby's campaign to take Jerusalem required carrying a pipeline across the desert to supply his army. The water for this actually was chlorinated water from the Nile. It passed under the Suez Canal in a great siphon. The line was continually extended until the walls of Jerusalem were reached Before General Allenby entered the city, he had the line run thru the gate so that Nile water was actually flushing the gutters of Jerusalem before he entered, reverently, with his staff all on foot.

"A LONG CAMEL CARAVAN"
Near the Sermon-on-the-Mont we spent the night on the hillock at a tiny inn. At eventide there filed thru the narrow street of the village a long camel caravan. When tethered the "Ships of the Desert" ate grass and "lilies of the field" indiscriminately.

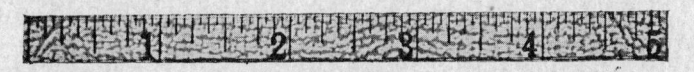

PECANS

The pecans illustrated in this photograph were purchased from the keeper of a back country general merchandise store in Oklahoma. His store displayed a sign "PECANS . . . PAPERSHELLS, 18c lb. . . . RUNTS, 8c lb." Inquiry as to the difference brought a suggestion:—"If you want the yarn, turn off on a side road 2 miles west of here, go north about 6 miles. There ask for Jim Jackson. He gave us just enough tantalizing information that we called on Mr. Jim. Following is the yarn:—"Yes, I sell the storekeeper both his Papershells and his Runts. The little negro boys around here go out in the woods and gather pails of the runts. It gives them spending money. I do not care to make a profit on it."

My own 3 "40s". Folks tell a tale around here of another man that owned 3 "40s". A stranger came along and said, "I want to buy a farm. Will you sell yours?" We made a bargain, he was to pay me $120 for the "40" and $100 extra for the shanty and well. He could neither read nor write so when I made out the deed I slipped in 2 other 40s and got rid of them because I wanted to be shut of them to get out to California."

Jim said, "Of course I can read and write and no such trick was played on me. I did, however, buy these 3 "40s" many years ago, almost just about that price per acreage. They are along a little stream that then was covered with young wild pecan trees. The land seemed worthless to induce any clearing. My wife and I had 4 stairstep of kiddies. We dreamed of a college education for them but it seemed hopeless. Then it occurred to me to put my savings into these 3 "40s". A friend of mine who was interested in our youngsters agreed to give me all the papershell grafts I could use. He had specialized in improving the stock of pecans up from the hardshell runt to these giant paper shells. By the time the first boy was ready to go away for college, already I was getting the beginnings of income from papershells which then commanded an unusually high price, because of their novelty. Each year the income increased. These crops added to our other earnings made it possible to send all 4 of our children to college. The boy is beginning to build up a practice as a doctor. The oldest girl has a good position as a bacteriologist assistant. She is helping toward the education of the last 2."

California grows most of U.S.A.'s almonds. One is indeed wealthy if, being in California, his garden has an almond tree. One tree yields enuf for not only his own table but for those of a score of neighbors and friends. Thus a whole circle enjoys almonds for Nutcrack Night or Hallowe'en, for salted almonds, for almond-raisin-mutton pilau, Armenian style, for that toothsome Sicilian

ALMOND TREE dish *mandelli con frigholli* (sliced fresh string
NEIGHBORLINESS beans with sliced almonds). Then there are the sliced-almond-decorated *kaffeekuchon* for the *kaffeeklatch*. A neighborhood with an almond tree, judiciously admin-

istered, is a neighborhood that truly is neighborly. Verily, if one wants friends one must be friendly,—and, if one wants kindly neighbors one must be neighborly.

With a properly-aged almond tree, (ours has been bearing heavily since World War I) the human biped that has an annual surplus of almond blossoms and almond nuts also has, as appreciative neighbors, feathered bipeds and furred quadrupeds. It was our almond tree that first attracted one of the latter. This squirrel overate for a full month and apparently never worried as to what that meant in threats of thrombosis or diabetes. By the time the frost had come and the last almond was devoured the neighborhood kiddies had adopted this acrobat. Just now, three of them interrupt this scribble with, "Mr. Goethe, he jumped from the oleander to the cypress!"

The almonds also are magnetic for crows. Every fall, our outdoor sleeping porch needs no alarm clock at almond-ripening. They hold a convention as saffron-gowned Dawn Goddess yields to Sunrise of the rosepink robes. And it is a convention. They all talk at once. There seem to be no parliamentary rules. Why should there be? A Parlia-ment is where folks parley—is it not? The other bird that is vocal at the almond tree is our California jay, and his family. Crow-time limited to breakfast hour but Jay-time, despite a late *dejeurne,* is all day long.

WEYANG-WEYANG, JAVA
When botanizing in Java, We-2 used daily to feed mangosteens and jakfruit to the monkeys. One evening a nearby village held *weyang-weyang*. The actors seemed even more weird than our guests, the monkeys.

Food 97

CEYLON FRUIT MARKET

To the lover of color, the Fruit Market from Tokio to Teheran, Timbuctu, Tangiers always is fascinating. The Orientals long have known the profit-strategy of colorful fruits, just as they have been most canny in color-use in the jewelry trade. Is it not curious that, only within lives still in being, this has been grasped by U.S.A.'s marketmen?

"She can make a cerry pie
Quick as a cat can wink its eye"

The commercial value of color appeal has long been recognized by the fruiterers of the Latin countries as well as Paris. Perhaps there is something about the Land of Bright Skies as against that of the Land of Overhead Gray that has awakened this love of color. It may perhaps even be racial, perhaps something very primitive. An octogenarian can recall that it was not utilized in U.S.A. in the 1880's. Such utilization came with the heavy Italian and Greek immigration just before the turn of the century. Many years ago We-2 were living at a certain point in Rome because of its convenience to the work in which we were engaged. Near us in the Piazza de Spagna was a line of young girl fruiterers. Their baskets were always attractively ornamented with greenery, often with flowers in the interstices of oranges or figs or peaches.

A cosmopolite becomes interested in the comparative progress or lack of progress in improving wild strains. The head tenant on one of writer's ranches a half century ago was a beloved old Japanese. His loyalty was of a type characteristic more of Chinese than of Japanese. He accumulated enough wealth from his tenancy to return to the Land of Midnight Sun. On one of our trips to Japan we visited him. We told him we would like to sample the famous Japanese pears. He seemed reluctant to obtain these for us. Finally I said, "Takahashi, why no pears?" His answer was:—"Boss-man, you no like him. Not like Sacramento River Bartletts. Japanese pear, him no good taste." Then his face broke into a smile and he added:—"Mebbe you eat him for turnip, then I think you like."

The Garden is a Place of Great Expectations, (apologies to Mr. Dickens). They even tell of a moron who planted dogwood, expecting a litter of puppies. May a gardening philosopher have faith that better success will come to the Mississippi Parkway, also Sacramento River Park Plans.

To raise flowers or food one naturally needs soil. In deforested Korea, your editor found, after the Russo-Japanese war, Japanese utilizing Germany's Schwartzwald Forestry School technique in an effort to restore Korean forests. His Korean experiences paralleled earlier explorations under Governor Pinchot. Following this, the Governor inaugurated U.S.A.'s system of National Forests. We-2 found in Korea, as his people found in North China, mountain valleys whose silt-laden rivers meandered in gigantic "S's" from mountain wall to mountain wall. The heavy rainfall eventually had eroded all soil to the bare rocks. It was then we saw "human taxicabs" as in this photograph.

Cannon-fodder needs then ended Japan's birth control. Lust for world power came to the Japanese militarists after Nippon's wars with China, and, later, Russia. As a consequence thereof, Japan's rulers abandoned the old folkway of maintaining a stationary population thru infanticide. The militarists yearned for *kamakatzies*. One warlord declared Japan was "willing to spend 10,000,000 lives to secure world domination by the Yamoto people."

All this, of course, paralleled the bluster of the Kaiser in World War I, of Hitler in World War II. In Italy, also, Mussolini boasted that he knew exactly how many Italian lives, how many lira, he must invest to restore Rome to her ancient glory. One curse of uncontrolled population pressure is this cheapness of human lives, particularly when a Dictator is in the saddle.

HUMAN TAXICAB, KOREA

"YOU CAN'T EAT PARKS" Our beloved Botany Professor had drifted a wee bit toward Utilitarianism in his philosophy. We, his students, yearned, however, for a feast of the beautiful. Perhaps we never had quite forgotten our childhood glee when gathering golden California poppies and purple larkspur. Let us admit we would soon be distressingly hungry if all sun-energy were shortcircuited away from chlorophyll-stored leaves. We had just won a fight to keep our authorities from slicing off some acres of one of our most-used city parks. In it, there had bobbed up the extreme Utilitarians' old argument: "You can't eat parks". And yet—cannot one have both beauty and food? Once, enroute to Melrose Abbey, we followed Sir Walter's advice to "go visit it by the pale moonlight". We stopped to chat with an aged God-fearing Scotch gardener. The shillings for his plaid shawl, his oatcakes, his lassie's tartan, for the learning his bairns were absorbing at school in time-honored Caledonian manner, all came from growing strawberries. His were luscious as well as large. One might be exaggerating a wee bit to say his Tam O'Shanter could hardly cover three strawberries. Each strawberry bed was bordered on all four sides by St. Patrick's Cabbage. The red-and-green of this saxifrage reminded one that even a strawberry bed could "put on its jewels."

Everyday, for a full half century, our own garden, which increasingly has given us food, also has yielded the 7 daily bouquets in dining room, living room, entrance hall,—and at My Ladye's dresser. Have we not been happier because of these "extraordinaries"—something beyond food—but still really essential?

EVEN YESTERYEAR'S KOREANS USED "ROCKEFELLERS"
Water for domestic use over much of the world is not obtainable by the mere turning of a kitchen faucet. Thousands and thousands make their living transporting water for domestic purposes as in above photograph. Coal-oil cans of American companies, often locally known as "Rockefellers", are used for this purpose. Water the world over is essential for continuance of life. Does our literature anywhere contain a more poignant cry of distress than:—"Water, water everywhere, and not a drop to drink!" The adjustment of plants evident in "leopard's hide-spotting" is the result of the necessity of living on and reproducing despite an ever-restricted water supply.

BAMBOO JUNGLE, JAVA

Even the grasses of one's lawn can stimulate study of their cousins overseas. Our Kentucky bluegrass, along with the wheat of our bread and the maize of the redskin—all are cousins to Asia's bamboos. In Java are giant bamboos. Imagine a "grass" with a stem one foot in diameter and 120 feet high! When We-2 were botanizing in Java, our bungalow was on a cliffside, above a clump of native huts. At sunrise, their population, (men, women, children) all dove off their bamboo porches into the river for a pre-breakfast swim.

GARDENING THERAPY

Gardening can restore the afflicted to health. Following may be worth reflection:—Many years ago We-2 went botanizing in San Diego County. Among our objectives was finding, because it might have some hybridization value, California's wild peony. This trip strengthened our conviction that the only way to really see a country is by what the Germans call *"fusszug"* i.e. foot-railroad or tramping. This, whether one wants intimately to know New Hampshire or Norway, Tennessee or the Tyrol. One morning, we stopped where, in the desert, a spring made possible a garden. Across its stone fence was a flaxen-haired, blue-eyed girl of 18. She was weeding strawberries. Here, another opportunity for trailside gossip. The conversation was promising. Then she said: "Where will you lunch?" We pointed to the desert beyond. "In another hour, we can get dry yucca stalks for fuel, I will make a pot of coffee. Lunch is in our rucksack". She said: "why not share it with me? The teakettle already has water boiling for midday tea. You shall have giant strawberries. Our honest-to-goodness cream they tell me, is like 'N'Orleans molasses at New Years'."

Food 101

At that luncheon she told her story. Her father was a British earl. They had a London townhouse, a manorhouse somewhere in England's South, a Scotch castle. From childhood she never had been allowed, in their family Rolls-Royce, to even tuck in the robe. Trained servants did everything. She later developed pulmonary trouble. This, London fogs aggravated. Her family allowed her to come out with a trusted servitor to San Diego's backcountry desert. She joined a group of 3 American college girls. They bought this tiny oasis. She not only milked the cow, but weeded carrots, strawberries. Two years of such outdoor gardening had brought practically complete recovery. IS THERE NOT SUCH A THING AS GARDENING THERAPY?

U.S.A.: NATURAL-GAS STOVE ... KOREA: WEED STALKS VIA HUMAN TRUCK

$5,500,000 planned for new recreational areas in national forests in California alone. The data, on this desk, recalls certain efforts, a half century ago, of one man of the eugenically highpowered type. Gifford Pinchot, with his fine Huguenot imagination, envisioned conserving what remained of our forests after more than a century's ruthless timbering.

It was Governor Pinchot who asked Us-2, about to depart for Japan, to volunteer to detour into Korea and North China for field data of complete deforestation. We were there in winter. In places the only obtainable fuel was weed stalks. A coolie outdoors fed these into a wall opening. From this a flue serpentined under the papier mache floor. There were of course no chairs. As guests, however, we were waved to squatting places on the floor. These were just over the weed stalk intake, hence gave, not maximum of warmth as much as minimum of chill as possible.

Governor Pinchot was canny. Probably nowhere else could be found an area so impoverished as to complete aboreal exhaustion. This committed Us-2 for lifelong struggle for Conservation.

AS SAME DEVELOPED, WE CAME TO CONCENTRATE MORE AND MORE UPON EUGENICS, i.e. CONSERVATION OF HUMAN ASSETS. This included reduction of such part of crushing taxation as was channeled to care of human weeds.

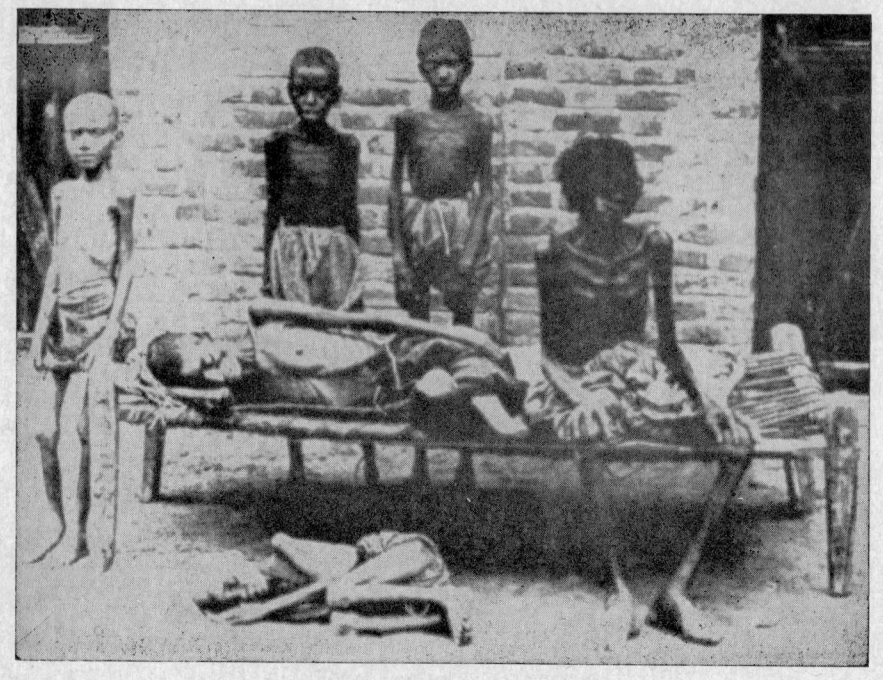

HINDU FAMINE VICTIMS

A famine was raging in Hindustan when We-2 went there to try to do our bit to lessen child labor injustice by American supervised play technique. Could there be a more eloquent tale of overpopulation illiteracy, and superstition. Agricultural lands have been cropped for 3,000 years with apparently no idea of soil conservation.

Any one, philosophically inclined, can hardly cross his garden without observing proofs of the Will-to-Survive, of the Will-to-Progress in evolution—in a word, of *Zeilstrebigkeit*. One example thereof is the sweetpea.

In our "Geogardening" wanderlusting, We-2 finally located the original wild pea in Sicily. The blossom (1 to a stem), was so small it would not cover the fingernail of ones little finger. Bailey says "much modified in color, size, conformation." On this desk is an announcement of a sweetpea to be introduced next year with 8 blossoms to the stem! Cannot what had been gained with peas and poultry, be accomplished with humans.

Today we face an almost unique test of the Will-to-Survive. Children in Soviet Berlin were summoned to stand in its squares. They were told to pray to God to drop chocolate packages. No sweets fell. A quarter-hour later they were told to pray to Stalin for same. Planes appeared, showered down the silver-foiled goodies ... We-2 made field studies of similar indoctrination of children under Hitler, Mussolini,

ZEILSTREBIGKEIT

Food 103

Japan's militarists. Japan's war-lords thus obtained their Kamakatzies. . . .

James Fenimore Cooper wrote (1851) "The Towns of Manhattan". He foresaw U.S.A.'s immense commerce expansion, "despite yellow-fever epidemics". He imagined "Towns of Manhattan" netted by bridges into one city. Estimating THEIR population as 500,000, he records several thousand immigrants landing DAILY. Cooper was disturbed by paupers, criminals dumped on us. He mentions "an insignificant but entrenched German prince GETTING RID OF HIS SURPLUS RASCALITY." Writer, one of little group creating public opinion toward enactment of 1921-22-24 Quota Acts, wonders how much taxpayers' money today is for paupers, criminals, traitors descended from Cooper's undesirables. How many DPs in Truman's years were properly screened? We drew traitor Klaus Fuchs. Earlier came Scarface Al Capone. He built a commercialized vice machine, allegedly paying him annually $200,000,000. Today Hyphenates demand Congress scrap McCarran-Walter Immigration Code.

Should not the extinction problem have careful thought of every patriotic American? Our leadership stock, largely of pioneer group, racesuicides. Morons breed like rabbits. The Differential Birthrates Law works far more speedily than most grasp. We have many extinction examples such as moa, bison, great auk, passenger pigeon. Fortunately, the pronghorn antelope, also the egret, show comeback is possible.

29, and mother of 11. Possible fecundity illustrated. (From a French newspaper.)

Copyrighted cartoon, courtesy Des Moines Register and Mr. J. N. Darling.

THE ONLY KETTLE SHE'S GOT

The deepseated Japanese love of gardening is well illustrated by a happening at the Plum Blossom Festival at Sugita. It was attended by nearly 400 blind shampooers. They went holding a long rope to "see" the beloved plum-blossoms. Some had memories thereof before blindness came. Many, however, had been blind from birth.*

BLIND SHAMPOOERS "SEE" PLUM BLOSSOM FESTIVAL

Education can lack balance, as with the biologically-illiterate

---

* Sightlessness is a problem that especially intrigues a garden philosopher interested in human genetics. It was discussed not a little at the last World Eugenics Congress at The Hague. At same this author was one of the speakers. The opinion of especially the Continental geneticists was that much blindness is a matter of heredity. One world-famous scientist stated that, of 200 children of a certain type of mating, 192 could be expected to be sightless. WHY CLOSE THE BARN DOOR AFTER THE HORSE IS GONE?

Food

domestic science student who thought "lioness" was a way of cooking potatoes.

 A pair of squirrels came to live as our garden guests. We never invited them. They, however, were most welcome nevertheless. It gave us a tie with the primitive. We thus became interested in the Junior Museum's pet library. It is Daylight Saving shift, and we have "gained an hour" but cutting last night's sleeptime accordingly. Stanford President Dr. David Starr Jordan used to exhibit his very accurate Swiss watch. He would comment: "I like it. It always tells the Truth.' 'Today, however, all clocks do not tell the truth. They say "6:22 when it is 5:22." From this office window can be seen the Italian cypress "apartment houses" herein elsewhere described. Their tenants, both housefinches and Brewers blackbirds have commenced their 12-hour work. The fledglings double weight daily. Hence the parents work like 1903's steel mills, on a 12-hour day. ...

BIRD FOOD
SQUIRREL FOOD

 An amazing burglary is reported over the radio. It happened to be at a castle We-2 visited long ago. Robbers broke into the vaults of Hohenzollern Castle and stole everything but the Russian Crown. The radio tells of the generations of Hohenzollerns from those early counts just north of the Swiss Border, thru the Dukes of Brandenberg, the Kings of Prussia until finally—the German Kaiser ... and 1918!

 We can almost match those generations in another line of the golden-crowned. A half century ago we commenced planting sunflowers to attract the goldfinches. They have been our guests every autumn since. Their generations must rival in number those of the proud Hohenzollerns.

 There are many items that can be planted to let birds know one is friendly: — Sunflowers, also French marigolds for goldfinches and sparrows,—elm buds, elm seeds for certain linnets and finches,—a sycamore for cedar waxwings, toyons for robins, redhot pokers for hummingbirds. Making a bird sanctuary of one's garden is a practical hobby because, properly planned, it can pay daily dividends in bird visits. They eat insects and weed seeds.

GOLDFINCH
GRUB

 The time to implant such a hobby-urge is in childhood. This week a visit to an old acquaintance seemed a duty. Four months ago he reached retirement age, grabbed the chance. He was in his front porch's rocking chair. His greeting was "I'm a fool. I had the option of 5 years more before retirement and then would have had a better pension. I was tired of work and took the first date. Now I am miserable. I have no hobby. I read the morning paper—then rock, back and forth, all day—waiting for Death to come.

Why not give your child a hobby? There's no better one than a garden that likewise is a bird sanctuary.

When the Norsemen and then Columbus "discovered" America they found people here—people with bronze skins and straight black hair. Because he thought he sailed across the world and found a sea passage to India, Columbus called these people "Indios". He was wrong, but we still call them "Indians." It is now generally accepted by scientists that the first humans arrived on this American continent some thirty or forty thousand years ago. It is believed that they came from the islands at the westernmost tip of Alaska. To the easternmost tip of Siberia is only 59 miles. In clear weather you can see from land to land. In ancient times there may have been a bridge of solid ice between the two shores, or there might have been an actual land connection between the two continents. But even if there were a 59-mile gap of water it could have been crossed in primitive canoes by hungry people hunting for game. HUNGER HAS BEEN THE MAINSPRING OF CIVILIZATION."*

* (From "The First Americans" Nature Bulletin, Forest Preserve District Cook Co., Ill.)

PLACE ATAB, CAIRO

Note the poultry cages. Then go up-Nile. Later, continue into the African jungle. You will find that this Cairo poultry is not far removed from the jungle-fowl type. Is it not a test of the present lack of imagination of the Egyptian *fellahin* that there has been practically no improvement of such stock for centuries.

Food

December fifth brought the first tinge of frost. We regretfully curtained the bougainvillea, still a mass of bloom. There had been a succession of ever-cooler nights. The flowers now apparently have ceased honey-making. Thus is inaugurated famine. For several days, the grasshoppers have moved as if they would welcome grasshopper crutches. Now beeflies try to find enuf chrysanthemum honey to keep body and soul together. Soon they too will be, in Victor Hugo's words, "eating dandelions by the roots." There is an acute food shortage in Hexapod Land. Little 6-footed friends are dying everywhere from cold and hunger.

INSECTS HAVE FAMINES

All this awakens memories of the first visit of Us-2 in Hindustan. Famine then stalked with Apocalypsian Four Horsemen ruthlessness. It was illuminating to note the varied reactions of parents. Some sacrificed their last crust to their offspring. Others abandoned their children. We saw one father put his baby in a neem tree's forks then stagger forward. Thus a garden, as honey-stores are lowered, remind one of how terrible a famine can be.

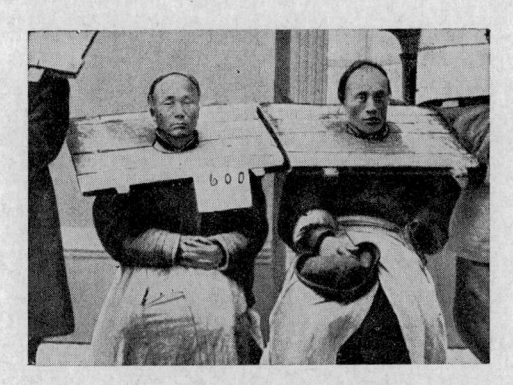

PILLORY PUNISHMENT

The pillory, (not unknown in our own New England in colonial days), was a common method of punishing Chinese garden thieves. Most such stealing concentrated on fruits, such as the *lookwahs*, also peaches, or in the south, oranges. There were also thefts of bamboo shoots, of vegetables, like the long white Chinese radish, even of salable potted plants.

We of U.S.A., with telephones, electric lights, radio, and abundance of food forget that more than half mankind is always half starved. A Turk, who had earned $1 an hour, $1½ if overtime, in an Ohio plant, was called home by his family. He retained his allegiance to Turkey and cannot now return. He told the writer his daily wages there are now ½ his hourly wage here. While in U.S.A. he had ham-and-eggs or beefsteak every breakfast. Now his diet is bread, greens, an occasional onion, with mutton once yearly at Eastertide. Should we marvel that such as he do not hesitate to commit a crime to gain admittance to this Land of Gold, of American Know How?

We have learned from Chinese gardeners. In fact all agricultural China in one vast garden, utilizing techniques based upon centuries of folk experience under increasing population pressure. One must see with his own eyes how same has crowded vast numbers to where they are born, live, and die even on river boats to grasp how intelligent, thrifty are, for example, the Cantonese. No wonder the Occidental observes "There are no gulls in Chinese harbors". There is no refuse for seagull food.

On writer's ranches 50 years ago, the 1-crop custom was the rule. In China, writer saw land raising good crops after 4,000 years rotation. Today in all writer's ranching rotations practiced.

THE WORLD'S MASTER GARDENER-PHILOSOPHER

In a half century study of gardening and gardening-philosophizing may the writer venture the opinion that the acme of gardening philosophy was attained by M. Dachert, creator of Les Jardins Ungemach in Strassburg.

The Maginot Line already was manned when the author visited Les Jardins Ungemach . . . German workmen, crossing the Rhine bridge from Kiel to Strassburg, complained of two years of butter routed into ammunition . . . The French, however, even then had not awakened to their population menace. The League of Nations' announcement came a few days later. It said: "France's birthrate curve has passed below the replacement line." Then came nation-wide hysteria. The Code de la Famille* was quickly enacted.

---
* See "Sierran Cabin . . . From Skyscraper". Pages 180-181.

Sodden Heinrich was snoring, beast-like. His head had fallen upon his arm, extended over a rickety table. At his side was an empty bottle of *kirsch*. His slatternly, ragged wife, half-intoxicated, swilling sour beer from a can, nursed her third child. The elder two quarreled on the floor....

The aged, spectacled professor, stood in the doorway, sighed, then exclaimed: "Alas, the apple falls not far from its tree-trunk". He recounted that Heinrich's mother had been a prostitute. Heinrich's father, rotted by alcohol, had died in the penitentiary. "I found the family," the professor continued, "when I was less wise than now. Heinrich then was about the age of little Heine there. I worked some years with him. I shut my eyes to the Good Book's warning about gathering figs from thistles!"

**LES JARDINS
UNGEMACH**

Young Heine's seventh birthday was approaching. Already one could almost predict the future of this anemic, undersized boy. Neighbors said his parents, during his babyhood, had silenced his whining with doses of soothing syrup. His was typical slum-inheritance, slum-environment.

Heinrich's 2-roomed, ground floor flat was as gloomy, even on a June afternoon, as a mid-November eve. When eyes became accustomed to its dark, one saw paper peeling off mouldy walls. Broken windows were stuffed with filthy rags. One's feet sank into a sponginess of dry rot. One trod on a sheet of rattling tin. This, as well as bits of a chest of drawers which old Heine had knocked to pieces, covered crumbling joists where the bedroom floor had fallen in.

In Heine's tenement lived 28 families. About 150 people shared the public-landing sinks. There were only 2 lavoratories to each 10 families. "Impossible to find a spot to put the beds free from leaks when it rains," one of Heinrich's co-tenants said. He added: "We find the driest spot, then hang up cooking pots to catch the drip." Another neighbor complained, "My flat is at its worst during winter rains. The yard then floods 2 feet deep, almost up to the window-ledge. Drains become stopped. One can hardly eat for the stink." Bugs crawled from filthy, decaying skirtings. Tenants who can afford insecticides, they said, syringe these. The weekly 2½ pints cost a half dollar.

Outside, the professor showed how, in places, finger-tips could touch simultaneously house-walls on both sides of a narrow street in this Strassburg slum area. A questioning voice was heard behind. Turning, one saw a six-foot-four, tawnyhaired, blue-eyed man, with that Viking build common among Texas Rangers. "Say, pardner," he drawled, "Do you reckon they keep humans in them-there rabbit hutches? Why, where I live, up in the Panhandle, when anyone moves in on us, even ten miles way, we jes' naturally clear out. We don't like breathing polluted air...."

Similar conditions were found to be characteristic during 25 years' studies of both European and Asiatic slums. These included, not only Middle-Age trade-centers like Strassburg, but also Mediterranean tenderloins. They likewise covered yesteryear-London's Whitechapel when horrified folk still whispered: "That's where Jack the Ripper killed another woman." Like a surgeon after an assassin's bullet, there had been probing, probing, probing, trying to understand the beginnings of poverty. In all these centers of rotting humans, from Liverpool, Constantinople, Marseilles, Naples to Calcutta, Shanghai, Tokio, there seemed one underlying cause.

THIS WAS: IT IS NOT THE SLUMS THAT MAKE THE SLUM FOLK. IT IS THE SLUM PEOPLE THAT CREATE THE SLUMS.

For example: In the early '20s model California bungalows were erected in a devastated area of France. In these were enameled bath tubs. The miners there used them for coal bins. They wanted thir semiannual bath in the good old way of their greatgrandfathers. To test British cynics' sneers about "3 generations from shirtsleeves to shirtsleeves," it was found that the slum descendants of country squires came generally from families that admitted that each generation had a "black sheep" weakling.

As these studies across Eurasia proceeded, there came persistent rumors of a promising attempted solution of such slum conditions in a Garden City in Alsace, Les Jardins Ungemach. A letter was mailed to the Alsatian professor. An invitation to visit followed. This said: "We will go most wisely toward this new suburb via Alt' Strassburg. The old town-core has a maze of crooked streets environing its towering cathedral." Street names there, like "Goldschmiedsgasse," recalled mediaeval guilds. One can best appreciate the housing progress made since the Middle Ages by strolling first thru these crowded quarters.

Slum tenements as high as 9 stories clustered around the cathedral. Into the lowest of these the sun's rays, even in midsummer, penetrated only about 1 hour daily. "From September till April," said the scientist, "'tis as dark here as a North Pole New Year's." There were some pathetic attempts at flowerboxes, mostly scraggly geraniums in old tins. One house, dated 1753, had an oleander. The rickety tenements often were inhabited by near-morons, slatterns, alcoholics. A friendly gendarme said, "Here are congregated most of Strassburg's parasites. They range from petty thieves to miserable males willing to gain a few francs for their vices by exploiting fallen women."

From cathedral-ward slums, a taxi whisked the professor and his guest to Les Jardins Ungemach. Here, in contrast to foul slums, were streets flooded with sunlight. Into its open spaces came cool, stimulat-

Food 111

ing breezes. Here were flower-fragrance, flower-color. Here housewives were preparing healthful, appetizing meals, based upon fresh, homegrown vegetables.

In this, the world's first Eugenics City, there was almost rural quiet. Here, near the castled Rhine, one felt one could sniff the Texan's "unpolluted air."

> Efforts to increase natality in France will be made through a "code of the family" containing 170 articles. Included are a prize of 2,000 to 3,000fr. for the first child born within the two years that follow marriage, medical aid and special taxes on unmarried persons and childless couples.

BATCHELOR-SPINSTER TAX

Just as a garden-philosopher grasps that sunlight also soluble food salts in the soil are necessary for his flowers' growth so he knows that taxes are necessary to support government. This author has written much about France's 1939 Code de la Famille. Here is one clipping from a Paris paper about the tax on bachelors . . . and spinsters.

It again is May Day. In Moscow's Red Square, thousands noisily celebrate one anniversary dear to most revolutionists. In our garden there is peace and quiet. The baker's dozen of watsonia clumps add their brightness to the massed color of peonies, iris, roses, clove-pinks, sweet peas, snowball and broom.

A neighbor has dropped in to gossip. "Are you finding the old friends, one by one, go, as Victor Hugo put it, to 'eat dandelions by the roots'?" One admitted that one of the disadvantages of being an octogenarian is the passing of one boyhood friend after another. He said: "Will you clip me a watsonia stalk?" Wondering why, one did. Four down-stem blooms had withered. Six were in full glory. Eleven more buds gave promise that the magenta masses would continue to brighten the garden for another fortnight.

THE GARDEN, NEIGHBORHOOD ASSET

He then remarked:—"This matter of friendship is like the watsonia stem. When Woodrow Wilson was on the Princeton faculty, he used to comment, a bit pessimistically perhaps, that one could count one's TRUE friends on his 10 fingers. One day I took stock. I was popular and had many 'friends'. Could I so classify them as to decide as to the precious 10? I was surprised my quota was not quite filled. I thereupon selected those needed to fill the gap. I cultivate them assiduously. I tried to give more than I received. But I held my "Quota" at Dr. Wilson's Ten.

"Then as one moved away, or perhaps went into the Great Beyond, I systematically filled THAT vacancy. Instead of a lot of just acquaintances I have maintained my half-score of Dependables. "Selfish", you say, yes, perhaps there has been that. I have conscientiously endeavored however to remember it is more blessed to give than to receive."

ONE-FAMILY COTTAGE, LES JARDINS UNGEMACH

"Across the 3,000 miles from Washington's Seattle to Florida's St. Augustine, one can buy standardized parts for a Ford, a Cadillac. That's American mass-production." "Yes," responded the Frenchman, "and the glory of France is exactly the opposite. You cannot do such things with French automobiles! France boasts of her carefully conserved individualism". . . Papa Dachert criticized English Garden Cities as crowding too many families under one roof (See Port Sunlight photographs). Above cut shows how, with characteristic French individualism, Papa Dachert built one-family cottages, improved on the British many-family houses. (Insert: A street in Strassburg's slums.)

Kindly, tolerant Papa Dachert recognized the good in the arguments of both Environmentalists and Hereditarians . . . He knew healthy children could not be expected from sunless, bug-infested slum quarters with rotten floors, clogged drains. He also expected neither "figs from thistles," nor highpowered children from social inadequates.

NOT FROM A MERRY-GO-ROUND

That phallic worship is widespread in Hindustan is perhaps an index to the immensity of what has been called "India's Insoluble Hunger." Such rites as your editor studied near Bombay were more than disgusting. Sarasvata, (or Vach), is, in the Rig Veda, the personification of Speech. By same, Knowledge is conveyed to Man. Degenerate Hinduism substitutes, for the sublime Vedic concept of the Goddess of Wisdom, that of female energy. Sarasvata thus became the wife of Brahma....

It is characteristic of those of American pioneer ancestry, when a problem arises, energetically to act toward its solution. Never had We-2 been more profoundly impressed than with what we saw in Hindustan. We had herein perhaps an unusual keenness because we had behind us some 18 years' strenuous after-office-hours work at Sacramento Orphanage Farm. This had yielded note books crammed with juvenile-behavior observations, with a percentage of juvenile delinquents. Like those whose fever makes hearing more acute, we sensed what might help overcrowded Hind. It was thus we came to estimate that the principal irritant was tragic overpopulation of the illiterate, superstitious masses.

There seemed to be, within Hindustani population mass, Kiths which eugenically could be used to rebuild that important area. One wonders, however, whether here again there may be under way dissipation of precious assets—in other words, trends of UNDERpopulation within OVERpopulation. Is there a parallel here to Gresham's Law in economics? (It is: Gold goes into hiding before worthless paper currency.)

BOERBOEDER TEMPLE, JAVA
"This temple is a seed symbol. Down on the first level, is Man-in-the-Underground. In its dark, he has the urge to reach upward for Light, like a planted seed."

    Beating against windowpanes is the mid-January rain that makes gardening (and ranching) possible. Seed catalogues arrive. Now the thrill of discussion, selection, listing, buying. Truly, hope DOES "spring eternal in the human breast." Later, comes seed boxes' preparation. After Java, We-2 never worked at seedboxing without discussing our adventures in South Java's jungles.

BOERBOEDER SEED SYMBOL There was the *passer* at each village. At same, turbaned, barefooted natives squabbled between the giant *kanari* trees' enormous buttresses. Roadside carvers made buffalo-horn fans. Batik workers ornamented sarongs. At dusk, above the *aloon-aloon*, flying foxes winged their black shapes against the dusk. Kindly, tolerant Major H............., son of a Holland-born navy Admiral and of a native Sultan's daughter, taught us more about Comparative Religions than ever We-2 learned in that university course.

    This graduate of a Netherland's university, (of also the university of the jungle) taught us tropical nature lore:—"Tigers and teak, rattan and rats, flying foxes and fruit of jak-tree, durains and devil dancers, mangosteens and monkeys, *orangs* and oranges, *weyang-weyangs* and wood lore. He would repeat the Golden Rule in its varied wordings of all religions. He could quote the Koran, also Confucius, could explain why the lotus root of pond bottom's black muck reaching

Reproduction

skyward could bloom into the Resurrection's symbol. We-2 would troll along Boerboeder's terraces. "This temple", he would explain, "is a seed symbol. Down here, on the first level, is Man-in-the-Underground. In its dark, he has the urge to reach upward for Light, like a planted seed."

The Major would jump from Demosthenes to Darwin, from Konfucius to Kant. His inheritance from his hardheaded, practical Dutch father, his imaginative, but superstitious, Javanese mother blended in this his tolerant, kindly, yet discerning man. In later years, as we planted the catalogued seed, We-2 often spoke of the Major's interpretation of Boerboeder as a giant symbol of seed potentiality, of progress from Darkness to Light. . . .

> "By the streams that ever flow,
> By the fragrant winds that blow
> O'er th' Elysian flow'rs:
> By those happy souls who dwell
> In yellow meads of Asphodel."
> (Pope—"Ode on St. Cecilia's Day")

"FOOD, THAT THERE MAY BE REPRODUCTION"
Gardening at first was by those less interested in Asphodel than in "Food that there might be Reproduction." The race-survival urge, however, is at times, even more profound than the yearning for food. To control both these, one must be as "quick-on-the-trigger" as California Gold Rush's "3-Fingered Jack." Simultaneously he fatally shot two enemies. They had plotted that, by entering by opposite doors, tho' one died, 'tother would kill 3-Finger. Said 3-Fingered Jack was part of those who pioneered, over 10 generations, across U.S.A. This, from James River, also Plymouth Rock until the California Gold Rush. During much of this period, Uncle Sam offered a food-producing farm to newlyweds. Those pioneers, to survive, had to be physically powerful, mentally alert. Thus arose "American Know How". May this be illustrated by following Hindustan anecdote:—

During writer's first visit there nearly a half century ago, a Western Aggie senior, just before graduation "done got religion." He abandoned agricultural engineering for Y.M.C.A. work. He was successful in raising funds for several overseas Y's. He then was sent to Hindustan to raise 1,000,000 Rupees. He obtained pledges for R820,000, dependent upon raising the entire sum. He "milked the cow dry." Not another rupee was in sight. Discouraged, he was about to sail home. Then an Englishman suggested a possible solution:—A semi-independent ruler, let us call him "the Sasushan of Swank" was itching for more initials after his name. The Court of St. James' honors soon were to be gazetted. A conspicuous gift probably would catch the Viceroy's all-seeing eye. He, in turn, might whisper to the King-Emperor at Buckingham. The British friend advised:—"I can obtain an invitation to next week's houseparty. These despotic courts' etiquette is exacting. In the morning, wear a cutaway, thin-striped trousers, violet boutonniere. Evening, tails, white tie, camellia. Thereafter, to use your American slang: 'It's up to you'."

Our Aggie graduate was dismayed. The opening dinner had 400 guests, seated by rank. A mere "Y" undersecretary, he was near bottom. All week, not one word with the Susushan, always surrounded by fawning courtiers. The last breakfast, our Y man nervously commenced eating mangoes from one of the table's center line baskets. The Susushan called out, "My young American friend evidently is a mango connoisseur. Why? The Y man blushingly stood his ground: "These mangoes have good size, much pulp, excellent flavor and ARE NOT STRINGY! In the tropics, I acquired mango-eating. Hindustan's remind me of my first Equator's ocean-crossing. Neptune's minions thrust into my mouth a rope's end, smeared with whale oil soap and tar."

"Good," cried the Susushan. "Perhaps, my young friend, out of his Occidental wisdom, can solve my garden problem. Some guests have seen my Treasury's piles of moonstones, turquoises, sapphires, rubies. Nothing therein do I value more than the tree in palace garden whence came these mangoes. It was planted by Greatgrandfather. Each year Grandfather, Father, then I religiously planted its seeds. My garden has become veritable forest of mangoes. NOT ONE TREE EVER CAME TRUE TO SEED ... WHY?"

"That's easy", answered the Y man. "On our peach orchard, father never used seeds. He budded. He grafted." He explained the processes. The excited Susushan adjourned that hardly-commenced breakfast. Coolies were summoned for the "donkey work," Midday tiffin, later, was ignored. The Y man grafted, budded until dark. His hands, now unaccustomed to such work, were blistered, bleeding. No talk of Rupees ...

At 6 next morning, the Chamberlain knocking at his door, said:— "His Highness dispenses justice in the Throne Room. He requires your presence" ... There the Susushan asked: "Why did you want an invitation here?" "To beg 180,000 Ruppees for the Y." Turning to the Court Treasurer, who stood near, the Susushan said:—"Give our truly-learned young friend a draft on our London Bank for Rupees 180,000."

An ever-improved "AMERICAN KNOW HOW" can come from constant study of one's garden biota. This can concentrate upon im-

Reproduction

provement of plants thru reproduction. Same can be by use of grafting or budding to maintain favorable strains, or by being alert to desirable mutations.

Such mutations do occur. Often they are not conserved. On the contrary there are intelligent gardeners who give us assets like the Thompson Seedless grape, the Youngberry, the Boysenberry. Occasionally there is a man of genius who devotes his life to such efforts such as Luther Burbank. His list of "creations" is too long to attempt here.

A CHINESE PROVERB SAYS:
中華諺語說得

"My brother's quite an inventor, too. He's a second Burbank." "How's that?" "He crosses cucumbers with sweet potatoes so that the pickles won't be too sour."

"WHEN THE TREE IS FELLED, THE SHADE IS GONE." (Here is a bit of philosophy about Extinction that may be 2,000 years old. Is it not an impressive folksaying?)

"This slave-mother, whom we are inclined to pity, may be indeed a great amorist, a great voluptuary, deriving a certain enjoyment, an after-taste, as it were, of her one marriage-flight, from the union of the male and female principle that thus comes to pass in her being . . . Nature, never so ingenious, so cunningly prudent and diverse, as when contriving her snares of love, will not have failed to provide a certain pleasure as a bait in the interest of the species. And yet let us pause for a moment, and not become the dupes of our own explanation. For indeed, to attribute an idea of this kind to nature, and regard that as sufficient, is like flinging a stone into an unfathomable gulf we may find in the depths of a grotto, and imagining that the sounds it creates as it falls shall answer our every question, or reveal to us aught beside the immensity of the abyss."

(Maeterlinck, The Life of the Bee)

The last chapter was on Food. This author, years ago, coined the expression:—"Food, that there might be Reproduction." Lower animals' reproduction is amazingly simple. Fission gives two individuals where before was but one. With Man, at the ladder's uppermost rung, reproduction is highly complex. All up that ladder, the gardening nature student finds fascinating phenomena. When **SEXUAL SELECTION** Mother Nature accelerated Evolution thru Sex,* hers was a marvellous concept. Thus became possible ever increasing progress. Offspring, inheriting both parents' desirable genes, were better equipped for the Survival struggle. This, as long as there was no highpower's interference as Excessive Birth Control.

Amazing is the acceleration of Evolution, once, by sex mechanism, two individuals' survival-fittest genes merge in their offspring. With only above cited fission-evolution, process necessarily must be slow. Once there was inheritance from two, in lieu of a single parent, progress tremendously was speeded. Of all this, the gardener daily is reminded by his plants, by their pollenizing insects. He continually pauses in contemplation. Then he reverently repeats the Psalmist's "The Heavens Declare the Glory of God, AND THE FIRMAMENT SHOWETH HIS HANDIWORK."

Every garden has a rather complete series from the primitive non-flowering to the flowering's peak, i.e. the composites. Such a series stimulates reflection. The algae, even today, (a billion years after the Huronian iron beds were deposited), are present in all gardens. If you doubt this, leave an open glass of water in your garden. Before many days green algae will become apparent. Among the living fossils, (you may have some as weeds in your garden), are the marestails. Their forerunners, the calamites, were on earth millions of years before the dinosaurs, consequently long before Man. Fossil marestails were common in Coal Beds. They extend back to the Devonian, say, 280,000,000 years ago. The largest living species, tropical Equisetum giganteum, reaches 40 feet in height. It is, however, runtish besides, with its 60-foot forerunners, the Paleozoic calamities. These exceeded one foot in diameter. Just as the giant dinosaurs could not survive, so the true coal-forming days' calamites. At the modern horsetail's tip, the spore-bearing cone, gives off tiny spores. These single celled are much more simple and primitive than seeds, which are composed of thousands of cells.

---
* A garden devotee, who also has invested much of a half century in fighting Commercialized Vice, can testify that few means of ruthless profit can excel exploitation of the sex urge in weaklings. This, particularly, as to those whose education has been deficient in spiritual values. Reader is referred here to the pamphlet "Red Light Abatement" by Senator E. E. Grant, author of the Grant Act. Is it not significant that this 1914 California law alone has persisted in what has been dubbed "Moral Legislation" of the first quarter of this century? The vice masters evidently feared feminine public opinion.

HATHOR, COWHEADED GODDESS OF THE SKY, ALSO OF LOVE

Hathor was the Egyptian original of Venus. On our yesteryear French-African camel trips down the "Trail toward Timbuctu", we came to appreciate why the shepherds of old worshipped the Heaven-gods. Few spiritual experiences can surpass the glory of the planet Venus, seen on the clearest of nights from Saharan sand dunes. Many of the inventions that daily make our lives worth living were born in the land of the Pharoahs. The Gifted Child, Champollian, properly educated, unlocked, for all time, innumerable secrets of Egyptian wisdom.

Observing such plants as the primitive marestails, one acquires a profound appreciation of the evolution from generalized ancestors of his garden flowers. It is not alone among one's garden plants that one observes the beauty of this law of Reproduction.

MARESTAIL'S PRIMITIVE REPRODUCTION The birds in one's garden also exhibit same. Is there any more fascinating sexual selection than that shown by our common house finch. Several dozen pair nest annually in our garden. Afront our home's facade are some 8 cypresses, our "Housefinch Apartments." Each contains perhaps a half dozen nests. Some trustingly are within reach of a tall man's hand. The male is brilliantly colored with crimson helmet, shoulder cape. Apparently his evolution has preceded among the lines of pleasing his mate.† After bird-

DARWINISM IN HOUSE FINCHES ing under nearly every flag, writer can testify he never found a more convincing example of mottled-feather pattern‡ than that of the female of California's housefinch. This, especially when contrasted with the striking coloration of the male.

---

† This, of course, is parallel evolution with the socalled "wedding dances" of such species as hummingbirds, also the remarkable feather-displays writer saw in Australia's Birds of Paradise. On the other hand his ladylove most inconspicuously is feathered.
‡ Thayer reminds us that camouflage is gained in one of 3 ways:—(a) mottled feather patterns; (b) iridescent plumage; (c) appendages.

To the garden philosopher, these manifestations of sex on every hand are fascinating. One sees it in the coloration of male birds, in various phenomena among insects. Even with the flowers. The evolution, over untold millions of years, toward progress in the transportation of millions of "renewal of life" elements from the anther of one flower to the stigma of another blossom is fascinating. One's absorption grows deeper when one contemplates such a transfer of inheritance of the possibilities of improvement thru heredity from one flower colony, as in any composite to another such colony-flower.

When one develops these thoughts toward a species wherein an individual possesses reason, as in the case of Man, the wonderment increases enormously. A world traveler cannot help comparing the freedom of courtship in Britain and U.S.A. with that of Hindustan. In Kipling's "Cupid's Arrows, Barr Saggotts," Commissioner with letters after his name," had hung the prize diamond bracelet, in the blue velvet case where it blinked in the sun. But Barr Saggotts was ugly and Miss Beighton's arrows went 1 "gold", 1 "red" but 5 "white". . . . Even she married, later, the boy she loved, Cubbon of the Dragoons.

Now, such occurrences do not happen in Hindu families. At the royal pre-wedding festivities (where We-2 occupied the 2 thrones) the bridegroom was present, of course, and his uncle, the Regent. The bride—oh! oh! she was not there. She and her bridegroom would see each other for the first time at the actual ceremony. In fact, in many weddings in Hindustan—(and Ceylon and indeed in certain places in Europe) the Go-Between sees much more of bride and of groom than do either of those whose wedding is to be celebrated. . . .

A phase of above that often carries humor in the form of the ridiculous is seen in what Browning calls "A Male Land." It was what was being completely forgotten that stimulated this author to write, for the 1949 Centennial, "What's In A Name?" with such items as Illinoistown, Bedbug, Pokerville, other "Male Land" incidents. . . .

For eloquent William Jennings Bryan, a watermelon seed was not too lowly for parable strategy. This famous 16-to-1 free silver philosopher ate, in Ohio, a delicious watermelon. He saved its seed to give to voting Nebraska farmer friends. To a group of these he said "I have brought you presents. They are seeds from a deliciously flavored watermelon I ate in Ohio. Reaching Chicago, I weighed its seeds. They ran some 5,000 to the pound. The mother watermelon weighed about 40 pounds. I reflected:—Someone planted a little seed. Given sunshine and showers, that watermelon seed had gone to work. From somewhere it gathered 200,000 times its own weight. It forced that enormous weight through a tiny stem to build that watermelon. Each of its many seeds was capable of repeating that miracle. What Architect drew that plan? Whence that seed's tremendous strength?"

Reproduction

SITE OF PRAIRIE HOUSE, PRAIRIE CITY

Stage houses were numerous along Gold Belt turnpikes. The locust trees, grown from Covered Wagon seed, are all that remain of Prairie House. It was named from nearby PRAIRIE CITY. When the Autumn winds play on these locust trees like the French poet's "violins" one can imagine one hears the ghosts of stage drivers, passengers, hostelers, stableboys whispering about the good old days. Then every winter storm uncovered more nuggets, even in rutted roadway of our photograph.

A gardner, watching his seed boxes notices the opposite growth of root and stem. This beginning at germination, continues through the plant's whole life. While yet in the soil, in total darkness, as soon as it begins to grow, the stem-end of the embryo points towards the light. It will curve quite round if it happens to lie in some other direction. It stretches upwards toward free air and sunshine. The root-end as uniformly avoids light. It bends in the opposite direction, ever seeking to bury itself more and more in the earth's bosom. How the plantlet makes these movements, we cannot explain. The object of this instinct however is obvious. It places the plant from the first in the proper position:—Roots in moist soil, from which they absorb nourishment. Leaves in the light and air, where alone they can fulfill their office of digesting what the roots absorb....

Writer finds October excellent for his Neighborhood Children's Nature Study Class to go exploring for seed wanderlusters. Most normal children have the hoarding instinct, enjoy collecting. It is fun to put different kinds of seeds into small bottles. They never, even at four-score years, outgrow such fascination of watching evolution toward reproduction.

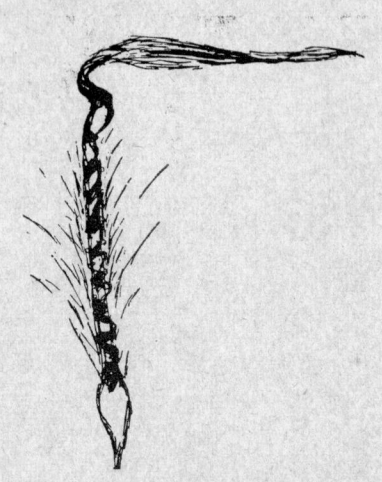

FILAREE SEED

It is midMay. Have just felt a prick at the ankle. Even before removing the offender, one knows it is a filaree seed for one has been cleaning up the "weeds". Yes, the prophecy was better than the average astrologer's. It WAS a next year's filaree plant, thumbing its way, under *Zeilstrebigkeit*, to an area with possibly less overpopulation. Even as to these seed travel-devices, "Mother Nature as always is first at Patent Office."

Seed travelers include those that (a) air travel (dandelion, milkweed, thistle, cattail); (b) sail (maple, elm, pine); (c) skate (linden, locust); (d) jump (violets, jimsonweed); (e) steal rides like a hobo (cockleburr, filaree); (f) float, (cocoanut); (g) do acrobat s t u n t s (tumbleweed); (h) gain transportation tickets by offering "goodies" (walnuts, pinenuts) ... Among the air traveling seeds is the Biblical "green bay tree," which is our oleander. One in bloom peeps over a wall, say Fez, or Damascus, or Peshawar. One knows at latticed windows in second stories above, black eyes watch. Arabian Nights atmosphere ever is present. A passing gust of breeze. Was it Ali Baba's flitting ghost? Harun al Rashid's? A great fleecy, drifting, sunset-tinted cloud,—was it really the Magic Carpet? On it, was there riding the shade of Fatima? The little clouds near it . . . were they wraiths of Janisaries, Christian-born, captured in boyhood, trained in Mohammedanism for the Sultan's bodyguard? That spinning dust-devil, was it a tenuous whirling dervish? Surrounded by oleanders, you ARE under the Crescent Flag. The lure of the Desert IS around you. Sunlight is blindingly brilliant in Oleander Land. One winks and blinks. In the warm breeze, 'tis easy to drop into Dreamland.

WANDERLUSTING SEEDS

One item about one bird transported seed* may be given here. It is myrtle. We plant it for several reasons, greens for interior decora-

---
* For bird transport of seed see also Chapter 7.

tion, shelter for native sparrows, fruits for cedar waxwings. We also make a jelly of the seed's pulp. The myrtle crown was awarded Greek games' winner. It thus ranked at Pythian Games with laurel, at Olympic Games with wild olive, at Nemean Games with wild celery. Moore sings of the charming pearl-like myrtle flowers among its green leaves: "The wreaths of brightest MYRTLE wove with sunlit drops of bliss among it." Myrtle probably would not have its delightful leaf odor were it not adjusted to semi-desert conditions. Adversity, in plants, in humans, brings out sweetness....

One day, We-2 were on a coasting vessel from Beirut to Smyrna. The freighter's loading time permitted a short inland excursion to Biblical Antioch. It was late winter. The Steppes' North Wind froze one to the marrow. Every few miles was another Turkish police station. This meant unbuttoning a heavy-mountain overcoat for passport. In that overcoat pocket was an old menu card, with crossed Turkish and British flags. This was offered as a passport. The police could not read. A few moments discussion at the first station, then a rubber-stamped "O.K." over "Soup d'Ognion."

———o———

Yes, this 4th-of-July we have a hitherto unobserved example of the Adventitious Bud. The World traveler has seen the most impressive examples in the tropics, in the trunk-buds of Java's jakfruit trees or in its cocoa plantations. Always a plant's *zeilstrebigkeit* operates another fruit. Survival is imperative. Otherwise comes Extinction. One thinks of tribolite and crinoid,—of brontosaurus and tricerotops—of dodo, moa, passenger pigeon, Carolina parakeet, ivorybill woodpecker.

———o———

An acorn becoming an oak, whose acorns later grew into another generation is paralleled by Sacramento's first playground. At first the early times of our 18-years' volunteer after-office work in Sacramento Orphanage Farm's supervised recreation. Thus came the determination to start a demonstration playground in our native city. We, with some friends, at first financed this privately. This, until taxpayers were convinced it was a good investment, if only for reduction of juvenile delinquency. From that seedplanting came Sacramento's present municipal chain of playfields. Writer was the Volunteer Commission's president during all years of private financing. He resigned only when his task was completed as the municipality took over.

A Garden Philosopher is fascinated watching a second generation of plants springing from seed he planted in an earlier generation. Lessons were learned conducting this education-thru-play experiment on Sacramento's 10th & P Plaza. Followed the expedition to the Orient, to start supervised playgrounds there. To this desk today comes a report transmitted to writer from the President of the Philippine Republic. It shows the playground which We-2 succeeded in getting established almost a half century ago in Manila's Tondo has grown to a total of 59 playgrounds.

ISIS WAS EGYPT'S MADONNA

Isis was Egypt's Motherhood Goddess. Her child, Horus, is here pictured in the hawk-headed manifestation. The Madonnas of a thousand mediaeval oil paintings represent an eternal adoration. One senses it existed in the worship of the thinkers at Nile-bank temples. The Gifted Child, Champollian, properly educated, was able to unlock for all of us many secrets of Egyptian wisdom.

Calendula's high fecundity stimulated my Sweetheart's thinking about the injustice of child labor. Shortly after our marriage, We-2 were gardening to get quick results in newly-broken soil. We had planted in January a plot of both golden and orange calendulas for contrasting bright color. It was in lush virgin soil.* Those calendulas,

FECUNDITY AND CHILD LABOR in that new soil, that spring, profusely bloomed, seeded. Annuals, they withered. Cleaning out the dead plants for the mulch pit, dropped seeds, under our sprinkler irrigation, had sprouted. In an area covered by my hat were several hundred plants. My Beloved observed:—"Note the biological parallel between the crops of Orphan-

---

* Our first home faced what now is Sutter's Fort State Park, which was across a streamlet called Burns' Slough. It was, therefore, what we ranchers call "Second Bottom". Sacramento then was so sparsely settled we could see, from our sleeping porch, the tops of the giant cottonwood at Sutter *Embarcadan* on the Rio de Los Americanos de Jedediah Smith, now American River.

Reproduction 125

age Farm† also Fairhaven kiddies and the calendula plantlets. All are largely unwanted. Our civilization scraps them".

That calendula week our house guest was a missionary. Our houseboy serving dinner almost dropped his tray when she addressed him in Cantonese. She described what we soon were to see with our own eyes—the teeming Orient's child labor. In Macao or Portuguese Chinese wee bairns eyestraining at blue kingfisher feather inlay. In this many children become blind. With loss of sight they "graduate" to the firecracker factories.

We-2 philosophized about struggling calendula seedlings, about Sacramento child labor, and in Japan, China, Hindustan. Thus came resolution to translate into action our garden philosophy. Hence our visits to Japan after the Russo-Japanese War, also to China, (where we saw Dr. Sun Yat Sen overthrow the Manchu dynasty). In Hindustan we studied the crowds at the Temple of Kali, dread Goddess of Hate. Thus, with Calcutta friends, was established Hindustan's first American-supervised-type playground. It was planned as an opening wedge to end child labor.

† Before our marriage, her restless Viking type of intellect, (inherited from her Virginia Tidelands ancestors of the 1600's) had urged her into astronomy as elsewhere described. With our marriage, came acceptance of Board Membership in Sacramento Orphanage Farm. Then she also accepted a Directorship of Fairhaven (home for unmarried mothers). It had been founded by our family.

**SUTTER'S MILL
GOLD DISCOVERY SITE**

Our first garden was opposite Sutter's Fort (built 1839). When first planted, it had a view of the American River's cottonwoods. Upstream some 30 miles was Sutter's Mill. When General Sutter built the historic fort, less than two decades earlier Jedediah Smith had discovered his "great California Valley with room for 100,000 farmsteads."

From our garden seat, We-2 used to discuss the ingratitude of Democracies. A monarchy rewards its heroes with titles. French towns under their Kings raise monuments to distinguished native sons. The great Roman Church grants sainthood to its devotees. Our nation actually forgot for 100 years Jedediah Smith. This tho, when all the historical records are published, he will be credited with having (in a remarkable crisis of world affairs) jolted into action what made U.S.A. a transcontinental power.

At least we lived to see the conversion of Department Store owner who had complained our Sacramento playground at 10th and Q would dry up his supply of "cash boys" and "cash girls". One August Sunday morning he breakfasted at our Sutter's Fort home. My Sweetheart took our guest out to the calendula bed. There was the annual fecundity—scores, hundreds of sprouting seedlings. "We have been discussing nature study" she said, then continued "There is a playground this very minute in Calcutta because 'We-2' philosophized about calendula seedling here, almost in the shadow of Sutter's Fort."

One's garden thus constantly reminds one of Overpopulation.* This, only recently has caught worldwide Intellectuals' attention. Is this fruition of seedplanting by a few Neopopulationists?†

---

* Eschscholtzia seeds 319 to 1 pod, 11 pods to radial stem, 9 stems. Thus one-1952-seed in 1953 yielded 31,581 potential plants. Wheat: 12 stalks at 60=720 fold but Crabgrass 200,000 seeds from one plant, which a year ago was but one seed.

† Credit here to the late Guy Burch. He devotedly, unreservedly spent failing energies, trying to awaken Mankind before the overpopulation menace became uncontrollable. Mention likewise should be made of the self-sacrifice of the brilliant geneticist Mr. Robert Cook. Already overworked with his duties as editor of the Journal of Heredity, he cheerfully undertook to also "carry on" the Burch work when, at latter's death, no other leader could be found.

27:729 CONTRAST

Defectives breed like rabbits. One moron, son of a narcotic addict father, sib to 4 illegitimates by 3 different fathers, murdered, in a drunken rage, his 9th child. In contrast, majority of those of creative minds have 2, 1, even no children. If all live, above moron, at the 9 rate would have 729 grandchildren.

"I have learned how," said one of two women, German immigrants, discussing birth control. The wise (?) one thought she "knew". Neither supposed a little boy was listening. Because of quackery, she had the care, until her death, af a child, later born deformed. In those 1880's, U.S.A. saw a new folkway beginning. The 2-child family ideal soon became custom, still persists in most **UNDERPOPULATION** advertisers' illustrations. Vice of above was, family limitation practice by the Desirables. A doctor said:—"We try to educate the morons. Too ignorant or too lazy; they continue to breed like rabbits."

Our nation already has suffered herein. During 1890-1940, some millions of highpowers, (under a 2-child folkway), never saw daylight. Were we alert to UNDERpopulation within OVERpopulation? Above loss is irreparable. What further height might we not have gained with those births. U.S.A.'s living standard is World's highest. We glory in our skyscrapers, airplanes, Panama Canal, a thousand other achievements. Was not the germ in one highpowered intellectual? This group expanded from Jamestown, Plymouth Rock until late 1800s, because of the high birthrate. 1890-1940 our intellectuals, the kind so able to pioneer they built our nation, racesuicided with 2, 1, 0 children.

We still can save our civilization, if voters inform themselves as to recent research gains in human genetics, eugenics. Why not use

Reproduction

same to reverse above dysgenic trend? How Differential Birthrates Law works is shown by the 27:729 vignette on page 126.

1890-1940, the 3-child family was the exception. Is it any wonder scientists say our national intelligence is lowered each decade? With more than half the world lacking population control, yet demanding U.S.A. feed them, may we, for survival, be forced to create A LEAGUE OF LOW BIRTHRATE NATIONS?

Must we not be ever alert as to human erosion?

Photo: Courtesy French Press & Information Service

THE OVERPOPULATED ORIENT'S SURVIVAL REQUIRES CHILD LABOR

Jokesmiths ridicule the baldheaded barber who, with a pate like an ostrich egg, shamelessly extolled the hairgrowth possibilities of his tonic to the customer in his chair. The lad with the tray to left knows the virtues of HIS product. The tray bearer to the right carries his baby brother, papoose-style.

Child labor is the rule in the Orient. There are so many mouths to feed, the oldest must quickly earn. Your editor, (volunteer child-labor-legislation worker at the century's turn) has described, out of his field studies, such instances as 5-year-olds at Morocco-leather-dyeing in such centers as Rabat and Fez.

Extreme overpopulation spells child labor and, as a consequence, illiteracy. A boy tying Oriental rug knots, commencing at 6, gets absolutely no schooling.

O O O O

Is it not curious that the seed of the giant sequoia is so small that any of the above O's would cover 1 seed?

Garden Philosopher

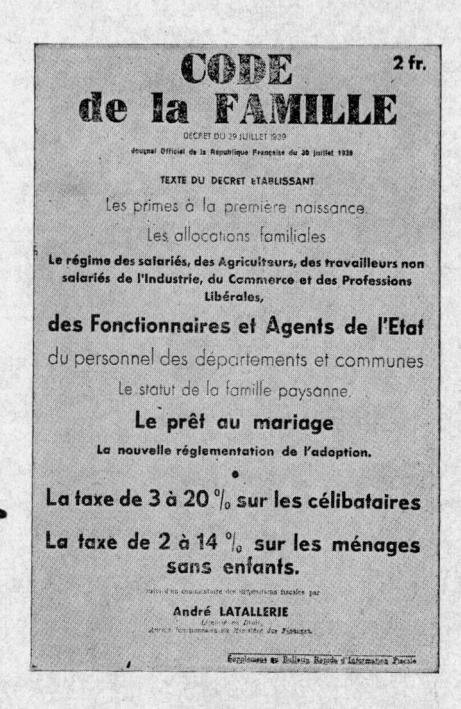

> **CODE de la FAMILLE** 2 fr.
> DÉCRET DU 29 JUILLET 1939
> Journal Officiel de la République Française du 30 juillet 1939
>
> TEXTE DU DÉCRET ÉTABLISSANT
> Les primes à la première naissance.
> Les allocations familiales
> Le régime des salariés, des Agriculteurs, des travailleurs non salariés de l'Industrie, du Commerce et des Professions Libérales,
> **des Fonctionnaires et Agents de l'Etat**
> du personnel des départements et communes
> Le statut de la famille paysanne.
> **Le prêt au mariage**
> La nouvelle réglementation de l'adoption.
>
> **La taxe de 3 à 20 % sur les célibataires**
>
> **La taxe de 2 à 14 % sur les ménages sans enfants.**
>
> André LATALLERIE

NOTE THE BACHELOR TAX

After all, does not the garden persistently tell us that all life is a constant struggle for survival? That seeds are vastly overproduced is shown by the example herein elsewhere mentioned of one crabgrass plant yielding 200,000 seeds. This, in an area already crabgrass-populated to saturation. One seed had space for survival. The other, say 199,999 starved to death. Does this not remind us that **SURVIVAL** we of U.S.A. face a constant struggle for survival in our endeavor to maintain our living standard? That it is the world's highest is due to American Know How.

Asiatics, with living standards at the opposite pole from ours, often have but 2 meals daily. We-2 found some Chinese rice growers who dared not even eat their rice. Its sale price invested in cheaper millet, yielded a margin covering cost of a few primitive needs:—a loin cloth, a pellet of opium.

Buying oranges in China, We-2 found, does not carry title to the peel. In China, tens of millions live on rice, rice, only rice. Any flavoring has a market value. In West China, sunrise-to-sunset toil earned less than a 3c postage stamp. Small wonder such folk hesitate at nothing to enter a land where a few hours' wage equals a weeks' at home. In Shanghai a piledriver's power was the muscles of women. A score circled it. At a signal all pulled together to raise the weight. Wages 5c a day, dawn to dusk. Asked why an American machine was not used, the boss said: "Here we make each job support as many as possible." In East Europe, not long ago, the writer found women earning only 12c per day. Such folk may hesitate at nothing to enter U.S.A.

On the trail from Nikko, with its worldfamous red lacquer bridge to Lake Chuzenji, we met coolie women carrying chunks of quarried rock. This was after the close of the Russo-Japanese War. We were surprised to find among them a blind burden-carrier. Even loss of sight did not prevent her having to carry the load. For this work we were told she earned, for a 12-hour day, less than 1 cent per hour.

Motoring across Turkey-in-Asia, we found the tariff for chauffeurs was 40c daily. 10c daily additional secured one speaking 15 languages. The reward of education was a daily wage increase equal the price of a large ice cream cone. With that much effort worth 10c, can one marvel at a willingness to bribe smugglers to gain admission to a land where wages are ten times Turkey's. Many of these Turks pass here as Greeks.

Too often Americans forget the chasm between our living standards and Europe's. In Greece, an American asked for an English-speaking chauffeur. 25% higher wages. 40c daily raised to 50c. This driver had lived in California. His brother's wife there ordered food over a telephone, cooked with gas, hot water thru a faucet. The wife in Greece had to haggle at a market for a quarter hour to buy a fish. Fuel came only thru picking up dead olive twigs. Water was carried by jar on head, Rebecca-like, from the village well a half mile away. Any wonder such folk break laws to enter our "Land of Gold."

With an American mining engineer, have been discussing wages in Rhodesia. Working, for years, with an English company there, he said he paid his No. 1 boy, (comparatively high I.Q., capable of leadership), one English pound a month. His cook earned $1.25 monthly. Common run at hard-labor boys, $1.50. Any wonder all who learn of our living standard want to enter U.S.A.! Municipal Ordinance here:— Painters $2.65 per hour, $5.25 per hour in overtime.

CAMEL PUMP, EGYPT

When writer, with 250-foot-boom clamshell dredgers, was throwing levees around Sacramento River swamp lands, he was reclaiming land that never had been tickled by the plow. . . . Once the levees were completed, it was necessary to install giant, electrically-driven pumps to pump out the swamp water, and to keep the land free from seepage, that it could be cropped.

These pumps were said then to be the world's largest. Their volume, pouring into the canal beyond the levee, made a stream enuf to float a boat. Compare such an operation with the above primitive camel pump. Its type was never improved since the days of Moses.

Ranching, which is but gardening on a greater scale, stimulates philosophizing as to American Know How. Same was born of 10 generations of pioneering by the old American stock.

Dad was Australian-born. Kin "Down Under" sometimes ask us to entertain Australians crossing U.S.A., enroute to Britain. One was a packer of canned foods. Approaching his first California cannery, he criticized sharply:—"Too much overhead." Writer questioned:—"How do you know—you have not been yet inside." He answered:—"This half-mile of automobiles, parked both sides of street!" Then I learned he thought only an executive could afford an automobile. He was unwilling to believe cannery labor force owned these cars. He said, "In Australia, such folk utilize bicycles, streetcars." Australia has, after U.S.A., world's next best living standard. Yet the Hyphenates who fought 1921-Quota Act opposed restriction ever since. They now demand McCarran-Walter Immigration Code repeal, despite the override of President Truman's veto. These Hyphenates insist on "liberalization" immigration legislation. That means, reducing U.S.A. toward coolie-wage standards. . . .

Reproduction

Armistice Day comes to the Garden. With it, the first sprinkles of California's rainy season. This obligingly telescopes precipitation into some few months. Thus we gain rainless summers for outdoor exploring. . . . The earthen paths had small pools of last night's rainwater. Already dried, sulphur-colored margins showed where, for a few hours, there had been minature lakelets. That **OVERPOPULATION** sulphur was pollen from the garden's deodar clump a hundred feet away. Similar yellow margins last midsummer were on a hundred glacier-gouged Sierran lakes. Six deodars thus coated a 100-foot radius with pollen. It were unnoticed, had it not been for that overnight shower. From half a dozen conifers, millions of pollen grains. The gardener thus has insight into Mother Nature's Law of Fecundity:—OVERPRODUCE, THEN FIGHT FOR SURVIVAL.*

Over a half century this author has ding-donged about Intellectual's interference with human reproduction. Man's natural birthrate is adjusted to a thousand centuries of primitive life. Only since Pasteur have we really commenced to accelerate the reduction of deathrates. It was impressive, on writer's first visits to Paris a decade before World War I to hear Academicians recount the worries of battlefield operations in the Franco-Prussian War. Amputations carrying 60% mortality:—"They often hardly dared operate. This, when even an injected pinprick sometimes resulted fatally." Now our researchists are steadily increasing life expectancies even among Backward Nations.

One pair of California's native whitefoot mice can become ancestors, at the end of the second year of 340,575 mice at the 5-litter rate. A yesteryear comedian observed "two is company, but three is a Board of Directors." If so, how about the 200,000 seeds of one plant of crabgrass. How about 340,575 garden mice at the end of the second year? Both are examples of Nature's method of fecundity, then let the fittest survive. Crabgrass, mice have been on our planet for, probably, the ten-millions of years. Pithecanthropus, perhaps our first man-like creature is sometimes credited with having lived in Java 1,000,000 years ago. Man has reason, can he learn from garden mice, garden crabgrass to correct today's tragic overpopulation from Japan, to Hindustan? This, without the natural checks of war, famine, pestilence?

To the gardening philosopher, few happenings, in his outdoor laboratory are more persistently impressive than weed invasions. Garden weeds remind us that one type of plant CAN displace another.

---

* Elsewhere this author has written repeatedly about adjustment of bird egg clutches to survival needs.

This is evident when coarse Bermuda, from insignificant beginnings, destroys a prized bluegrass lawn. Crabgrass penetrates the violet bed, displaces those dispensers of delightful perfume. On the ranches one sees parasitic dodder shouldering out the milk-valuable alfalfa. Prolific Johnson grass can destroy the profit of a tomato crop. On the sheep ranges, Klamath weed outs forage grasses. Bindweed CAN displace sugar beets also tomatoes so much as to almost eliminate the profit necessary to continue ranching. Wild radish, thru impure seed, unless controlled by airplanes' selective spraying can so thoroughly monopolize sunlight and soluble soil-salts that a grain crop can be killed 100%! Neglect to weed your garden and bindweed (European wild morning glory) can oust your chrysanthemums.

IMMIGRATION CAN PREVENT OLD STOCK REPRODUCTION

Many human weeds have come here as immigrants from overseas. If homogeneity is a prime factor in civilization's progress, (as seems evident in all Scandinavia), then are not the findings of a former Census Director* worth reflection? He declared admission of any immigrant to U.S.A. meant just one old stock American never was born. Our living standard is the world's highest. Those whose wage standard is anywhere from ½ to perhaps 1/100 of ours, become successful competitors here. The old Americans had to practice excessive birth control. This, which spelled race-suicide, was synchronous with our industrialists' acceptance of cheap, docile labor from the Mediterranean, also Eastern Europe. This, to fill the vacuum caused by the tragic 1861-65 Civil War deaths.

A U.S.A. Immigration History has arrived today. It declares immigrants entered thusly:—1780-1820 (40 years), 250,000 . . . 1820-1880 (60 years) 10,000,000 . . . 1880-1914 (34 years) . . . 30,000,000. It reports that the 3rd or 1924 Quota Act permitted annually 154,000, and that actual admissions during some years was less than ¼ of the quota. In other words, THE PRE-WORLD WAR I DELUGE OVER A CONSIDERABLE PERIOD WAS REDUCED 97%. Before World War II broke, one statistician estimated the Quota Acts had blocked (1921 to 1939) an influx of over 25,000,000.

May a gardener, a rancher, a grower of seeds for the seedsman, a dairyman, a stockman, a world traveller, an ardent immigration restrictionist, testify out of all above practical experience as to his reactions to above. This writer lived in both Constantinople and Athens during the Exchange-of-Populations. He saw much of the refugee camps of Russian exiles on Black Sea's shores, also of displaced Armenians in the Grand Leban. He also had an illuminating insight

---
* For Walkers Law data, see Cook's "Human Fertility", p. 85.

into the philosophy of the Druses. (They rebelled because of the French injection into their ancient land of both Armenians and of Tonquinese. They declared French policy was to exploit their holdings of centuries thru substituting heterogeneity for homogeneity. They insisted France expected, by the use of highly vocal minorities' competition, to break down their Nationalism. Is not parallel of this in Grand Leban painfully evident in U.S.A. today?)

In discharging his duty herein, writer also studied *Massenpsychologie* in Germany and, in France, the invention and development by the University of Paris THE PAMPHLET as a means of public education. We were advised by French friends that THE PAMPHLET technique was responsible, in no small way, for France's world leadership for several centuries until World War I.

With absorption of above, we then used the strategy of "The Education" of Henry Adams. He declared he cared nothing for the masses as long as he could gain the ears of America's 10,000 who created U.S.A.'s public opinion.

BUTTRESSED KANARI TREES

In Mohammedan Lands, the life of any wife often is made miserable by the continual plotting of other wives, and even more so when a new and young concubine is introduced into the harem. Moslem thinkers themselves are beginning to conclude polygamy makes for weakness of the social structure. It still obtains from Morocco across Egypt, and Hindustan to Java and Malaysia. It is not uncommon in China.

SHE CANNOT PHONE: "INCLUDE A LOAF OF WHOLE WHEAT"

"It is not wise for the Christian man
To hurry the Aryan brown,
For the brown man smiles while the white man riles,
And it weareth the Christian down,
And the end of the fight is a tombstone white,
With the name of the late deceased,
An epitaph clear:—" 'A fool lies here,
Who tried to hurry the East'." (Kipling)

Learning to respect the garden wisdom, accumulated over untold centuries, of the Orient, is helpful in adjusting the thinking of an American with Covered Wagon background. We of the Far West, who have survived the rigors of 10 generations on the Frontier, have come to have faith and optimism that make us unpleasant companions for those who have, may we use the term, stagnated by being tied generation after generation, century after century, to one location. Was there anyone wiser than Hindustan-born Kipling, who became saturated with ideas out of the subcontinent's folkways. The impressions of his childhood were carried over into his life as an adult. His writings therefore, at least to this author, are worth some rereading weekly. How much he has telescoped into his observation:—"East is East and West is West and never the twain shall meet." How much there is in the quotation credited to him, on the headstone of a Far East cemetery given in the lines above. How much wisdom is concentrated into his estimation of Asia.

"THE SAHIBS HAVE NOT ALL THE WISDOM!"

Reproduction 135

A FAR CRY FROM U.S.A.'S TEXTILE MILLS
Hindu wife still spins as in New England of the 1600's.

Our family's contacts, since the 1870's, had been as persistent with Hindustan as with China. 1858's Sepoy Rebellion then was about a decade past. Its rebels had been ruthless, especially as to British women. The "punishment" also was something about which to shudder. One must admit, however, the "reforms" the **SUTTEE** *babus* demagogically demanded had proceeded as rapidly as *Brahmin* opposition permitted. A classic example is British ending of the *suttee* or widow-burning.

One means of birth control was this very *suttee*. Its cruelty happily was ended by the stern British raj. Was it not just another phase of what we see when scores of calendula seedlings, sprout in the area occupied by one mother plant?

Our family, over 3 generations, had above connections. We-2 after successful privately-starting present Sacramento Playgrounds, carried "American Supervised Play" to the Orient. Our Calcutta center still serves.

Few today alive knew the Far East of the Russo-Japanese War's close. Of these, those interested in genetic aspects of flower-breeding, also in Eugenics can be counted on one's fingers. This testimony may be worth recording:—The Far East had some folkways of high eugenical worth. One: Intense passion for homogeneity. This, as to Korea, will be discussed elsewhere herein. Others, like Japan's wrestling matches, were of debatable worth. One bout writer then attended opened with Shinto ritual. Present were Japan's masculine "400". None were accompanied by wives, only geisha girls. Participants were of a breed writer never elsewhere has seen. Enormous mountains of fat, of flesh, they, stripped to the waist, wore skirts. Encircling the champion were 6 hopefuls. To retain championship, he had to down one after another without one moment's respite. . . .

GEISHA GIRLS

So with immigration restriction. One old-stock American in, say the 1880s, could compete with one Scarface Al Capone-type alien. Abovementioned Director of the Census said, "Every alien arriving prevents birth of one oldstock baby." On this desk, a case history of one alien with 16 sons. (He didn't count daughters.) The Hyphenates demand abolition of immigration restrictions. Does that not mean a trend of pioneer-stock toward extinction like the bison's? Ought we overstrain severely, (like the Japanese wrestler-champion) the type that built U.S.A.?

To a eugenist, also earnest feminist, above emphasis on absolute male dominance must always be biologically unfortunate. IT IS TO THE GLORY OF RECENT RESEARCH IN HUMAN GENETICS THAT WE KNOW THE MOTHER CONTRIBUTES EXACTLY ONE-HALF HER BABY'S GENES. This is something every garden flower whispers. In the unscientific Far East custom is, therefore, say only 50% efficient. How much upon our unique respect for womanhood is our unique American Know How based?

JAPAN'S CHAMPION WRESTLER, WITH 2 OF HIS 6 CHALLENGERS

In our worldwide travels, We-2 often remarked that nowhere else does womanhood command the respect that it has in Saxon America. . . . At Japanese wrestling matches, no spectator thinks of taking his wife. Geisha girls, however, ARE numerous there.

Reproduction

"LOBSTER CLAW" INHERITANCE

This "Lobster Claw" photograph dramatically illustrates the danger of hereditary diseases, (see next illustration.)

Is not this problem of best type of reproduction dependent upon the number of truly happy marriages. Experience of Us-2 herein has been rich. Our family founded Sacramento's Unmarried Mother's Refuge, "Fairhaven". We paid its early recurrent deficits. Source of income formerly December rug sale. Girls, awaiting **HAPPY** confinement, wove rag rugs. One winter's sale failed **MARRIAGES** to total $20. How writer, practical businessman, solved marketing problem is told in writer's book "Seeking to Serve." My Sweetheart's continued knowledge of Fairhaven kiddies' fatherhood, plus use by Us-2 of Sacramento Orphanage Farm as a Child-Welfare Laboratory, was most helpful. Author's lectures at Ione Reform School gave additional insight. Such after-office-hours' work brought conviction California needed juvenile legislation. Enactment of 1909 Juvenile Court Law was secured.

The tragedy of the child from the broken home is impressive. The kiddie where father and mother lead a cat-and-dog life is destructive of many spiritual values.

Is not most encouraging, eugenically, the progress being made in opening across U.S.A. Marriage Consultation Centers? In this matter of mating, cannot humanity be divided like the Biblical "sheep and goats"? Morons, in even the great 1930s Depression, continued to breed like rabbits. One scientist then estimated that 20% taxeaters on relief produced more children than 80% prudent taxearners. These Marriage Consultation Centers usually have an Advisory Board. Thereon is one eugenist or, at least one physician really trained in Human Genetics. Such an expert often can end worries. A couple truly in love may be fearful of transmitting to any children a hereditary taint.

True, certain diseases, such as Huntington's chorea*, haemophilia, certain mental disorders seem to "run in families". Writer was delegate to last World Eugenics Congress at The Hague. It

MARRIAGE CONSULTATION CENTERS

there was asserted certain blind by inheritance tend to marry other blind. One great scientist reported his research showed, of a group of 200 such children, 192 have defective vision. It now seems possible a competent geneticist often can advise marriage need not be avoided. This is a matter for highly trained technical minds. The battle for such Municipal Marriage Consultation Centers progressing as favorably as another parallel movement, a half century ago. In this, a small group of us fought to substitute supervised playgrounds for child labor.

An ancient Arab proverb says, "I complained because I had no shoes, until I met one who had no feet." ... As shown in above illustration, such a deformity CAN "run in families." One of the priceless services of a good Marriage Consultation Center is the advice obtained from the Geneticist member of its staff. When a prudent couple is in love, but has fear of transmitting a trait to offspring, in most cases such anxiety can be removed. An expert geneticist knows—as mere layfolks cannot. All this has high eugenic value. The prudent refrain from marriage, often unnecessarily. "Morons always breed like rabbits."

* See "Huntington Chorea", from Genetics Research Program. (Pouch A. Rochester, Minn.), printed under a grant from Mary Glide Goethe' Fund, Minnesota Human Genetics League. It may be helpful ot those organizations on Marriage Consultation Centers.

Insects

The visits of bees are necessary for the fertilization of some kinds of clover . . . 100 heads of red clover (T. pratense) produced 2,700 seeds, but the same number of protected heads produced not a single seed. Humble-bees alone visit red clover, as other bees cannot reach the nectar. It has been suggested that moths may fertilize the clovers; but I doubt whether they could do so in the case of the red clover, from their weight not being sufficient to depress the wing petals. Hence we may infer as highly probable that, if the whole genus of humble-bees became extinct or very rare in England, the heartsease and red clover would become very rare, or wholly disappear. The number of humble-bees in any district depends in a great measure upon the number of field-mice, which destroy their combs and nests; and Col. Newman, who has long attended to the habits of humble-bees, believes that "more than two-thirds of them are thus destroyed all over England." Now the number of mice is largely dependent, as every one knows, on the number of cats; and Col. Newman says, "Near villages and small towns I have found the nests of humble-bees more numerous than elsewhere, which I attribute to the number of cats that destroy the mice." Hence it is quite credible that the presence of a feline animal in large numbers in a district might determine, through the intervention first of mice and then of bees, the frequency of certain flowers in that district! (Darwin)

"I wish also, . . . Alleys, enough for foure to walke a breast; Which I would hau to be Perfect Circles, without any Bulwarkes, or Imbosments; And some fine Banquetting House, with some Chimneys neatly cast, and without too much Glasse. For Fountaines, they are a great Beauty, and Refreshment; But Pooles marre all, and make the Garden unwholesome, AND FULL OF FLIES, and Frogs. Fountains I intend to be of two Natures: The One, that Sprinckleth or Spouteth Water; The other a Faire Receipt of Water, of some Thirty or Forty Foot Square, BUT WITHOUT FISH, OR SLIME, OR MUD . . . the Maine Point, is the same, which we mentioned, in the foremer Kinde of Fountaine; which is, that the Water be in Perpetuall Motion, Fed by a Water higher then the Poole and Deliuered into it by faire Spouts, and then discharged away vnder Ground, by some Equalitie of Bores."

(Bacon's Essays)

Let us reflect upon human dependence for food on flowering plants. This, even in the Hunting Age. Buffalo, camels, sheep, ate largely flowering plants, i.e. grasses. Same still have place in certain gardens as the pampas grass clumps, fashionable in yesteryear gardens. As population pressure increased and leaders invented new food production techniques, our dependence on flowering plants increased. An example on writer's ranches one important crop is alfalfa. At times we shipped highly-compressed bales of this nutritious clover via Panama to New York. This, that Manhattan babies might have milk. Dependence of flowering plants on insects is illustrated by above Darwin quotation.

OUR DEBT TO INSECTS

Garden-philosopher Bacon did not like the Diptera. He specifically mentions "flies." Anyone summer-botanizing in New Hampshire's birch woods will say "Amen". When Glacier National Park trails were being pioneered, we saw a stretcher coming out. Its sufferer was near unto death from infection. He had scratched a horsefly bite.

The mosquito, another of the Diptera, has an unenviable reputation: Unforgettable is the wisdom of "Willoughby Rodman 'awkins, Sir . . . Jamaica darky, Sir . . . Britisher, Sir." Mr. 'awkins was this author's chauffeur when birding in Panama. HE KNEW! "Bossman, someday when we start for Jungle, I show you French boat. Frenchman, he try dig Big Ditch. He no-can-do. He dredger, he rust in he little ditch. American he come—he chase Yellow Jack away. He stop chills-and-fever. AMERICAN, HE JUST LIKE GOD." Was there ever a more beautiful tribute to "American Know How" than Mr. 'awkins' admiration of our control of insect-born disease?

———o———

In Grand Canyon National Park, Tonto Platform is classified by some geologists as an old penaplain. It is rich in fossil trilobites. These are held by some geologists to be the ancestral stock from which the insects were evolved. This is just another example of the ever-growing value of the National Park as an outdoor museum offering education in sugar-coated form. (See the Trilobite illustration, page 141).

Our knowledge of these insect visitors, constantly increased, will be more widened as our young folks (as they increasingly are) learn to READ A GARDEN. For example, Dr. Pirsson reminds us we now know some 13,000 species of living butterflies and that, of fossil forms, only 22 are known. Of these half are from Florissant. It was the remarkable work of the writer's friend, the late Dr. Cockrell at Florissant, that induced Us-2 to invest a summer session at the nearby University of Colorado. He was a member of its faculty.

ORIGIN OF INSECT METAMORPHOSIS

Insects

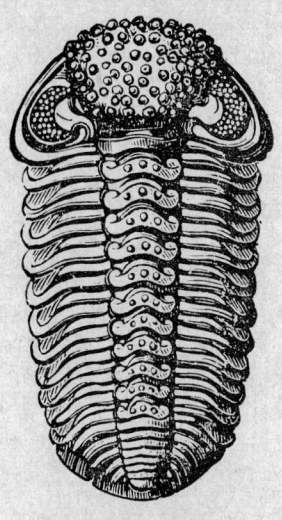

TRILOBITE

Your garden insects supposedly sprang from these Trilobites. They were creatures of the lobster-and-crab brotherhood. As marine organisms, under population pressure, moved landward, came the transition from these Trilobites to the first primitive insects. Trilobites stimulated, as far back as the late 1600s, one beginning of our science of paleontology. They first were supposed to be a kind of fossil* fish. Linnaeus recognized them as crustaceans. Writer saw colonies of these fossils in Canadian Rockies' strata. They once were foremost among the animals. They lived in ocean shallows. They lost out in competition with the "brainier" fishes as latter were evolved. (See also page 140.)

---

* Elsewhere this author has described the Cockerill prediction, the cause of extinction of elephants and camels in North America might someday be proven by finding a fossil tsetse fly. The Doctor himself, later, did find, at Florissant, said fossil tsetse.

"You DIRTY boy!" Perhaps five years old, I still remember my Aunt's saying this when I was caught making mudpies. I had found my clothing the most convenient napkin. I WAS DIRTY. And a year later I recall an immigrant Polish peasant woman gossiping:—"Her mantel piece was so neglected one could write one's name in its DUST." DIRT . . . DUST, and yet:—Today September opens. At 3 P.M. the goldenrod swarms with hexapods:—bee flies, bluebottles, syrpids, bluet butterflies, several species of wasps, microhymenoptera . . . and honeybees. The honeybees seem nervously busy—as they sense Winter is not far away. They are collecting honey. That honey is based upon, eventually, DIRT, DUST, soil. Hidden in the garden's sleeping porch one watches flicker also bluejay, to use Pepy's words, "delousing themselves". Later watching house finches taking for the same purpose dustbaths in the garden, one is stimulated to go a-rummaging for some line drawings of various mallophaga made years ago. This, by a friend who specialized in their study, and insisted research as to this group because it might throw light on certain problems of evolution.

In the search, we also found a portfolio of other line drawings. Latter are of trilobites. They were made more than a half century ago when writer became absorbed in studying these fossils. Even then the geology Professor was wondering if they were the ancestral stock that expanded into the vast and varied aggregation of our modern insects. There does seem to be a semblance between trilobites of the Devonian to the Carboniferous and the mites that annoy the garden's flickers and bluejays. One thinks of folksaying of the Ozark hillbillie (who never heard of a gene or of a chromosome) "Little Jim is the splittenest image of Big Jim."

The ancestors of our garden insects appeared long before the first flowering plants. Some geologists think insects evolved from the trilobites in the Devonian, or Age of Fishes. Other geologists fix their rise simultaneously with that of the Coal Age reptiles. They, along with landcrabs, seem to have been our first air-breathers. By the Pennsylvanian we have several hundred cockroach species. **FOSSIL** Giant dragonflies, some with a wing-spread of 2 feet, flew **INSECTS** among Coal Age sigillarias, lepidodendrons, calamites, and tree ferns. These plants were to rot into our coal. By Comanchean Time, appeared hymenoptera, (bees, wasps, ants), also beetles, flies. . . .

One path in our garden angles into Japanese anemone clumps. Some are white, some magenta, some pink. We-2 planted them years ago, returning from our first Nipponese trip. They somehow ever reminded us, at their annual flowering, to be alert for opportunities to serve. We had seen them blooming along a certain rickshaw path in Japan's hinterland. They were unforgettably attractive grouped at a Torii of lichened granite. Crossing above rickshaw path was another trail with a queue of plodding maidens. Each had atop her head a cruelly-heavy block of ore from the mine uphill. Where my father, at his mines, used ore cars on tracks, here girl-labor, at a couple-of postage-stamps daily wage, was cheaper. (How a little group of us fought in those years, to elevate Oriental womanhood!) . . .

On one white anemone alights a skipper. Here we have a living fossil. Writer's friend, the late Dr. T. A. D. Cockerell, once told him the skipper was one of Mother Nature's first attempts at butterflymaking. Compared with similar-sized bluets or bronzelets, one senses Mother Nature has progressed toward beauty. The wise Doctor was world authority on certain fossil insects. He had collected most of the peerless finds of Colorado's Florissant shales.

Now comes to the anemone's honeyfeast, a yellow-and-black tiger swallowtail, also a brick-red monarch. What progress from tiny skipper to these two lords of butterfly world! Did you ever wonder how the

Insects 143

word "butterfly" originated? On this desk is data that it first was suggested by the butter-colored excrement of a European sulphur. This butterfly's body wastage, butter-yellow in color, butterlike in texture, is supposed to first have been used to name such a fly. One record gives the original Anglo Saxon as *"butterfloege"*, adds Old Dutch *"boter-schijte"*, (literally *"butter-voider.")"*

JURATRIAS BUTTE, GRAND CANYON NATIONAL PARK

This photograph illustrates passage of Geologic Time. The butte against the skyline is JURASSIC of the Age of Reptiles. With the exception of some such buttes that resisted, the strata have been eroded, are now sediments in the Colorado Desert, or say in California's Imperial Valley. The flat surface upon which the butte rests is Paleozoic (Carboniferous). In the Canyon, hundreds of feet down, is a formation with numerous trilobites. Some geologists hold they are the insects' ancestors. By the time the Jurassic was deposited, uncounted millions of years had intervened. Along with gigantic reptiles (Stegosaurus, Tyrannosaurus, Tricerotops, Brontosaurus) were cockroaches and dragon flies. One of latter had a 29-inch wing spread.

The locusts and grasshoppers arose in the Jurassic. Here is a bit of grasshopper history:—A Tennessee hillbilly once taunted a Lake Tahoe Pah Ute. The Redskin hungrily was munching dried grasshoppers. This Amerind, (American-Indian), retorted:—"Ugh! Paleface, he eat 'um shrimp!"

Our California grasshoppers preach eloquently of efficiency. Some in our garden are leaf-green with golden lines and dots. Here is just enough disruptive coloration to confuse a hungry bluejay. Some are mottled like gravelly soil. Some have crimson underwings, some canary-yellow, some wings flash silver. These underwings might be puzzling as much as the camouflage of brightly-colored birds of the Amazon or Orinoco jungles.

GRASSHOPPER TRIBE

Defense mechanism of such seems to parallel that of underwing moths. Like moths with red underwings, contrasting with perfectly-camouflaged wing-covers, so our garden grasshoppers have above-described conspicuous underwings. As to the value of such striking colors beneath camouflaged upperwings, watch a half-wild cat. Note a sparrowhawk, its lookout a dead Sabine pine. Pussy, or falcon, either strikes at bright color in flight. Presto! It is gone. The camouflage now all concealing has been increased in efficiency by that very instantaneous shift from bright color to concealing hues.

Enjoy late Indian Summer grasshopper observations. Five weeks ago was Equinox, but no traditional equinoctial storm, as New England-born 49'ers persistently predict. For five rich weeks there have been cloudless days with wonderful afternoons to observe maximum insect activity. Today whitecrowned sparrows from Alaska call from the brush shelter We-2 planted to protect them. An accipter is atop the court's great elm. The "French", the "African" marigolds, the Korean chrysanthemums, the zinnias swarm with the 6-footed. Grasshoppers are there in varied camouflage as abovementioned. Other 'hoppers are mottled protectively in disruptive coloration. Some have colorless underwings that give a flash of silver in flight. Others are canary yellow or scarlet. All 3 brightnesses are, indeed, part of their survival mechanism.

―――o―――

If the garden has a eucalyptus windbreak, it offers rare winter opportunities to improve the gardener's insect acquaintances. In January one finds hidden beneath the "stringy barks" a zoo of the 6-footed. Adult hemiptera make same their wintering Palm Beach or Honolulu. Perhaps there will be found a hibernating mourning cloak. Or, there may be the earthenware jug of a wasp, containing an unhatched egg atop a paralyzed spider. When you contemplate that Mother wasp's ability to sting exactly that spider's tiny nerve ganglion, so that it will live until the next spring's hatching, thus supplying her baby's food, you will be ready to sing, with the Psalmist: "The firmament showeth His handiwork." Perhaps the most fascinating of all the life awaiting a gardener's stringy bark exploration are the fuzzy moth cocoons. It's lots of fun to collect a garden's various cocoons. These hairy ones may yield surprises. Sometimes a parasitic fly has intervened. Your hatchings may be Diptera, not Lepidoptera! All this stimulates the gardener to philosophize upon parasitism. The Florida gulls' example was used by idealists there to educate moronic crackers. These lazy hillbilly boneheads were the tools of demagogues who preached that Government owed them a living.

RAISING PARASITIC DIPTERA

Insects 145

The zoologist Hertwig, always preaching *zeilstrebigkeit*, reminds us that some parasites are so tough they can live in alcohol! The philosophy of the Niche warns humans that, when the tax-earner turns tax-eater, his parasitism transforms him. This just as surely as Florida gulls, grown dependent upon fishery-scrap, now no longer can gain food by foraging.

The successful conduct of a neighborhood kiddie garden nature study class depends upon ever maintaining fresh interests. There are few fields more promising than mimicry. One starts competition as to who can exhibit at the year's end the best collection. One of the first finds will be the bee flies. These mimic honey bees most successfully. This writer, after seventy years of collecting, cannot bring himself to grasp with his bare hands a bee fly. This, tho he knows it has no sting. Memories of painful bee stings are too persistent. . . .

Mid-July's sun, still away North, casts late afternoon rays thru an opening in the elms that once shaded the packing house of the mile of cherry orchard which now is Elmhurst. As late as 6:30 one can observe, in that searchlite beam, the enormous number of insects otherwise usually unnoticed. A square yard of illumination may show several score in action. Only in one other spot did We-2 ever observe the like. It was when, to get local color for the educational program to acquire, for a State Park, the North Calaveras redwoods, We-2 sleeping-bagged a fortnight under those peerless Sequoias. . . .

What most impressed us, in sunbeamed Sequoia as well as our garden elms, was the manner in which flycatcher vision parallels that of humans. Even to it the number of hexapods visibility must have been enormously increased:

BUGS:—
(BEDBUGS,
STINKBUGS,
MEALYBUGS,
TOADBUGS)

Asiatics, with living standards at opposite pole from ours, often have but 2 meals daily. This author found some Chinese ricegrowers who dared not eat their own rice. Its sale price, invested in cheaper millet, yielded a margin covering cost of a few primitive needs:—a loin cloth, a pellet of opium. Such folk, however, still have the yearning for pets. If they cannot afford a dog, a cat, even a song bird they can at least twist bamboo into a cage for a cicada. . . .

At October end, the golden chrysanthemums (which are literally CHRYS-ANTHE-MUMS) swarm with skippers, and other butterflies, thread-waisted wasps, honeybees, ants, 12-spotted flower beetles, half a dozen kinds of wild bees. There are also flies that

BUTTERFLY
TONGUES

mimic the bees . . . As to said butterflies:—Our family, decade after decade, bought its watches in Switzerland. Only there could one buy that quality that was the wisest investment. One thus came to have glimpse of those miracle-working watchmakers in their shops. One saw the marvels of watch parts, such as the coiled main springs. Today we watch a cabbage butterfly. It feeds, this November morning, at a chrysanthemum. Its marvellous tongue is stabbing one ray flower after another at the rate of 5 to 1 second. Note, however, that tongue when coiled. Again one grasps that Mother Nature always was "first at the Patent Office". The butterfly tongue is a perfect model for that mechanical marvel, the watch spring.

A CHINESE PROVERB SAYS:

———o———

"THE CICADA CAN FLY BUT 10 PACES, BUT IN THE TAIL OF A NOBLE STEED, HE CAN GO A THOUSAND MILES."

"Ole Man River
Ole Man River
He doan' do nothin'
He doan' say nothin'
He just keeps a rollin' on."

Up-Nile negroes sing in another language. One does not know if it is a Sudanese version of Ole Man River rolling along. The Nile, like the Mississippi, does "keep rolling along." And on its banks, the scarabs roll their balls of camel dung just as they did in the days of Moses. We-2 were strolling under the gingerbread palms in an Egyptian garden with Blank Pasha. A scarab beetle crossed our path. It was rolling its ball of camel dung, just as its ancestors had done for 5,000 years since the First Dynasty—just as its even more remote ancestors had for 45,000 x 5,000 years. For the beetles arrived in the Triassac. Some geologists estimate the Triassic with its dinosaurs as 225,000,000 years ago. This would be 45,000 times as long as the years since Cheops built the pyramids. Great is the expanse of geologic time!

EGYPT'S SCARAB

We have scarabaeidae in our California gardens, where one can witness Father Scarab and Mother Scarab doing commendable teamwork rolling the ball of dung that later is to be baby food. Why do scarahoids roll the balls of dung? This writer's friend, the late Dr. Comstock wrote: "Many predaceous insects frequent the masses of dung from which the balls are obtained in order to prey upon the larvae which lives there. The more intelligent tumble bugs remove the food for their larvae to a safe distance."

Nothing We-2 ever brought from our Egyptian work was more prized than a ring-sized scarab exquisitely carved in turquoise which we found Up-Nile. The Egyptian superstition was that the ball was the earth—the beetle the sun,—its antennae sunrays—their segments —the days of the month.

> "Male stag-beetles sometimes bear wounds from the huge mandibles of other males; the males of certain hymenopterous insects have been frequently seen by that inimitable observer, M. Fabre, fighting for a particular female who sits by, and apparently unconcerned beholder of the struggle, and then retires with the conqueror." (Darwin)

At October-end, the Garden's insects never were more fascinating. The creamy Korean dwarf-mums still attract many. Afront these, dwarf magentas' buds give promise for Thanksgiving color. Big Monarch butterflies wing their leisurely way, reminding **INDIAN** one of Brazil's Golden Monkey Jungle's big "blue-**SUMMER** silk Morphos flight." There also passed a Viceroy.* **BUTTERFLIES** Some thistle butterflies, also an occasional buckeye stop for "coffe-and". Some fritillaries remind one of veteran Dr. Cockerell's find of their Miocene ancestors at Florissant. Also cabbages, some sulphurs.

Now are scores of Microlepidoptera. There are many handsome bronze midgets, interrupting feeding for lovemaking. A few blues, but mostly coppers. Studying their behavior, one wonders about such inherited size-patterns. These microlepidoptera always are thumbnail editions. The skippers, too, are dwarfish. The monarchs, the swallowtails to them must seem giants. Why are bumblebees clumsily large, like clodhopping ploughboys, when honey bees adjusted to a size as uniform as their comb cells? Why is the bee hummingbird so small? (Writer, picked up a dead one in Jamaica. His negro guide asked: "Him baby?" answered, "No, Him papa.") Why was the moa twice a man's height. Note, too, the bee hummingbird persists. The moa is extinct.

Our midOctober garden is colorful with thousands of giant orange African Marigolds, contrasted with canary varieties. A dozen species of butterflies suck nectar from their small disk flowers. Skippers

---
* The Viceroy, a Basilarchia, mimics the Monarch in a remarkable, (and puzzling) manner. Most other California Basilarchia have strikingly different coloration.

are as oldfashionedly garbed as a matron in leg-of-mutton sleeves or
a bustle, Bluets are like winged turquoises. Peacock butterflies with
circled designs as fascinating as that of their jungle-camouflaged god-
father bird. Sulphurs, the first gave us our word "butterfly" based as
above noted, on an Anglo Saxon word we today call "obscene". Cabbages in white, with an immigration-violation record so costly, we
ranchers wish some Bertillion of Fabre's time had invented hexapod-
finger-printing.

Swallow-tails, as markedly yellow-and-black striped as a Bengal
tiger . . . a brick-red monarch. He flaps his wings as lazily as said blue-
silk Morpho. He commences feeding on our African Marigolds as
leisurely as a Paris boulevardier enjoying *coc au vin*. One notices, on
this Monarch however, something unusual. IT IS BANDED, the 3rd
banded butterfly seen in our Sacramento gardens this month. The one
caught came from Ontario, some 3,000 miles away. The power for the
journey? Even more wonderful than the refining of Ethyl gasolines
from ropey, crude petroleum. It was the daily ration of honey, usually
pumped, by uncoiled tongue, from a composite's disk flower. . . .

Autumnal senescences become impressive at Halloween. The air,
when the Dawn Goddess dons her "robes of saffron" is nippy. Virginia
Creeper now is scarlet-gowned. Scales of thistle butterflies are faded.
They show the same carelessness about grooming as an elderly dame,
overgenerous with rouge, with powder, whose failing eyesight causes
geographic errors. Grasshopper movements have
HALLOWEEN slowed so perceptibly, one feels an urge to invent
BUTTERFLIES orthopteratic crutches. In the last composites, the
outer, hence greater circles of disk flowers, are be-
ing translated into seedings. Only the few at the center seem to offer
their minimum of nectar to beefly, to bluet. Both already are weak
with increasing famine.

That undesirable alien, fecund prickly lettuce, flourishes in an
adjoining vacant lot. It persists in sending wave after wave of its
parachute troops to gain a foothold among phlox and zinnias. On one's
knee-desk, are two sad letters, one in English, one in German from
distant professors. Adjustment to retirement both find galling. The
German friend reminds one there also were postwar concentration
camps, in one of which he suffered even more keenly. He recalls a
French noblewoman's observation when en route to the guillotine her
trumble jolted on Rue St. Honore stones. "Liberty, liberty, how many
crimes are committed in thy name".

A third letter is one from a vigorous, middleaged friend, already,
because of his brilliant intellect, Dean, long before his years. This

Insects

author has tried to awaken in him a consciousness he too some day must become Emeritus. (Dear Bishop Block, with a humorous anecdote for every occasion, would say "E-meritus, oh! yes 'e' is 'out-of-it' 'meritus,' he deserves it.") Writer's rare privilege has been to have had a wealth of friends in academic life here and overseas. Some consciously, intelligently have self-directed their mellowing. Thus came in retirement years mental dividends so great, Shylock would rub his hands gleefully. In contrast, others allowed themselves to be so absorbed with the daily grind they experience a cruel shock as Retirement Day comes. Then follows little output—and that tinctured with bitterest gall.

The afternoon before Halloween one is at the garden seat. Basking in the sunlight, one watches a big green grasshopper. He creakingly, with death already evident, tries to ape youth. One notices too, a bee busy at a golden-wedding chrysanthemum. Pollenpockets packed, it hums contentedly with assurance of its sheltering hive. Does not garden insects' behavior parallel that of us humans, even professors? The grasshopper, as far as human can guess, led a careless life. It was bent on eating and reproducing. The bee was disciplined to a life of service, worked for the community of its hive. Has selflessness, too, perhaps a survival value?...

> "So work the honeybees, creatures, that, by a rule of nature, teach the act of order to a peopled kingdom. They have a queen, and officers of sorts. Some, like magistrates, correct at home. Others, like merchants, venture trade abroad. Others, like soldiers, armed with stings.
>
> (Shakespeare: Henry V, Act. 1, Scene 2)

"God gave us Memory", once wrote a philosopher, "that we might have roses in December." May not some of life's fleeting hours be well invested in accumulating rare memory pictures? One writer enjoys is of Dr. T. A. D. Cockerell. Well into his 80s, his leisure, while directing Palm Springs Museum, was spent at his lifelong interest, wild bees. We-2 once happened in when he was bent over his microscope. The cacti were in bloom. He explained how certain ferral bees were adjusted to foraging only at certain cacti. . . . This August day, observing bee's problems, one sees that they have their troubles as much as do we humans. Today garden shows certain South-Africans in abundance bloom. The bees know honey is there. They are not built for its harvest. One can almost imagine in their buzzing a bit of hymenopterous profanity. Our garden's bees herein are not resourceful. Into New Zealand it is different. Bumblebees from England were introduced there. They, too, could not

NATIVE BEES

reach the honey of the native tree-fuchsia. Being "inventive", they systematically bit their way thru the floral walls when they found they were too big to down tube. That our native California bee was indulging in "swear-words" posed a question. We had displaced native blooms with alien ones. This meant starvation. . . .

"I AM CONTENT . . .
Send the deed after me
And I will sign it."
"Merchant of Venice"

When Shakespeare made Shylock say "I AM CONTENT", he unconsciously reminded us of how close the English intellectuals of the Elizabethan Age were to the French of the days of William The Conqueror. He gave us literally the English for the similar French *"Je suis content"*.

Is there any philosophy that more continually recalls the ideal of contentment thru happy labor than that of gardening? Just now some dozen or more clumps of Michaelmus daisies **CONTENTMENT** spotting the flower beds are musical with the hum of contented busy bees. On a warm Autumn day, is it not worthwhile sometimes to rest from physical gardening and enjoy the gems of wisdom offered us by the Bard of Avon? This matter of contentment, and then of happiness thru labor is one that intrigues the criminologist. One versed in penalogy insists that the worst prison riots are by men who are denied the privilege of creative work.

Mounting juvenile crime is another stimulus to the Garden Philosopher. On this desk are recent statistics. They disclose that, while California's population last year was up 5%, juvenile delinquency increased 15%. Should we not watch closely the high birthrate of the type that finds it cannot meet the strain of life without the resort to narcotics? They resort to consequent crime to cover the actions of their heartless exploiters. THESE USUALLY ARE ALIEN-BORN. . . .

"A bug's a bug—but a yellowjacket's a whole baseball nine of the other fellows" (Beautifully-stung investigator of a hornet's nest on a Yosemite National Park Nature-Study Field Excursion.)

The garden-philosopher day after day becomes overwhelmed with amazement at the ingenuity displaced by Mother Nature in her task of evolution of the insects from those primitive trilobites hundreds of millions of years ago. Of all the animal groups that visit one's gardens, none are more fascinating than that section of the hymenoptera commonly dubbed "wasps".

Insects

This despite the assertion of a geographically illiterate passenger on a French liner in the Mediterranean. One morning at daybreak We-2 were on deck taking our pre-breakfast stroll. This fellow passenger approached excitedly "There's land ahead. It's an island called Corsica because its women were the first to invent corsets!"

The wasp originated the corseted waist type of feminine beauty. Dr. Comstock puts it thusly: Muddaubers' "most striking characteristic is, that the first segment is generally narrowed into a long, smooth round petiole", i.e. a true "wasp-waist". The mud-

WASP WISDOM dauber is one of the spider-storage wasps. Muddaubers are "speck-to-die's" (SPHECIDAE). There is another social wasp that has quite a reputation of ferocity. It is Vespa or yellow-jacket. Its nest is not exposed like Polistes. It consists of bee-like combs enclosed in what looks like a castaway Japanese lantern. If one only could hope for the years of Methuselah he could profitably invest a decade or 2 thereof studying the behavior of the wasps of his garden.

Another of our garden wasp is said Polistes. It makes apartment houses. (There is no record of any tenant complaining about a midnight radio thru paper-thin walls). Polistes' walls truly are of "paper" —gray paper. You can have a lot of fun studying these guests of your garden. Another interesting wasp is the jugmaker. It is one of the Eumenidae. It is a mason-wasp using mud for its nest, as do swallows. Couriously both make jug-shaped homes. . . .

Your Maeterlinck's "The Bee" is thumbed to near-illegibility. Your garden's hymenoptera are worth said Methuselah's lifetime of study. The twelve months you planned to concentration on bees, wasps, and ants was just *hors d'oeuvre*. Of course, (if only to remind you of happy days in Italy and in Greece) your garden has its grape arbor. What can be more colorful than autumn's pendant

OAK "APPLES" purple clusters? What fun to pickle spring's grape leaves for an exotic Armenian *pilau* of mutton (tho' fattails be unobtainable) with your own garden grown raisins also stonepine nuts, (really Piute-gathered from Nevada's pinyons) and, lastly, that *pilau* has airplane-sewn rice from your own California ranch, in lieu of Oriental hand-planted paddy. The wasps thieve some ripe grapes. These you begrudge them no more than a few ripe cherries to the Western Tanagers.*

Fortunately for this authentic history of just one single California garden, it possesses an oak. It is in an unobtrusive corner and is not yet of offensive size. How it got there is a puzzle. Perhaps a crow

---

* These repay us doubly,—In forest insects consumed next week, and in that glorious flash of gold, scarlet and black that you think spoils all camouflage theories. This, till someone far more observant reminds you how perfect it is in the land of lichen-draped silver firs and ponderosa pine.

may have dropped an acorn. And, perhaps, it is a chance sprout from one of this author's experiments each autumn, with Elfin Forest seed-travellers. Acorns travel too. If you doubt, watch squirrels also California jays. This oak is accommodating. It is hardly a teen-ager. It has, however, several "oak apples"* or weeping-oak galls.

"Go to the ant thou sluggard" said King Solomon the Wise. With all his wisdom, he never had heard of the Argentine ant. He knew nothing of the Argentine. He never dreamed of the glamorous Evita, politically more powerful than her dictator husband. Solomon did not even know there was a Western Hemisphere. He could anticipate neither Eric the Red nor Columbus. He, however, had **ARGENTINE** heard rumors of islands out near the Jumping-off **ANT** Place. They had ferocious, gigantic dogs. (We still call "Can-ary, really Can-ine, Islands".) Solomon heard in those islands there lived one-eyed Cyclops. Was that single eye in the middle of the forehead or at the shoulder-blade?

Tho Solomon never had seen a Pampas ant, he, however, did know his Eurasian, his African ones. From these he drew wisdom. Perhaps his "sluggard" was a servant with 18 kids, yet not much to show in work beyond thumbprinting his relief check? Now, after 3,000 years comes Argentine ant data from South Africa. There Argentine ant has displaced all native ants. U.S.A. now has research on this Argentine pest. Within the year, a dossier reached this desk, of studies of Argentine's arrival in Alabama, some decades ago. Came Father Argentines, Mother Argentines. Soon there were plenty of Baby Argentines. They, as with their cousins, in Africa displaced Alabama's native ants. Dixie's could not compete with the compact, tremendously-efficient Argentine ant's social organization.

Since low-wage areas immigrants replace oldtime Americans, can we not today profitably ponder Solomon's advice as to ants? DO they not illustrate need of adequate immigration control?

On one Christmas afternoon, our garden still had some 20,000 chrysanthemum blooms. One clump, like giant daisies, was in a sheltered corner. On its diskflowers ants,† despite the chill, still gathered food. They worked slowly, however, as if every movement brought pain. They stimulate memories of a dear old German Professor of yesteryear. Long past 70, he always had lived in a University town. There his father, his grandfather had been faculty members. We sometimes talked for several hours. He knew, and he knew he knew:— "Along here is one of the best Neanderthal Man stations. The great

---
* Children enjoy "Insect Stories" by writer's friend, the late Dr. Vernon Kellog. Especially interesting is its "Houses of Oak."
† For thrillingly-illustrated "Consider the Harvester Ant" see Natural History 6/ '53.

ice cap came down this far." Then he would dilate upon the conditions under which Neanderthal Man lived. Today I watch these benumbed ants. I think of that savant. They have been foodgetting, that there might be reproduction, during the millions on millions of years since the Jurassic. Man has been at the same task for a short 1,000,000 years. WHO CAN PICTURE HIS STATUS WHEN HE HAS BEEN HERE AS LONG AS EVEN TODAY HAVE BEEN THE ANTS? HAVE WE NOT HERE A LESSON IN HUMANITY?—Blessed are the Meek.

The garden's survival battle progresses hourly. Note native ant's competition with the alien Argentines. This particular survival-struggle exhibits important phenomena, (always with bearings upon human problems). The Garden Philosopher, therefore, sometimes neglects weeding, fertilizing, irrigating because of his absorption.

One problem that continually forces itself upon one's attention is the parallelism of these tiny alien Argentine's ants and the larger native ants. (Note the flickers which feed on the latter). One remembers when there were no Argentines. . . .

> Remember March, the ides of March remember:
> Did not great Julius bleed for justice's sake?
> What villain touch'd his body, that did stab,
> And not for justice?
> What, shall one of us,
> That struck the foremost man of all this world
> But for supporting robbers,
> Shall we now
> Contaminate our fingers with base bribes,
> And sell the mighty space of our large honours
> For so much trash as may be grasped thus?
> I had rather be a dog, and bay the moon,
> Than such a Roman.
>
> (Shakespeare's "Julius Caesar".)

The Ides of March are here. We-2 go into our garden to gather calendulas, orange contrasted with golden, for the diningroom table. This in memory of when, at the Ides of March, we, for boutonnieres, gathered some tiny wild ones, weeds in the Forum at Rome. It was the very Forum where Caeser once strode.

As we gather our posies, we find one calendula with a bee fly. It mimics the true bee. He seems asleep. Picking the flower where

THE IDES OF MARCH he has been feeding, the bee fly corpse falls into one's hand. Still hanging to it is a crab spider. Its golden color blended so perfectly with that of rayflower and diskflower one was deceived as fatally as was the bee fly. On this same 15th of March, a white cabbage butterfly on a white narcissus. It does not move. It is dead. Sucking its life blood, a WHITE crab spider. Have we here two cases of AGGRESSIVE COLORATION? The Garden Philosopher thinks,—and thinks—and thinks!

The garden is rich in the 8-legged predators. Today are crab spiders. Later there will be wolf spiders, also attids, arrayed in a crimson jacket like yesteryear's organ grinder's monkey. Then will come funnel weavers, likewise the Argeopies, magnificent orb weavers.

All are, indeed, predators. The garden also has other predators. The ladybird beetles, (welcomed because they prey on noxious insects), nevertheless are predators. The hawks, too, are butchers—sparrowhawk, the occasional redtailed,—and the swift bullethawks or accipiters. So, too, are the owls, likewise the venerable gopher-snake. One of the lessons Mother Nature continually repeats in the garden is that, except the bullethawks, most garden predators should be made welcome guests.

She reminds us that, excepting some cannibalistic spiders like the Black Widow, NOTHING IN THE GARDEN PREYS ON ITS OWN KIND. Here is one of the most profound bits of philosophy over which the Gardener ponders. This for two reasons: (A) War. (B) Commercialized Vice.

(A) As to war, had the small, power-lusting group that hid behind Wilhelm II (whose very name of "Kaiser" was the Teutonized one of "Caesar") not distorted Darwin's "Survival of the Fittest", there would have been no *Flottenverein,* no World War I. Hence, there could never have been the Bolshevik Revolution when it was needed by our enemies. Britain could never have lost the flower of her young leaders when "The First 100,000" held against Von Kluck in those successive critical days at Liege, Samur, Mons, Charleroi. Thus France could not have had to sacrifice the residue of world leaders that could have fathered a French intellectual renaissance. Go into your garden. A sparrowhawk will pounce upon a grasshopper, but not another falcon. A snake will gulp down a mouse, not another reptile. An owl's noiseless strike will gain him an unwary gopher, as your automobile lights unexpectedly showed. He will not, however, eat even an owlet.

(B) It is in Commercialized Vice that one sees the most ruthless profiteering. The booze baron, the "mac" who lives off the earnings of fallen women, the card shark, the narcotics vendor—each and all prey upon fellow humans.

Birds

Paralleling the marvellous variety of garden's insects is the similar diversity of its birds. This is especially so if one plans the garden shall yield, amongst its other uninterrupted dividends, the joy of its being a bird sanctuary. Even a window garden in California can entertain a certain range of bird guests. These, from the finches, even jays, (that soon come, too, for a regular meal of birdseed or crumbs), to the tubes with artificial nectar for the hummingbirds. In observing behavior of garden insects, even more so of garden-visiting birds, one often can find answers to some human behavior questions. Then, too, natural curiosity about insects, and again even more so about birds, can be utilized in education of children and of children-become-grown-ups.

SAINT FRANCIS AND THE BIRDS

One who was most wise knew, centuries ago, what an educational asset were his garden birds. Gentle St. Francis tho't of them as his brothers. As Auduboniers, We-2 made pilgrimage to his Assisi. The kindly saint had a true gardener's insight. He loved his flowers. He also loved the birds that visited his garden. He called them his "little brothers." The climate of Italy, with its vines, chestnuts, olivetrees, citrus groves resembles California's. In our garden we do have neither St. Francis' nightingales nor his singing blackbirds.* We do have, however, mockingbirds, chats, and that beloved vocalist, the house finch.

The garden indeed is a living museum, with daily change of program.

A museum, in the original Greek sense, is a place in which to MUSE,—to meditate. One's garden always remains a "museum" in that sense. It is also an aviary, a botanical garden, a zoo as well as a museum. This is testimony of a gardener, a geogardener, a wanderluster. An octogenarian, he recalls field studies from the scanty vegetation next the Polar Ice Barrier to that of Brazil's Golden Monkey Jungle. Also adventures from Saharan camel trips to studying alpacas and vicunas at 16,000 feet in the Andes. His camera work included little kangaroos in the fringes of Australia's Never-Never. He has journeyed in slippery Manchurian dugouts, in out-riggers, in Java's tiger infested jungle, also with Paumoto's pearl divers.

BOTANICAL GARDEN, MUSEUM, ZOO, AVIARY

After above, he finds his native California's home garden suffices as aviary, botanical garden, museum, zoo. Here is an example:—The great elm rises above the wellhead he had reproduced from that in Venice's Doge's Palace. Towering above all else in the neighborhood,

---

* The European blackbird is a thrush. America's is of the oriole family.

it is a favorite bird roost. Cedar waxwings use it November to February. The garden has been planned for plenty of berries to offer them hospitality.

This is written in August in a shady north corner where nothing else but ivy will grow. It recalls Melrose Abbey, also beloved spots in Brittany. That ivy bed is also a museum. It illustrates Mother Nature's success in cutting transportation costs. She does not bother with Diesels, with red-and-green lights on signal towers, with train dispatchers. Her transportation system runs smoothly, efficiently, inexpensively. She never grumbles about a strike, such as the recent one which has tied up transportation for more than a month for the hundred thousands. One of Mother Nature's jobs IS transportation of seeds. Cedar waxwing's droppings into that ivy bed winter after winter result in its becoming a nursery bed. Today a bride and her groom have decided their new garden's shrubbery—myrtles, cotoneasters, toyons, cretagus, pyracanthas, all can be trowelled out from the ivy-bed. Yes, the garden is Aviary, Botanical Garden, Museum, Zoo—and money-saving nursery for newlyweds.

THOUT, IBIS-HEADED GOD

Thout, Goddess of the Moon, was also the Scientists' deity . . . (The Egyptians had profound reverence for the little group that constituted their researchists.) The ancient Persians asserted their Moon Goddess ranked in power next after the masterful Sun God. Thout's worship apparently paralleled that of the Roman Diana. A gifted child, properly educated, unlocked, (for all time), secrets of the religious revolution of Amenophis IV. This must have reduced exploitation of the illiterates by the multiplicity of the priests, just as the preaching of Saint Paul affected the revenues of another Diana, she of Ephesus.

Birds

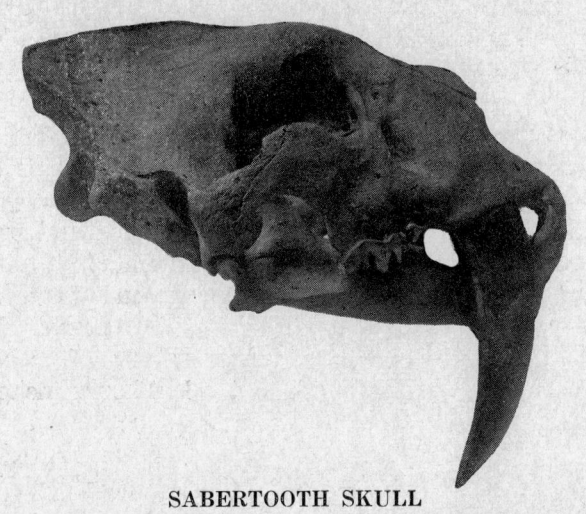

SABERTOOTH SKULL
The Sabertooth was contemporaneous with Asphalt Stork, California Turkey, California Peacock, Terrible Bird and Incredible Bird. Remains of all are found fossil in the asphalt pits of La Brea. Our knowledge of these is based largely upon the brilliant research of this author's friend of many years, noted avipalaentologist, Dr. Loye Miller.

FOSSIL BIRDS

True, America lacks Europe's nightingales; songster-blackbirds, also the cuckoo's call. Other Eurasian avifauna members now are extinct—Asphalt Stork, California Peacock, California Turkey. Also disappeared here, several *sauvage* species persisting to our East, or to our North. The California species of wild turkey also is gone forever, along with that ferocious cat, the sabertooth "tiger", likewise the Terrible Bird, likewise the Incredible. If one, however, wants to learn ever more about his garden's flowers, his garden's insects, his garden's birds, he can hardly find any subject more fascinating than our Golden State's fossil birds. Dr. Loye Miller, pioneer in California fossil avifauna research, has contributed much herein; for both adults, and by children's stories.

One thus does gain insight into human problems. Once one actually knows his garden birds (writer listed 78 species visiting his garden) he is qualified to explore further. There is, for example, Birdsong. Here is a garden item that fascinates the genetics' student. Most ornithologists agree birdsong, characteristic of the nesting season, is hardly what poets fondly believed. It is rather a "NO TRESPASS" announcement.

Project your garden-bird studies beyond its borders—learn "to read a trailside like a book". Go to forest, desert, overseas. In contrast with nearly all the other birds, so the jays, (ordinarily so noisy they are dubbed "the Warners")—are silent while nesting. Moreover this is true of California Jay of our gardens and of the Bluefronted Jay of the Ponderosa pine forest. Just as the pharalope is a dominating feminist.

Alphonse Bertillon, anthropologist, was called to be Chief of the Bureau of Identification of Paris police. His 1880 method of applied anthropology to crime control with not one error in some 700 identifications over 6 years was credited with "a remarkable reduction in crime throughout France." He netted many criminals once clever enuf to continue lawbreaking. The real discoverer of fingerprinting, however, is said to have been Galton. Did either Bertillon or Galton have as much fun as Sherlockholmes-ing footprints in the dust of one's garden paths. At Octobers-end, there are telltale prints:—Scotty and Laddie, neighborhood dogs. Cats. Most fascinating of all are the birds,—California Jays, Robins, the last housefinches and goldfinches. Latter are leaving this week for Guatemala as the white-crowned sparrows are arriving from the Yukon, also from Lake Tahoe. One is rewarded for having created a bird sanctuary by their contributions to his entertainment....

FINGERPRINTS
FOOTPRINTS

"Amongst birds, the contest is often of a more peaceful character. All those who have attended to the subject, believe that there is the severest rivalry between the males of many species to attract, by singing, the females. The rock-thrush of Guiana, birds of paradise congregate; successive males display with the most elaborate care, and show off in the best manner, their gorgeous plumage; they likewise perform strange antics before the females, which, standing by as spectators, at last choose the most attractive partner."

(Darwin)

Research as to the behavior of the lower animals is illuminating our race-old darkness as to certain problems of human behavior. Studies of mentality of rats is becoming increasingly helpful. Dogs, particularly, are of value because many of their reactions parallel those of men. Observation of bird guests in one's garden is a neverfailing source of interest. Soon we will discuss certain phases of nesting, of song, of flocking.

BIRD BEHAVIOR

"Mallard ducks can be tamed in captivity while black ducks do not tame. Wild rats and half-breeds from them, even though the latter were bred and reared in the laboratory, were significantly more "wild" and "savage" than quarter-breeds, yellowhooded animals and pure albino rats. These differences persisted throughout their lives, even though they had spent most of the time under the uniform environmental conditions of the laboratory, and the strains bred true. This ". . . strongly suggests that the differences arise from hereditary rather than environmental factors."

Above is quoted, condensed from Professor R. W. Russell's paper at a Eugenics Society of England Member's Meeting. Dr. Russell states:—

"That the behavior of living organisms—like their morphological, neurophysiological and biochemical characteristics —is influenced by HEREDITARY FACTORS. In no way did this deny that behavior could be modified by environmental factors. Recent research has provided some grounds for the belief that the limits of the capacity for such modifications are themselves INFLUENCED BY INHERITED PROPERTIES OF THE ORGANISM.

WAXWING BEHAVIOR

Halloween. The white crowns and golden crowns are calling. A Quebec postcard mentions the first snowstorm. That is why the cedar waxwings are arriving for winter quarters. They have been away for the summer. They are here without warning, expect us to be ready even to meals. The garden's myrtles indeed are laden with their purple fruits, all deliciously ripened. The waxwings' sibilant notes say they do approve of our fidelity. Those call-notes are so high they cannot be heard by some human ears. All this, these garden waxwings whisper, is to remind us that there are such sound waves that some folks cannot hear. Some light waves, like the ultraviolet and infra red, also are invisible to practically all men.

Our garden was planned as a midurban bird sanctuary. Hence it has abundant berry-fruiting shrubs. These are for the whole range of feathered guests from waxwings to robins. Many insectivorous birds seem to accept above diet when midwinter lowers hexapod activity. In the center of our garden is a clump of tall elms. To the top of these the waxwings flock. Suddenly one of them makes a dive from the elm top to a clump of our myrtles. These are about 150' distant. Quickly a part of the flock follow. The others start straggling by. In ten minutes their minaret in the big elm is vacant.

This waxwing behavior stimulates reflection. The birds, like most humans, are gregarious. The flock dive, however, includes about half the individuals. The others remain. Here again, have we not variation?

From overseas scientists, as this is written, comes data about hereditary influences on behavior. It includes studies of dogs, of ducks, of rats, of even Japanese waltzing mice. American investigators recently have suggested that light might be shed on problems of childhood by research into the behavior of dogs. In these notes of The

Garden as a Bird Sanctuary, may not an occasional item be repeated that one's garden, a bird sanctuary, also may be a laboratory for studying bird behavior, and its parallel to human behavior. . . .

> "By The Company's permission,
> And the Governor's Commission
> I've made the Grand Tyhee.
> Of this entire I-la-hee.
> Famed in Song and Story
> I've attained the Heights of Glory.
> By 'Saginaw' I'm known to Fame.
> 'Jake' is but my common name!"
> (Epitaph at Saginaw's Grave)

Our sleeping porch overlooks our garden. Successor to one built some 50 years ago earlier at our Sutter's Fort Park home, latter was prototype to hundreds of Sacramento Valley outdoor dormitories. We-2 had enjoyed mockingbird singing from one during a winter San Diego visit. Our experiment induced friends to do likewise. All so evidently enjoyed all fresh air slumber, we carried on a systematic educational campaign therefor.

FLICKERS HAVE PROBLEMS

Our present one is high in our giant elm. Our bird sanctuary garden makes on said sleeping porch a rare vantage-ground for bird behavior study. Last year's redshafted flickers raised a brood of 5. The illuminating flash of fire-colored wings daily recalls a flicker-feather decorative headdress years ago at Killisnoo, Alaska, on the grave of Chief Jake, ("Old Saginaw"). It reverently had been placed between two Chilcat blankets. These were of epilobium or fireweed silk interwoven with wild-mountain goat-wool and dog hair.

One flicker juvenal is eliminating irritating mallophaga from its plumage. (A cynic observed it was good for a dog to have some fleas. It made him forget he was a dog. Perhaps it is good for a flicker to have some bird-lice.) Same give an overworked business executive something else to think about, beyond neverending problems. The flicker explores under one wing, then another, almost twists off that black-collared neck. He tries to reach an itching spot at his rear collar button. If asked why he scratches, he might answer, as did the schoolboy:—"No one else knows where it itches."

Mallophaga CAN become a study. One friend understands why We-2 budgeted a year to studying our garden's fungi, another to its spiders, another to its grasshoppers. He thus comprehends, because he is investing a whole lifetime on the Birdlice. He says an owl's markedly are different from a flicker's, insists any research, even his, has great possibilities. After the data we found overseas about Pasteur's encouragement, in the 1860's, of a povertystricken student working on *penicillium glaucum*, also after Madam Curie's inquisitiveness about that something in St. Joachimsthal sphalerites that we now label "polonium", also "radium", who shall say "fool" to this researchist devoted to his mallophaga? Flicker footprints, in the dust of our garden path, are beside an ant hole. Read Beebe's: "The Bird" for the marvelous adaptation of the flicker tongue in gaining his dinner out of an ant nest. All this reminds one that, just as a lifetime profitably can be invested in the Mallophaga so too could one invest fascinating years in studying the tongues of birds. . . .

Just now the drama in our garden is Brewer blackbird courtship. Was ever more exaggerated Ego packed into the antics of this melanistic male? Was ever more understanding of masculine weakness telescoped into the coyness of his apparently indifferent mate? She knew, all the time, exactly where she intended to go. His net assets consisted of bluff and bluster. One of the most profound intellectual experiences We-2 ever had was attending Rostrand's "Chanticleer" in Paris. Perhaps, eugenically, only the Gallic imagination could have created such unique drama.

**THE EGO,
AVIAN,
ALSO HUMAN**

If we are truthful, has not each one of us a fairly developed Ego? What we observe in birds is what we ourselves feel. May there be recorded here another anecdote?

Across San Francisco's Union Square from the St. Francis Hotel is a florist's. It specializes in orchids. Its window display was a background of gorgeous Cattleyas. In the foreground a vase with 3 sprays of yellow butterfly orchids. A young miss, of say 9 years, and her uncle passed. She exclaimed: "Oh, let's stop and look at the orchids." He impatiently answered "Those purple things!" "No," countered the lassie, "those yellow ones." "Those are not orchids, they are just yellow flowers." "But, Uncle, don't you see what wonderful orchids they are?"

All this was too much for one who enjoys childish appreciation of Nature. "Pardon me. The young lady correctly has identified those orchids. I have collected them myself in the jungles of Central America." Then writer told them about the Cloud Forest where they grew *sauvage*. As they moved on it was impossible not to overhear—"Uncle, didn't he know just lots?" It must be confessed it was music to a certain Ego. . . .

Ein Vogel ruft' im Walde
Ich weiss es wohl wonach.
Er will ein Hauschen haben,
Ein greunes laubig Dach.
                   (Heine)

(A bird sings in the Forest.
And I know why.
He wants a nesting home
One well hidden in the leaves)

    During 300 years, our highpowered ancestors had large families. U.S.A. thus acquired its greatest asset, its resourceful Intellectuals. These, 1890-1940, deliberately reversed nature, racesuicided. Morons meanwhile multiplied like rabbits. With our native resourcefulness, there still is time to reverse above. This, if every collegiate learns Differential Birth Rates Law's eugenic significance. The third child is needed for more replacement. Is not mating behavior worth study?

    With World War II's housing shortage most American families knew about housing problems. We-2, as pioneers in U.S.A.'s City Planning movement, had offered years before to go to Europe as well as to U.S.A.'s Atlantic Coast. This, to try to interpret for our Sacra-

NEST MAKING

mento the solutions of housing problems by more mature municipalities. Our native city's "Gold Rush" was still a strong movement when this author was born. Since we both had training in biology, we continually found inspiration in watching our feathered garden friends as to their behavior while solving avian "housing" needs.

"All the world loves a lover" is a folksaying that records how deep is our instinct for the beauty that glorifies mating. Today, as perhaps never before, Mankind is faced with tensions that threaten destruction. On this desk is the mismating record of one U.S.A. city where the rate is 4 to 1. Is therefore time wasted when the philosophizing gardener tries to evaluate the mating phenomena of his garden's feathered guests? Even in the center of a city it is possible to coax quail if adequate shelter be given. Our sleeping porch in Springtime is musical with the love-notes of Valley Quail.

BIRD ROCK, POINT LOBOS RESERVE STATE PARK

Seabirds, because of bird rock nesting immunity from snakes, also rodents, have evolved a natural rate of, often, but one egg annually. Compare this with quail clutches in our garden of up to 16. Note also the great laying capacity of domestic poultry, descended from ground-nesting Jungle fowl.

Several score linnets are singing. The eight cypresses are their apartment houses. They are more successful in neighborliness than Capitalism and Communism. The linnets live harmoniously with the blackbirds, nest in the same cypresses. The garden's Birdsong is of continued fascination. The poet Heine would have you think all those redheaded housefinches are ardent Romeos singing to their Juliets. Hardheaded ornithologists, however, record the facts. Those birdsongs are "No Trespass" warnings, in music, not signboard, to all other girl-hungry males. They mean "You shinny on your own side!"

BIRDSONG

Competition of males is apparent throughout the avian world. A widespread sport (cockfighting) is based upon the evolution of rooster spurs. The wedding dancing of rival hummingbirds of our garden is described elsewhere. Writer can never forget an aerial battle he witnessed in a garden near the Taj Mahal. It was long before Mig and Saber-jet ever tangled in mid-air over Korea. It was between 2 lovely green male parakeets. They fought and fought until death came to the weaker. Then the watching hen, apparently well contented, flew away with the victor. Here indeed was Darwin's "Survival of the Fittest". If he be alert, the Garden-philosopher will see much, watching the feathered guests for whom he has planned his garden.

Courtesy American Museum of Natural History.

EGRETS NESTING

At the century's turn, these beautiful birds approached extinction because of plume-hunters. Their comeback resulted from brilliant strategy of National Audubon.

"The crow doth sing as sweetly as the lark"
(Merchant of Venice, Act V, Scene 1)

Attempts to reduce birdsong to human syllables vary. Here is one of the writer's interpretations. It is of the "Oh dear me" of the goldencrowned sparrow. It like many of us is "Seeking to serve" in the effort to abolish poverty:—

"Oh dear me! Oh dear me!!
This is what the goldencrowned
Sings to me.
Oh dear me! Oh dear me!!
If only I could make the world from sorrow free—
Little Puritan songster in your coat of brown,
Surely you have earned the right to golden crown.
Oh dear me! Oh dear me!!
If only I could set the world from sorrow free."

With a garden planned for a bird sanctuary, then a notebook consciously kept, one can accumulate fascinating data on birdsong. It is interesting to listen to the varied vocal imitations of mockingbirds, also thrashers. The top ventriloquist is the chat. One pair nests annually with us. Their numbers include everything from a laddie's whistle to the croaking of a frog.

"Hear how the birds on every blooming spray
With joyous musick wake the dawning day."
(Pope)

PRONGHORN ANTELOPE WARNING-SPOTS

The white flash of a startled pronghorn's rump-spot jolts the entire herd into flight. Note parallel between junco and antelope.

Photo: Courtesy California Museum of Science

Few bird behavior phases fascinate the Garden Philosopher more than their flocking. The value of flocking as to birds is illustrated by juncos, bushtits, cedar waxwings, also wild geese overhead. The flash of the white tail feathers of a junco is just as effective as a red light at a busy automobile intersection. Its value depends upon

JUNCO'S WARNING SIGNAL

the tendency to variation as to nerve-responses of various juncos. Darwin declares this tendency to variation always is present. One of the most fascinating winter bird studies is of above junco behavior on the garden's lawn. This signal of white is seen also in herds of certain deer, likewise antelope.

Flocking seems to have a survival value among the waxwings. The varied I.Q. of humans seems to be paralleled among certain birds. One individual has keener food-finding sense. The dullards, by joining the flock, thus gain the food necessary for reproduction.

Bushtit flocking also has high survival value. A flock of these tiny birds was cleansing, of its insect pests, the great elm of our garden. Upon warning by their leader of the approach of an accipiter, they promptly fell into scatteration formation plus the confusion chorus. All this was so effectual the bullethawk whizzed past without even one feathered midget for *hors d'oeuvre* for his dinner.

As to behavior of certain flocking birds seen from his garden, writer finds himself repeatedly absorbed in studying them. Frequently a pigeon flock overhead wheels like cavalry on maneuvers. On a northwindy January day, white pelicans circle high in Heaven's blue.

In migration, particularly, the value of wild goose flocking long has been observed and admired. This by even the Ancient Greeks. We know today only too little about the mechanics of migration. The value of a seasoned old honker in directing his "V" is, however, most evident.

As to wild geese following their leader, said Ancients did marvel at such wild goose leadership. Euripides noted "The ordered host of **WILD GEESE "V"s** Libyan birds avoids the wintry storm, obedient to the call of their old LEADER, piping to his flock." Aristotle wrote of the leader of wild geese keeping watch at night, also of his position at the head of his "V". The ancient Greeks knew much about the scarcity of leaders. They took their examples of eugenic leadership from Mother Nature.

From Aristotle and Euripides to Denmark's wee bairns is a far cry. Alice Nordin caught the wonder in childish eyes and ears. All this she transferred to unforgettable sculpture.

Birds

Among others that flock are robins, blackbirds, white-crowned sparrows, goldfinches, bushtits. All are examples of the kind of survival that apparently impressed Darwin. Survival chances are increased by cooperation within the flock. They are not, as the Nazis and Soviets interpreted it, furthered by mass-murder. Having lived under Hitler, also Mussolini, having been at the Russian *grenze* the week of the worst Soviet blood purge, having also "played chess" with the warlords of Japan (to block their propaganda with U.S.A.), writer has had some insight as to how cooperation can make for human advance. Darwin was impressed that survival chances were increased by cooperation within the flock. One example of present day cooperation is Protestantism's Ecumenical Movement. Said groups of robins, blackbirds, whitecrowned sparrows, goldfinches, occasionally bushtits are all examples of a kind of defense mechanism which apparently impressed Darwin. He declared survival chances are increased by COOPERATION with the flock.

Courtesy American Museum of Natural History

The Ancients marveled at wild goose leadership.

From said experiences comes a profound conviction that frightfulness destroys even those in power. Must not those who have the responsibility of leadership win their victories thru Love, not Fear? If the leadership of Love is to be maintained, generation after generation, do we not need the 3-child family that is necessary for replacement? With that, and with the power of Love, can we not hope to prevail over Communism that would destroy Christianity? Need we then fear the Heroic Mother medals for those who bear eleven Super Heroic sons?

THE PEAK, AND CANARIENSIS PALM, CANARY ISLANDS

Goldfinches are called by our neighborhood boys "wild canaries." Here is a onomatological study that would delight Archbishop Trench. The goldfinch is the color of our caged canary. The canary takes its name from its habitat, the Canary Islands. These, in turn, gained that name, (based on Latin *canis*, dog), because of their fabled giant dogs. These islands, just at the edge of the dropping-off place of our supposedly-flat earth, were assertedly inhabited by great one-eyed monsters, the Cyclops, who kept these formidable dogs. Incidentally, botanizing in the Canaries is one succession of thrills from their wild Cinerarias (which this author elsewhere has described) to their remarkable euphorbias. These, in arid volcanic ash soil, parallel our cacti, but are without thorns.

Mayday and communities of housefinches from Cuernevaca and Taxco are arriving, as whitecrowned sparrow clans leave for Alaska. Autumn brings goldfinch flocks to the planned composites, sunflower, African marigold, French marigolds on whose seeds they gorge. Hardly a month but the garden is a laboratory of behavior of bird cooperation thru flocking. These studies, started 60 years ago, stimulated thinking about certain centrifugal forces at work in that Protestantism that was the basis of our Declaration of Independence and our Constitution.

"Blessed are the Peacemakers."

"Man is an animal, but a SOCIAL animal". (The Next Million Years. Sir Charles Galton Darwin)

MONTEREY GULL FLOCK, FISHING FLEET IN BACKGROUND

The value of flocking is evident with the gulls overhead in the garden, with the blackbirds that winter-roost in the eucalyptus-tops, in the telegraphic flash of one nervous junco's white tail-feather telling of stealthy approach of Tabby. The bushtits in the garden's giant elm survive because their alert leader warns of a nearby accipiter. They quickly go into scatteration formation plus the confusion chorus. The bullethawk whizzes past without even one feathered midget for hors d'oeuvre for his dinner.

Flocking is a constant motion picture in our garden with no parting of pennies for admission tickets. Sometimes, on a northwindy winter day, it is a flock of pelicans wheeling and wheeling, white against the sky's cobalt. Then, with spring's quail nesting, one observes how much the family (human or avian) is a matter of instinctive flocking. Father quail stands guard on the tip of a bush. He spies a bullethawk, sounds the warning. Mother and young scatter to various nearby shelters. Sometimes Dad has to make the supreme sacrifice.

QUAIL FLOCKING

Thus one has not only a study in avian Sociology—the tendency of a family to flock until next Spring's mating—but also the value of cooperation thru flocking, as with blackbirds.

One then projects his flocking studies beyond his garden fences. In all the precision of yesteryear's cavalry maneuvers was there ever such marvellous coordination as that of said flock of bandtail pigeons speeding up stream to their acorn banquet in a clump of oaks at canyon head. Or the perfect wheeling of a flock of sandpipers on a wave-rippled beach?

Over our garden there flew, just now, a flock of 11 gulls. They were working—working at food searching, food getting. Their perfect maneuvering was a demonstration of cooperative teamwork's value. It also recalled the danger of underestimating the need thereof. Such flocking is repeatedly evident in the garden's gulls, blackbirds, robins, finches, bees, and wasps.

Humans cannot safely ignore flocking. A dramatic example of such a danger is Kipling's "By Word of Mouth". It of course is an outstanding mystery story as to why round little sleepy Dr. Dumoise came to die of the cholera in pestilent Nuddea. It also is a story (which the Garden repeats often) of why the NONFLOCKING of the Dumoises brought the death of Mrs. Dumoise. Truly, as Kipling cannily observes:

> "Few people can afford to play Robinson Crusoe anywhere—least of all in India, where we are few in the land, and very much dependent on each other's kind offices.

Photograph Courtesy American Museum of Natural History.

EGRETS FLOCKING IN EVERGLADES

Above shows "Comeback" possibility. This author repeatedly has described the near extinction of the Egret until National Audubon inaugurated its brilliantly-successful protection campaign.

Americans cut the Panama where others failed. Americans made deserts, dry for millions of years, fertile with orange and grapefruit orchards, date gardens. Americans harnessed millions of horsepower

Birds

where, for untold ages, had been only waterfalls. THE BEGINNING OF EACH OF THESE WAS ONE HIGHPOWERED HUMAN BRAIN. Since the days of the first settlement in Virginia and New England, until recently, the brainiest parents were noted for their large families. 1890-1940 our intellectuals tragically reversed this favorable birthrate by having families of only 2, 1, 0 offspring. Meanwhile morons always multiply like rabbits. With our still high percentage of pioneer blood, which never quailed at any menace, we can still stem this unfavorable tide. It needs only a clear understanding by every American of the eugenic significance of the differential birthrates law.

NATURE STUDY CLASS
Feathers dropped in our garden were collected and utilized in the Neighborhood Nature Study Class. (For fascinating data on tarpoon scale, peacock feather, and shark's tooth as diversified structures derived from the skin—also attractive illustrations, see Chapter on "Feathers" in Dr. Beebe's "The Bird".)

"What! Is the jay more precious than the lark,
Because his feathers are more beautiful?"

(Taming of the Shrew, Act IV, Scene 3)

A famous chef, (whose earnings allegedly exceeded the salary of the President of France), wrote, at the century's turn, a cookbook. It was very popular throughout his native France. In its introduction he asserted "no one can be a truly successful cook who does not appreciate the value of color in foods he prepares."

At the Goethehaus at Weimar, a German scientist, said to the writer "Some of us think his researches in Color showed more vision than any other one of his manifold ventures on the frontiers of knowledge." This author elsewhere has testified to his own belief that color* is the principal stimulus to gardening.

COLOR IN GARDEN BIRDS

Supplementing the hues of flowers, (and incidentally the problems of the Why of flower-color) is the great variety of shades and tints in garden birds. Do they not cover the Vibgyor of the rainbow? Violet of the Violet-green Swallow. Indigo of Western Bluebird. Faded Desert Blue of California Jay. The blue-green or turquoise of Arctic Bluebird, which, in years of heavy snowfall, ventures into the gardens of our Valley floor. Green of mallard camouflage. Yellow of Summer Warbler, Orange of Tanager, of Oriole. Red of House Finch, Flicker, of Hummingbirds. This week an overhead mallard dropped a feather. Because a bird feather is ever a wonder, it was saved. Today, another feather falls from a jay in the big elm. It is placed beside the duck feather.

Both have much in common. This gardener wanders off into philosophizing about an outstanding trait in both. Mallard camouflage is green. Bluejay is blue. Both color areas, however, are restricted to that part of the vane where color is useful. Not one pinpoint more. This, just as if Mother Nature was buying Easteregg dye at the corner drugstore at so much per.

This benjaminfranklinese tendency, so apparent in Scotland, (an environment where thrift has high survival value), is evident everywhere in the garden. It is fun to post to a pad every new example of Mother Nature's Caledonian ancestry!

> Dost thou love life?
> Then waste not time,
> For time is the stuff
> That life is made of.
> (Benjamin Franklin)

That color is an important factor in bird behavior will be apparent as soon as one commences to philosophize about his garden's

---

* Note "Foreword" in "Geogardening". The book, tho out-of-print, is in most U.S.A. libraries, public or collegiate.

Birds

birds:—As to flicker-color "All us ranchers shoot yellerhammers on sight." "Why?" "Well, one of 'em bored a hole under the eaves of Bradford's barn. And—well, I guess we're jest agin' 'em on general principles."

Another example of biological illiteracy. And here is why:—One spring, some years ago, a pair of redshafted flickers decided to nest in our garden. True they WERE enthusiastically noisy during the siesta hour. And they DID bore a hole in our broad eaves (our home is North Italian Renaissance) tho no serious damage. In due time We-2 were able to indulge in typical grandparental behavior. This, because Mamma presented Papa with quadruplets.

Flicker color has appeal to the savages. When We-2 were in Alaska at the close of the Klondike Gold Rush, we found flicker feathers used in Tlingit warbonnets. One, indeed, was of the grave, at Killisnoo, of Chief Jake, "Old Saginaw." It was between the two Chilcat blankets herein elsewhere described.

With the Yankee blockade of the South during the unnecessary Civil War, dyes for Confederate grey became scarce. Alabama matrons, with characteristic Dixie ingenuity, boiled hickory nut skins. These made a grayish-yellow dye for the cotton. Thus the Southern soldiers came to be dubbed "yellowhammers." . . .

One, who, as a 5-year-old kiddie, had already been inaugurated into Nature Study, is amazed that, as an octogenarian, he continually finds new and delightfully absorbing material in his garden. Just now a redshafted flicker flew to a perch on a branch of the Great Elm. His flight was like that of an underwing moth or of one of the bright underwinged grasshoppers. This, in that there was a flash of brilliant color followed by a landing with complete camouflage.

The mottled feathers of the flicker are of themselves worthy of long study. In this bird we have 2 of the 3 types of camouflage described by that Master Nature-artist Thayer. He divides both protective and aggressive coloration into 3 classes:—a) mottling, b) iridescent, c) appendages. The appendages of the flicker, (bill and, even more so, the long tail), together with a mottling the color of the tree bark constitute a remarkable example of concentration, in one bird, of 2 of said 3 types of camouflage.

Possessing a garden is like ownership of a private library with every book one desires. In one's garden one can delve and delve like the famous picture of the spectacled old biblophile up his ladder. He has one book between knees, another under his arm—is peering myoptically into a third.

One similar fascination the garden offers its alert philosophers is color variants. Elsewhere this author has described his own success, following the suggestion of his friend, the late Luther Burbank, in isolating color variants of California native wildflowers. It is his garden's feathered guests, however, that offered the most tantalizing problems. There is space here to hint at only two:

COLOR VARIANTS

HOUSEFINCHES. One February end, these welcome linnets commenced arriving from their Mexico winter quarters. That year they were plague-stricken. The garden showed over two dozen that dropped dead on arrival. Among these were eight which, in lieu of the normal crimson feathers, had yellow like a goldfinch's.

ALBINOS. Even more interesting was the evident loneliness of an albino English sparrow. Our garden's population of this species averages perhaps 100. Among them one year was a part albino. It was most evidently ostracized. Have we not here a parallel as to how humans (except the martyr type) find it more convenient to have their behavior conform to the norm? Whenever our albino attempted to join a flock, all pecked at it as angrily as the blackbird we once saw fend off an eagle! English sparrows are notorious for prolonged breeding. Ours are nesting most of the year. It was evident, however, this poor albino could find no mate.

Primitives always have had legends of the white buffalo, the white deer, the black tiger. Was there not a Black Dragon Society? One European friend of yesteryear became intensely interested in Milanism. On our visit with him, the highlight was his taking us to see a mounted black leopard.

These notes are ventured here as an example of the treasures one's garden contains, if one is intent on "reading that garden" as if it were a shelf of books.

One experienced something similar when he attempted substituting playgrounds under supervision for child labor.

When St. Francis called the birds his "little brothers", was he noting they, like humans, were bipeds? Their behavior includes often the need for security. In planning the garden as a bird sanctuary, each garden bush also can do double duty. It can be more than an ornament. It can be a bird refuge. There is need, for timid finches and sparrows, of quick cover for quick dashes to shelter from seed-rich areas. If the gardener be Scottishly-thrifty, he will select berry-yielding bushes. Robins seem to exhaust native toyon berries first. They will, however, then proceed to cotoneasters or pyracanthas. After meals of myrtleberries, cedar waxwings gain variety with their favorite planetree seedballs.

BIRD STUDY AND HUMAN PROBLEMS

The California garden bird sanctuary by planned strategy also can attract some of our various hummingbirds. TUBULAR flowers for these are needed. The golden State has such a wealth of species. Atlantic U.S.A. has only Rubythroated. California has Allen's, Rufous, purplethroated, Anna's, Costa's and Calliope. As this is written, one wonders which was more exciting,—the magnificent staging of Aida at Milan's La Scala or the wedding dance of two male Anna's before a demurely-coy, and apparently absolutely uninterested female perched on a nearby branch. Have we not here a typical cinema triangle?

A few Asiatic buddleias can attract a whole series of butterflies. In fact one folkname for the species with abundant violet-hued racemes is "Butterfly Bush." Garden planning thusly is again almost as thrifty as the Aberdeen lad who brought home, as bride an Edinburgh lassie. She was chosen for cheeks like red apples, so "she'll nae be a-wasten' thrippence o'mine at the chemist's for rouge!"

Then, too, almost without planning, one has the usual range of composites for the fall migration of both greenbacked and willow goldfinches. Crows, too, show up at almond harvest. Brewer's blackbirds say "thank you" for a few Italian cypresses. Nesting atop these, they "mind their own business." Thus one cypress also may hold a halfdozen housefinch nests. Policing jays find plenty of forage over which to emit loud warning to all the furred and the feathered when an unbelled cat sneaks into the garden. Our garden is at approximately the geographic center of Sacramento's quarter million humans. In this urban, but carefully-planned bird sanctuary, some 77 species have been noted on the Audubon check list....

Leaving these comments on our garden birds for the next chapter:—"Humans". May there be inserted here just one of many notes about the garden's mammals?

The garden does contain mammals, even wild mammals. Most of them, however, are adjusted to nocturnal foraging. A note about one of the bats, therefore, seems appropriate to be selected from many observations of our furred friends:—

In a clump of forsythias, we found, this morning, a hoary bat. It was broad daylight. He was sleeping, characteristically, head downward. Most of the bats of our garden are the smaller variety. This large bat was gray in color as his name indicates. One wonders how much human progress could have been accelerated had there been some means of better understanding our feathered and furred friends if we could have had, which of course is impossible, a common language. These bats knew much about radar long before our discovery thereof.

Do you recall the sinking, by radar, during World War II, by the United States submarine Sailfish, of a Japanese super plane carrier? The big flattop was out of sight and miles away. The radar controlled torpedo, it was alleged, was used so speedily and, withal so accurately, that the Kamakatzies on board never knew that death had come.

We-2 intently studied this giant bat as it slumbered in our forsythias. We gardeners philosophize as to what enormous amount of material will be worked out laboriously, even painfully, by the researchists of generations to come, which would be in use today if only we knew what they instinctively know.

> Second Witch:—"Fillet of a fenny snake,
> In the cauldron boil and bake;
> Eye of newt and toe of frog,
> Wool of bat and tongue of dog,
> Adder's fork and blind-worm's sting,
> Lizard's leg and owlet's wing,
> For a charm of powerful trouble,
> Like a hellbroth boil and bubble."
> (MacBeth, Act IV, Scene I)

We Occidentals, today, almost as much as in MacBeth's time, are often superstitious about bats. The wiser Chinese class them as emblems of good luck. We-2 found a bat clan among Guatemala's Indians. It wears a bat design of black-sheep wool outlined against the white wool. They breed for black-sheep in the Guatemala highlands because of a premium on such black wool.

> "Cuando yo tengo dinero,
> Se llabaman:—"DON Tomas,
> Pero, cuando no tengo dinero,
> Se llabaman:—"Tomas" . . . no mas".
> (Mexican folksong about the Pulqueria)

A rough translation of above peon's verse about the vendor of pulque is

> "When I have me plenty of money,
> They flatter with "DON Thomas,
> But when I'm dead broke without money,
> They snub me with "Tommy." (That's all!)

The big elm is a muchly-used outlook for various birds. Just now an accipiter has flashed to the ground. That speed spelt efficiency. No wonder the boys call him "bullethawk." A spurred towhee was his prey. A friend, veteran in the fight against those who exploit—also create—alcoholics saw the helplessness of towhee before accipiter onslaught. He compared it to the adroit propaganda of those who are ruthless about their human wrecks as long as profits can be gained from such wreckage.

Followed that day quite a debate about worldwide efforts to eliminate alcoholism as one of the principal causes of Poverty. Thus the Garden becomes a Forum for Garden Philosophers. Flowers, birds, even insects stimulate discussion.

A CHINESE PROVERB SAYS:

Neither Confucius nor Lao Tze ever heard of a gene or of a chromosome. They, however, out of what we call "common sense", (and which seems none too common), philosophized eugenically.

"IT IS MOST UNWISE TO EXPECT A DUCK'S EGG TO HATCH A PHOENIX."

The Greeks, with their love of gardening, respected the owl as the BIRD OF WISDOM. This so much so that the writer's coin collection has an ancient Athenian drachma with the imprint of an owl. Our garden, despite its being at the very center of the city, has 2 regular owl visitors. One is the barn or monkey-face owl. It does the screeching. The other is screech owl which does not screech but hoots. Occasionally a third owl passes. It is the big great-horned. Its call is a deep "hoot, hoot." In New Zealand, writer found a Maori dictionary with the words for owl given as "mo-poke". One would hardly class that as a mimetic name until he hears it pronounced by a Maori. It then becomes an exact imitation of the call of the common New Zealand owl. . . .

> For the Ordering of the Ground, within the Great Hedge, I Leaue it to Variety of Deuice: Aduising nevertheless that whatsoeuer forme you cast it into, first it be no too Busie, or full of Worke. Wherein I, for my part, doe not like Images cut out in Iuniper, or other Garden stuffe; they be for Children.   (Francis Bacon, p. 191-2.)

Of the two bipeds that inhabit the Garden, Sir Francis thought little of the one that is feathered. Its leg-scales ever remind the Garden Philosopher of its reptilian ancestors—of its "cousins":—Over-armored Stegosaurus . . . Tricerotops, who specialized too much in weapons . . . Dimetricon of excessive backbone . . . Tyrannosaurus, afflicted with a Mussolini-complex . . . and Brontosaurus, who neglected a slimming diet, even after his doctor warned:—"Your love of tummy is bad for your heart." The other garden-biped is not feathered, has no scaled feet and legs . . . possibly once, despite baldheaded males, was quite furred. (This, we can judge from orangs, chimpanzees, gorillas.)

That state of being 2-footed, not 4-footed, suggests a brotherhood tie—even tho, say, not 2nd, but 99th cousinship. Perhaps we can learn from observing avian behavior. This, just as we contemplate dinosaur extinction. Much light, indeed, can be rayed on human behavior by observing that of birds. So much is this true, one is amazed at National Audubon's and A.O.U.'s membership rolls are not jammed with names of psychologists, sociologists, yes, of clergymen.

Was it not cynical Diogenes-of-the-Lantern who forced Plato to think biologically? Plato, it will be remembered, was in The Garden, (proper environment for any philosopher). He discoursed of Man, described him as "a biped without feathers." Diogenes slipped out the back gate to a poulterer's stall for a plucked rooster. This he threw on the ground before the Master. Sarcastically, he exclaimed, "Plato! There's your man!"

PLATO, AND DIOGENES' ROOSTER The great philosopher may have been thinking a bit carelessly as to biology. Plato had to add a limitation as to human fingernails. But is it not Diogenes, with wounded Ego, who attracts our attention? Is he not entitled to words of praise? Think of how long it is taking to reduce U.S.A.'s biological illiteracy! Remember the resultant tragic blunders in lawmaking. They mean billions in taxes. The real cost however is in human hopes, human lives. If only some in high places had been Auduboniers!

> Flowers have an expression of countenance as much as men or animals. Some seem to smile; some have a sad expression; some are pensive and diffident; others again are plain, honest and upright, like the broadfaced sunflower and the hollyhock.
>
> (Henry Ward Beecher—Star Papers.)

MOJEDSKA FALLS

Just over the ridge from Modjeska Falls are the headwaters of *El Rio de los AMERICANOS de Jedediah Smith* (now AMERICAN RIVER). That stream twice is a historical example of American Know How:—(a) Bible Toter 'Diah Smith camped his wounded *Americanos* on its banks downstream. (b) At one American River waterfall, Gallatin and Livermore developed the world's first long distance hydroelectric line.*

---
* See "Side-whiskered Gallatin and His Little Cascade" in "Sierran Cabin . . . From Skyscraper" (p. 150). Tho out-of-print is available at most U.S.A.'s public also collegiate libraries.

TRIAL AND ERROR We criticize the "Trial and Error" method. True, 'tis time-consuming. Mother Nature herself, however, has used it for one thousand million years, still does. But you object "How few men can hope for even one century?" True, not yet, but we are on our way. The expectancy of life in Rome-of-the-Caesars is supposed to have been about what Hindustan's is today. Sweden's is more than double that of Bombay or Calcutta. High I.Q. counts!

Mother Nature using her Trial-and-Error method produced above two remarkable types of bipeds, bird and man. Both are found in our gardens. In fact without one there would be no gardens. We gardenphilosophized about birds in the last chapter. This will be devoted to that other garden-loving biped, Man.

Mother Nature indeed has, for said thousand million years, been experimenting, inventing. After she had a rather successful crinoid, she wondered whether it was too much isolationist. She then created free moving starfish. On another shelf in her laboratory she had the beginnings of backboned creatures. (Many of us humans lack "backbone" even now.) The fishes were quite good,—but she restlessly moved with ever new attempts. Her abovementioned reptiles, gigantic, armored, powerful, she found to be of too low I.Q., so she attempted improvements. Thus quadrupeds became bipeds—feathered too—and there came the birds—(These still have said scaled legs to remind us of their ancestry). In another line where she emphasized intelligence. Instead of armored dinosaur bulk, came brainy mammals, eventually another biped, Man. He was not feathered but more or less hairy —until, with males in maturity, came bald heads.

And so a baldheaded gardener works with his plants—watches his 6-legged insects that visit his garden flowers—studies his 2-legged birds that are his garden's guests and dreams of transplanting the lessons of flower, insect, bird into solution of human problems—such as Reduction of Poverty....

The gardening, or botanizing instinct is strong in most of us. Even a busy military commander like Fremont did not overlook its possibilities. Thus his own name came to be honored in an Order new to U.S.A.

Down in the tropics are found, sometimes exclusively, certain botanical orders. One is Sterculiaceae, named for Sterculia, Rome's God of Manures. The ancients worshipped anything they could not understand. They knew that barley around camel droppings produced 10 times any on other terrain. Here was Magic, and a manifestation of Fecundity. Hence it was to be worshipped.

Sterculiaceae, (order almost entirely tropical), includes the silkcotton trees. One genus, however, ranges out of Mexico's tropics into California. (This Mexican element in our flora includes highly fascinating turpentine weeds, tarweeds.) The first California Sterculia was collected by Fremont, while blazing the trail Jedediah Smith had recommended to Government. Smith discovered the map's white blotch marked "Great American Desert" represented ignorance. Sacramento River did not rise just west of Utah's Great Salt Lake. Between, Smith found the Sierra Nevadas. Smith also discovered Sacramento-San Joaquin Valley. Lone survivor of his 23 men, he stumbled into the Wyoming fur post. He gasped:—"I found virgin land enough for 100,000 farmsteads. Send a military expedition to blaze the trail, then start the Covered Wagons rolling!"

Fremont, crossing above Sierras, found growing, in the interstices of Mount Fremont's summit's granite, a new Sterculia. He collected specimens; still called "Fremontia." Writer collected his first at this very type locality. Later, birding for condors in the semidesert straddling Kern and Los Angeles' border, he again found it in sandy arroyos. Covered Wagon folks used Fremontia in lieu of Atlantic coast's slippery elm, for poultices for sores. This, as figs are employed by oldwives in Persia and Turkey.

CHINESE KNEW VALUE OF GREEN VEGETABLES

Gardening is ingrained in the life of a Chinese to the very marrow. Here is a picture of a Chinatown in the Gold Belt. The Chinese had learned to work over the tailings from which already the 49'ers had extracted most of the gold. The frugal Chinese, though they never heard of vitamins, knew the value of adding to the diet plenty of green vegetables. Writer learned from his own days in China that the affection extended not only to the vegetable garden but to such items as the narcissus at New Year's time.

Is not interesting radiation of propaganda in even Western Europe when illiteracy was so common a king considered it a waste of time to learn to read and write? King John could not read the Magna Charta. He had to depend upon his ecclesiastical clerks.

We found a Scandinavian monk story when we made the pilgrimage to Sweden to University of Upsala's Linneaus Garden*. This monk made the pilgrimage from Stockholm to Constantinople or Byzantium. There being even no bridle paths, the journey was by boat thru the forests. This monk must have been quite convincing with his propaganda. By begging in Constantinople, he accumulated enough to purchase 3 slaves. His eloquence probably was increased by his **VOLGA** knowledge that his return on River Volga was upstream against its mighty current.
PEARS He recorded many observations. Some seem fairly accurate, some slightly imaginative. One, his tale of the pears he picked at Volga bend. They were as "large as a tall man's head. Cut into halves, each had inside a steaming pork chop!" ...

---

* By thus going to the actual spot where gardening history has been made, one is able to picture how translations of ideals into actualities can become history.

Propaganda is most effective among illiterates. Corrupt officials use it to retain power. Writer landed one morning at a certain South American wharf. A man, unlighted cigarette between fingers, begged a match. Writer, nonsmoker, regretted he had none.

That evening, in our steamer's 2 men's cabin, he was greeted with:—"Were you separated from 50 bucks?" Noticing his surprise, they told each one similarly had been approached. Upon complying, the smoker threw back his coat lapel and showed his police star:—"You are under arrest, carrying matches with match tax unpaid." The officer in each case, enroute to the jail, enlarged upon missing the steamer, also discomforts of incarceration. (Most jails south-of-the-Rio Grande supply prisoners with no food. The officer hinted that the jail's drinking water was infected, also much vermin in the cells. Then, melting with pity, he said he would risk accepting a gift of 50 *pesos* for the judge. This, to cover tomorrow's fine.

MATCH-OF-ECUADOR

Above occurred where less than 10% of the population are literate. Have we not also the responsibility to reduce what this writer has come to designate as "biological illiteracy", "geological illiteracy", "astronomical illiteracy"? One's garden's flowers, insects, birds tell fascinating stories useable in reduction of all three.

The very soil of one's garden made up of particles of Coal Age sea bottom, of Jurassic-granitic batholith, of the whole series of lavas from rhyolite thru andesite, dacite, to basalt. These stimulate thoughts of reduction of geological illiteracy. Our home garden, most of our ranches, are all parts of the great Sierran piedmont fans with all the above rock materials resulting from the erosion of the Sierra Nevadas and of the Coast Range into the great trough of the Sacramento-San Joaquin Valley. These sediments have been accumulated to a depth of several thousand feet. Then at night when the air is laden with scent of daphne or violet or clovepink or gardenia, one gazes up into the stars, then one thinks of the words of Longfellow:—

GARDENING, ANTIDOTE FOR PROPAGANDA

> Spake full well in long quaint and olden
> By one who dwelled by the castled Rhine,
> When he called the flowers, all blue and golden,
> Stars that in earth firmament do shine.
> Stars they are, wherein we read our history,
> Like astrologers and seers of eld,
> Nor are they wrapped about in the awful mystery
> Of the burning stars which they beheld. . . .

Into Iowa Hill's name is intertwined two biographies. Uncle Andrew was an Aberdeen native. Nephew Donald, was born in Iowa Hill. Uncle, a '49er, came to Iowa Hill when it "had more voters than any other California city, except Frisco and Sacramento." As conservative as Aberdeen granite, he disapproved of "this newfangled hydraulicking." Its mountain-ripping monitors incensed him. He preferred his rocker. It bought his tea, oatmeal to his dying day. A bachelor become "a-gin' travel," he never had left Iowa Hill for San Francisco, even Sacramento.

Andrew's younger brother had followed him to Iowa Hill, there married a newly-arrived Scotch lassie. In due time, young Donald was born. A young man, he clerked for a Scottish grain-exporting firm in San Francisco. Donald long had invited Old Andrew to San Francisco "just to see how that village had grown." The Uncle finally yielded. Donald invited him to a de luxe hotel dinner, ordered a la carte. Uncle's appetite was prodigious. The real tragedy came with the French pastries' tray. Commenting "They sure give you plenty here," the veteran miner took a cherry from one, a candied violet from another, a morsel of green anglica from a third. Then he teaspooned the frostings from a half dozen petite fours. The resultant check consumed a half-month's salary at the grain-exporter's. That hurt.

Iowa Hill was one of the California's great hydraulic mining centers. Today one can view, from across American River Canyon, a mountain side was cut in twain. The scars are a mile long, almost a quarter-mile deep. The power of a great "head" of water, concentrated into an adequate brass nozzle can tear away, in a few short weeks, half a peak that, for 30,000,000 years, had towered against the skyline.

Have we a parallel in human institutions? Some have weathered many storms. May they however, fail under concentrated pressure of adroit propaganda? When writer, in Europe, was studying *massenpsychologie,* he vacationed in Switzerland. One day he climbed a mountain with an Italian cleric. Latter boasted: "Give me control of education, children in the schools, adults thru the printed word. I thus can change permanently the course of history." This, as surely as the California gold mines' hydraulic monitors rip away half-a-mountain!

There has developed worldwide, since the century's turn, a new force in U.S.A. A Californian of the late Gold Rush days, in describing it declared his best simile was the hydraulic monitor. This so concentrated control of the snow waters from higher-up, it could rip away,

to get the golden nuggets a whole mountain side. That force is what
the Germans, (who borrowed it from the Italians)
GOLD BELT'S call *massenpsychologie*. There is in English no word
HYDRAULIC yielding an exact translation. The nearest we get to
MONITORS it is "propaganda" if it's our enemy's. If it's of
friends we dignify it as "public education." When an
alien is granted citizenship, makes a fortune in commercialized vice,
then buys a newspaper to control public opinion for selfish propaganda, have we not given him, thru mistaken generosity, a force as powerful as California Gold Belt's hydraulic monitor?

It was better to have no opinion of God at all, than such an opinion as is unworthy of Him . . . Superstition is the reproach of the Deity. Plutarch saith well to that purpose: Surely (saith he) I had rather a great deal . . . Men should say there was no such man at all as Plutarch, than that they should say that there was one Plutarch that would eat his children, as soon as they were born . . . Superstition dismounts all these, and erecteth an Absolute Monarchy in the minds of Men . . . The Master of Superstition is the people; And, in all Superstition, wise men follow fools; and arguments are fitted to practice in a reversed order . . . The Causes of Superstition are . . . our great reverence of traditions which cannot but load the Church.
(Francis Bacon Essay on Superstition, 1625.)

One of the pearls of wisdom to be enjoyed in one's Garden on a dewey morning is Discrimination between Truth and Superstition. In learning to read his garden's pathside as if it were a book, one comes to grasp the eternity of Truth, to understand how ephemeral is Superstition. . . .

Giovanni, our gardener, could have gained a fortnight's growth in planting the calendula seed. That would have given a growth to
brighten Christmas. The terrace above the fa-
PIANO DI cade's dwarf myrtle hedge could have their
GRECCHI'S orange bloom contrasted with canary-yellows.
MOON-PLANTING With the extreme conservatism of his native
Piano di Grecchi, Giovanni insisted we must wait
until crescent new moon.

To demonstrate that here was superstition, I planted some of both orange and of yellow calendulas at the early time. Giovanni's seed boxes followed a fortnight later. My seeds yielded the expected galaxy of composite color at Yuletide. Giovanni's, missing those precious two weeks of October sunshine, did not bloom until St. Patrick's Day.

Humans

Giovanni still watches the moon. He will not walk under a ladder. He shudders if a black cat darts across his path. He could not be induced to sit down to a meal, were he the 13th.

As guests in the garden of Bing of Singapore, we acquired, if not Merit at least Wisdom. Our host was fond of quoting Confucius:— such as, "One gathers no lichi nuts off sprouts of bamboo . . ." Above is an ancient folksaying. The Russians word it differently:—"Acorns do not grow on pinetrees." Do not both testify as to Heredity's power?

BUBONIC PLAGUE BACILLI

Biologist on research as to parasites on ground squirrels, University of California's Hastings Natural History Reserve. California ground squirrels now continually harbor bubonic plague bacilli.

In midMarch, violet seed sprouts are so thick one's thumbnail will cover a score. In the Middle Ages, violet seeds were supposed to be the eggs of fleas. (The capsule does eject its seed to a distance). This so much paralleled a flea's leap the "biologically-illiterate" of those days saw in them a remedy for fleabite. Of course, being thus biologically-illiterate, they never dreamed that the flea could be a carrier of bubonic plague infection.

Violet sproutings also are an example of overpopulation. Perhaps the extreme parallel to this is one of the grasses. The space occupied by the plant can receive, it is estimated, up to 200,000 seeds. Since the previous year saw the terrain already overpopulated, there was no room for more than one to sprout. Mother Nature always has sufficient reserves, even in human fecundity.

"And he told them tales of the Loup Garou,
And of the spider shut up in a nutshell."

We plant no totem poles of Raven-atop-Bear-atop-Seal at our front doors . . . We load no long-dead ghostly Himalayan deodar with prayer rags, believing the Wind Gods will carry out petitions to Those Above. We string no blue beads on the donkey bridle to avert the Evil Eye. We scoff at a bandannaed Jamaica Mammy's insisting "Duppies" live in the silkcotton tree. We sneer at Elfin Forest fairies.

BUT,—are we really so superior? We DID guillotine Lavosier, (who gave us the Agricultural Experiment Station). We DID liquidate Vavilov, (who had enormously increased Russia's food supply). We did not hang the disciple of Pasteur who first experimented with *penicillum glaucum*. We DID deny him, however, the few franc's worth of fuel needed to continue his experimentation.

We likewise, only yesteryear, were somewhat violently intolerant of those who dared suggest that what Pasteur had done for 19th Century Medicine might be paralleled in our 20th Century by research into such diseases as affected the Czarevitch. This very year there are those who scoff at trying to learn from Elfin Forests "leopard-spotted" areas. . . .

SUPERSTITION IN ARCHITECTURE
The Chinese gardens in the old days practically never had straight paths. As in the little wayside temple above, it was assumed that any curve would detour an evil spirit. One from the air landing on the tiles above could not crawl out to the end and drop off to harass the people below. His course would be projected back into the air by the curved roof. (See page 13)

Does not Reduction of Poverty require substituting, for corroding superstitions, the facts accumulated by the researchists? One's garden work continually poses that question. Elsewhere is mentioned the cosmopolitan extent of superstitions based upon faulty interpretation of natural history philosophy.

In Burma, most lives are under influence of their Nats. These spirits personify natural forces, winds, monsoons, eclipses. Only recently a press dispatch related a high government decision there only was made after their astrologer "read the Stars".

SUPERSTITION SOLVENT

In Paris, We-2 made pilgrimage to the seldom-visited spot where Catherine de Medici obtained similar advice. How much of such bloody strategy, (as razing Issoire by her son, the Duke of Alencon), was due to avarice and bigotry of court astrologers can be imagined. The domination of the late Czarina's will by that crafty monk gives some idea of how Catherine de Medici could herself have been in constant terror. That, in an age when often even Monarchs did not trouble to learn to read and write. Nothing like Issoire since has been seen until Nazi destruction of Ledice.

Elsewhere this author has written of his studies of duppies in Jamaica. These spirits, for example, live in the silkcotton trees. Fascinating also is the serpent cult in groups from ancient Greece to the Mayas' Quetzalcoatl. Even West Europeans ground yellow lichens into pills for yellow jaundice cure. A great botanical order, SCROPHULARIACAE, is based upon superstitious belief of its herbs' potentcy in curing "SCROFULA" or "King's Evil." (Venereal disease's ravages, during Britain's general illiteracy was "scrofula"). When you pick your garden's giant, rustproof snapdragons, or enjoy yellow mimulus filling old Californian mining ditches with golden bloom, (where once flowed the water for hydraulic monitors ripping mountains for their gold nuggets) think of the name-history of their Scrophulariacae.

Our garden is bisected by an "alley". When Goethe Bank financed subdivision of Elmhurst, wherein is our garden, it was during the end of horse-and-buggy days. Alleys usually are eyesores. Ours was kept clean of deceased felines, tin cans. It, however, always bordered both sides by alien weeds—cheese mallow, foxtail, locoweed. One day came the concept, clean all these overseas undesirables into a seed-destroying bonfire. Substitute a patch of eschscholtzia gold, emblematic of our Golden State. That truly was a BON-fire. Weed-seed mortality must have been incalculable. Borders then were raked clean. As each golden poppy in our garden produced seed, it was carefully lifted for deposit in that cleansed alley border.

BEAUTIFYING AN ALLEY

Next spring that once unattractive alley had many poppy plants. WE LABORIOUSLY WEEDED OUT FOXTAIL, CRABGRASS, KLAMATH WEED, BERMUDA. Those last year's poppy seeds were most prolific. That alley each springtime is one golden ribbon. Until frost there is continued bloom—with contrasting lovely glaucous foliage.

Is this not our task as citizens—eliminating the human weeds? That is what Italy did under Mussolini. After dumping his Black Hand on trustful Uncle Sam, Il Duce sneered, "America, Gangster Land." Some years ago We-2 watched the netting of Mediterranean criminals. The constabulary crossed the district like an advancing battle line. Anyone without a registration card was arrested. Inability to produce same, was, under their law, equivalent to a plea of guilty. The judgment uniformly was: "Sentence to an island desert rock penal settlement or a passport to Cuba or Mexico. Thus we accumulated gangsters.

Have not we of the West an unusual responsibility as to Eugenics? The Pacific Coast has probably the largest percentage of pioneer stock in the United States. We are the descendants of men who, for 10 generations, one after another, braved the dangers of the Frontier. The weak went down. The strong remained. As carriers of these genes, have we not a very unusual responsibility?

WOMEN, VEILED YESTERYEAR, TODAY VOTE

To the Viking nations belongs the credit of having lifted half the human race from abasement to a voice in Government (see item on Finland, page 189). In such villages as above, during writer's visit a few years ago all women wore veils. Must one expect too much from one's folk when, on this desk, is a dossier of items from Deans of Medical Colleges regretting the lack of knowledge, among physicians, of human genetics.

> "The most vigorous males, those which are best fitted for their places in nature, will leave most progeny. But in many cases, victory depends not so much on general vigor, as on having special weapons, confined to the male sex."
>
> (Darwin)

THE FISH MARKET OF HELSINKI

Within sight of this market is the building where the Finns started a maledominated world on the road to Woman's Suffrage ... The garden teaches Genetics and Human Genetics ... that the mother contributes equally with the father, their child's genes.

Men-folks, however, are not all-wise. Here, a masculine frailty item:—Early this morning, writer motored to one of his ranches. More than 10 miles of the road were beautiful with chicory's blue blooms. Same stimulated memories of introduction of this European plant into California. This, in pioneer days, when our first levees were built by mulepowered Fresno scrapers. (No one then dreamed of a 250-foot-boom dredger, its clamshell biting a ton of earth). San Francisco's French colony wanted chicory to mix with their coffee. One riverbank rancher planted experimentally. His ranch became "The Chicory

Ranch." This alien became a roadside weed. It displaced native wildflowers. Thus, complete displacement of native flora by this one outlander.

In yesteryear's Sacramento, an attorney was Scottishly thrifty. He yielded, however, to his wife's entreaties for money for a party. Discussing costs, she mentioned floral decorations.

THE GARDEN AND FEMINISM He said: "We can save THAT expense. I'll get something to startle your guests." He decorated their home beautifully with armfuls of blue chicory blooms. Biologically illiterate, he did not grasp its flowers close at noon. At luncheon time, it was too late to substitute from the florist's. That mansion contained vases of wiry, stiff, ugly stems, with withered, colorless blooms. . . .

Gardening philosophers appreciate the laws of sex. Mother Nature does not overvalue the male. There is harmony, equality. We grudgingly corrected injustices by granting the vote to women. Finland herein led. Japanese women gained same only when McArthur arrived.

RAJAH'S FAMILY GOES TO A WEDDING

Above *howdah* is not a school bus. It contains a Rajah's harem, going to a royal wedding. (Where we attended this, we also did birding—Sunbirds, parakeets, ioras, bulbuls, minivets, paradise flycatchers, tailor birds . . . We made accelerated progress, as with paradise flycatchers, because of knowing from our garden California species. This also with sunbirds, because of years of study of the hummingbirds feeding at our flowers.

Respect for Womanhood diminishes West to East. It is somewhat higher in U.S.A.'s Far West. (In California, a kind of chivalry persists from the Gold Rush. The Golden State then was what Browning called

"A Male Land"). Writer repeatedly has described tales of his Sweetheart's visiting Hindu *zenannas*, Moslem *harems*.
WOMAN'S SUFFRAGE Depth of contempt was Korea, also Japan. TODAY WOMAN HAS A NEW STATUS:—HUMAN GENETIC RESEARCH NOW DISCLOSES MOTHER CONTRIBUTES ONE-HALF HER CHILD'S GENES. How different from Merejowski's "Peter and Alexis" with its "My Father, Author of My Being."

LODGEPOLE PINES, USED BY BLACKFEET FOR TEPEES
In the Glacier Park hike of some 250 miles, we occasionally met groups of Blackfeet.

On a 250-mile hike with some guests thru Glacier National Park there one day approached on the trail, a Blackfeet Indian party. This when the Park was young, and without campers' facilities. Though hiking, we took packhorses with dog tents, sleeping bags and month's supply of grub. Horses loaded to proper limit, each man carried a 60 pound rucksack. We therefore suggested our ladies have light rucksacks for their toilet accessories.
REDSKIN FEMINISM At one point I was at our party's rear. After said Redskins had passed us, one squaw looked back, saw our feminine rucksacks. She ran back, patted me on the forearm. She said:—"Heep smart buck, make 'em squaw carry burden."

Often since, writer has reflected upon Amerind status of women. One who remembers when California hills still held a considerable "squawman" population, recalls squaws gladly "married" palefaces. They said no white man could possibly be as cruel to his squaw as was the average redskin. His subsequent Amerind studies were from Totem Pole Land's Tlingits. Also Haidas, to way down the Cordillera, thru Arizona, also New Mexico pueblos, then on across areas of the old Maya-Toltec Mixtec, or Aztec Empires, down thru the old Inca Empire to Chile's Araucarians. He is convinced that the squaws of Glacier, and of the California Gold Rush were unerring in their estimation of the status of Amerind womanhood.

BUFFALO SKINS FORMERLY WERE USED FOR TEPEES
Most of the work of preparing buffalo skins, like nearly every job except hunting, fishing, were gravitated to the squaws.

Request Indian Birth Control

NEW DELHI, India — (Æ) — Indians were urged yesterday to restrict their families to three children to prevent "the present enormous annual population increase of more than 3,000,000."

The 1951 census report on maternity data said "while the incidence of improvident maternity is steadily decreasing in other countries, there are no such signs in India."

The report said the average number of children by every Indian mother up to the age of 45 was 6.6. Of those, an average of 2 died and 4.6 lived.

The report suggested later marriages as one of the antidotes to overpopulation. It added:

"The theory, based on European experience, that there are more children among the poorer sections of the community is not borne out in many parts of India."

HINDUSTAN FINALLY AWARE OF OVERPOPULATION

'Twas only yesteryear Hindustan's Commission of native pundits reported their overpopulation problem was beyond control. Demagogic *babus* then shouted "Rich America has no moral right to allow us to starve!" Some even declared since U.S.A., under the Truman Administration, had enacted two Displaced Persons Acts (nibbling at the Quota Immigration Law) America became bound to accept their Displaced Persons, result of the Hindustan-Pakistan partition. (These were estimated at 20,000,000.) President Roosevelt's representative further reported above as "Insoluble". This writer suggested a "500 Year Plan", insisted that, with birth control of most Hindustan elements, there were groups of promise. Upon their normal birthrate, a powerful Dominion could, in time, be built. Progress would be accelerated when Hindustan came to appreciate the mother contributes half her child's genes.

Egypt Women Stay on Strike

CAIRO — (Æ) — Doria Shafik and eight of her supporting suffragettes entered their third day of a hunger strike yesterday determined "to continue until the end" unless Egyptian women are granted electoral rights.

Mrs. Shafik, looking pale and tired, said proposals received so far from Egyptian officials here were far from satisfactory.

"They ask that we give up the hunger strike and promise that they will 'study' our demands," she said.

"We shall not leave this place (the press syndicate where the hunger strikers have established their headquarters) until our demands are fulfilled."

She said three other women had gone on hunger strike at Alexandria, Egypt's second city.

HONDURAS GRANTS WOMAN'S SUFFRAGE, 1952

Of all the 10,000 sermons Mother Nature offers in garden insect, garden bird, garden leaf, garden flower, none continually intrigues this garden philosopher more than the fact the whole biota evidences that the female's contribution toward the offspring exactly balances that of the male. Is this not particularly impressive as to humans? Despite the centuries of injustice of the man-made civilizations across Eurasia, it has taken human genetics' research of the last few decades to demonstrate that what a few fanatics tried, commencing 1900 to accomplish, has a sound basis in the Nature's laws.

Few in Honduras, even today, grasp that the mother contributes one-half her child's genes.

(See page 194.)

EGYPTIAN SUFFRAGETTES' HUNGER STRIKE

Activities, March 1954, of Cairo feminists recalls similar strategy of yesteryear London suffragettes. Same included such tactics as dropping vials of corrosive chemicals in mailboxes. . . . The status of the wife under English law, at that time was based upon glaring injustices. These increased in number as one crossed The Channel. From France to Egypt, Hindustan, China, Korea, Japan, Eastward there always was accelerated lowering of the position of womanhood. One remedy for this, suffrage, originated in Scandinavia. It also was only the biological research of the last few decades that established the fact that the mother furnishes exactly one-half the genes inherited by her child. MOTHER NATURE TEACHES THAT BIOLOGICAL TRUTHS ARE EVERYWHERE IN THE GARDEN. Only a few Egyptians are informed as to Human Genetics.

> "The treatment and transport of food consumed by urban people unquestionably injures its nutritious value."   (Osborne, "Our Plundered Planet".)

Is there any substitute for carrots, parsnips, green peppers, tomatoes, beans, peas fresh from one's garden? Is not real "millionaire" he whose dinner asparagus that morning was cut from his own bed, whose corn was on the stalk twenty minutes before serving! U.S.A.'s population already is 16,000,000 beyond what is considered ideal saturation point. This means ever fewer enjoying fresh tomatoes, fresh corn from their own gardens. Blundering American idealists insist Hindustan's expectancy of life be increased to Sweden's. Would this not enormously increase their misery? Nature automatically reduces overpopulation by pestilence, famine, war. Mortally wounded in battle, death comes soon, better than starvation's long drawnout torment. Should the Occident not teach Hindustan first birthcontrol before modern sanitation? Is not our own Puerto Rico a warning herein? From an upriver junk journey, then overland by sedan chair, a friend sent a photo of a father, 3 children. Later an epidemic struck their village. 2 of 3 children died. The nearest doctor, 100 miles away, could not begin to serve his painfully overpopulated area . . . thus characteristically backward.

OVERURBANIZATION

When We-2 landed in Korea, we were shocked Fusan taxicabs were chairs lashed to coolies' backs. A rickshaw man as a human beast of burden was bad enough. At this Korean system, we rebelled, preferred walking to participating in such human slavery. IS THIS AGAIN NOT AN INDEX TO THE ORIENT'S OVERPOPULATION?

Honduran Women Will Vote For First Time in December

By JANE EADS

WASHINGTON—(AP)—Senora Emma de Moya Posas, Honduran journalist and a leader of the Honduran feminist movement, says that only after next December will she be able to sleep nights with no worries. At that time the women of her country will at long last gain the right to vote, a privilege for which she has been fighting since 1948. Outside of Honduras, the only Latin American countries where women do not have suffrage are Nicaragua, Paraguay and Colombia.

"Honduran women missed by only three votes of getting suffrage last year," Senora de Moya Posas, columnist, magazine writer, and radio commentator, told me. "When we have suffrage our chances of being appointed to high office will be better, though we will have to keep fighting to break down the barriers set up by the men."

WOMEN STILL DENIED THE VOTE IN NICARAGUA, PARAGUAY AND COLOMBIA

THE SACRAMENTO BEE, FE

Lebanon Decree Gives Women Right To Vote

BEIRUT, Lebanon —AP— Prime Minister Khalid Shehab's government issued a sweeping new election decree last night giving educated women the right to vote, cutting the number of parliamentary seats almost in half and drastically revising the basis of representation among lawmakers.

Educated Lebanese women now not only have the right but the duty to cast ballots in elections. Voting for all eligible is compulsory. Non voters can be fined from 50 to 100 Lebanese pounds ($13.50 to $27)

LEBANON GRANTS WOMEN'S SUFFRAGE, 1952

Honduras, also Lebanon, clippings here reproduced, show the almost meteoric women's suffrage advance. Meteoric, because in history, a century is hardly a month. In biological evolution, 100 years is hardly more than a passing moment.... This author remembers clearly his native California's fight for Women's Suffrage. The victory came only within this half-century. In the early stages, advocacy, on a public platform, of women's votes was a signal for a volley from hoodlums of very ripe tomatoes. These attacks were not spontaneous. They evidently were plotted by extreme conservatives. These tried to thus silence those believing in women's suffrage as simple justice.

Canny Prince Bismarck knew the danger to the Germany he was building of revolution. He invented the *Kleingartenvertrieb*.

It was this writer's good fortune to be frequently a guest at a certain castle in Germany that had often entertained the "3 Kaisers": Wilhelm, Franz Joseph and the Czar, also Prince Bismarck. It was not those Emperors that intrigued this student of European History as much as the yarns his host would spin during a long evening about Fuerst Otto. That statesman was one of the most far-seeing that ever served an Imperial master. The tale about what happened when the startled Russian Grand Duke sud-

CANNY PRINCE BISMARCK

denly grasped that Prince Bismarck understood Russian,—well, as Kipling would say—"That is another story." It was not the stories of 1866 struggle between Austria and Prussia over the Dutchy of Schleswig-Holstein, it was not the trap he baited for Napoleon III at Sedan that he might translate into an actuality the Bismarckian dream of a united Germany. It was the profound insight into the strategy of social service legislation. One evening We-2 were in their library chatting with the Count and Countess, when the former said:—"How often, in that very chair, the tired Prince used to sit and enlarge upon his schemes to check German unrest." He had never forgotten the Revolution of 1848. He always insisted that the petty German princes were unwise in acting like Oriental despots. That particular evening the aged *Graf von* _____ said "You are so tremendously interested in social legislation I advise you to study current manifestations of a Bismarckian invention—the *Kleingartenvertrieb*. Go to our industrial centers and learn how actual 'ownership' of a tiny garden works to satisfy the longings of the German artisan." Prince Bismarck used to insist that a GARDEN plus security against illness and old age was a sufficient prescription against revolution.

BRETON BUTTERDISH

A garden is mentioned in the opening lines of that Philosopher Victor Hugo's "Les Miserables." It is the garden for the convalescents. The hospital manager is astounded at the Bishop's offer to exchange his Palace, with rooms for 60 beds, for the hospital with space for 20. The Bishop learns that when typhus, also "military fever" strikes the hospital sometimes has a hundred cases. . . .

Is there, in all modern literature, a more vivid description of the mistress system than the chapter of Les Miserables with the coldblooded, heartless letter from the four blades to the mistresses they, after two years, abandom? That, then the story of poor Fantine, of little Cosette and of Jean Valjean. . . .

That same heartlessness is evident in the Breton butterdish in writer's collection. It is a constant reminder of the injustices women long suffered from Britany to Bologna, Budapest, Bohkora, Bagdad, Bombay. The only sword to sever that Gordian Knot was Woman's Suffrage!

RICE GROWING IN CALIFORNIA

On writer's rice fields, sowing is done by airplane, in lieu of hand planting of seedlings. Fertilization is also aerial, just as tomatoes are plane-sulphured. Likewise, with biological intelligence, land infested with ALIEN* cruciferous weeds (mustard, radish) can be controlled by selective air-spraying so that grain (Graminae) sprouting later is not weedchoked.

* Any farmer, knowing how ALIEN weeds constitute "taxation without representation" will fight as vigorously as did the Boston Tea Party at the Revolution outbreak, to prevent Hyphenates destroying U.S.A.'s Immigration Control.

RICE PADDY PATHS Our garden is ALL beds—not one square production foot is wasted. Hence paths are limited to footways. One who has lived in the Orient knows how narrow are the rice paddy paths. Thus has been consolidated a folkway of what our pioneering forefathers called "Indian file".—Blackfeet today in Glacier National Park chatter over shoulders as did redskins since time immemorial. Papuaans, clearing jungle ways for automobiles might make a highway twelve feet wide. They themselves would traverse it, "Indian file". (no holding hands there—you teenagers). In World War II, at one U.S.A. university the G.I.'s learning Cantonese, did their classwork similarly in Chinese file back and forth across the campus. Speech and walk made one think of Kwantung.

As this gardener-philosopher sits on his asparagus lug box athwart his rice paddy-sized garden path he recalls the Rough Riding Colonel of San Juan Hill. A halfcentury in advance of his fellows in thinking, he once asked, on a visit to Sacramento: "Leaving the railroad station this morning, our carriage passed thru several blocks of your Chinatown. Your Chamber of Commerce boasts of your population growth. Why? Do they yearn for the Chinafication of California? Do they forget how many of these queued Orientals are forced to accept damp cellar housing? Do they grasp that results in a tuberculosis death rate the highest in any U.S.A. group? You'all are happy with your present numbers. Why sweat to have 10, 20, 100 individuals where today you have but one".

The Beloved Teddy was canny. Overpopulation brings famine, epidemics. It is THE cause of war. A vigorous young man prefers the risk of death on the battlefield to slow starvation when he sees over the Frontier the stuffed warehouse of an Outland.

If China ever decides upon a highway system like U.S.A.'s,—to gain space for same, it must "liquidate" just so many Chinese as today gain food from land thus converted to roads.

And who can say we do much better in U.S.A.? Adjoining some of writer's ranches, acres of the world's most fertile land is being converted to factory sites!

> "Ye field flowers! the GARDENS eclipse you, tis true
> Yet, wildings of nature, I doat upon you
> For ye waft me to summers of old,
> When the earth teemed about me with fairy delight
> And when daisies and buttercups gladdened
> Like treasures of silver and gold my sight."
>
> (Campbell)

Was there ever a more canny Gardening-philosopher than one of our yesteryear Cantonese hosts? Long ago he has gone to his Ancestors. We biographed this Fountain-of-Wisdom as Mr. "Bing of Singapore."* An earlier generation of our family pioneered in human betterment in China. Its aim then was to break the shackles of Chinese womanhood. Analyzing our success therein, writer profoundly is convinced this educational work succeeded because of concentrating on EUGENICALLY HIGHPOWERED CHINESE GIRLS. With several decades of such work, we contributed something to the long understanding between China and U.S.A. Hundreds of "our" girls, with Christian ideals, married men who governed China 1911-1941. This could not have happened had our work been among the lowest coolie girls. Then came our tragic, and I believe unnecessary, loss of China to the Soviets.

GARDEN-LOVING CHINESE

While in China, a Mandarin invited Us-2 to introduce the American supervised recreational idea into his area. He said frankly there always is such a thing as Public Opinion in China. He added that any-

---
* For biographical sketch of Mr. Bing see Eugenics Pamphlet No. 78, in your local library.

thing relating to children peculiarly was attractive to Chinese. He offered to contribute playground sites and salaries for the 2 expert supervisors we always recommended if we could procure such talent from U.S.A. This for every city in his province. Unfortunately, such trained leaders were not available when our country's own playground movement was in its infancy.

Indian Summer has begun as this is written. A magnificent tiger swallowtail comes over the 12-foot escallonia. Same has been planted as greenery-contrast for the bright, tall goldenrod, the Michaelmas daisies, the colorful zinnias afront. Papilo ignores all this honey feast. He has more important business. He wings his way to a camellia bush for a landing that spells "REST." I take out my watch to time him. Seconds become minutes. The lepidopterous muscles ARE weary. Finally, recuperated, he returns to zinnia's honeystores.

PHILOSOPHY OF REST

The Lapp eats his reindeer-blood cakes. The Guatemalan gorges on iguana stew. The Eskimo feasts on seal blubber. Have not all inherited instinctive behavior tendencies based upon untold out-of-doors centuries? Humans today have been crowded into unwieldy, inefficient, monstrous cities. Many lack all gardening opportunities. We then wonder at crime. With such shifts of environment, ought we not be amazed at so little unsocial doings? ...

It is August-end and early morn. The roses are most satisfying. Dozens of pink buds and fullblowns awaken memories of a score of European rosegardens. Writer recalls Empire Day celebrations by exiles. Lord _____'s bouttonniere was his Lancastrian red rose. Three of us, two Commoners, and the writer, (a mere American, not even a Colonial), wore the white rose of our Yorkshire ancestors. That War of the Roses ranks with our Civil War of 1861-65 in tragically dysgenic destruction of Leadership. Both those wars were unnecessary!

EUROPE'S BELOVED ROSEGARDENS

Throughout Europe, one is impressed with the high value placed on Rose Gardens. This folkway seems to have been consolidated when royal patronage did much to fix customs.

One glorious rose clump this August end is of coppers. It recalls the tragic life of one of France's great rose-creators. When World War I broke he was working on crosses of certain yellow wild roses said to be Persian. Both sons were called to the colors. Both fell in action. He named his two best products for his lads. Then he said:— "Now my life work is ended". We wonder why France has lost world leadership in so many fields . . . Writer can never forget the finding by his friend, the late Dr. T. A. D. Cockerell of a fossil rose in the Florissant of Colorado along with his butterflies and other Miocene insects. Among his friends was a Parisian, owner of a great department store, and of a rose garden boasting every known species. Dr. Cockerell forwarded the unique Florissant fossil to Paris with "Of course, this rightfully is yours!"

ALMOST MOBBED IN CONSTANTINOPLE

The intensity of isolation of Moslem women may be illustrated by an experience We-2 had living in Constantinople after World War I. We entered a streetcar headed toward Yedi Kalu. At the next stop a veiled woman, evidently elderly, boarded the car. All seats were taken. I instinctively offerd her mine. That I was sitting in the first row of men's seats and that the forward part of the car was reserved for women was something that I, then newly arrived in Constantinople, did not grasp. Almost a riot started over my "insulting a Turkish woman." Then one man in the crowd quieted them, then told me "I have just convinced them how ignorant you are." Then he explained to me how I had offended.

It is rather difficult to believe that there could be just a few years ago such occurrences, not out in the extremely conservative hill area, but actually in Constantinople itself, also that now, not only are women's veils discarded, but they actually have women's suffrage. One encouraging factor in today's perplexing world is that Turkey has telescoped into few years changes that our Western civilization spent centuries in making.

On one of writer's ranches, some acreage is devoted to raising sunflowers for the seedsmen. In fact, also are crops of lettuce, carrot, onion, pea, beet-root seed. Sunflowers are a problem. They run to height, like yellow-moustached Vikings of old. Since mechanical harvesting is increasingly forced upon us, it now is essential to breed a runtish plant. This, like the Brookville turkeys for apartment house couples, or like the substitute of handsized "nutmeg" for the football-type muskmelon of yesteryear.

MUTT AND JEFF SUNFLOWERS

The researchists are responding to our S.O.S. In fact, this is written in sight of rows of both Mutt and Jeff sunflowers. The dwarf sunflower is coming as surely as writer's friend, the late Luther Burbank, isolated milkwhite also rosepink, also crimson eschscholtzias from his million golden poppies.

To create such strains, however, does it not take more than good soil, sufficient moisture, sunshine? Is there not behind it all a kind of intellect as rare as, say, one crimson bloom in a field of 100,000 California poppies?

Here at the sunflower experiment the writer has been discussing the problem of the researchist birthrate with Bill, a young student worker. A letter has arrived from a biology Dean down in Dixie. With him has been correspondence about the collegiate birthrate. That Dean has 5. His President has 4. The student and the writer have been computing family size of the professors we know. The average is plus 1. We also have been tabulating the drunken driver convictions in our neighborhood. They average 8 to the maladjusted couple! Bill is soon to be married. His sweetheart insists they, both with very high I.Q., must have 5 children. CAN THEY? . . .

In one Latin American city, a group of sociologists of which this author is a member, made a study of the salaries paid the police. Apparently, the stipend was practically a zero. Moreover, not only did he receive practically nothing, he was required to squeeze out of his beat, by corruption, a certain monthly amount to the Higherups before he was allowed to keep anything for his own family. This writer happened to know some of these policemen. They were practically all illiterate. When one has neither the ability to read or write, and, further, is biologically illiterate, how can such a government be expected to be genuinely interested in the Reduction of Poverty?

The garden can be a base throughout the year, for radiation of acts of kindness. In January, a little violet bouquet to say, a gentlewoman almost a nonagenarian, a "shut in" at a Rest Home. Its perfume over several days will stimulate memories of the Long Ago.

"BREAKING THE ICE" GARDEN STYLE

In February, a spray of acacia gold to an elderly Australian loosens his tongue. He thereupon talks entertainingly of cockatoos in the Back Blocks, of kangaroos in the Never-Never. . . .

Canny Papa Dachert was founder of the world's first Eugenical Garden City.* This deeply spiritual Chocolate King projected into the planning of that remarkable experiment, (now donated to Strassburg), various devices for human betterment. One was the use of gardening for increase of neighborliness. We-2 long ago also had paralleled this in our garden and made it a part of our garden philosophy.

LA FONDATION
LES JARDINS UNGEMACH

met en construction
SEIZE VILLAS

LES JARDINS UNGEMACH CONTINUED GROWTH

Announcement of sixteen additional "villas" to Les Jardins Ungemach.

"Love? Love?? What am Love?" Why love am de insane desire on de part of one man to pay de board an' lodging of another man's daughter fo' de rest of her natural life."   (Yesteryear Minstrel Show.)

Is not cooperation but another manifestation of Love? Cannot Love be increasingly substituted for antagonism? Is not any marriage

---

* "Les Jardins Ungemach", described in "War Profits and Better Babies". The book, now out of print, is, nevertheless, obtainable at most college, also public libraries in U.S.A.

of Love, of compatability based upon attainment of such adjustment that two can live together harmoniously? Do not the compositae of our gardens, tho' speechless, preach this by example. And does not such near-perfection of adjustment make for SURVIVAL?
LOVE Love, indeed, is the greatest, the most beautiful mystery of all. Can anything teach it better than gardening? What can grow out of it may be illustrated by this incident:—

The adjoining owner having died, We-2 promptly bought his estate's vacant lot next our home. We thus acquired an unsightly but useful and necessary shed. How to make it attractive instead of being an eyesore! Some climbing roses and other vines were purchased. Two years later the shed was entirely covered. Honeysuckle and ivy gave perennial greenery. The roses, carefully selected for periods of long bloom, yielded attractive variation of color from time to itme. Is it not worthwhile to reflect upon how a tiny investment can accomplish such a miracle?

In this century's opening years We-2 noticed the loneliness of native California's scattered rural school houses. Our string of ranches extended from the cattle range in the Mt. Shasta region, north of the great Sacramento-San Joaquin Valley to Kern County where that valley ends at Tehachapi Mountains. We-2 then started distributing rosebushes to these pathetically-naked countryside school houses. It seemed no one ever had thought of beautifying all these often-unpainted frame boxes. We selected roses best fitted to survive midsummer vacations, because Nature watered them in the October to May rainy reason. Some schools became truly charming.

OBI ADDS TO IRIS' COLOR CHARM

On the trail from Nikko, with its worldfamous red lacquer bridge, to Lake Chuzenji, we met coolie women carrying chunks of quarried rock. This was after the close of the Russo-Japanese War. We found one blind burden-carrier. Sightlessness did not relieve her having to carry her load. For this work, we were told each girl earned, for a 12-hour day, less than 1 cent per hour.

That garden fashions shift is shown by disappearance of the yellow rose popular in California Gold Rush gardens. This, probably, because a later generation disliked its peculiar odor. The tree-of-heaven first planted at Chinese joss-houses has become naturalized. The osage orange of the Ozarks persists because, the garden-hedge of Gold Rush days, it still is as useful as the desert's *ocotillo* as a living barbwire. The locust will long be the street tree of the ghosttowns, even to the edge of precipitous cliffs made by the hydraulic monitors.

———o———

"Man does not live by bread alone, but by the fragrance of roses, the scent of orange blossoms, the smell of new-mown hay, the clasp of a friend's hand, the tenderness of a mother's kiss."
(The University Presbyterian ... R/D1/'54.)

When U.S.A.'s biological illiteracy is reduced, our voters will commence to grasp the Philosophy of The Niche.* They will learn much from a species' radiation into new food areas. This depends upon OBSERVING, not IGNORING, laws governing same. We then will have better lawmaking. Our people, for example, then will become more alert to the menace involving their liberties by "amending to death" the Immigration Quota Acts of 1921-2-4.

Why does one garden? Ask one's best friend, one's neighbor, a dozen, a score of folks from various walks of life.

As to VEGETABLE gardens, the answers revolve around the Food concept with our Victory Gardens, many said "Helping Win the War". . . . Additional comments are: "It's lots of fun" . . . "Everybody's doing it" . . . "Relief to work with one's hands" . . . "Back-to-the-soil" . . . "Thrilling to watch something grow." . . .

COLOR LOVE STIMULATES GARDENING

If, "Why a FLOWER garden?" the response frequently is:—"Always did like wildflowers." Further questioning elicits: "Their color attracted." . . .

The joy of color IS all embracing. It is deeply primeval. . . . Note a savage's pleasure in beads of jade, of gold, of even brightly-colored glass. Observe the frankly uncontrolled urge in certain races, as the Burmese, to dress in bright colors. Study the highly refined balancing of color values in women's gowns, millinery. This reached new heights in Paris before World War I. Fascinating it was there to see world-famous designers' efforts in attiring:—(1) The tall, blue-eyed, golden-haired daughter of an English earl, (2) A velvet-eyed, jet-haired odalesque from old Constantinople, (3) The spoilt,

---

* For much data on the Niche, see the file of Eugenics Pamphlets in your local library.

Color/Scent

already obese, young wife of a Colombian emerald-king. Dubbed *"mestizo"*, she probably only 1/16 Castilian, with 1/16 negroid, 7/8 Amerind.

Color HAS appeal, indeed, both to the savage and to the sophisticated. It is no accident that one of the best French cook books of the Cateau Age opened with. "The first essential of a successful chef is an imagination sufficiently vivid that he can sense the color values of the food he prepares when it reaches the master's table.*

> "Around her neck
> She wore a yellow ribbon.—
> She wore it in the summer time
> And in the month of May,
> And when they asked her
> Why-in-the-world she did it,—
> She said she did it for her lover
> Who was fur, fur away."
>
> (Calvary song of the Yellowstone, when the Army policed our then few National Parks.)

Since all men are egocentric, the Garden Philosopher tends to interpret Gardening happenings in human terms, as in the last chapter. Color-appreciation today is evident in humans from the most highly cultured to the lowest primitives. It even extends to those other bipeds, the feathered folk, as note at the close of the last chapter.

COSMETICS, 777 (?) B.C. Nature probably utilized color in the interaction of flower and insect as long ago as the Miocene, say 30 million years ago.

The story of human use of color goes far back into history. We stumbled across an early criticism of color-use by the Greek philosopher Hesiod. The yarn IS stale, say 777 B.C. It may, however, stimulate a chuckle:—We-2 were traveling in Greece in the days when one still saw occasionally, a Beau Brummel in pleated skirts. With a thirsty radiator our chauffeur paused at an ancient monastery. One priest, some years in U.S.A., spoke far better English than our attempts at Greek phrases. We tarried a wee bit. He told of a water pipe faithfully supplying his monastery since time immemorial. A recent earthquake intervened. Searching in the crypt for the break, they discovered what supposedly was living rock was a

---

*Above condensed from "Geogardening". Tho out of print, the book is obtainable at most U.S.A. libraries.

wall. Behind it was a box with parchment. One recorded the wail of Hesoid:—

"Our young females have discovered they can make a cosmetic by mortar-grinding a green rock.* With same they smear their cheeks. When a virgin deports herself thus brazenly, to make herself attractive to our young men, civilization is doomed."

———o———

What a fine start in conquering the Greek language these scientific names give. They are fossils, too, for they remind us that, once, education wisely included Latin and Greek classics. What have we not lost in our contemptuous discard of these reservoirs of rare wisdom. Into Greek was concentrated the centuries of contributions by the giant Greek intellects in drama, philosophy, medicine, biology, architecture. Into Latin was embalmed the rare Roman ability to administer, to govern, and particularly to make laws!

CHLOROPHYLL,
SIDEROPHYLL,
XANTHOPHYLL

On a recent gum counter are attractively arranged spearmint and peppermint, juicy fruits and pepsins. All sell at 5 cents. In their midst is a haughty newcomer, chlorophyll, at 19 cents. It is the vogue for its chewing makes one "kissable." It is competing with those dangerous perfumes:—My Sin, Night of Delight, Irresistible.

Mother Nature must have learned, centuries ago, how valuable is chlorophyll. She is as Scottish as a Highland tartan. A maple leaf has fluttered to the ground as this is written. Once it had chlorophyll, siderophyll, xantophyll. Now it is a mere mummy of skin and bones. All its spring and summer chemicals have disappeared.

———o———

Today opens the Fortnight-before Christmas. The cherry tree's golden leaves flutter one by one to the ground. Thru the brown of the baring branches is the background of the green of the Acacia. AND THAT ACACIA HAS READY-TO-BURST FLOWERBUDS. It has been a mass of fluffy yellow bloom on New Year's Day. The leaves flutter one by one and an octogenarian feels his thoughts also flutter one by one.

A CHINESE PROVERB SAYS: **"OUT OF AN INDIGO VAT, ONE DOES NOT DRAW WHITE CALICO."**

---

* It was malachite, green carbonate of copper.

Once, We-2 were at our vessel's rail watching varicolored-coiffured Negroes loading the captain's purchases of palm nuts. The venerable botany professor philosophized: "That there comes over the vessel's side a steady stream of palm-nut baskets is because our vessel* is stocked with junk colorfully dear to the savage negro heart." There were barrels of black highsilk hats, from secondhand clothing stores of London, of Paris. There were also strings of brightcolored beads. What seemed, however, most attractive were flimsy, near-silk kerchiefs. Some flashed brilliant purples, striking yellows, flaming reds. A few had that color dearest to Islamic souls, Mohammed's sacred green. From one boastful darky, just back from wondrous Mecca, these extracted triple trade of palm nuts.

COLOR IN SOMALILAND

The whole day had been like what, some years later, could be described as a motion picture's unfolding. The dominant note, to this writer, seemed to be savage color love. Opportunities to thus observe primitive origins of human behavior, are disappearing as rapidly as the melting of a Spitzbergen glacier's nose under the 24-hours-per-day sunlight of the Midnight Sun.

> "What would the rose with all her pride be worth,
> were there no sun to call her brightness forth?"
>
> (Moore—Love Alone)

One February early morning started with fog. Same gives variety to flower color. The massed tazetta-white and calendula-canary, also-orange is pleasingly softened by fog gray, behind, between. Here IS charm.

One thinks of a German philosopher encountered on a Himalayan pass into Tibet. Persistent was his enjoyment of everything from poppy-color to the irregular form of a wind tortured deodor. He would say *"Ich bin materialist."* He then would add: "There is no God, There is no Hereafter, While living I propose to enjoy, enjoy, enjoy!" Well, even his Teutonic philosophy would en-joy the joy of midwinter flower color filtering thru fog-smoke.

FLOWER COLOR IS PUBLICITY

Do not we who garden, also think, however, perhaps a bit materialistically (or shall we say not deeply) about flower-color? Do we look deeper to try to fathom why flowers have color as a dominant

---

* Our freighter ran inshore as close as possible. Out came a few native *dhows*. Fuzzy-haired negroes had clambered up our side. Good trading ashore soon was evident. The freighter's long boat, first mate had charge, was lowered. Somaliland's male citizens quickly had their respective harems at work. These had gathered ivory-palm nuts, later coat buttons for Europeans. The lazy menfolk leaned against palm-tree trunks, directing the work. These ebony Apollos by midday strutted around in high silk hats. A half-dozen kerchiefs were around one buck's neck, little other clothing, save a G-string. Leftovers, beads, kerchiefs, went rather unequitably, to his youngest wife. This, tho the elder ones worked far more efficiently!

factor in their defense mechanism? Color to them is PUBLICITY. It signals to bee or butterfly:—"I have honey for you. Come, for I know your hairs will rub some pollen. I know that SEX is one of the most beautiful of all Mother Nature's inventions. I flash my color-lanterns in hospitality—thus inviting your visit!" ...

Of all garden colors has not yellow a peculiar sphere? An octogenarian remembers discussions, at the century's turn, of "The Yellow Peril.* Kaiser Wilhelm II was fond of emphasizing same. At the Boxer Rebellion, German strategy was: "So terrorize the Chinese, the German there will be feared for 1,000 years!"

"YELLOW PERIL," YELLOW THERAPY

Is there not another phase of yellow's value? It perhaps is more pleasant to contemplate. Has it a high value in building morale? We-2 once were planning to climb Uri Rotstock. With us were an Atlantic Coast couple. The husband was one of that day's great nerve specialists. They then were so few, they could be counted on one hand's fingers. This healer said:—"My first prescription invariably is:—'R/x—Daily: A vase of yellow flowers'." He believed in yellow blossoms' therapeutic value.

As this is written in mid-May, our garden is most attractive with its yellows. The brooms everywhere are in full bloom. Masses of yellow flowers also are in the beds. Coreopsis remind one of geogardening in Arkansas. The rich golden-brown of our home interior's teak finish makes a pleasing background for dishes of contrasted orange and golden calendulas. These also bring up fond recollections of other geogardening, i.e. in Sicily, also in Greece. Is not most fascinating the sleuthing garden flowers to their sauvage beginning?

> Tulip-beds of different shape and dyes,
> Bending beneath the invisible West-wind's sighs.
> (Moore: Lalla Rookh.)

A neighbor, knowing our garden from narcissus gold in February to acacia gold the next January remarked:—"The only way to enjoy flower golds contrasted with foliage green or, in fact, any garden color is from a lowflying airplane." ...

Again, aboard that trader off Somaliland, the veteran Botany Dean of a European university, said:—"After all, the dominant stimulus is color. Look at these Somali dandies," he continued, "One's

---
* One wag said "The real Yellow Peril's the yellow streak in the American politician."

kinky hair is dyed red as a rose, another is as yellow as a sunflower. That skinny negro, within the year, has made the Mecca pilgrimage. His hair has a new-clipped lawn's hue. Green, the **REACTIONS** plant's color, still stirs profoundly the desert-dwelling **TO COLOR** Mohammedan's soul."

That professor was, to steal a Freemasonry metaphor, a 33° geogardener. From his own little, but world-famed, botanical garden, he had gone awanderlusting across Siberia, to revel in days of journeying thru orange-red Oriental poppies. He had threaded narrow, snow-choked Himalayan passes, to descend into Tibetan meadows carpeted with blue poppies. These, he declared, seemed, at a distance, mountain lakes reflecting Heaven's blue. He had botanized in Java's purple lantana tangles. Penetrated deeply into Ecuador's rainforests, he had studied the color attraction blossoms held for hummingbirds. He was positive that color dominated, not only primitive man, but lower vertebrates, even insects....

"If man can, in a short time, give beauty and an elegant carriage to his bantams, according to his standard of beauty, I can see no reason to doubt that female birds, by selecting, during thousands of generations, the most melodious or beautiful males, according to their standard of beauty, might produce a marked effect. (Darwin)

At our mountain cabin's Lookout Point, the Geology Professor's wife, an artist, was eloquent about the sunset coloring. Beyond and below us, the mountains, as Kipling would say, were huddled like sheep. The various distances, also elevations gave a mosaic of blues and lead-blues, and purples that was charming. The professor complained:—

"All you see, my dear, is color. To me much more wonderful is the exhibit of force. Away to the left is a lava-**COLOR VS.** flow mesa. Over to the right a volcano's crater. Below **VULCANISM** it, a cinder cone. The two parallel canyons are faults of crushing. That hot spring evidences the forces, the senile, nevertheless are not dead. And all you can see, Dearest, is color!"

As Charlie Yuen, of the San Francisco Chinatown drama, said to the Boston tenderfoot:—"You miss a lot-in-life." But perhaps all that is necessary to color. Is that not the primal urge in flower gardening? How many successive Februarys would we thrill over the newly arrived seedsmen's catalogues, if all flowers were even Islam's sacred green. Hence we plant for flower color. With accumulating years, however, it dawns on one that, like the Geology Professor's jig-saw puzzle of a skyline, there is another, even a more satisfying joy.

The Garden Philosopher is necessarily somewhat hedonistic. He revels in his garden's pleasures. Of these, color, also perfume, are among the dominants.

> Here are sweet peas, on tiptoe for a flight;
> With wings of gentle flush o'er delicate white,
> And taper fingers catching at all things,
> To bind them all about with tiny rings.
> (Keats—I Stood Tiptoe Upon a Little Hill)

It is mid-January of an almost frostless Sacramento winter. Already our Filipino asparagus cutters are moving into the cabins on writer's ranches in anticipation of an early harvest. In writer's garden, a Japanese flowering apricot is a mass of pink bloom contrasted with green of escallonia, broom, and honeysuckle. The cerise color is morale-building, especially on grey days. Below is the bronze of forsythia whose buds are itching to burst into blossom.

JAPANESE FLOWERING APRICOT That Japanese flowering apricot stimulates thinking about our little-appreciated debt to Oriental gardens. Indeed, how much we accept of happiness, of convenience, of health, of invention, because of some forgotten man who spent his very lifeblood in, say, propagating a better-hued apricot, in proving malaria is not mal-aria, in forcing the power of a mountain cascade, as at Folsom, into a 22-mile wire to turn Sacramento wheels, thus giving mankind practical hydroelectricity.

Jedediah Smith, Forgotten Man, is an example of our ingratitude to those who slave, suffer, die for us: It is timely because the Sacramento State College campus now is being planned. Its situation on *El Rio de los Americanos de Jedediah Smith* is unique. As a banker of 50 years ago, the writer made loans on parts of *Rancho Rio de los Americanos* east of the campus. Smith ferried three-fourths ton of beaver pelts across the river near the campus site.

Years ago while at the university We-2 were doing historical research on original documents. Mrs. Goethe found the words "Bible Toter." We started digging and finally covered most of Smith's trail from his Ohio River birthplace to his second massacre. In tracing his trail we followed the Smith River, now a state park boundary. We found no one who knew why it was called "Smith River." One settler said: "When I was a boy someone asked Granddad. He said, 'It's named for all the Smiths that vote'." Jedediah Smith was forgotten.

We determined to restore his place in history. Hence our gift of his redwood grove through the Save The Redwoods League. The state

Color/Scent

park board afterward extended the same to cover the 10,000 acres of sequoias in the Jedediah Smith State Park. That board showed rare appreciation of Smith's unique character. He succeeded where even Lewis and Clark reported "Impossible."

After the second massacre, Smith, the lone survivor, staggered into the Wyoming fur trade outpost and gasped: "In that desert I found a valley (Sacramento-San Joaquin) with room for 100,000 farmsteads of good land. Send a military expedition (Fremont's) to blaze the trail. Then start the Covered Wagons rolling." (See page 74)

CEYLON BULLOCK CART

These Singalese bullock carts carry citronella grass for perfume (just as trucks carry alfalfa on this author's ranches for the dairies.)

> The daisies are rose-scented,
> And the rose herself has got
> Perfume which on earth is not.
>
> (Keats—Ode)

Buying oranges in China, writer found, does not carry title to the peel. In China, tens of millions live on rice, rice, only rice. Any flavoring has a market value. In West China, sunrise-to-sunset toil earned less than a 3c postage stamp. Is it any wonder such folk hesitate at nothing to enter a land where a few hours' wage equals a weeks' at home?

VIOLET CULTIVATION IN FRANCE

The canny French have bred violets for maximum perfume. (Would that they had shown as much concern about breeding humans. This author has written much about the tragic results eugenically of The Dot, also of the French Revolution. He made the first English translation of the 1939 Code de la Famille.)

PERFUMERY, FLAVORING
Perfumes have been distilled from gums, such as myrrh,—from seeds, as vanilla—from roots as orris,—from flowers, as attar-of-roses, violets, — from grasses, as lemon-grass oil — from leaves, as bay oil,—from even wood, as cedar oil. The produce for market takes many forms. Rosewater, orange water go largely to Oriental *harems* and *zennas*. Pomades, or perfumes in grease, were popular yesteryear for masculine hairdabbing, as well as for bristling martial moustaches.

Planted for fullmoon's perfumed air effects, our garden last night had massed clovepink in its borders. Another dividend-paying perfume-bearer is honeysuckle. Why not also plan for delightful indoor scents. A vase of a dozen roses, selected for odor, or of certain violets the French perfumers grow, will fill an entire room. Remember, too, such effects as the Daphne Path at a certain swanky Spa.

The garden-devotee, when overseas, should visit the perfume farms at Grasse. True, they today may not be as well cultivated as before when Madagascar and other imperial French colonies commenced competing. Also, synthetics are formidable rivals. Grasse, however, is still worth a visit. Count de Grasse was Washington's friend in 1776. And Grasse today still has plots of perfumery roses, of violets of jessamine, as well as carefully-bred orange-perfume orchards. Those Gauls of yesteryear knew how to obtain results by following genetic laws, tho they never had heard of chromosomes.

The flowers at Grasse are pressed down into great copper vats. Then hot lard is poured over them. When cool, alcohol is allowed to permeate the grease to leach out the perfume-oils. This is drawn off for processing for the attractively shaped bottles of "My Sin", or "Midnight Delight". Such alluringly-selected names attract the dollars of American tourists in Paris. The resultant grease is a valuable by-product. It is the base of perfumed soaps. In their manufacture, France long dominated world markets as successfully as in women's gowns, also millinery. The education of no gardener is quite complete until he has made pilgrimage to Grasse.

LAVENDER CULTIVATION IN FRANCE
What does not "Lavender and Old Lace" recall? One lavender bush has an honored place in our garden. It is valuable for, not only perfume, but as a remarkable source of niche study. It is a plant adjusted to that forbidding NICHE, the arid-limestone semi-desert of Southern France.

It is not possible to worship God in one's garden as devotedly as within the walls of a church? God-in-Nature is adorable. Never in the garden does one hear there the theological wranglings that humans sometimes indulge in. Never have three violets quarrelled as to how many angels can stand on a needle's point!

NATURE'S LAWS WORK AS UNCEASINGLY AS OCEAN'S TIDES

One gazes at the marvellous coloring of a pink rose. One contemplates the unbelievably-efficient cooperation in the floral head of a sunflower. One is lost in admiration of the adjustment of a hummingbird feeding at a fuchsia. One remembers with profound reverence a honeybee circling a disk flower of a Coreopsis, recalling it was largely thru interaction between insects and the then newly created flowering plants that played such a part in their displacement of the lower orders at the time the little mammals were edging out the giant dinosaurs over the precipice rim into extinction.

One sees friction in the garden. Two elm limbs rub in each wind storm. They finally crash. One wonders at the effect on unfortunate children in homes where Discord has supplanted Love. One recalls the classic study of the dog who, under systematic irritation, could not digest his meat scrap.

ALGIERS DATE GARDEN
Fascinating was the study of the gardens of French African oases. It meant the use, however, over short periods, of nothing but dates as food. On our camel trips down the "Trail toward Timbuctu" it was not safe to drink camel milk. The only exceptions were those few military posts where one could obtain Pasteurized milk. The only meat, stringy tough camel flesh, was exposed in the bazaars. It invariably was disgustingly black with fly swarms. As a result, our food was dates. We boiled these because of bacteria. The same *harems* that bid for the choicest *Deglet Noor* dates consumed great quantities of rosewater and orangewater from the perfumery farms of the domains of the Count de Grasse.

The garden stimulates much thought because of its miracles of color, of form, of scent as survival mechanisms. Thus the garden philosopher feels the urge to explore the possibilities of testing these evolutionary trends to ascertain whether they can throw light upon certain human problems. He asks himself how can above be applied to such age-old matters as Reduction of Poverty? And, even more so, the now-understandable and new knowledge of genetics? Has not our generation a new responsibility herein? More discoveries have been made thru research in above in 50 years, 1900-1950, than man ever accumulated in the one million years since Pithecanthropus gulped jakfruit while alert for any lurking maneating tiger in the jungles of Souerakarta.

THE GARDEN DISPLAYS SURVIVAL MECHANISMS

Watch the "wedding dance" of 2 checkerspot butterflies. All the honey feasts the garden offers, from sweetpea, sown columbines, or highly-perfumed clovepink are ignored. In the garden's life, SEX apparently outranks FOOD. All evolution of flower-color, of flower-perfume, is in response to this fundamental instinct. So, too, is, the coloring of male birds. Note the crimson "nuptial plumage" of the Elfin Forest's male housefinch. Observe its blue jay's splendor when he dons his wedding clothes. The sex urge, expressed in desiring to please the Lady Love is evident, too, in the so-called "wedding dances". Did you ever see that of California's State Bird, the plumed "valley quail"? Only once in some 70 years of bird study did this author ever have this thrill. He witnessed it when he had remained motionless for an hour where he had crawled under Elfin Forest chaparral. In fact, this single record duplicates his "only" Down Under of the lyre bird's wedding dance. Australia is proud to feature same on her postage stamps. For further evidence of the sex urge resulting in courtship, be alert near tubular flowers like the pentstemon for the wedding dance of Anna's hummingbird. YET HOW HOLLYWOOD HAS BEEN PERMITTED TO EXPLOIT, FOR PROFIT, THIS PRIMAL URGE! DOES SAME NOT OFFER A HEAVEN-SENT OPPORTUNITY TO STUDY POSSIBILITIES OF RACE BETTERMENT?

The pages of American History contain few more convincing examples of acceleration of progress thru planned cooperation than the Ecumenical Movement in U.S.A.'s Protestantism. IT PARALLELS THE MANIFESTATION OF GOD-IN-NATURE IN THE SUNFLOWER FAMILY.

Arriving in Korea at the close of the Russo-Japanese War, we were amazed at the sanitation conditions. We also learned we could support a Korean medical student thru 4 years of college at $25 per year.

These men, of course, had not inherited the "American Know How". They could, however, at least substitute scientific knowledge for corroding superstition.

We-2 lived in Seoul for a while. A friend suggested a climb to a hill overlooking Korea's capital city. He said:—"You can still see there the soot-blackened stones of the old Emperor's telegraphing by signal fire. This is the same as mentioned in Scott's "Lay of the Last Minstrel". Arriving at the summit a Japanese sentry at a turn of the trail poked his bayonet into my face. Above those blackened stones was the latest in military telegraphic equipment. Were not the Japanese adepts at imitating "American Know How"?

One day we walked down Seoul's main street. It is part of Great East-West Road. Crossing it is Great North-South Road. Our companion, an American geologist. Americans then were beginning to obtain mining concessions. Mining had been tabu. At above crossing, a granite out-crop. Even flowerpot-hatted aristocrats, in long grass-linen robes of lavender and applegreen, held that granite was the vertebrae of a great dragon. On it Korea rested. Skin punctured, this dragon also showed displeasure by earthquakes.

Gypsy moth caterpillars were imported to U.S.A. in 1869. Biologist Trouvlot put them on some bushes to feed. He covered the plants with a cloth to prevent escape. A sudden wind blew off the sheet. The caterpillars escaped. Trouvlot asked the authorities for $100 to collect the dangerous pests from overseas. They refused. Before two decades had passed, Massachusetts was spending **PEST RESISTERS** a million dollars in unsuccessful control... Today the Bay State has sunk herein over $25,000,000. Today the alien pest is being fought in the hope of preventing it invading the Western hardwood forest. The Federal Government entered the struggle in the early 1900s.

The cost of having admitted undesirable alien humans has cost Americans daily so many dollars that probably few realize the heavy expense. Government at last is alert trying to bar these undesirables. When will the American taxpayers awaken to the blunder of dysgenically remaining asleep as to undesirables that are still not barred by our faulty immigration control?

"Speak of many things, of ships, and shoes, and
SEALING WAX and cabbages and kings."

Some of us are old enuf to remember the sticks of varicolored sealing wax, the candle to melt same, even the seal intaglio pressed into the warm wax, as a secure identification. When the gardener thinks of such security, does he remember here again, Mother Nature was first at the Patent Office? An example is the miracle of the morning glory. It unravels its beauty to the risen sun. A passing bee crawls down its violet funnel for the honey down there and emerges coated with white pollen like flour on a baker's bare arm. Once fertilization is gained, it proceeds to gain a security as cannily planned as the intaglio impressed into the heated sealing wax on a yesteryear's loveletter's flap. At noon, the big corrolla commences to roll together toward the stem thus SEALING the ovary against damp. . . .

SEALING WAX

Our Houston host was spinning Amarillo yarns. That Panhandle, may it be remembered, is at times rather arid. They tell of one inhabitant boasting of his daughter of 7. She still believed in Santa Claus. His neighbor cut in with "Shucks. That's nothing. My kid is 9 and he still believes it can rain!" The Houston host's yarns included one about a prayermeeting. The brethren had prayed on three consecutive Wednesdays for "showers of blessing". Deacon Jones' petition, an hour long, must have done it. The cloudburst,—well, this author once saw 5 inches within an hour, and was willing to believe that, after midnight, there was no let up for the flooded congregation. The minister groaned "Oh! Lord, don't you know there can be too much of a good thing!" There are scientists who think they could have improved upon the creation of man. We have some structural weakness, certain anatomists show faulty planning. This garden philosopher thinks, however, that Mother Nature should not be criticized. One of the most persistent happinesses is her succession of bloom. Acacias in January, sweet peas in February, trumpet narcissi in March, lilies of the valley in April, poppies in May, phlox leading the floral procession all midsummer. Tazettas in November, violets in December. One must daily be grateful to the Giver of All Good that flower bloom color is staggered thusly from New Year's Day thru to Christmas. . . .

ENDLESS SUCCESSION OF BLOOM

Mayday's hours have been invested in decorating our home with one from writer's ancestral coat-of-arms, the *fleur-de-lys*. We have been fortunate in enjoying, over the years, the friendship of the Lloyd Austin's, long successful plant breeders. Of rare vision, they have applied genetics to improving pinetrees, also iris. Today, largely because of rhizomes from their Rainbow Gardens at old Hangtown, our entrance hall, dining room, living room, library are charmingly colorful, (and odorful) with "sweet flags." Half the iris are as golden as the nuggets, thefts of which brought into being old Hangtown's Vigilantes. The other half runs the gamut from

IRIS GENETICS, IRIS-TIMING

almost baby-blue to royal purples, (so different from the classic crimson once dubbed "royal purple").

The iris breeder searches for a mutation with very tall stem with many blooms today and buds promising more. Note the iris' willingness (if one may use a human term,) patiently to offer its scent for pollenizer visits. There are several blooms on this stalk. The shriveled ones tell of those 10 days ago. In 10 days more, more will flaunt color, perfume. The last buds will start opening to welcome the sixfooted. These pay for color-thrill, scent-thrill by being living airplanes. They carry to other *fleurs-de-lys* the pollens that give the cross-fertilization which is evolution.

WHAT INTRIGUES THE GARDENER IS, the "PATIENCE" OF IRIS-TIMING. Here is a floral rendition of the old folksaying: "If at first you don't succeed, try, try again." Iris *zeilstrebigkeit* needs no dominant leaders to ever build morale. It has no morons that whine "the Government owes me a living." It goes on, a bloom every few days. Some days may be foggy, perhaps, some cold, some rainy. All this means insect inactivity. But, with patience, there comes sunshiny days. The hexapods then are warmed into the essential activity. Work with patience—ever work with patience—and over the years that become aeons have been evolved blooms welcomed for decorations for one's coming guests.

This matter of color, seemingly dominant cause of gardening of many, grows in absorbing interest with the years. Van Dyke, most sensitive to our arid Southwest's gorgeous tints, once remarked: "They make no impression on the Amerind." And yet! Once We-2 were living on a Mexican *hacienda*. We daily strolled along trails, studying desert biota. One morning we met a peon funeral. They were too poor to buy the baby a coffin. Father carried the little bundle, wrapped in a tattered *zerape*. They were pure Amerind, but spoke Spanish. We joined them, put a few wildflowers on the grave. Their grief seemed almost too heavy.

Returning that evening, we stopped at their unfloored abode to say a word of comfort. Coming thru their cactus hedge, we saw grandmother seated outside the door. We tried to express sympathy. Thru her tears she pointed westward to gorgeous desert coloring. She said simply, "But, senor, I still have the sunset!" Was Van Dyke right?...

MEXICAN BABY'S FUNERAL

In Guatemala we used to watch Mayan skill with native dyes. Their native indigo, different from the Asiatic plant, was grown for blue. Cochineal from *nopal* gave scarlets. Yellows came from boiling fustic. Browns were carefully brewed over mangrove charcoal. Thus they dyed their cotton.... Even warlike Apaches had a well-developed color technique, with every rainbow shade. Use of red, also yellow ochre was common among Amerinds from New York's Iroquois to Montana's Blackfeet. Aztec garden's color use has been described elsewhere by this author.

Sir Grafton Elliott Smith told writer he was convinced widespread Oriental appreciation of jade, with belief in its magic properties, was a manifestation of color-love. Certainly use of inlaid emeralds in interior decoration of Cuzco's Temple of the Sun was based on appreciation of their green, contrasted yellow of gold wallplates. This writer can forget neither the charm of a headdress of macaw feathers he once excavated in Peru, nor of the Montezuma feather cloak he located in a German museum. . . . Watch the great Paris designers, from Worth to Schaparelli. They are as much Grand Masters of color as were Italy's or Holland's mediaeval oil painters. They produce marvelous gowns for as varied subjects as an English earl's daughter, a Cairo odalesque or an Ecuadorian *haciendado's* squaw-like wife. . . . Was Van Dyke right? And do we not grow our garden flowers because of a very deep spiritual urge?

In these days when our U.S.A. is continually extending its imitations of canny Prince Bismarck's ideas about old age security, there is one form of senescence insurance that is tragically seldom considered. It is happiness insurance. Its premium? Adopting a hobby in at least early middle age.

FLOWER DECORATION HOBBY
One that CAN commence in childhood is rooted in juvenile nature study in the garden. Then when Romeo and Juliet commence homemaking, it becomes very useful. It is floral decoration. Today our home is colorful with masses of golden acacia bloom, broad fatsia leaves in the foreground. Backstage are long branches of myrtle foliage. For the focus-point the canon requires, a bunch of purple heather. All this with the acacia-gold color scheme projected thru the rooms with table bowls of Soliel d'Or narcissus, blended with emphasizing paperwhites or tazettas.

This hobby is as useful in making and holding friendships as any studied parlor trick. When your chateline's friend is planning a luncheon or a dinner, offer to take an hour from your desk to furnish and arrange her floral decoration.

And when you are deeply absorbed in this hobby, as you easily can become, some summer vacation, take the plane and your Sweetheart for Japan, and get their ideas about not only gardening in general, but about floral decoration. It is reduced to a Code over there. No *"noblesse oblige"* in the days of chivalry was more exacting.

"If you have your nose on the grindstone rough,
And you keep it down there long enough,
In time you will say there is no such thing
As brooks that babble and birds that sing,
Then these will all your world compose:—
Just you, that grindstone, and your poor old nose."

One's garden, with "miracles" at every yard along the trail, is a salve for a painful "grindstone nose". Am studying a lush Eschscholtzia plant. It has a 2-foot diameter, glaucous-green foliage with some 30 deep ORANGE blossoms today. Its beauty is gripping. An 8-year old enjoys it as much as an octogenarian. There is, nevertheless, a something even more gripping, very tantalizing. This, however, to the octogenarian—not the kiddie:—Why is that foliage glaucous green, those petals, ORANGE? Nearby grow calendulas also with ORANGE flowers. Beyond in the vegetable garden carrots-roots, ORANGE. Still further, an ORANGE tree.

Beside that poppy are BLUE forget-me-nots, BLUE scabiosas. (We had planted, indeed, for an orange-blue contrast. We can gain this color effect. We cannot however produce BLUE poppies (tho' Tibet can). We cannot obtain orange forget-me-nots tho' Amsinka, (a native borrage), comes always true-to-seed with orange corollas. Yet the soil is the same. Just for experiment, the exact 1952 poppy area was planted 1951, also 1953 to forget-me-nots. Not one poppy could extract blue dye from the soil!

As this is written, one reflects upon a container of branches of a rosepink gladiolus from the garden. The original sprays were of a lovely deep cerise. As the flowers toward the tip developed indoors and without sunlight, they became first a sickly anemic pink, finally pure white. In other words, denial of sunlight meant a real loss. Does this not stimulate reflection upon a similar anemia in the civilizations of such countries as Hindustan and Ceylon? The Orient is a vast man-dominated area. Women's place in the scheme of things is simply that of what might frankly be called a breeding machine. Even in the Moslem lands the theory that she no more has a soul than a burro or a camel.

A CHINESE PROVERB SAYS: "TIGERS AND DEER DO NOT STROLL TOGETHER." Does this not hold as to any reconcilement of Soviet and our ideals?

THOUSAND-HANDED KWANNON

Did some longforgotten Buddhist priest, contemplating the philosophy of an aster bloom, grasp that cooperation made for more human happiness than antagonism? This question arose as We-2 one day, stood before the shrine of Kwannon, the thousand-handed.

> Of all the floures in the mede,
> Than love I most these floures white and rede,
> Soch that men callen daisies in our toun.
> (Chaucer—Canterbury Tales)

Chaucer loved the daisy but probably never thought of it in terms of cooperation. Life in England then was parochial. It took the centuries from Chaucer to Kipling to give us the concept of "The everlasting teamwork of every bloomin' soul". In all English literature is there any sentence more pregnant with possibilities than this?

Man is learning from the biota of his environment the value of using such survival mechanisms as scent and color. One example of latter is his use, only as recently as this 20th century, of camouflage in war. Another result of learning to read in Mother Nature's book is recognition of tendency to flock. We are learning that gregariousness has a survival value for humans as well as for a herd of tusker elephants, for a flock of blackbirds, for even a school of fish. Dr. Ross (Principles of Sociology) in chapter on Cooperation mentions collective hunting of forage by the buffalo, and, in humans, common upkeep of highways and bridges. The expanded family, the Roman

MAN IS GREGARIOUS

gens, the Highland clan, the Chinese village (usually kin) gives one we-feeling and sense of security. Of course there are individuals who feel safer alone. Hermits for example. And some lone-wolf criminals. Do you recall the darky in New Orleans police court charged with stealing a timepiece? The jury found him not guilty. "What's dat mean, Judge?" "It means you go free". "Does dat mean ah gotter gib de watch back?"

> "Gardener, for telling me this news of woe,
> I would the plants thou graftest would never grow."
> (Richard II, Act 11, Scene 4)

Acacia has an honor post in our garden. Dad, being Australian-born, secured years ago, from kin "Down Under" an early-blooming strain. We call same "New Year's Acacia." More than once it has showed some golden bloom at the year-end. Thus, in January, we know what Cuthbertson meant by his lines, "The Bush": "Give us the wattle's gold". We cut and distributed to friends dozens of bouquets. A passing motorist from Chicago kodachromed his redcoated subdeb daughter with that cascade of gold as a background.

MASSED BLOOM

Today I am trying to estimate, by counting a sample area, the number of our New Year acacia's blooms. The computation? In that one tree, of the dainty fuzzy that Aussie artists convert into babies with dots and dashes for eyes, mouth, nose, there are 12,000,000 flowers. We humans are fascinated by the color mass. What about possible pollenizing insects—or, even birds.

My Australian field notes mention treeferns, eucalypts, bottle-brush trees, flocks of red parrots, cockatoos, wallabys, even a platypus. Curiously these jottings make little mention of insect-flower interaction:—a matter always elsewhere of fascination. The other Australian problems, such as relation by Down Under fuchsias with those of the Andes—of the evident connection of the floras of Australia and South Africa to have blotted out the 6-footed. However, writer asks himself whether, in worldwide botanizing, did he ever find a 12,000,000 flower concentration on one plant. Imagine the value of such concentration. Elsewhere he has described the color power of toyon or California Christmas berries in attaching a flock of robins across a couple of miles of the American River canyon. If that made for survival thru seed transport, imagine the magnetic effect of 12,000,000 colorful, sweetscented blooms on 1 tree.

Selection, Survival   223

"BEFORE" AND AFTER'S "BEFORE"

A half century ago writer was in the saddle for days on trails thru forest like this. Many of these trees climbed 200 feet into the Blue. Today they are gone— and, on his ranches in the Great Valley below, each year there is new heavy expense for ever deeper wells, even heavier pumps. The water table annually drops because no great sponge of forest litter longer holds snow or rain.

Cooperation thru conservation is replacing the former waste in lumbering. Our National Forest system has been created. Few lumber companies longer cut, slash, burn, then abandon acreage as not worth paying taxes. Today they cooperate with timber farms on which lumber becomes a crop.

> You cannot forget, if you would, those golden kisses
> all over the cheeks of the meadow, queerly called
> DANDELIONS.
>
> (Henry Ward Beecher—Star Papers)

While We-2 were on field study at CroMagnon, we paused to rest on a couple of wayside boulders. Across the road, stonemasons were working. Along came a tramp. One mason was about to light a cigarette. The hobo snatched it from him, snapped it into halves, gave him back one half, kept the other. Then he growled: "The world's wealth is too concentrated. You have a cigarette. I have none. I equalize matters by force!" Here was class hatred, by a typical unsocial, noncooperator.*

COOPERATING COMPOSITES Of all the enlightenment the gardening philosopher wins from contemplating his garden's biota, nothing, perhaps is more impressive than the evolution of flowering plants. Many botanical keys place Renunculaceae at the column base, the Compositae at the summit. Carnegie Institution's Dr. Clements' "Flowers of Coast and Sierra", has a front piece in colors. It shows the evolutionary rise, from Buttercups, thru Roses, Saxifrages, to Composites' tribes at the summit.

The Buttercups usually have one blossom at the stem-apex, like St. Simeon Stylites, atop his pillar. Compare any Composite, such as Dr. Beecher's "golden-kissed" dandelions. They not only exhibit cooperative herding, but division of labor between ray flowers and disk flowers. The constant succession of massed composites in the garden reminds one how those who cooperate are surviving, while those who do not tend toward extinction.

Further evidence of survival thru cooperation is in our illustration of CroMagnon wild horses of Caveman Time. A hungry lioness might successfully battle with one wild horse. Equine survival depended upon strong herd instinct. Note strategy of circled horses, biting and hoof weapons all toward the enemy. This mathematically, is the technique of African elephants. This method also was successfully employed by our Covered Wagon forbears against Indian attack. Scouts warning of an approaching redskin war party, Covered Wagons swung into a circle. Women, children in the center, the riflemen lay prone beneath the wagonbeds, fired thru wheel spokes. (See page 248)

March faded yesterday into April. This morning, at 10:30, has sufficient WARMTH that the black carpenter bees are at work at the cascade of Wisteria racemes. There is an 18-foot waterfall of the lavender blooms which contrast beautifully with the cream colored climbing roses at its side. At sunrise no bees were there. WARMTH is necessary to stimulate the 6-footed into activity.

What a part WARMTH plays in human life! Victor Hugo writes of an elderly man basking in the WARMTH of a cottage's sunnyside. A friend has just been praising the "WARMTH OF GREETING" when she arrived for a house party in the country. Then later she observes. "Mrs. .... is probably the ugliest woman in the valley. But one soon forgets it. She has almost unique ability TO BREAK THE ICE when things drag at a gathering.

---
* Why not reread Harvard's Dr. Lothrop Stoddard's "Revolt Against Civilization?"

Selection, Survival

The Garden Philosopher watches the sufficiently WARM bees at the wisteria. He thinks of how the fireplace has cheered **WARMTH** since the Caveman first scratched a mammoth on Cro-Magnon cave walls. He dreams of a brotherhood of all living things,—of even babies and bees—a brotherhood possible because of what is enjoyed in common. If we can learn this, can we not achieve the War-less World?

NATCHEZ DUELLING GROUND

One charming Chateline said:—"My grandfather's brother, a brilliant young man, died on Natchez duelling ground in an affair of mistaken honor." She continued "You, also, see philosophy in your gardening. Dare I suggest you complete your Natchez visit by going out to our old duelling ground? It may inspire you to redouble your efforts to work to lengthen the periods between wars and toward someday the outlawing of war as a means of settling national disputes as completely as has been the Duel as a way of settling individual quarrels."

Sunflowers instinctively turn to the Orb of Day. Daisies close when skies become gray ... Goethe Bank and its subsidiary corporations had a clerical force of considerably over one hundred. It was this author's responsibility to manage that staff. It was the largest force of its kind in the West of that day. Especially so for a backwater town like Sacramento, still fighting to retain its State Capitol, and with but one sizeable industrial plant, the Southern Pacific Shops.

BY FEAR? OR BY LOVE?

One day the Sacramento principal department store owner called. Writer's private secretary in a sudden emergency had to interrupt for instructions. As the secretary left the merchant commented "Studied you intently during that interruption. Your technique spells eventual disaster. You evidently have never learned how to rule by fear!" The answer was "In the Goethe staff, we 'rule' (tho' we do not like that word), NOT BY FEAR BUT BY LOVE."

Anyone who has seen in his garden the momentary agony of a towhee too far from cover as a bullet hawk (Accipter) strikes ...

anyone who has seen sunflowers turn lovingly to the risen sun knows, in a way never to be forgotten, the difference between management BY FEAR contrasted with BY LOVE. Gardening philosophy, carried into office management, is worthwhile. It gives spiritual contentment. Even with the type whose only sensitive nerve leads, not to his heart but to his billfold—administration based on LOVE, in lieu of FEAR, pays material dividends. There are "extras" too, if one can appreciate the spiritual dividends.

It was in a Natchez garden that its Chatelaine remarked: "Before you leave, go out to our old duelling ground. We have learned from our sunflowers individual cooperation instead of duelling." Vicksburg up the Mississippi ever reminds us how we lost forever thru that avoidable Civil War some of Dixie's best human strains. "How long," she asked, "will nations learn the less of our golden Coreopsis that cooperation pays that we can avoid wars as we have duelling. My grandfather's brother, a brilliant young man, died on Natchez duel ground in an affair of mistaken honor."

"HOLD THE FRONT LINE TRENCHES" . . .
"THEY SHALL NOT PASS!"

Shortly after Armistice Day 1918, this author stood, with a French officer, (who had served in Verdun fortress), on the rim of this trench. This Gaul came from an old Royalist family—loathed the Bonapartists—was skeptical about the French Republic. He was one of those brilliant intellects that brighten French salons. He said "We vowed, as to the Crown Prince's troops:—'THEY SHALL NOT PASS!' Nor did they! But at what cost to France! Much of what was left of French leaders stares out of the eye sockets of such skulls. We have had war after war—mostly needless, as for Bonaparte glory. Napoleon ever took our best—left the stupid man-with-the-hoe to breed morons. The mobs of 1789 guillotined not only Lavoisier and Malesherbes, (of whom you speak so admiringly), but thousands of those who made France intellectually supreme before all the world. That old stock had adequate families."

Selection, Survival

SHRAPNEL FROM VERDUN (WORLD WAR I)
Above is a paperweight on this writer's desk. Walking across Verdun battlefield shortly after Armistice Day, 1918, it was given him by a French officer. "That bit of shrapnel ended the life of my dearest friend, one of France's most brilliant intellects. Take it with you to America. You may find it of value in stressing the need of longer periods between wars!"

Any garden-philosopher knows it is the COOPERATIVE flowers that are winning out in an evolutionary sense.

It is Washington's Birthday. The garden is gorgeous with Calendulas, golden contrasted with orange. This wealth of bloom, because of careful planning:—(a) buying the best seed from seedmen successful in selection (b) planting in August with the aim to have opening buds at St. Valentines Day.

WAR Careful planning? The Garden Philosopher asks himself. Can mankind not do as well in outlawing war? In Switzerland, birthplace of the Red Cross, is an art gallery aimed to educate with oil paintings. In Sweden, Nobel instituted the Nobel Peace prize.
The world however has seen, since 1914, World War I and II, the Cold War with our dead in Korea, France's in IndoChina. What is faulty with our planning?

Is it bad seed? Is it a lack of eugenic vision? The 1954 Berlin Big Four Conference has just ended in another deadlock. The trouble is at the Kremlin. This writer, who was at the Russian Border at one of the worst blood purges, dares ask, as he looks at the cooperation of calendulas in his garden of daisies a-bloom in his lawns, whether the ideal cooperation can be expected from Moscow.

Can 3,000,000 intelligent Kulaks be liquidated, can the Katlyn Massacre destroy Poland's intelligentsia, can leadership in Czechoslovakia, Hungary, Roumania, Latvia, Esthonia, Lithuania be systematically destroyed, can the Kremlin plot the elimination of 15,000,-000 Chinese who dare think . . . can all this occur and there still be between Iron Curtain and Bamboo Curtain a trustworthy populationmass—a peoples intellectually capable of detesting the brutality of war?

The ruthless type that could destroy a Vavilov cannot be expected to be free from Lust-for-Power. Ask the daisies, the Coreopsis, the Gallardias, the Sunflowers. If you can hear their voices, they are telling you only COOPERATION spells progress.

In Seville, We-2 were studying bullfighting. This, with the aim to try to substitute therefor the less cruel American baseball. My Beloved became ill with Mediterranean sorethroat. She was confined to her room in our hotel facing the Plaza de San Ferdinando. As a little girl, she had enjoyed the music of yesteryear's organgrinder with his little red-capped monkey who collected the donations. As she was suffering considerable pain, writer used to toss out coppers to the organgrinder below. This brought him regularly every afternoon.

ORGANGRINDER WAYS

On Sunday, however, 2 grinders appeared. Apparently one owned the route for Monday, Wednesday and Friday. The other had Tuesday, Thursday and Saturday. Sunday being a day when crowds were more numerous, they both appeared. One played Carmen. (The Plaza de Toros was but 2 blocks distant). The other ground out, simultaneously, selections from "The Barber of Seville". This disharmony was so excruciating, this author finally had to pay both of them to go elsewhere. Is not lack of harmony at the bottom of many marriages, often hastily made, which wind up in the divorce court? . . .

The success in cooperation of the sunflower family stimulates philosophizing about the races which have or have not learned to cooperate. This author's family's dealings with the Chinese, both in pioneer California and in China and the visits of Us-2 to the Celestial Empire, make more profound this admiration.

Chinese cooperation is based upon a sense of commercial honor that may be worth reflection. Dare there be recorded here an anecdote? One of our family's ranches is a Bartlett pear orchard in the Sacramento River Delta. It was leased to a Chinese outfit on cash rent. The rent was payable in the fall after the crop had been marketed. One day the head Chinese came to the family dwelling with 2 sacks of gold twenties. (This was when our Government was on an honest hard money basis and when the possession of gold had not become a crime). Chan laid on the table 1 sack, holding the other in his hand. He said:—"Please count it". It was the stipulated annual rent. Then

Selection, Survival

he said:—"Now please count this" and laid down the other, and larger sack of double eagles. When questioned as to what he meant, he replied:—"This year pears catchee good market. We makee pay what we think more better".

It is that sense of cooperation—this time thru honesty, that one learns is successful in sunflowers and in commercial life. Writer in various parts of Japan noticed that the tellers in Japanese banks at the turn of the century always were Chinese. Asking an elderly Chinese the reason, he replied simply:—"It is not your Christianity, it is just survival. In China the man who does not cooperate, who tries to substitute stealing for honest labor becomes blacklisted in public opinion . . . He gets no job. He and his family starve to death."

KAFFEENEONS
Here is an item about a Constantinople wisteria at a *Kaffeeneon* . . . and about a sunflower. U. S. A. today has "Koffee Kups" from Delaware to Oregon. England had them when Charles II tried to suppress them as "centers of treasonable plottings." The real coffee house is Mohammedan. In fact the scientific name of the bush with the stimulating "bean" indicates its type locality was Arabia. George Ade's yesteryear's "Fables in Slang" contained the history of a married couple that failed to "MOCHA and Java."

When We-2 lived in Constantinople our favorite was the *Kaffeeneon* of the Wisteria. Just how old was its twisted vine no one knew. In Spring it had 10,000 lavender racemes. There, to sip coffee together, we met our friends, the Intellectuals. They were British, American, Turkish and a few Armenian Christians. Thus one had, finally, a composite picture of Byzantine life. Of all that we heard, we saw, nothing was more indelibly impressive than the history of the Crescent displacing the Cross of Sancta Sophia. It is a tale of failure to cooperate, a failure that damaged, and still damages the Christian Church.

The *Kaffeeneon* of the Wisteria was out near the Golden Gate, built by Theodosius. This emperor called the assembly of 345 bishops. They were to decide who was the foremost among the Bishops of Rome, Antioch, Jerusalem, Alexandria, Constantinople. There WAS a truce but the quarrel continued. This, until Bajazet's scimitars in 1396 cut to pieces 100,000 Christian Knights at Nicopolis. Bajazet boasted he soon would stable his horse in Rome's St. Peters. For 57 years the Greek Church appealed to the Roman Church for aid. ROME FAILED TO COOPERATE. In our own lifetimes we were at Sancta Sophia during the celebration of Ramadan and of Biram.

The Christians by the Tiber might, in the 1450s, have learned something about cooperation by studying a sunflower.

Marxism must eventually fail because it preaches Class Warfare. This, unless it succeeds in world wide liquidation of ALL leaders. We-2 were in Korea after the close of the Russo-Japanese War. The Japanese militarists then were in ruthless control. Their policy was to absolutely exterminate all Koreans. This, to fill up the country with Japanese, possible with their "baby-a-year" strategy. The distressed Koreans were abandoning Buddhism. Barnacled with superstitions, it did not satisfy. Christianity did give them hope.

THE CHURCH'S ECUMENICAL MOVEMENT Unfortunately, the 4 Christian denominations were competing at all strategic points. A conference was held in Seoul. They there decided on "the Cross over Korea." A remarkable granite outcrop marked the crossing of Great North-South Road with Great East-West Road. The cross formed by these 2 grand trunk highways should delineate areas assigned to each of the 4 denominations.

Beloved Bishop Harris said: "You youngsters go back to U. S. A. and tell them how we are making ecumenical American Church history out here in Korea." Out of that came the founding by Us-2 of the Sacramento Church Council, also California Church Council, likewise, later, our participation in financing a City-and-State Commission of the Federal Council. Its plans resulted in hundreds of councils across U. S. A.

"The seed I have scattered
In springtime with weeping,
And watered with tears
And with dew from On High
Another shall shout
When the harvesters, reaping,
Shall gather my grain
In the Sweet Bye-and-bye." (Old Hymn)

A Glasgow man tells this story of an Aberdeen lad:— He was courting a pinkcheeked lassie. He suddenly became silent. Maggie said:—"A penny for your thoughts, Sandy." "Was thinking I would like a kiss." . . . Thereafter, another silence. Maggie, hoping for that all-important question, remarked:—"And of what be ye a-thinking noo, Sandy?" "Was wondering how long ye'd be keeping me awaitin' for that penny." As to the part Thrift plays in Survival, can one not learn much from plants, both garden and *sauvage?* Note how thrifty

THRIFTY MOTHER NATURE, BEAT THE SCOTS TO THE "PATENT OFFICE" Mother Nature is with some polygonums, also sedums. The radical rosetted leaves do all the work thru one summer. It thus gets ready for next summer's flowering. This, so that there can be efficient seedmaking. Note, however, that when the plant is ready for flowering that the stalk which shoots up, (sometimes 1½ to 2 feet), is often absolutely leafless.

Thrift is "preached" everywhere in one's garden. One sees it in the moisture-conserving, rosette of radical leaves of the artichokes. It is apparent in the amount of blue coloring on the feather a bluejay drops in the path. It has just enough and no more azure for camouflage needs.

When the garden-philosopher adds item to item like above (sedum, artichoke, blue jay) to his note book, he is puzzled as to how long his native land can be as prodigal as that son of scripture who, inheritance gone, was reduced to eating the husks of the seed pods right now dangling from the Saint John's Bread tree in his garden. Such national waste includes the bill for alcoholics (greater than that for education), for gambling (many times that for either church support or for research that can reduce disease).

Is there any lesson that impacts more deeply, more persistently upon the garden-philosopher's thinking than that of the SURVIVAL value of COOPERATION? Constantly he is reminded, by his garden flowers, that the dandelion tribe, thru cooperation, is distancing the ranunculus and the poppy clans. This, just as these two shouldered the algae into insignificance. One forgets a glass of water on a sunny toolhouse shelf, comes back after a fortnight's vacation and notices the green spirogyra growth. The sunflower outside the tool house, nine feet high and assertive with golden blooms, boasts "we cooperated and we are the successful!"

ALGAE, THRU POPPIES, TO THE SUNFLOWERS

Any couple who saw years fade into decades, trying to do their bit to weld into a fighting weapon the various elements of their Protestantism, know that the Path Upward (paralleling the path from algae thru ranunculus to sunflower) is beset with thorny weeds. In that task, it is necessary to have Faith — Faith and Hope. And, moreover, to never forget the precept "Be not weary in well doing." The gardener knows the need of intelligent discrimination in order to obtain the best results. So, too, the Gardening-philosopher comes to understand the strategy of Selection that there can be Survival. . . .

The jungle roof, seen from a plane, is like a gigantic Oriental carpet unrolling along endless miles of color. This is due to evolutionary struggle upward, for sunlight energy, also insect pollenization, out of often midnight-black tangle of vegetation between jungle floor and jungle roof. This lush growth is so matted that, in Java, we found rattan palms of amazing length. They snaked their way thru the vegetative

JUNGLE ROOF

congestion, always toward some light. Some such rattans, though indescribly slender, sometimes actually had a length double the height of California's tallest Sequoia.

But why go to those disease-breeding South Java jungles to observe this reaching for sunlight, — this *zeilstrebigkeit?* One can find it in one's own garden:— One August we observed a hitherto unnoticed stray gray growth in an 8-foot myrtle screening hedge, in its massed emerald green. "Hello! Here's a discovery. A fungus disease on myrtle. Something new to Science." It was, however, no fungus, indeed no myrtle. It was a glaucous-green Tibetan cotoneaster. Some robin, or waxwing, had finished his dinner atop those 8-foot myrtles, dropped a cotoneaster seed. It sprouted. Then, under *zeilstrebigkeit,* it followed its urge toward sunlight until we had 5 feet of a leadpencil narrow cotoneaster. The garden continually exhibits new evidences of the struggle for survival.

The German botanist Strassburger describes certain research by Saussure and du Trochet and the disbelief therein of Liebig. Dr. Strassburger then asserts emphatically "Plants MUST breathe in order to live". A simple experiment in plant respiration can be made by taking two "teel" bottles. These are conical, having a 2½ inch base and at the cork, a "lead-pencil" sized stem or a 3/8 inch one. Both bottles were brimfilled on a 103° shade temperature July day. Into one was placed an acanthus stem. While this is not as much desert-adjusted as a cactus, this stem had 11 flowers. The other bottle had no flower. After 24 hours, the flowerless bottle, level had lowered 1/8 inch thru evaporation. That with the acanthus stem had dropped 1¼ inch. Would not the difference of 1 1/8 inch represent the respiration that the great Liebig doubted?

On this desk is a comment, (and accurately so), on alien Klaus Fuchs as "the deadliest spy in all history". In this connection one dares question the philosophy of certain Hyphenates in our midst. Coming from European areas where living standards are far below ours, they persist, year after year, in criticizing Immigration Control. When the Quota Acts of 1921-22-24 were being debated, they objected to any U. S. A. registration of aliens as "insulting" to the "unfortunates to whom we had granted asylum." This, despite all, even native born, having to register to vote, or to obtain an automobile license. This powerful group, numerically small, but masters in politics, blocked any Registration of Aliens Act until World War II was imminent. Congress then was forced to enact same for security reasons. Actually we trailed even Turkey, yes, Persia herein! Today millions of Americans still gulp down Hyphenate propaganda.

Selection, Survival

Wallflowers, which grow wild in France, stimulated memories of how France's coal area furnished this one act drama:— Shortly after World War I, We-2 made certain Western Front studies from Flanders and France to the Tyrol. Puzzled as to a byroad's direction, I had our chauffeur stop at a gate, side entrance of new home. Its cost had been contributed by a charitable but fanatical American environmentalist. She insisted better surroundings solved all problems. Hence, the cureall was:—replace the miserable, war-destroyed coalminers' huts with Los Angeles' bungalows . . .

CONSERVE HUMAN MUTANTS

In answer to my knock came, to this side door, a coalminer's wife and a brood of children. It was impossible not to see the bathroom. Its enamelled tub was filled with coal. Writer expressed surprise. She countered with "Why not? We chastise ourselves once a year in Lent with that awful annual bath. Isn't that enuf? But, that thing built into the house, IS handy to store coal."

One thought of the environmentalist widow, also remembered the observation of a sage:— "It is not the slums that make the slum-people. It is the slum people that make the slums . . ."

As We-2 left that bathtubbed cottage, we discussed a conversation long forgotten. Visiting our friend, that wisest of Gardeners, the late Luther Burbank, he conducted us along a garden path. In his eschscholtzia area, he watched for desirable color-mutants. Author of "Training the Human Plant", he said:— "ONE THING I KNOW, (BUT I CANNOT HAMMER IT INTO OTHER HEADS). WATCH FOR MUTANTS!" He had worked out for himself, (and independent of DeVries), the whole Garden Philosophy of the mutant. As to humans, it was the philosophy of the Gifted Child.

In another part of California, beloved Dr. Lewis Terman also was absorbed in similar research. Mr. Burbank "couldn't hammer it into other heads." At this writing one senses that herein Dr. Terman has succeeded. At least one thinks one sees beginnings, in Eastern U. S. A., of a change. The movement holds as much promise as did the supervised playground movement as a substitute for child labor a half century ago. . . .

WATER HYACINTH CHOKING IRRIGATION CANAL
The delicate lavender of water hyacinth HAS color appeal. This, just as much as the sob-stuff stories about Displaced Persons which proceeded bullying Washington into rushing shiploads of aliens into U. S. A. without what some students of immigration control consider proper screening. It is noticable that the names of most traitors betraying U. S. A. military secrets to Russia are those of aliens. Among first generation ones is Displaced Person Klaus Fuchs. Among second generation one the Rosenbergs, also Harry Dexter White, whose real name still is a matter of debate. What billions would have been saved American taxpayers if the Soviet had needed four additional years to solve the secret of our atomic bomb.

"Nothing teems, but hateful docks, rough thistles, kecksies, burs, losing both beauty and utility." (Henry V, Act V. Sc. 2)

"Other seeds fell upon thorns, AND THE THORNS GREW UP AND CHOKED THEM." (ST. MATTHEW XIII:7)

THE "BEAUTIFUL" WATER HYACINTH

Whether a plant reproduces by seeds or by slips, a nation must ever be alert to watch its migration past our borders. An American woman, traveling in yesteryear's Java, saw a "beautiful" wildflower. It was a water-lily. It had numerous spikes of lavender blooms. Delighted, she had "slips" sent to her Southern garden. Her fishpool always thereafter brought exclamations of pleasure from enraptured guests . . . Being an idealist, she wanted everybody from Savannah and Palm Beach to Memphis, New Orleans, Galveston to share in her find. She was wealthy. She was quick to translate ideals into action. She employed men, therefore, systematically to drop water-hyacinth slips into rivers from South Carolina to Louisiana. . .

Today any garden-owner from Miami to Shreveport can have Javanese water-hyacinths from nearby streams. The pest has spread even to the sloughs of California's hot Sacramento Valley. Recently your editor went to Florida to bring his Everglades data up-to-date. On his first visit there, the Everglades had not been drained. There

Selection, Survival 235

were only trails thru the ripping sawgrass. Transportation was by tiny steamers. These threaded the bayous. Trees brushed cabin windows. One COULD, however, traverse Florida by water. Our photograph shows a hyacinth-blocked stream. The wild turkeys along its banks once were startled by steamer's whistle. Today, it is abandoned to the highly prolific weed from Java.

Floridians fought a costly war against the water-hyacinth. They first tried poisoning the plant. They then found they were losing their fisheries. They next sunk tens of thousands of dollars cutting. "Worse'n skunks" the "crackers" complained. They finally resorted to pasturage. The cattle seemed to relish the coolth. However, "no milk, no meat" grumbled the cattle owners. As this is written, Florida has hung up the white flag of surrender. The water hyacinth has walloped the flag of Dixie.

Should not the above story warn us that there can be BLUNDERING IDEALISTS? . . .

HOARY CRESS CAN REMOVE RICHEST LANDS FROM TAXROLL

The Gentle Carpenter of Nazareth often spoke in parables. He reminded his countrymen who tilled the soil not to expect a crop of "grapes from thorns, figs from thistles". Eugenists find much in His teachings. In fact your editor's conversion to investing his life therein came from reading his pocket testament where the Sermon on the Mount was preached.

Is not all life a struggle of Seeds against the Weeds? Hoary Cress, undesirable alien, is one of California's most detested weeds. There is almost no successful eradication technique. It is said one county is offering ranchers 5 years excused from taxation when fighting hoary cress. One method is drowning as per above illustration.

Hoary cress never should have been permitted entry here. Is it not the same way with humans? Scarface Al Capone would never have entered U. S. A. had we had immigration control such as long was suggested by the late Dr. H. H. Laughlin. He insisted "Admission is equivalent to the gift of a fortune. Therefore, we have a moral right to demand family records of 20 blood kin. This, overseas, would locate gangsters."

NOTICE TO DESTROY WEEDS

Notice is hereby given that on ——— JUN 1 1943 ——————
the City Council of the City of   passed a resolution declaring
that noxious or dangerous weeds were growing upon or in front of
the property on this ————————— ———— Street.

WEED NOTICE

In Barbados, where they serve delicious flying-fish dinners, this author was told that island is the only area in the entire world that is absolutely free from weeds. The boast there is that any sprout never lives long enuf to produce its rapidly-multiplying seeds.

Recently some thinkers were discussing the abuse by naturalized American citizens of their admission to our land of highest living standard. The remark was made:—"We give these people hospitality, then they want to grab everything in sight." It reminds me of a current story of a platter of 2 fish served a couple of Scots. Sandy helped himself to the biggest fish. Donald said:—"Where are your manners, Sandy? I would have taken the smaller." Sandy replied:—"Well, you have it, haven't you?" We invite some of these people to the table. They grab the bigger fish, to-wit:—want all restriction abolished.

WATER HYACINTH EQUIPMENT

Just as California ranchers are taxed to provide equipment to control the alien water hyacinth so they and all other Americans also are taxed the thousand-millions we now glibly quote as "billions" because there the treason of aliens granted American sanctuary, and their sons—our atomic bomb secrets were betrayed to Moscow. This enabled them to save 4 years in their race to overcome our lead with the atomic bomb.

Selection, Survival 237

"Now 'tis the Spring, and weeds are shallow rooted
Suffer them now and they'll outgrow the GARDEN
And choke the herbs for want of husbandry."
(Henry VI, Act III, Sc. 1)

In all the gospel of SELECTION, is any parable more persistent than that of The Weeds. The worthless chaff-growth that consumes as much sun-energy, as much soil energy as the wheat-plant has been with the suffering gardner since Biblical times. The lawn's Kentucky blue grass is choked out by Bermuda and Crabgrass. In the flowerbeds, dandelion, redstem compete with and displace asters, phlox, sweet william, larkspur. On the ranches hoary cress, milk-thistle, star thistle, Johnson grass, dodder, sometimes reduce earnings until red ink also displaces the black ink of profit. On our cattle and sheep ranges here Klamath weed and now halogeton* destroy pasturage as prickly pear similarly reduces profits in Australia.

"THE ETERNAL FIGHT SEEDS VS. WEEDS"

NILE WATER-JUG, CARRIED ON HEAD

Note size of jug compared with housewife's height. Filled, it makes a heavy load. "Bear ye one another's burdens." In Hong Kong cemetery this editor once was shown a famous gravestone. On it was inscribed this epitaph: "A fool lies here who tried to hurry the East." The story of that "Christian man" who "tried to hurry the Aryan Brown" is comedy . . . likewise tragedy. In Hong Kong, one is told that, like the California Gold Rush place names, this grim humor was a shock absorber. This, because of the stress of a decimating epidemic. At that time few tropical disease problems had been worked out by our researchists. . . . Why not reread Kipling's Gunga Din? On the battlefield, the "regimental bhisti, Gunga Din" brought water to the man "chokin' mad with thirst an' a bullet where the beltplate should 'a' been." The wounded soldier welcomed the "arf-a-pint o' water, green and crawlin' and it stunk". After recovery, he testified "of all of the drinks I've drunk, I'm gratefullest for one from Gunga Din." As to above researchists:—Whether in tropical disease or other pioneering on the frontiers of knowledge, they make sacrifices. These noble men, however, have to commit race suicide. This because an ungrateful world ignores why they dare have only 2, 1, or 0 children.

---

*See Readers Digest (12-53). As this is published a conference of cattlemen is being held to combat this food-destroying alien weed.

How many grasp the significance of California's population rise? 864,694 in 1880, 10,586,223 in 1950. U. S. A. already has passed the Optimum Saturation Point, where Living Standard declines. Despite this, the Hyphenates continue fighting Immigration Control. They almost prevented enactment of the 1921-22-24 Quota Acts. (Writer was one of the small group that built public opinion to secure their enactment). These Hyphenates failed about their boast "Quota Acts will be amended to death by 1930". They did delay until 1929 National Origins enforcement. They blocked, 1921 to 1939 Registration of Aliens. Now they attack McCarran-Walters Immigration Code, passed over the Truman Veto.

RADISH CONTROL TO PERMIT GROWTH OF GRAIN CROP
This illustrates the manner in which botanical plus chemical knowledge, (i.e. American Know How) can save a food crop (grain)* from choking by a weed (wild radish). Dr. Jepson's Flora of Western Middle California notes that Linneaus named Wild Radish "Raphanus" from the Greek word for "quick-appearing" on account of "the prompt germination of its seeds" . . . (It is a prime grain-choker on our ranches). Dr. Jepson further says, "Common weed, NATURALIZED FROM EUROPE".

* Read Buller's "Essays on Wheat" for history of Marquis wheat, "one of the most valuable food plants of the world." It is dramatic.

In our garden also are "Koreans". They are low, creamcolored, many-flowered chrysanthemums. They are the border for a mass of orange plus canary yellow African marigolds contrasted with clumps of lavender likewise pink Michaelmas daisies. There are some 7,000 blooms now on the massed Koreans.

Daily, since the plants were slipped last March has proceeded the back-breaking labor of weeding this border. Each sunrise means several hundred weeds of all kinds must be pulled to keep that Border ready for maximum bloom. The garden lover becomes as fanatical as to weed elimination as a wooden-shoed Volendam housewife for cleanliness. You can see one on her knees, brush, bucket and soap bar, scrubbing the dyke afront her cottage.

BARBADOES
PERMITS
NO WEEDS

Selection, Survival 239

Tired of stooping, one rests for a minute to study grass fecundity. From the matted Siberian iris has been pulled a grass in seed. It is a strangletop. The panicle has 6 arms. One has 48 seeds. After five months of daily weeding, one sneaking grass, almost unseen among the Siberians, has fruited toward trouble for next year.

Years of costly weeding both in the home garden and on author's string of ranches has brought profound admiration for the Barbadoes folk, even more than flying fish dinners and "women's tongues." On that island are permitted no weeds. Would U. S. A.'s immigration policy were such that human weeds like Traitor Klaus Fuchs were not permitted here as Displaced Persons.

One reason one enjoys one's garden is that there is only one way to travel therein—and that is—afoot.

STAR THISTLE

Star thistle is another alien weed that sneaked into U. S. A. Then, because of its high fecundity, plus its defense-needles, (discouraging any use as a forage plant) it displaced food-crops. In a reclamation district in which some of this author's ranches are situated, there was a heavy assessment for star-thistle eradication tax. Despite the expense, a few years later the infestation again was heavy . . . The most costly weeds however are humans. Scarface Al Capone allegedly enjoyed $200,000,000 ANNUAL (!) income from his commercialized vice empire with not one gangster-murderer ever hanged.

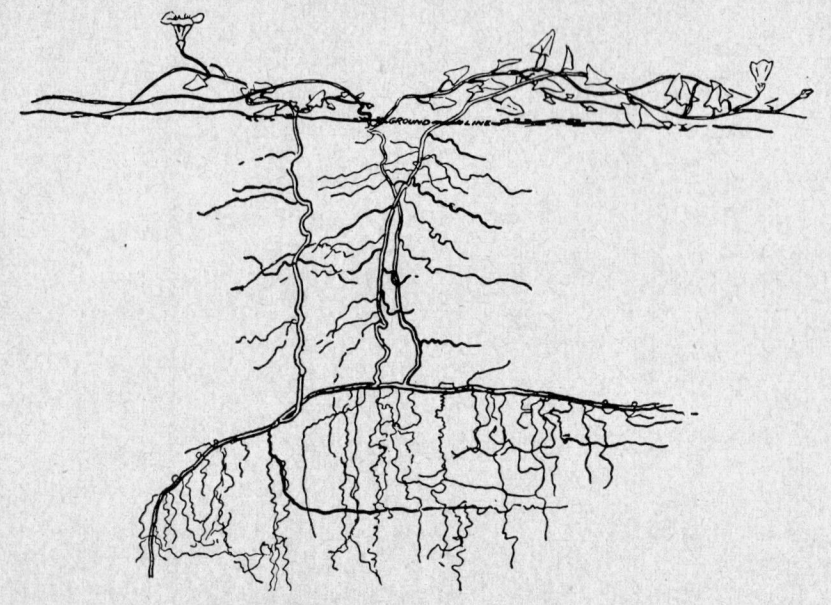

BINDWEED ERADICATION DISTRICTS

On this desk is data about the legal formation of Bindweed Eradication Districts. This alien member of the morning glory family has become a costly weed across U. S. A. Expensive tho it be, a thousand species of overseas weeds could not pile up for U. S. A.'s taxpayers the staggering national debt because one human weed, one Displaced Person, convict Klaus Fuchs, repaid our hospitality by betraying our atom bomb secrets to Moscow. Thus the Soviets gained four priceless years in overcoming our lead . . . and, with that debt, we eat hamburgers instead of yesteryear's beefsteaks.

The water hyacinth's injection into the flora of our semitropical states (Florida, Louisiana, California) is an example worth risking inclusion here because of its double value. It is a weed. It arrived thru blundering idealism.

CONTROL OF ALCOHOLISM   As to the weeds which plague the gardener and the rancher, the gardening philosopher constantly reflects upon human weeds and the manner in which they hinder Reduction of Poverty. At the present writing drunken driver deaths mount. Estimates as to their percent of highway fatalities run from 25% to 80%. This author has had more than a half-century of combatting Commercialized Vice*. There has been discussion recently as to who is more powerful — the Government of California or the Liquor Lobby at its Legislature. This week Local Option has been again voted down. The liquor profiteers were clever enough years ago to so confuse voters that latter parted with the right of local communities to deal with the control of alcohol.

The use of *massenpsychologie* strategy herein would be amusing

---
*See Senator E. E. Grant's "Red Light Padlocking." It is available at most local, also college libraries in U. S. A.

Selection, Survival 241

were it not tragic. This writer asked a church woman of great influence why she was advocating voting as the liquor profiteers wish. Her answer was, "Look at those beautiful billboards that read 'Let's make it a clean sweep' ". (They had a painting of a housewife and her broom). A prominent liquor lobbyist is alleged to have said, "Smear on the Mother stuff with a shovel and you can win enuf votes to tilt the election scales our way."

A garden-philosopher thinks of the ceaseless struggle to eliminate weeds in his garden. He recently signed a check for taxes, part of which covered cleansing the irrigation canals on his ranches of water hyacinth. And he groans under the burden of Blundering Idealists, from the woman who brought the water hyacinth from Java to the other one who worked strenuously to induce church women to vote "wet" because of "those beautiful billboards." ...

Down Under folks' rabbit problem arose because a homesick Briton, years ago, imported bunnies to remind him of "home". This caused a million headaches, annual losses of millions of pounds of sterling. Rabbit fencing across Australia failed to stop the ever-increasing horde. The rabbit, under Australian skies, is a real he-rabbit. He is as prolific as the old Tennessee Moonshiner who fathered 19 kids. The old man would boast he had "refused his mother's milk before his eyes were open, and called for a gourdful of good corn likker". U. S. A. has passed the Population Saturation point. This means sliding toward everlower Living Standards. Instead of scrapping the McCarran-Walter Immigration Act, (as alien-born Hyphenates demand), WHY NOT, FOR 10 YEARS, BAR ALL IMMIGRATION? ...

Is U. S. A. not a very different nation from 1917/21? We then had a population about 2/3 toward SATURATION. Today, we already are millions beyond saturation. Thus any addition of lowpowered morons means drift toward Chinafication. Am profoundly interested in birth control in Japan, Hindustan, Latin-America and some day, China. Do we need a League of Low-birth nations?

The Himalayan "Hills" were intensely fascinating around this century's turn because of their flora's contributions to Occidental gardens. These included "butterfly bush" (Buddlea), most valuable to one absorbed in the lepidoptera. Also from India, Tibet, Yunnan, came pyracanthas and cotoneasters that give berry-color to feast human eyes—and berry-food to fast waxwings. Some of that area's herbaceous plants also are highly prized, such as the rare blue Tibetan poppy, likewise the now very popular December-blooming pink Tibetan saxifrages.

THOSE HUMAN WEEDS:
THE GAMBLERS

We-2 hired a string of Nepalese for one expedition. Their wives and children tagged along. Midday halt meant pay-time. We had 24 coolies in our outfit. Luncheon was postponed until the gambling was over. That lasted each day until some coolie had won all. Then he would lend (at 10% monthly) to each loser the family rice-money.

Half-way around the globe was a similar occurrence in Mexican-Californian history. A certain well known family bears the name of a Spanish family, the founder, an army lieutenant. The government at Mexico City lacked silver—paid the soldiers by a land-grant. They gambled their shares among themselves until this young officer won the whole *rancho*.

Gambling in U. S. A. is almost entirely in the hands of aliens. One such, granted citizenship, allegedly "cleaned up" $9,000,000 in a few years in one type of gambling. One racketeer some years ago admitted such investments must promise 100% per annum to take the risk. If undisturbed for two years they have their capital returned and 50% per annum for the biennal term. "After that" he remarked cynically, "it's 100% per annum as long as church folk snore." Human weeds! And most come from certain areas overseas as did our first halogeton seed. If one works efficiently for the Reduction of Poverty, he soon finds himself alert as to Immigration Restriction.

The Caribbean studies covered (1) displacement of an originally white population from France's Viking departments, by a negro one, (2) The status of Puerto Ricans, hoping to prevent history repeating itself herein as to another group, (3) smuggling of aliens from Cuba. The slogan was:—"Avoid New York. Enter the open back door via Cuba". Registration of aliens has become imperative in view of increased unemployment during the 1930s great depression. . . .

"Every jackass, he t'ink he pickaninny gwine be race horse"
(Jamaica Negro folksaying)

"Heredity is what every man believes in until his only son commences to make a fool of himself." However, much the jokesmiths poke fun at Heredity, are we not piling up more facts as to its possibilities? This, from sugar beets to strawberries, from cows to carnations. One field of great promise seems to be in the elimination of such inherited diseases, as hemophilia, also Huntington's chorea.

Eugenics research has proven perhaps 16 types of blindness to be inheritable. A blind man married a woman born blind with the same disease. These had 5 children, all born blind. They, now again marrying blind mates, just as in Spain, the inherited 6-finger deformity folk always marry the same deformed type.

The displacement of yesteryear's big, family-size muskmelon by

Selection, Survival 243

the nutmeg cantaloupe, is a dramatic example of the possibilities of breeding ability in the Garden.

"Sir, didst thou not sow good seed . . . from whence . . . hath it TARES?" (Matt. XIII, 27).

Thus to the Rose, the Thistle:
Why art thou not of Thistle-breed?
Of use thou'dst, then, be truly,
For asses might upon thee feed.
(The Rose and Thistle from
the German of F. N. Bodenstedt.)

UNIVERSITY OF CALIFORNIA, DAVIS, STUDENTS IN SELECTION RESEARCH

Annually on writer's ranches are raised vegetable seeds, (carrots, lettuce, beets, peas). Seed companies may provide their experts in Selection. These uproot all low grade pea-seed plants. (Have we not Darwin's Artificial Selection?) Said experts work in gangs of 10. Your editor has accompanied them along rows of growing peas. After 60 years ranching, he today still cannot see what these keen-eyed men find in plants uprooted before seeds are set. Upon such selection depends seed companies' survival. Truck farmers quickly observe any seed company's lowered standard.

When will we use similar technique with markedly-unsocial humans? Sicilian Scarface Al Capone came to use here his Blackhand criminal methods. He built a commercialized vice machine which allegedly yielded him $200,000,000 yearly. U. S. A. blundering idealists demand relaxation of immigration screening. Such blindness is giving American taxpayers much of their present burden. Displaced Person Klaus Fuchs also was not screened. Should he ever have been allowed to enter, to betray our atomic secrets to Russia?

Those who know amoebic dysentery in the Orient shudder at unrestricted Mexican immigration. This disease gained a foothold on Mexico's west coast. Dr. Holmes writes: "At Berkeley we examined Mexicans from the quicksilver mines. About 33% had amoebic dysentery, a tremendously serious thing. When aliens come who know nothing about sanitation the tendency for all their endemic diseases to spread among our population is very great. . . .

Dr. H. H. Laughlin, eugenics expert, often consulted by Congress, gives good advice. He insisted that, to any immigrant, admission to this land of highest living standard, of greatest happiness, is the equivalent of a gift of a fortune. He declared, therefore, we should searchingly examine the history of, not only the applicant, but his family. He says this is necessary that we may accept no one as the potential parent of future Americans who does not represent a real asset.

MASS BURNING OF OPIUM PIPES

A professor in China in 1911 told this author:— "Chinese has no word for patriotism". However, true this may have been, there was a thrilling expression thereof at the 1911 overthrow of the Manchu dynasty. One manifestation of nationism was que-cutting. Another was mass-burning of opium pipes. It was thrilling to thus actually see history-in-the-making.

"There's lots of gold
In the streets I'm told
In the streets of
Sac-ra-men-to."

The only passengers on a little freighter off the Chittagong coast, We-2 had the delight of discussing the Reduction of Poverty with a canny captain. Until recently he had been, not only Captain, but Commodore of his company's entire fleet of Far Eastern freighters. His flagship was in Calcutta Harbor when orders came to load a cargo of opium for Hong Kong. He said:— "My conscience will not permit me to use my talents as a navigator to engage in the enslaving narcotics trade." The factor was furious, cabled Liverpool for instructions. The answer was "Demote him to the Karachi run". He was sentenced to command what was then called "the stinking reaches of the Persian Gulf". They say a thermometer up there, bulb in the sand can reach 160°. He remained on Karachi run until a consolidation of shipping companies brought a change.

ANOTHER HUMAN WEED: THE NARCOTIC VENDOR

Here was a FLOWERING of human character most admirable! On the contrary there are human weeds—the vendors of narcotics. One type is marihuana, the hasheesh of the Moslems. The trade in U. S. A. has grown enormously the last few decades. A garden of it allegedly was actually cultivated within a certain Western penitentiary. It was supposed to be just a weed patch. A garden-philosopher devoted to the elimination of human weeds knows that most of the *marihuana* trade is in the hands of Mexicans.

On this desk is data of an arrest of a marihuana smuggler. The article asserts that what he bought South-Of-The-Rio Grande for $150 was bringing $8,000 at retail. This, at a time when savings bank deposits pay say about 2%.

———o———

"God has framed men differently . . . Some for command . . . others husbandmen." (Plato)

A Savoy florist's showwindow was colorful with carnations. To him we showed wild clove pinks from their Savoy meadows. "One such meadow," said he, "witnessed much of plant, of human evolution. Brutish man lived there, perhaps a half million years. His progress was snail like. The lowly-revolving geological clock brought climates with faunas ranging from muskoven to hippopotami. Once he ate wild horseflesh. Later, chief food, reindeer meat."

CARNATION BREEDING

In this meadow's escarpment wall are *abris* once sheltering Neanderthaloids. A plowman there uncovered a Bronze Age axe mold for his copper-and-tin alloy. This meadow sloped to a lake. Its more intelligent Lakedwellers began to improve, by artificial selection, apples, pears, beans, peas, grains. With their fire-making and other discoveries, our airplane age was in embryo.

Prehistoric times ended. Gauls, with wild boar standards came, then Roman legionnaires tugged heavy catapults there. Later tall, goldenhaired Visigoths, blue-eyed Vandals, redbearded Burgundians, coasted, half naked, on their shields down snowy Alpine slopes. Their greatgreatgrandsons built castles. While man thus was evolving, tiny wild pinks bloomed there. Finally, up Paris-way, were kings. Warfare among nobles lessened. The arts flourished in royal castles. Gardens were started. Imaginative headgardners were alert for any larger, or more odiferous Savoyard pinks.

The contrast between today's florist's carnations and Mother Nature's work accurately is outlined in our cut. Savoyard peasants' gardens contain almost all size-graduations from small wild carnations to giant florist varieties. Some gardens there were so heavy with perfume that one noticed same when passing on a dark night, tho no blooms were visible.

Even today we have human contrasts as marked as the difference between the wild Savoyard pink and the gorgeous florist's carnation. Compare Australian blackfellow, Congo-jungle pygmy with the Franklins, the Darwins, the Pasteurs. . . . To grasp these differences DO exist, to come to know that humans CAN be improved as well as wild pinks is only the beginning. Just as man has learned to utilize the power of a distant mountain cascade to turn night into day, he now is beginning to master the mechanics of genetics.

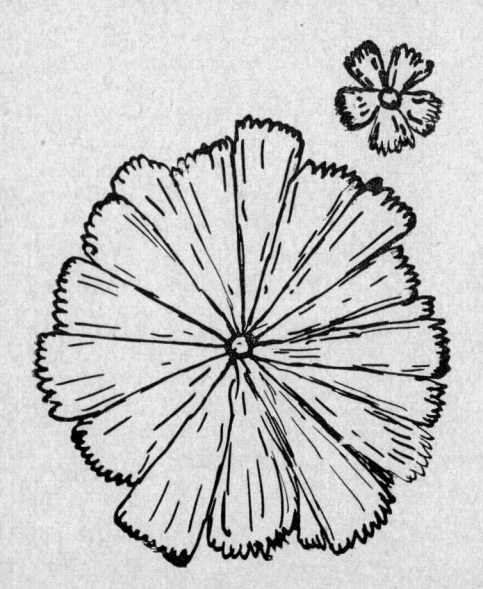

WILD CLOVE PINK, ANCESTOR MODERN CARNATION

The contrast between a wild clove pink collected by this author in Savoy, and a carnation he bought in a florist shop there is accurately shown above. That florist, (shown the wild clove pink), commented: "We French built up our fine carnations by long selection of that *sauvage* stock."

LE SEUL PAYS OÙ LA NATALITÉ ait baissé en 1938 c'est la France

Les impressionnantes statistiques de la S.D.N.

Une révolution s'est produite dans le domaine démographique : les statistiques que vient de publier la Société des Nations révèlent en effet que dans les pays « libéraux » (appelés ainsi en opposition aux pays totalitaires), où la courbe de natalité descendait d'année en année non seulement le recul a cessé, mais la courbe est redevenue ascendante. Ce redressement est vrai (comme on le constatera par le tableau des naissances ci-dessous), pour tous les pays jusqu'ici en forte dénatalité, sauf la France !

	1935	1938
ANGLETERRE	711.000	735.000
AUSTRALIE	111.000	120.000
BELGIQUE	127.000	130.000
ETATS-UNIS	2.155.000	2.300.000
FRANCE	640.000	612.000
Nlle-ZELANDE	23.900	27.200
PAYS-BAS	170.000	178.000
SUEDE	85.000	93.000

"ONLY DYING NATION IS FRANCE"

That is not exactly a translation of this clipping, but it conveys the idea. These headlines (from Paris Soir of July 25, 1939), evidence the nationwide hysteria when the League of Nations Population Office announced something startling had occurred. For the first time in West European history, a nation's birthrate-curve had dropped below the replacement level. Other headlines begged citizens to plan to have children to repeople the country. This, one editor said, "It is a question of money, also of dances and games."

THE BLUNDER IN FRENCH THINKING CONTINUES TO BE THAT IT IS COLORED BY CANNONFODDER PHILOSOPHY. THEY THINK IN TERMS OF QUANTITY, NOT QUALITY. THEY DO NOT CARE TO BE REMINDED THAT A FEW HIGHPOWERED GREEKS STOPPED THE ONSLAUGHT OF XERXES' HORDES.

HORSES WILD CIRCLE OUTWARD THEIR "DEFENSES" AGAINST ATTACKING LIONESS

In Cromagnon time, wild horses roamed France. As with zebras in Africa today, they were food for lions. When above lioness attacked the wild horses met her with what the French call the horses' **"defense."** This consisted in massing into a circle. It was, curiously, the strategy used by the Covered Wagon folk under redskin attack. It also is today the method instinctively resorted to by wild bull elephants against lion attack. They herd their cows and calves into the center.

Above Font de Gaume Grotto cave-painting is one of Man's earliest attempts at art . . . Cromagnon Man—like lions in France, like France's wild horses, (whose meat he also ate) became extinct. Should not such extinction stimulate American eugenists to consider the 1890-1940 fall of our own high-power birthrate? The census of 1940 came when all were absorbed in war. Someday one may shock us, like France in 1939, with a hysterical demand for "more babies and we don't care what kind!"

A noted Swedish eugenist cynically remarked "NO DEMOCRACY CAN BE EXPECTED TO GRASP WHAT IS HAPPENING TO ITS POPULATION UNTIL THE DAY OF DEBACLE. THEN IT WILL WILDLY DEMAND, NOT QUALITY, BUT QUANTITY." Of course he has France, (with its hysterical enactment of the Code de la Famille*) to substantiate his argument. The above is written in the Faith that there still exists in America enuf leadership to steer us past the Quantity Rock into the Quality Haven.

*See "Sierran Cabin . . . From Skyscraper". This book is in most U. S. A. public also college libraries.

"The Civil War persisted despite Dixie's food shortage" once said a Confederate "because, when hungry, we ate unripe persimmons. These so shrunk our mouths, we could live on less food!" Same results are obtainable with Europe's wild sloeplum. An Alabama negro, overseas in 1918, tasted one of its purple fruits. Spitting it out, he exclaimed, "Ah'm telling you'all! Dat berry am got a green A-la-bam' persimmon skinned half a mile!" This wild fruit, pea sized, its deep purple color helps insure distribution. Large birds gulp down its fruits whole. The tiny stone's fertility is not destroyed passing thru the digestive tract. Pits often are dropped far from the parent tree.

WILD, BITTER SLOEPLUM, FROM A ROADSIDE IN FRANCE

Selection, Survival

Neanderthal man may have been the first human to taste sloe plums. His women's repulsive hairiness, some scientists say, caused his extinction. Another theory is, that it was deficient brainpower. Dull, almost apelike, he never tried BY NATURAL SELECTION, to improve this bitter peasized plum. His successors, tall, artistic Cro-Magnons, despite their better brains, also did nothing herein. They did not invent agriculture, much less horticulture. Bronze Age man, however, had some HIGHPOWERS commencing to grasp Darwin's NATURAL SELECTION. Some European museums have found Lake Dwellings' carbonized fruits. Thus history dawns with HIGHPOWERS groping toward today's SELECTION BY BREEDING FROM THE BEST!

Since Bronze Age man hammered out swords, pins and axes of his hardened red alloy, we hardly have begun to apply this principle to humans. We, for centuries, used it on, from pigs to prunes and potatoes, from hens to horses. We CAN multiply human highpowers, as well as produce big sugarey Santa Clara prunes that disdainfully would refuse to recognize their sloe plum cousins from Southern France.

Recently research advances with such accelerated speed, we can now control the makeup of our future population-mass as surely as we can fly an airplane. Translation of above knowledge into action awaits only enlightened public opinion.

> "The males of carnivorous animals are already well armed; though to them and to others, special means of defense may be given through means of sexual selection, as the mane of the lion, and the hooked jaw of the male salmon; for the shield may be as important for victory, as the sword or spear." (Darwin)

Survival is a process under which the "seeds" displace the "weeds".

The garden's leafy, also leafless brooms* illustrate survival thru adjustment to dessicating temperatures. Such adaptations to various environments may be studied in a wide range of garden plants from stonecrop to cacti.

Here's a survival anecdote out of California's Gold Rush. Uncle Fred told about naming Dutch Flat. Hans, blond, blue-eyed German War partner to blackeyed Mike from County Kerry. (All Germans then

---
*For data upon how the buckeye, radiated under population pressure, from a moist-woodlands broadland, SURVIVES in California's hot Upper Sonoran Life Zone summers see Elfin Forest (pp. 5, 6). The book, now out-of-print, is available at most U.S.A. libraries.

SURVIVOR'S STEAK THAT FOUNDED DUTCH FLAT

were dubbed "dumb Dutchmen"). "Dutch Flat" more accurately was "German Flat." Above partner's placer was the first mining at Dutch Flat. It promised little. One morning Mike entered their cabin door. Hans was frying a bearsteak morsel. "Where's breakfast?" queried Mike. Hans woefully pointed to the 4-inch strip. "We'll cut it in two," said Hans. "No you don't" growled Mike. "It's only enough for one. We'll take it between our teeth and pull. Who tugs hardest gets it." Hans reluctantly agreed. Mike hissed between tight jaws, "Is yez ready?" Hans opened his mouth with a hearty German "Ja." Uncle Fred always insisted, however, Hans finally won. Mike, bearsteak in tummy, vamoosed for better diggings. Hans stubbornly stayed. He lived on such rabbits, quail he could shoot. Within a month he uncovered a bedrock seam. It ran into the pink rhyolite bank. Hans, tunnelling, "struck it." In about 20 feet it was full of nuggets. Dutch Flat eventually was named for this German discoverer.

ROSETTED FILAREE, NATIVE OF MEDITERRANEAN SEMIDESERTS

Botanizing in Andalusia, also Algiers, We-2 found the rosetted filaree. It has become an introduced weed on our California cattle and sheep ranges. Toward the end of spring, when most herbaceous plants had yellowed with drought, the soil below the rosette would be as moist as if it had rained yesterday. Filaree, a weed in gardens, also the cultivated artichoke, (which we found growing wild on the rock desert sloping southward to Saharan sand desert), both have evolved toward SURVIVAL thru rosetted leaf-bases.

Selection, Survival 251

Having French and British ancestors as well as German ones, this author dares record his belief that he always detested the propaganda of the *Flottenverein* leading up to World War I, also their slogan of *"Wir muessen Kolonien!"* In fact, speaking overseas for Peace, he was warned his statements regarding the Kaiser's approval of said Navy League's control of German public opinion if continued would bring his arrest for *less majeste*. His disapproval, further of Hitler, because of latter's Messiah complex, was even more deepseated. Despite this, he must ever feel sorrow because of our reported having to bomb to their death the 5,000 German scientists at Puenemunde.

That what happens in the garden is paralleled in human behavior is evident in German comments after World War II bombing. "SURVIVAL is that on which we Germans must concentrate. SURVIVAL now is all that matters."

Photograph: Courtesy American Museum of Natural History
NESTING HUMMINGBIRD (See Page 253)

Can any child better be taught Conservation than seeing, above the mangroves, the pink of roseate spoonbills against a sapphire sky? The plumage of these beautiful birds was their undoing. Some always had been shot for food. The "Key People" however, were as instinctive conservationists, as were the Redskins. Only enuf were taken to supply food needs. Then came an everincreasing demand for their colorful plumage as milady's fan. Also half-frozen Yankees came out of the snowdrifts for winter recreation. Some of these, calling themselves "sportsmen," would shoot scores apiece just as targets. In one rookery, only 3 pairs were left. Then National Audubon moved into the land of Knockemdown Key, Whiskey Jug Key, No Name Key. Their wardens enforced protective laws, until Everglades became a National Park. Reachable inexpensively by automobile, there can many children enjoy tropical nature study....

Always fascinating are those feathered helicopters, the hummingbirds. Thru the year our garden has several species:—Annas, Rufus, Purple-Throated and sometimes Calliope. One can deliberately plan for their food supply. Especially visited are such tubular-flowering plants like the tritomas or redhot pokers. Herein one observes that Mother Nature, again, in the case of the helicopter, was "first at the patent office."

An illuminating example of the use of gardens, large or small, as bird sanctuaries is the Mojeska Hummingbird Sanctuary in Southern California. It is owned by the pioneering California Audubon Society. This is a Southern California group. When it was organized as the California Society, Dr. David Starr Jordan and the author were invited to become members of the Board in order to give northern balance geographically....

Someone has said "Education is what teaches one to successfully adjust oneself to a changed environment." One tree that failed herein in Western U. S. A. is the gingko. (The practical Chinese call it "duck's foot-leaf tree"). The leaves of a neighbor's gingko, Gingko siberica, sometimes are wafted over into our garden. Its very name fascinates the eugenics student absorbed in the problem of EXTINCTION. In Dr. Knowlton's "Plants of the Past" (Chapter on "Jurassic Plants") are several illustrations of leaves of this maidenhair tree.

EXTINCTION, GINGKOS, HUMANS

Extinction can come of even globe-girdling forests, as of the great Gingko Forest, also of the vast Sequoia Forest.* Each one almost circled the Northern Hemisphere, Alaska and California, thru Kansas, Pennsylvania then Greenland to Spitzbergen, Switzerland, Siberia. Deforestation in Hindustan is so complete that often the only fuel is dung cakes. In North China, also Korea, only weed stalks remain for fuel. This has been described elsewhere by this author.

Should not the problem of Extinction, from gingkos to humans,

---

*As an example of man's acceleration of the extinction trend in the case of Sequoia, of his wanton destruction of one of its "sylvan islands" (to borrow Dr. Jepson's designation thereof) see page 111 of "Seeking to Serve", also page 48 of "What's In a Name" for the tragic destruction of the finest of all Big Tree Groves, Converse Basin. Both books, tho out-of-print, are available at most U. S. A. libraries.

Selection, Survival   253

have the careful thought of every patriotic American? Our leadership stock, largely drawn from the pioneer group, has, for several decades, been race-suiciding. Morons always breed like rabbits. The Differential Birthrates Law works far more speedily than most men grasp. We have plenty of examples of extinction, such as the great auk, the moa, the passenger pigeon. Fortunately, we also have the examples of pronghorn antelope, likewise of the egrets, showing how the comeback IS possible.

NEW ZEALAND'S MOA DEVICE

Does size affect survival? Within the memory of man, according to Maori folktales, the moa reached extinction. These giant birds were approximately twice as tall as a man. In contrast, the hummingbird persists in hundreds of species. Elsewhere this author has described finding, in Jamica, the bee hummingbird the size of his thumbnail. (See hummingbird page 251)

MEINKOPING PUEBLO'S CORN GARDENS

At Meinkoping we found survival gardening adjusted to sandstorms. Around each corn kernel was a hexagon of 6 more. All 6 might fall to the sandblasts. The center one usually survived. Thus food was assured.

"The Rose saith in the dewy morn:
'I am most fair,
Yet all my loveliness is born
Upon a thorn'."
(Rosetti: "Consider the Lilies")

Shrubs with thorns as defense mechanism are typical of such deserts as Moses' Israelites crossed between the Red Sea and the Promised Land "flowing with milk and honey." A Holy Land pilgrimage makes one better understand his Bible. When We-2 were journeying to Bethlehem, we stopped overnight at an inn. **CROWN OF THORNS** Outside was a corral of thorn. As effectual as barbwire, it was the species that had furnished Jesus' Crown of Thorns. At dusk, a shepherd drove his flock into said corral. Then he slept on the ground across its entrance. Could one ever thereafter forget "I am The Door!" Christ also asked "Do men gather grapes of thorns?" . . .

Another defense mechanism making for survival is sticky leaf secretion. (Note certain California native weeds, also Spain's cistus, or rockrose). Two rockroses grow wild in the Near East. One is white, the other pink. Both have the red blotches on their petals. Each such conspicuous red spot guides insects to its honey stores. The cistus has narrow leaves. This is characteristic of certain moisture-conserving plants. Its stems, too, are as sticky as a Californian tarweed's. This is so much so that, after a wind-storm, grains of sand adhere to the foliage and stem.

REMAINS OF ANCIENT KIVA, GRAND CANYON NATIONAL PARK
Why these Amerind villages became extinct is a problem for archaeologists. A eugenist is tremendously interested however in the type of mind that can date a similar abandoned settlement as A.D. 1298. This is demonstrated by reading tree rings indicating the cause was long continued drought. This type of intellectual is comparable to that of Champollian*, France's gifted child.

*For data on Champollian see Eugenics Pamphlet No. 88 in your local library.

As to Survival and Fecundity, one might apply the classic remark of Railroad King Harriman:—"You can't unscramble eggs!" That survival can depend upon Differential Birthrates Law is illustrated by history of the seabird colony outside San Francisco Bay's Golden Gate.

"YOU CANNOT UNSCRAMBLE EGGS"

During writer's boyhood, a regular staple in San Francisco food markets were "Farrolone eggs". These were of guillemots and murres nesting on these oceanic islands. These large eggs were almost pointed at one end. As a result, they would spin, would not roll over the cliff-edge in the gales that regularly swept these islands. Under Dr. Grinnell's clutch-number law, birds lay the exact number of eggs necessary for replacement. Herein they were far "wiser" than American intellectuals with the "2-child" birthrate of 1890-1940.

The custom of the bird harvesters was to visit the island in a body and destroy every nest with any eggs it might contain. Thus, there was no danger of partially incubated eggs affecting market demand. Immediately nest-building recommenced. The only nest material available was seaweed and the nests were rather carelessly and hastily constructed. Then egg laying recommenced. The supply of fresh eggs was assured. The amount of eggs laid under such nest-robbing is unbelievably large. One ornithologist experimented with a flicker who laid 60 odd eggs before quitting. . . .

On the trail from Nikko, with its world famous red lacquer bridge to Lake Chuzenji, we met coolie women carrying chunks of quarried rock. This was after the close of the Russo-Japanese War. We were surprised to find among them a blind burden-carrier. Even loss of sight did not prevent her having to carry the load. For this work we were told she earned, for a 12-hour day, less than 1 cent per hour.

"JOSHUA TREES"

It is the end of June. The thermometer read 97° yesterday. The weatherman threatens 100° today. Oldtimers sagely comment:—"Warming up for the Fourth of July." This warming-up process has brought a new bloom into our garden. Our yucca is hung with 77 fairy lanterns. Thrice that number of buds promise more beauty. The yucca, (alias "Century Plant") illustrates the Life Zones' theory. Yankee ship captains brought it to Massachusetts gardens. In that climate it bloomed so infrequently folks thought its flowers came one hundred years apart. Survival of the yuccas is due to several factors. One is its unique fertilization by the Pronubia moth.

Garden Philosopher

"UNCLEAN WIVES OF MANY HUSBANDS"
Polyandry is common in Tibet. It may be one method of survival thru controlling overpopulation. Overfecundity presents problems because of the fixed number of food-producing acres.

Everywhere in the garden one is impressed with its *zeilstrebigkeit*. Plant, insect, bird, is incessantly moving toward progress. Well could Victor Hugo exclaim, as herein elsewhere noted: "My religion is PROGRESS". Everywhere, as in the mechanics of the unopened morning glory, in its unfolding of bright color, of its sealing the fertilized ovum is *zeilstrebigkeit*. It also is witnessed in the coiled tongue of the butterfly, in the differientiated silks of spiders' webs, in the brightcolored flash of a pursued grasshopper, then oblivion, to the disappointment of hungry sparrowhawk. Again here is *zeilstrebigkeit*. In the muscular development of a helicoptering hummingbird feeding at a red-hot-poker flower, its muscular development, its bill structure, its feather equipment, its reduced weight, its unique iridesence that earned the sobriquet "winged jewels"—again *zeilstrebigkeit*. Always, always, always, survival based upon ever-improving efficiency.

COLOR-SCENT PLAN AND EUGENICS

"Ivy climbs the crumbling hall
To decorate decay." (Bailey—Festus.)

Decay or Survival? Or, as Hamlet put it: "To be or not to be". The will to survive, which is a dominant factor in Hertwig's *zeilstre-*

Selection, Survival

bigkeit is ability, under population pressure, to discover a niche wherein survival is possible.

All December and January some 9,000 narcissus tazetta show their white blooms to brighten midwinter's grey, overcast days. And, now as February opens, comes above them the deep pink blossom of the flowering apricot. This color combination recalls Benjamin Franklin's comment on slavery: "Why increase the sons of Africa by planting them in America, where we have so fair an opportunity, by excluding all blacks, of increasing our lovely white-and-pink? But perhaps I am partial to the complexion of my country, for such kind of partiality is natural to mankind."

One's garden teems with examples of plants also animals that instinctively have solved, each its own peculiar niche problem. May a few examples be cited in the following pages:

THE "INCREDIBLE BIRD"

From one fossil scale, Agassiz built up a theoretical fish outline. The finding, later, of the entire fossil fish proved his judgment unerring. Today we have, not a fish scale, but a bird bone. Avian paleontologists christen it "Incredible Bird." This Incredible Bird was even considerably larger than the "Terrible Bird". Latter apparently was perhaps twice the size of the California Condor. We know nothing about Incredible Bird's birthrate. We do know it long has been extinct.

We have learned however that Condor lays one egg, biennially. Often it is infertile. Condor*, now confined to Southern California desert ranges, once had a much greater habitat. Lewis and Clark found it on the Columbia River. It must once have inhabited the Oregon apple orchard country. It also was seen by the Spanish explorers where now are the Salinas lettuce farms. One river there is still "Pajaro River", the "River of the Big Birds."

That the Condor race is ancient is revealed by fossil remains of birds in the La Brea Asphalt. Therein Dr. Loye Miller found bones of, not only Condor, U. S. A.'s largest bird, but Tetraornis, the "terrible bird".

We know only too little about the Terrible Bird and the Incredible Bird. We DO know, however, that, while even undesirable-alien birds (English Sparrow, Starling) increase, the Condor tribe IS so close to EXTINCTION.

---
*National Audubon tries to save Condor as it did Roseate Spoonbill. Perhaps, however, the Condor may drift to extinction like Passenger Pigeon, also the pretty gold-and-green Carolina Parakeet, (U. S. A.'s only parrot"), likewise Moa, Dodo. We-2 offered National Audubon $1,000 for a publicity campaign to save Ivorybilled Woodpecker. Apparently it also is extinct. Here was woodpecker UNDERpopulation amidst OVERpopulation. Are we alert as to such UNDERpopulation within OVERpopulation?

Photo: Courtesy French Press & Information Service. Photo by Therese Le Prat

JUNGLE ROOTS, ANGKOR THOM

This sculpture on a Brahmin Temple at Angkor, in French Indo-China, is framed by the roots of surrounding trees. It is possible to grow in gardens over a considerable area of the United States certain vegetation of the jungle. In writer's own garden are certain plants like gardenia, bougainvillea, magnolia, largostema, crepe myrtle. The latter has its flowers at the end of the branches, as is true also of many tropical trees. This author has described frequently airplane figs over jungles.

A CHINESE PROVERB SAYS:

中華諺語說得

Neither Confucius nor Lao Tze ever heard of a gene or of a chromosome. They, however, out of what we call "common sense", which seems none too common—philosophized eugenically.

WHEN THE TREE FALLS, THE SHADE IS GONE.

Camouflage

Photo: Courtesy of California Fish & Game Commission

TREE FISH CAMOUFLAGE

A Gardening Philosopher early finds his thinking directed toward the camouflage of his garden companions. This, all the way from insects to mammals. Here, as with many other items in the ever unfolding garden phenomena, he finds himself "irritated" in the original meaning* of that word. Thus he feels impelled, if he be of Viking descent, to go exploring to meadow, chaparral forest, desert, seashore — then overseas to jungle, cloud forest, — to probe further for Truth which is the worship of God-in-Nature.

*Read Archbishop Trench for the shifting of word-meanings, as "desultory" from the "desultor", or rider of two or three horses at once, in the Roman Circus.

Photo: Courtesy American Museum of Natural History

RATTLESNAKE CAMOUFLAGE

We encourage the snakes in our garden. (No rattlers however are invited). With the gopher snakes in daylight, plus the owls at night, we keep the mice to a minimum without cats. Both the former prey on rodents. Neither, however, molests the guest birds in our sanctuary. The gopher snakes, like the owls, also are fascinating studies in camouflage coloring. They are, in fact, as interesting as our garden's flowers.

To the realm of zoology belongs also Paleozoology or Paleontology, the study of the extinct animals. For between the extinct and the living animals there exists a genetic relationship: the former are the precursors of the latter, and their fossil remains are the most trustworthy records of the history of the race, or Phylogeny. As in human affairs the present conditions can only be completely understood by the aid of history, so in many cases the zoologist must draw upon the results of paleontology for an explanation of the living animal world.

(Translation from "Zoology," Dr. Hertwig, University of Munich)

Photo: Courtesy American Museum of Natural History

CAMOUFLAGED NESTLINGS

Present reduction of deathrates in the highly intelligent Western civilization countries has been due very largely to concentration on infant mortality. Herein Mother Nature again was "first at the Patent Office". Few births show more striking contrast than those of the Order which has yielded us our barnyard fowls. There is hardly a more remarkable example of this than the difference between the coloration of a cock pheasant and of his newly hatched young. The male has evolved along "beauty parlor" lines. This, to be as colorfully attractive as possible to the hen. On the other hand, the young are so successfully camouflaged, writer almost has stepped on them. This, because in addition to their protective coloration, they instinctively "freeze".

The garden philosopher studies the breast spotting of certain of his garden's juvenals, i.e. his robins, bluebirds, dwarf hermit thrushes. He recalls similar spotting of thrush juvenals elsewhere: — wood thrush, hermit thrush, gray-cheeked thrush, olivebacked thrush of East-of-the-Mississippi. Also, in Britain, and on the Continent again, among the thrushes, spotted-breast camouflage in the young, i.e.

Camouflage

missell thrush, redwing, field fare. This further occurs in juvenal blackbirds in Europe. (The European "blackbird" is a thrush, ours an "oriole". Here arises problems of phylogeny.

THRUSH JUVENALS CAMOUFLAGE These seem to substantiate what Dr. Fairchild has so convincingly written in his book "Race & Nationality." It should be read by every American.)

One eminent scientist has been courageous enuf to counter-attack against those who would for selfish propaganda purposes distort the facts and who deny there is such a thing as "Race".

LEOPARD CAMOUFLAGE
Nearly all the larger cats have concealing coloration. This enables them to stalk their prey. The tawny color of the lion blends with the African terrain. Stripe of tiger, spot of leopard, both are as much survival mechanism (through better food-getting) as the winter snow color of arctic fox, polar bear, snowy owl. Why not a notebook to record observations on camouflage in your garden. You will be surprised how it grows with the years!

Photo: Courtesy Calif. Academy of Sciences.

Years ago, this author learned to write anywhere:—in Paris' "Metro", London's "Underground", in steamerchairs, or on a convenient rock outcrop. Sun warmth also attracts. Thus, a stray lugbox from one of his ranches, plus some thick cardboard, makes a convenient desk. Thus authorship hours can be spent

THE FREEZE IN CAMOUFLAGE in the Garden. Is there any aid to accuracy more prodding than such field work? If one doubts one's observation, the correctory subject is at hand. This, like a painter in oils transferring scenery to canvas.

Onto this knee-high desk has just fallen from a deodar, a ladybug beetle. (Most Coccinellidae are beneficial.) The ladybug struck the to-it-unfamiliar desk. At first it seemed the fall had stunned it.* It had, however, only gone into a "freeze"†. In a few moments, it cautiously wiggled, then flew away. This "freeze" is common to animals from invertebrates, such as ladybirds, thru fledglings (young quail, pheasants, plover) to fawns. Said "freeze" has high survival value, especially if the animal be well camouflaged.

Have we not a parallel to the "freeze" among certain human societies in what Ghandi advised to his Untouchables, i.e. Passive Resistance? Is same not an Oriental force we must not underestimate?

---
*When one has waited for months, (as in the 1880's, for a shipment from Australia of a parasitic species), to rid one of a devastating, alien fruit pest, one is Scottish about avoiding wastage. A California entomologist then invented use of natural overseas parasites to control alien pests.
†This "freeze" is peculiarly effective in the case of camouflaged insects, particularly those with brightly colored underwings, including many grasshoppers with red or yellow wings, also with underwing moths.

Photo: Courtesy California Academy of Science.

CAMOUFLAGED GIRAFFES
Camouflage that may seem to be of a striking pattern often blends with the animals' terrain. This is true of giraffes, of zebras. (Note tick birds at arrows.)

Photo: Courtesy of Yosemite Nature Notes.

CAMOUFLAGED TWIN FAWNS

Fawns form a typical example of Elfin Forest camouflage. One would hardly expect a "forest", whose members seldom are as tall as a buck's antlers, to be "deer country". Dust or mud tracks, deer droppings, deer beds testify to the contrary . . . One may almost step on a camouflaged fawn before seeing it. It instinctively "freezes". We now are raising an orphaned one on the bottle at the cabin. It comes indoors as readily as its companion, the collie.

Another hobby perhaps worth consideration can be cultivated by having an alphabetically-indexed looseleaf notebook. Herein, year after year of gardening, also of geogardening, likewise of garden-philosophizing can be accumulated data about flower-names. Such labor will earn spiritual dividends if one conducts a garden column in one's local press. As insurance against boredom and consequent accelerated arrival of death, is it not also a good provision against the day when the sentence of retirement is imposed, as only too often it is, before one really is old.

Following are a few notes from this author's "Names" looseleaf: Some folknames are strikingly appropriate as BLEEDING-HEART, BOTTLE-BRUSH. Among the weeds, SHEPHARDS' PURSE is the exact shape of the *bursa pastoris,* with the drawstring holding the pathetically few coppers. COPA DE ORO, ("cup of gold") for California's state poppy is as Spanishly appropriate as BUTON D'OR (gold buttons) is for the almost globular, golden buttercups of the meadows where the French make their matchless Grueyere cheese. CENTURY PLANT, of the semitropic desert, is indeed well named in New England where one can see frost on the Fourth of July. On Cape Cod, whence roving sea captains transplanted it, it may bloom once in a blue moon. In our garden it is a panicle of glory every summer. DUTCHMAN'S PIPE also ELEPHANT'S EAR both show kiddie

"COLLECTING"
PLANT NAMES

imagination. PITCHER-PLANT also POKER-PLANT carry the kitchen out into the garden. WALLFLOWER to one who knows them in their native habitat, the hoary walls of old French *chateaux*, are exactly what any one would dub them.

When CATTAIL is shedding its million downy seeds, does it not look all the world like Tabby's caudal appendage. The garden flower, LADY SLIPPER, is a dainty term. It parallels with that remarkable orchid, SABOT DE VENUS, you may collect in the cork oak forests where Robert Louis, the well Beloved, wrote "The Black Arrow" despite cheeks flushed with telltale tuberculosis. FIREWEED not only looks like a persisting forest fire of yesterday but grows in "burns" from Oregon to Norway. DUSTY MILLER recalls yesteryear workers in our flourmills when the highly inflammable dust on the roof caught fire. In a few hours the whole structure was but ashes. EVERLASTING recalls West Australia.

STRAWBERRY's name reminds us of when Britain sold them on straws just as the *dulce lemonas de Guadalajara* were strung on twigs. HONEYSUCKLE, also Honey locust bring to mind the woolly-headed pickaninnies of Alabama, then Arkansas, who grew their own candy. What little girl missed doll parties with CHEESES made of mallow seeds, just as we buy them wrapped in silver foil today at the grocers. Is BABYS-BREATH not as dainty as a wee bairn's smile? Any farmer knows the cost of BINDWEED when that wild morning glory once gets a hold on his acres. FIDDLENECK, BUTTER-AND-EGGS, BLUE CURLS, SNOWBALL, TARWEED, TIGER LILY, MILKWEED, BIG ROOT, EVENING SNOW all are plants one almost can "see with his eyes shut" their names are so descriptive.

OUTWITTING THE U-BOATS

It was artist-biologist Thayer's sense of color values that was the basis of maritime camouflage. The ruthless U-boats were, as Admiral von Tirpitz had predicted, "bringing Britain to her knees". Then came counter-strategy. It included such devices as the submarine-detector,"* also Thayer's concealing camouflage.

*Invention of a biologist born in the South African leopard spotted scrub.

Camouflage

JUNGLE CAMOUFLAGE

In all the history of Biology has anything been more amazing than the accelerated speed of use of camouflage in warfare. As to the jungle phases thereof this was greatly stimulated by those natural born artists, our Japanese opponents. They quickly became past masters of effective jungle camouflage. This author has written much on camouflage . . . much about the rebuffs of its originator, artist-biologist Thayer . . . about protective, also concealing, camouflage. . . . likewise about snow camouflage from his experiences north of the Artic Circle to the first and highly successful snow camouflage of the Finns against the Soviets. Much of this data is in the author's books, also in Eugenics Pamphlets of which he was editor through all its some 89 numbers. (All above are available at most U. S. A. collegiate, also public libraries.)

"Hummingbirds' metallic color marks THE VERY CLIMAX of the development of iridescence" . . . all are flashing pictures of flowery and leafy landscape at uncertain distances." (Thayer: Concealing Coloration)

AVIAN CAMOUFLAGE The Garden Philosopher need not venture beyond his garden fence for almost the whole range of avian camouflage. He finds the leaf-shadow-resemblance type of Disruptive Coloration in robin, junco, blackheaded grosbeak. As to Obliterative Shading, he has his White-crowned Sparrows venturing timidly out from their shrubbery, then hastening back at the least alarm. Occasionally a Kildee will be seen foraging along one of his garden paths. Again he is treated to a study of the deceptions gained by that master artist, Mother Nature.

And, as examples of Iridesence, he has his garden's blackbirds and hummingbirds as above described.

As he studies these exhibits year after year, he marvels at human obstinacy as to accepting Progress. In his garden, with blackhelmeted junco, quail babies, iridescent grakles, and a whole opened jewel box of hummingbird gems, he is impressed with two impelling thoughts:— The first, the inventiveness and devotion of Thayer in working out war camouflage. The second, the pigheadedness of those in high places unwilling to scrap uniform's display for uniform's protective coloration. Anyone who has argued and coaxed and pleaded with little men in big jobs in government or in business knows how wearing it is to get progressive ideas into skulls that seem indeed to be of the proverbial solid ivory.

WATER TANK CAMOUFLAGE, WORLD WAR II

Camouflage as protection against bombing increased in World War II. Even iridescent coloration, such as that of the blackbird, may have high camouflage value. It was artist Denis O'Leary who taught us there was some bluebird in a blackbird. At the campfire, we were discussing avian camouflage. The monochrome male Brewer's blackbird seemed to show no disruptive coloration, no obliterative shading.* "One apparent exception to the rule," I admitted "was the male blackbird." "You're colorblind," exclaimed Denis. "There's some bluebird in every blackbird cock." The next day We-3 were resting beneath a stunted Douglas oak where the Elfin Forest trail traced the border of a tiny meadow. A father Brewers was foraging. Denis proved the play of sunlight on feathered evidence gave not black, but blue. He was inaccurate in saying "bluebird blue". 'Twas the hue of neither western nor Arctice bluebird. It was, however, so nearly a lazuli-bunting blue that it looked like a blue hole in the blackbird's breast and side.

---
*Note the varied concealing coloration of rattlesnakes,—from the diamond rattler, thru the "pink" rattlesnakes of Arizona, "Leopard-spotted" Painted Desert, to the sand-colored "sidewinder of California-Colorado Desert."

Observations of the Niche and its philosophy, its examples of adjustment, particularly under population pressure to new environments is a hobby that—commenced in one's garden—sends one a-

The Niche

PHILOSOPHY OF THE NICHE

wanderlusting over the Seven Seas to add to one's accumulation of data. One sees it in varnish of winter tree-bud, in thorn of rose, in weight reduction of hummingbird, in urbanization of the ant nest, in rhizome reproduction of iris, in needle-form of deodar, in remarkable camouflage of underwing moth, in mimicry of honeybee by bee fly.

As one goes afield he notices such adjustments as the protective mane of lion, the tearing-bill of hawk, even the poison of asp. He will notice the bright blue tail of the juvenal skink, (which it can lose and replace), in the water-storage ability of the barrel cactus, also the corrugations of the suhuaro, the pad of one's camel's hoof, as well as its fat-storing hump, the nice adjustment of yucca bloom and its pronubia moth, the ability of albatross to use wave-crest to save fatigue, the similar use of rising heated air by circling redtailed hawk, the weak bill of buzzard, that it can utlize carrion, Eskimo ability to consume usefully seal blubber, yucca cordage by Navajo before he could buy a ball of string at the 5 & 10. Yes, indeed, Mother Nature's surgery removes the gardener's cataracts of ignorance, he marvels when he sees the interlocking forces at work in his garden.

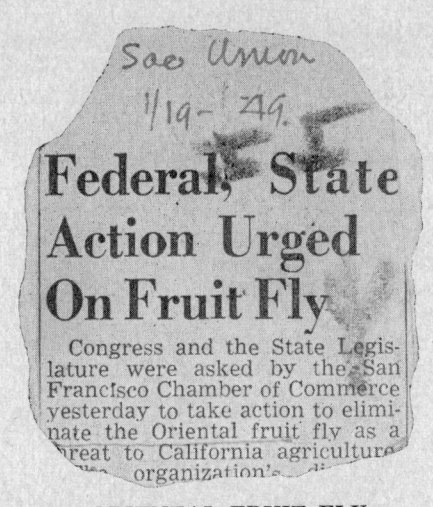

> Sao Union
> 1/19-'49
>
> **Federal, State Action Urged On Fruit Fly**
> Congress and the State Legislature were asked by the San Francisco Chamber of Commerce yesterday to take action to eliminate the Oriental fruit fly as a threat to California agriculture organization's

ORIENTAL FRUIT FLY

As to Oriental Fruit Fly, is not amazing the unbalance as to dangerous 6-footed aliens and alien bipeds? We are alert to such insect menaces as the Oriental Fruit Fly, yet we admit Displaced Person Klaus Fuchs, convicted traitor. We allow him access to atomic bomb secrets so carelessly that the Soviets overtake our 4-year headstart. Thus they hoodwink us into a Korean war, with more than 100,000 American casualties and a national debt boost till it hits the legal ceiling. WHEN WILL U. S. A. AWAKEN TO A REALISTIC IMMIGRATION RESTRICTION POLICY? A HANDFUL OF US HAVE BEEN CARRYING ON THIS LONELY FIGHT SINCE WORLD WAR I. WE COULD NOT PREVENT RUSHING MASS LOADINGS IN AMERICAN SHIPS OF DISPLACED PERSONS IN 1951 AND 1952. WERE THESE ALIENS PROPERLY SCREENED?

Two bluebird species periodically can be expected as guests in our bird sanctuary. Nearly every winter come the cinnamon-breasted Western and during occasional cold winters (as when the lake in Sutter's Fort Park became ice incrusted) the turquoise Arctic Bluebird (S. artica). Its rare visits suggest to a student of biology the part temperature plays.

CONTRASTED LEAVES SUN-LOVER, SHADE-LOVER

Cinerarias grow luxuriantly in the fog belt of the California's Transition Zone. This suggested to this author that, to find them *sauvage*, he must track them to some seacoast. One could guess, as with the thimbleberries of the Avenue-of-the-Giants, Humboldt Redwoods, what their broad leaves indicated. These seemed evolved, to utilize with Caledonian thrift, every bit of filtered sunlight. Note the ample leaf of shadowloving Thimbleberry in contrast with the reduced needle-like leaves of a gilia from the sunscorched, excessively-drained Sierran moraine.

Many desert plants have been successful in adjustment to an environment of extreme aridity by reducing their length of stem. This is one of the remarkable adaptations of plants to the forbidding desert niche. It is also seen in certain alpine plants, such as the Sessile Thistle of California's High Sierras.

Records noted from a maximum-minimum thermometer on the sleeping porch are helpful. We must admit our garden never has experienced the thrill described to Us-2 once by Death Valley Scotty. He said one day it was so blisteringly hot at Stove Pipe Wells that the maximum actually dropped lower than the minimum!

MAXIMUM MINIMUM THERMOMETER The garden however shows constantly changes evolved during adjustments to various temperatures. It can become a hobby, useful in senescence, to record observations of these. The two bluebirds abovementioned constitute an example.

Sacramento being Lower Sonoran, we, like the yesteryear song "Yes, We Have No Bananas", have no August bluebirds. With November's lowered mercury, however, they venture down into our garden.

The Niche

A January freeze makes the thermometer fall further. There is a heavy snowblanket on the high Sierras. Down come the *Artica's* to thrill us with that exquisite turquoise plumage.*

*For considerable temperature data see "Elfin Forest". The book is out of print but is available at most U. S. A.'s libraries. Those desiring to further explore herein will find thought provoking material in the "Botany" of Drs. Strassburger, Jost, Schenk and Karsten.

CONTRASTED LEAVES OF ROSALES

Dr. Jepson's "Flora of M. W. California" lists under "Roseaceae" these genera: (3) Adentostoma, (4) Cerecocarpus, (5) Rosa. Our photograph shows, left, Adentostoma or "Greasewood" . . . middle, cultivated rose . . . right, Cerecocarpus, or mountain mahogany. All 3 are rosales.

The wild species are natives of California's Upper Sonoran Life Zone. This has summer shade temperatures up to 110°. Greasewood's leaves, therefore, are so reduced they resemble needle points. Even mountain mahogany's leaves have hardly 7% the area of the garden rose. All 3, nevertheless, probably descended from a generalized Pre-Rosale ancestor.

Our cultivated roses, which thrive in California Coast Belt's moist coolth, retain their broad leaves. Thus Mother Nature strives for efficiency. Rosale Adentostoma, therefore, has adjusted thru evolution, to its NICHE. One of its devices is leaf-size* reduction: Such minute leaves do not waste moisture.

Mother Nature works always toward evolution of something better. She even had "bigger and better" dinosaurs until she created the enormous and powerful Brontosaurus or Thunder Lizard. It was, however, as poor in brains as is a moron of today. So Nature commenced anew with the tiny but brainy mammals. This, until she finally evolved Man, (who today harnesses waterfalls, speaks across the earth by wireless, flies the air like a bird, invents radar). All that is needed is an adequate birthrate of the Talented to insure undreamed of progress.

*The manzanita, another Upper Sonoran bush of the heather family, adjusts its LEATHERY leaves to intense sunlight by shifting them edgewise to sunrays, (like a Venetian blind).

A robin flock feasts on earthworms of the garden's glade. The spotted breasts of its juveniles are characteristic thrush-clan obliterative shading. Young bluebirds also visit our garden. A eugenist is fascinated by this persistence of thrush camouflage pattern. Similar spotting is in the European blackbird's* young. Theirs is a thrush, our blackbird is of the oriole family.

Adult robins show obliterative shading. The black head resembles a leaf shadow. This, too, has survival value. When, at Cooper's hawks approach, an adult robin flies for shelter to a nearby small oak, the dark head resembles the shadow of a leaf.

FLOCKING

This is just enough to confuse in those fateful few seconds before the bullet-hawk strikes. Note ALL the flock rushes to cover. Eugenists continually emphasize camouflage.†

A perfumer's ad, in a World War II magazine showed American soldiers fighting in the jungle. So well were they camouflaged, the illustration constituted a puzzle. Readers were asked:—"How many soldiers actually are in this picture?" Biologists continually marvel at ever new discoveries of Mother Nature's devices for SURVIVAL. Camouflage‡ is combined with flocking especially under a leader is most effective.

*Note, too, the song-inheritance of European blackbird. Compare it with the squeak of our redwing, even our Brewer. The spotted breast persists into adult plumage of some thrushes.
†This, because of its amazing history. The biologically illiterates in authority rejected artist-naturalist Thayer's theories. Latter was certain camouflage should be substituted for the brightly-colored uniforms. This, particularly of our British and French World War I allies. Every day's delay in above meant battlefield deaths. Eugenists are interested in the reduction of biological illiteracy. This, because thus the progress of eugenics program also will be accelerated.
‡An American nature-student, passionately idealistic, Thayer felt the urge to use Nature-lore to save soldiers' lives. Based on the mathematics of concealing coloration, he invented camouflage. . . . Into its very name is crystallized the tragedy of his months of disappointment. He tried to interest U. S. A. The final decision was made by a high official. This man was BIOLOGICALLY ILLITERATE. Thoroughly disheartened, he took his data to Britain. Same rebuffs then to France. The quick Gallic imagination saw that it was worth whole divisions to their decimated army. THAT IS WHY OUR WORD IS FRENCH, NOT ENGLISH. It is an example of the cost of BIOLOGICAL ILLITERACY.

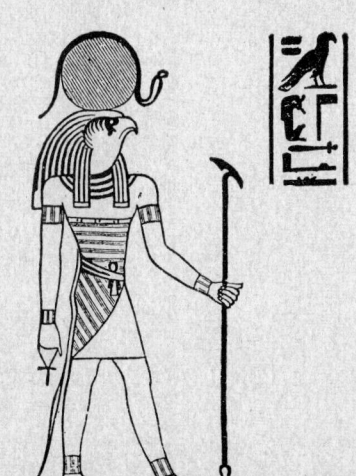

HARAKATE, HAWK-HEADED GOD

As one accumulates garden instances of niche-radiation then, leaves his garden to gain beyond further knowledge thereof, he comes to evaluate the protective mane of the lion, the tearing bill of the hawk, even the food-procuring value of the poison of the asp.

The Niche 271

CHAPARRAL OAK

The chaparral oak is the clump to the left of children and below the volcanic outcrop. (High bush against skyline is manzanita.) Many think of the oak as a magnificent tree. The British concept of "Hearts of Oak" parallels the affection with which Germans speak of their *"Eichenbaum."* Even California's great Sacramento-San Joaquin Valley was, before the Gold Rush, one vast park of weeping oaks. These, too, were spotted, because the valley floor lies in Lower Sonoran Life Zone. Their magnificence was possible because of the rich soil, semi-tropical climate, abundant underground waters from Sierran snows.

In the piedmonts of both Sierras and Coast Range, temperatures were even higher than on the valley floor. In addition, there was a rapid drainage, somewhat like that of Southern France's limestone semi-deserts. One finds, therefore, Elfin Forest's oaks become dwarfed chaparral, such as the oak to left in above picture of volcanic boulders.

Chaparral oak's foliage (above arrow) also shows adjustment to high temperature plus aridity. Latter is intensified by the rock-hill drainage above referred to. Middle photograph shows in center 2 Kellogg oak leaves. It is of the next higher Life Zone, the Transition, with greater coolth, less evaporation, there is more abundant water. The oaks are highly variable. This is demonstrated by Kellogg oak's large leaves compared to chaparral oak's tiny, closely-clustered foliage.

GARDEN NICHES Even the ordinary garden affords abundant opportunities to observe adjustment to various niches. Many California gardens grow successfully quite a range of desert shrubs from cacti to yuccas. Arid South Africa contributes remarkable pink amaryllis. Such drought-resisters as the sedums illustrate how they have radiated into such a niche as tiled roofs. Many gardens have plants from the edge of Austalia's Never Never such as acacia, bottlebush, she oak. The dry moraines of New Zealand's South Island give us certain interesting veronicas. From Andean rainforests come various fascinating fuchsias. The Arctic and near-Arctic present us with other varieties including Saxifrages, Iceland poppies. The alpines range from Tyrolese forgetmenots and Alp's primroses to the broad-leaved saxifrages of Tibet. Siberia's steppes offer us giant Oriental poppies. North exposure nooks are just the place to study the shade lovers from violets to ivy. In semitropical California one can have bougainvillea from Brazil's Golden Monkey jungle, gardenias, and avocadoes. The rock desert sloping southward to Sahara's sand dunes send our gardens the gorgeous skyblue-flowered artichoke — (unless the unopened bud entered the home via the kitchen door).

ERFURT, HOF DES EVANELICHES WAISENHAUSES

Erfurt is one of the world's most discriminating garden-seed merchandising centers. Often when We-2 wanted something special we could purchase at Erfurt when nowhere else stocked same. One colorful border effect we saw in a castle garden, we reproduced, via Erfurt seed, 24 years ago. These blue-and-gold perennials have reproduced themselves ever since. (Note how Europe has to resort to potting plants to give them a Niche.

"Boss Man, I bring gang to cabins now? You-think we cut 'grass *pronto?*" The questioner was Number One Boy of the Filipino asparagus cutters on one of our ranches. He had "bobbed up serenely" at mid-January, knowing some cutting would be under way by Valentine's day, almost a whole month earlier than average.

The acacia in our garden that day was a 30 foot-tall mass of

The Niche

golden bloom. The Tibetan saxifrages had thrice their usual bloom. Calendulas, orange and golden, planned for Christmas bloom, had been in flower already at Thanksgiving. In delightful contrast with their gold was the massed white of a thousand tazettas. These narcissus had become naturalized from stock We-2 bought in Holland almost a half century ago. Such wealth of bloom is to be expected to our south on the Santa Barbara Coast but not inland at Sacramento. The cause? Indian summer thru November, thereafter an almost-frostless December and January.

To one observing temperatures year after year on a high-and-low thermometer, the abnormal warmth is remarkably a matter of a few degrees. It is amazing how slight are the differences between the successive Life Zones, from reindeer moss on Spitzbergen, to the rainforest, with orchids and epiphytic cacti, of the Amazon.

AIR PLANT NICHE: A PHONE WIRE
Here is a true flowering plant, radiated under population pressure, to survival thru foodgetting on a Florida telephone wire. When more gardeners become garden philosophers, will we not produce leadership so intelligent we can help the illiterate stubborn, moronic Backward Peoples toward eugenic betterment without endangering our own nation?

There is so much to be learned after these centuries of failing "to read a trailside like a book"—so much to which we still are blind:— Tonight is Hallowe'en. The equinox is 40 days past. Of the several Michaelmas daisy clumps, only one offers honey. The shortened hours of warmth mean lessened honeymaking by the plants—lessened honey harvesting by bees, flies, wasps, butterflies. PRODUCTION DEPENDS UPON THE PROPER TEMPERATURE. There can be too much heat. Pies of fresh cherries are impossible in Ceylon. Strassburger records that European cherry, transplanted there, grows but produces no fruit. Light also is a factor worth the garden philosopher's study. Elsewhere herein has been mentioned this author's experience as to indoors' loss of color of gladiolus, also Nice stocks. One has much material for such observation in the ordinary garden. Ours has, as weeds, arctic stellaria in late winter, Mexican-originated tarweeds in August.

CYPRESS, JAYHAWK CEMETERY

The JAYHAWKERS must have been familiar with the quotation from Whittier's "Snowbound":

"Alas for him who never sees
The stars shine thru his cypress trees."

These scattered and almost forgotten Gold Belt graveyards are excellent sources of pioneer history. At least one California college is doing research therein . . . Our own gardens' eight cypress trees pay double dividends. They not only are "correct" for a mansion in the North Italian Renaissance, but they have become useful Bird Sanctuary factors. Each, becomes a "niche", has "story" after "story" of housefinch nests each summer. The Brewer's Blackbirds have made the summits of all eight cypresses "pent house" for their annual broods.

MANGROVE NICHE IS SEA WATER

Any gardener specializing in botanizing on salt pans and playas in saline arid regions, (such as Death Valley), marvels at adjustment to niches of high salt content. Wonderful is the radiation of the mangroves to existence on mudflats, seawater covered at high tides. It was Everglades' mangroves as much as anything else that stimulated Us-2 to persist until they were incorporated into a National Park. From our nature work with (a) Sacramento Orphanage Farm Kiddies, (b) the "2,200 schools", (c) the bringing from Switzerland what became National Parks Nature Guiding, we knew the possibilities of producing generation after generation of future scientists from the modest-income families that could study tropic biota via the "Tin Lizzie" in an Everglades National Park.

At one time, the nearest colony of a hated weed, prickly lettuce, was more than a half-mile away. Then its seed parachute, one of nature's miraculous efficiencies, utilized a winter **PARACHUTING** gale for transport. The seed dropped in the very **IS NICHE WORK** corner of our vegetable garden. It there sprouted. Its life was spared. This, for selfish, guinea-pig reasons.

It was an alien intruder. It came with late October gales with maize, tomatoes, potatoes still not fully harvested. Now, sentimentally, all three latter had right to garden space. All were American in origin. All three gave us very acceptable food. Said guinea-pig possibilities, however, saved it from uprooting. The soil was good. The prickly lettuce grew shoulder high to a 6-footer. In due time it developed on the summit of its stalk an inverted cone. This was of flowers. They were followed by seeding. Above mentioned height gave it a mathematical advantage over lowgrowing plants like oxalis, clove pink, calendula.

This stalk was worth observation. Fully 40 inches from radical leaf-crown to its reproduction cone atop, it had, nevertheless, less than half the diameter breadth of one's little fingernial. Prickly lettuce, because of great fecundity plus said height, CAN displace native wildflowers, also garden plants. That lettuce had 20 stems, with 15 laterals, each. These 300 with 4 flowers average, at 8 seeds, meant 9,600 seeds in that one alien intruder.

FECUND HUMAN IMMIGRANTS ALSO CAN OUTBREED LOW BIRTHRATE NATIVES.

If there is any one sermon the garden birds try to chirp continuously it is that of Food that there may be Reproduction. That is to say, the Philosophy of the Niche. Said Philosophy of The Niche, if it ever penetrates the consciousness of the majority of American voters, may solve one of our least understood national problems. THAT SOLUTION, PROPERLY MADE, MUST BE OURS IF U. S. A. IS TO DISCHARGE its unique and recently acquired world leadership.

As this is written two tragedies have come, within weeks of each other. One is that of Mexican wetbacks. The other is of Hindu pilgrims at Allahabad. Both are linked with American Know How.

Both incidents brought death thru trampling. The Wetback one

JAVA JUNGLE, WHERE "TERMINAL BUDS" SNAKE AROUND

An impressive example of adaption to a niche is that of the rattan palms of Spice Island jungles. Once sprouted, the terminal bud snakes around in the continual darkness toward light. Thus was found a record one whose length exceeded twice the height of California's tallest Big Tree.

The Niche

occurred at the Border where Wetbacks fought for jobs where they could earn in one hour several days wages in South Mexico.

The Allahabad deaths, with many bodies washed down the Ganges, may run from 500 to 1,000. The incident recalls the visit of Us-2 to the Allahabad area nearly a half century ago. It was during our stay in Hindustan to try to do our bit to lessen child labor by financing an American-type education thru play center.

The friend had insisted on our making studies of exploitation of the illiterate by fat, wellfed priests at the Temple of Kali, one-eyed Goddess of Hate. On our return he said:—"Now, to get insight of how astrology can become an instrument for exploiting the ignorant, go to Allahabad. It probably is the only place in the whole world where one can see a million humans in one mass."

Now, many years later, comes the story of the 1,000,000 pilgrims.

The real moral, not to be overlooked, is the Niche. . . .

Rubycrowned Kinglets this winter were cleansing the escallonias of their insect pests. Just below them, whitecrowned sparrows were scratching the fallen leaves for seeds. There was a little elf near them. His voice was highpitched as the sibilant call notes of the waxwings up in the garden's big elm. This elf was trying to call the garden philosopher's attention to the contrast between bills of Kinglet and whitecrown. The Kinglet's long pointed bill was evolved to food-getting by consumption of insect proteins. The sparrow's was short, thick, ideal for seed-crushing.

Someday some truly great author will write "the Philosophy of the Niche." He will draw his material from grosbeak bill and rose thorn, from lion mane and camel footpad, from humming bird lightness and clovepink scent. It will be the Epic of *Zeilstrebigkeit*.

Once that philosophy is translated in our country's folkways— once our citizenry grasps what competition it faces with an Orient inured to only "Morning Rice" and "Evening Rice", once our generation learns its own inherent weakness of "let Government do it" and yet grasps the power of our "American Know How" we shall return to the philosophy of our Pioneer forebears. They learned it conquering the Frontier. They made life so easy for our generation that we have approached the parasitism of the Florida seagulls. After a half dozen generations of gorging on the wealth of fishing-boat garbage, they lost the power of fishing for themselves. This, indeed, is the lesson of kinglet's needled bill, of sparrow's stubby one.

The Jungle, particularly its Cloud Forest type, is environment particularly fascinating to the gardening-philosopher. (His original garden stimulus may have been a home-garden orchid-house. Some day the wanderlust is awakened.) This cloud forest fascinates both bird lover and botanist. It long has suffered from ruthless lumbering. Some tropical hardwoods now are almost as rare as a primitive black walnut in Illinois. Such a heavy rain forest is a biological asset. In Venezuela, writer listed scores of hummingbird species. This, in lieu of the Atlantic coast's one, California's half dozen.

CLOUD FOREST, ALSO JUNGLE NICHE

The bat population also interests one. We now learn some of the Conquistadores' whoppers about bloodsucking vampires had some truth. The botanist revels in brightcolored air plants, also orchids. Epiphytic cacti grow high on trees. In similar rain forests in Java, writer found palms whose length was approximately twice the height of California's tallest big tree. This palm has a Malay name, *rattan*. It snakes its way through the jungle toward light until it reaches astonishing lengths.

Our national parks' brilliant success is having worldwide influence. From a Washington conservation group, (of whose board of governors this writer is a member), is released news of that republic setting apart a Cloud Forest National Park. It is about the size of Rocky Mountain National Park. It has macaws, also brightcolored parrots. Its toucans have bills almost as long as their bodies. Its ocelots' kittens make attractive pets until they grow to dangerous size. Not far from above writer watched a coffee "train," from a *finca* which was cleared jungle land. That train's "cars" were burros. Each had a sack of coffee on either side.

USA has tremendous high school, college population expansion. It has Everglades National Park as a base with tropical biota. Travel time-saving comes using airplanes in lieu of burros. Such parks, (which a few Americans today try to save from commercial exploitation), seem destined to become bases of important discoveries. One possibility: increased control of tropical diseases.

When U. S. A.'s biological illiteracy is reduced, our voters will commence to grasp the Philosophy of The Niche.* They will learn much from a species' radiation into new food areas. This depends upon OBSERVING, not IGNORING, laws governing same. We then will have better lawmaking. Our people, for example, then will become more alert to the menace involving their liberties by "amending to death" the Immigration Quota Acts of 1921-2-4.

---
*For much data on the Niche, see the file of Eugenics Pamphlets in your local library.

If the Garden taught nothing else, it would be a constant stimulus to the use of Mother Nature's devices in human invention. An example of this is the goldfish in the lotus pond.

Streamliners follow fish form. Note survival value in above fish's form. Automobile engineers learned much from nature study as to fish form. Side by side, lay a barracuda, a halibut, a trout, a catfish—yes, even a Moorish idol from Hawaii (who escapes into submarine cracks in reef or lava). Note how survival depends upon form.

Researchists study such matters—thus create jobs by the thousands. Do we not need an adequate collegiate birthrate?

Study, too, the series of early aircraft throughout Eugenics Pamphlets. Note the transition from inefficient unnatural architecture to ornithological types. MOTHER NATURE IS ALWAYS "FIRST AT THE PATENT OFFICE."

Human extension in radiation, under population pressure, is measured by inherited intelligence. The stupid stagnate, die under periodic famines, as in Bengal, also North China. America is rich in inventive folk. These, because of 10 generations of fierce selection on the frontier. The stupid pioneer died early, fathered few sons.

> "I doe hold it, in the Royall Ordering of Gardens, there ought to be Gardens, for all the Moneths in the Yeare: In which, seureally, Things of Beautie, may be then in Season. For December, and January, and the Latter Part of Nouember, you must take such Things, as are Greene All Winter: Holly; Iuy; Bayes; Iuniper; Cipresse Trees; Eugh; Pineapple-Trees; Firre-Trees; Rose-Mary; Lauander; Periwinckle, the White, the Purple, and the Blewe; Germander; Flagges; Orenge-Trees; Limon-Trees; and Mirtles, if they be stooved; and Sweet Marioram warme set."   (Francis Bacon p. 187)

BACON'S "ROYALL ORDERING OF GARDENS"

PARIS' Panorama from the Arc de Triomphe. It shows the Avenues of Bois de Boulogne and of the Grand Army. Many European business streets add to civil beauty by street forestry plus window flower boxes.

> "A little GARDEN, square and walled
> And in it throve an ancient evergreen
> A yew tree and all around it ran a walk
> Of shingle-and a walk divided."

Bacon spelled it *"Eugh"*. By Tennyson's time it was lettered *"Yew"* (anyone who has hankered after yew effects and attempted to buy matured specimens knows how dollars can be poured into a garden, if one does not have to count them).

Just as the very plants cultivated in one's garden are reminiscent of Travel*, past or anticipated, so into the names of such species is embalmed much biography and history. Just as an archaeologist excavates long-forgotten sites for Indian arrowheads, Babylonian cuneiform brick-recordings, or Egyptian mummies, so one can go "excavating" into the nomenclature of plant names. This is inexpensive recreation. All that is really needed is the garden, plus access to a dictionary and an encyclopedia.

"EXCAVATING" INTO GARDEN-PLANT NOMENCLATURE

Once We-2 were hiking along a trail in Alabama magnolia swamp. We met, at a cross trail, a New England spinster coming from one

---

*See "Geogardening". Though out of print, it is obtainable at most libraries throughout the English-speaking world.

direction. A little Negro lad came from the other. She stopped the boy, patted his kinky wool, said patronizingly:—"What a nice little boy you are. I know you want to grow up to be just like George Washington, don't you?" His answer was a "No 'mum". She countered with: "But why?" He answered:—"How can ah be LAK George Washington when ah IS George Washington".

We Garden-Philosophers recognized in that little colored boy a kindred soul. He was searching,—was he not,—for The Truth? He, like Socrates, was truly a *phyllis-soph.*

An example of how one can project his garden-philosophy beyond boundary fence and hedge is mimetic bird names. One commences by listing "chick-a-dee," "pee-wee," "flick-air," "or-ree-ool." Then the wanderlust prompts him to go to, say, Arkansas for the "teacher-teacher bird," to Indiana for "bob-white" to Virginia for "whip-poor-will," to Florida's Everglades for "chuck-wills widow."

MIMETIC BIRD NAMES, IN GARDEN, THEN OVERSEAS
Then that same Viking curiosity urges him to explore the overseas. It takes him to Brittany where he listens to the "chit-chat," to the Dolomites for "cuckoo," to the acacias below the towering eucalypts of New South Wales for the "coach-whip" bird's stinging call, to the tree ferns of Gippsland for the "cu-ca-bur-ra," to New Zealand's South Island for "ka-ka," and "mo-poke."

Let those who plot to make the word "Nordic" tabu in U. S. A. remember that it is the Viking urge, (once expended in world-exploration), that now is driving their very precious element in the world population toward new frontiers, the frontiers of Research. It is the basis of much we call "American Know How."

San Francisco-before-the-Earthquake (or, as its habitants prefer, "before the 1906-Fire") possessed a Chinatown truly Oriental. It was the scene of a play then produced. The star was a fat, goodnatured Chinese restaurant-keeper. He wore the traditional queue. A Boston tenderfoot strolled along old Dupont Street.

"YOU MISS A LOT IN LIFE!"
Yankee-like, he asked questions. The restauranteer responded with, "You no-know Charlie Yuen? He heap smart guy! He own two-tlee-six lest'lants in Chinatown!! He fliend evely P'liceman. And you no-know Charlie Yuen? Well, YOU MISS A LOT IN LIFE." Then, tapping his own ample blouse, he concluded with: "Me, Charlie Yuen." Charlie Yuen knew his name was respected in that fascinating old Chinatown, with

its preserved ginger, its dried ducks, its frosted melons, its desiccated abalone, its firecrackers at the annual devildriving. Names ARE important.

Do your garden flowers whisper to you about the eugenical highpowers that were friends of the early scientists who built the history of Botany and whose names they bear? If not, then, also, "You miss a lot in life."

SESHET, GODDESS OF WRITING, AND PROTECTRESS OF PAPYRUS RECORDS

This young lady is secretary to mighty Ammon Re. Her stylus is hardly as speedy as a typewriter. She personifies, however, a concept. Like many others out of Egypt, it has continued to our day. (Note, also, that half-socks long ago were invented in the shadow of the Sphinx.)

The Garden Philosopher muses about illiteracy reduction. The ancient Egyptians were pioneers herein. Papyri were entombed with royal mummies. Elsewhere is described the finding of a mummified crocodile stuffed with papyri . . . We North Europeans tagged far behind in appreciation of writing. King John could not read the Magna Charta — nor could he sign it. He "sealed" it.

Iceland, with rare eugenical wisdom, leads the world in attaining 100% literacy. This, by the simple expedient of denying marriage licenses to illiterate morons. U. S. A.'s own record herein is hardly a source of pride.

The Garden Philosopher contemplates his flowers, the insects that visit them, the birds that are his welcome guests. He dreams of these as aid in reducing also U. S. A.'s BIOLOGICAL illiteracy. Under foot, the soil that feeds his flowers reminds him of the history it contains of Sierras once seabottom with crinoids and brachiopods—of swelling granitic magmas that built mountains—of nights, thru millions of years, often brilliant with volcanic fireworks. Then he prays for an appreciation of the content of his garden soil reducing his nation's GEOLOGICAL illiteracy. Furthermore on moonless nights, he strolls along his garden's paths. He remembers "If the stars appeared but once in a thousand years how men would adore them!" Then he dares hope the spread of sky-facts, thru increasing numbers of amateur astronomical societies, and of planetaria, also of observatory research, will hasten the millenium when ASTRONOMICAL illiteracy also is reduced, and exploitation thru astrology outlawed.

Is not history embalmed in common garden plant names? We-2 were motoring along a new highway toward Brazil's Golden Monkey Jungle. It had one cut, say 600 yards long, with 100 feet apex. Both **BEGON-IA'S NAME** sides were shell pink with thousands of wild begonia seedlings. Hardly little-finger-joint-length, each had a bloom. This started us exploring genus Begonia. We went to London's Kew Gardens for information. We were advised to study the Caribbean, also certain Central American jungles. The Caribbean profoundly impressed with its changes.

Linneaus named the genus for a brilliant French thinker, Michael Bignon (1638-1710). Bailey lists him as a promoter of botany and superintendent at San Domingo. We crossed this island, found much wild begonia. Striking was the abyss into San Domingo's, also Martinique's former French plantations had fallen. Their estates, once producing enormous quantities of food, now, under unstable rule, are jungle. Begonias, as weeds, where once sugar cane, coffee flourished. A German trader told us he swapped, for wild coffee, bright colored beads with the voodoo-dominated negroes. He declared they diluted the beans with selected pebbles to increase weight. This blue-eyed blonde Teuton laughed sarcastically:—"They think they fool me. I know the percentage, reduce my price."

If the reader can find Dr. Lothrop Stoddard's "San Domingo," he probably will be amazed over the enforcement of the French Revolution's *Egalatie* philosophy. In same there was no real equality. Instead, mulattoes massacred whites, later fullbloods liquidated mulattoes. We there were told Haiti flag half red, half blue was the French tricolor, the white torn out. The insurgent leader there commented:— "Nothing white in Haiti".

A garden philosopher herein is troubled that much unbalanced *Egalatie* philosophy now permeates American life. With his considerable European experience with Communism he suspects Moscow. His friend above, Dr. Lothrop Stoddard, said he was required to cease further similar writings. He was dependent on them for bread and butter. In his "Revolt Against Civilization", he clearly had predicted much which corrupted American life in the 1940's.

Space limits permit only 3 other examples of biography crystallized into plant names:—

BOUGAINVILL-EA We-2 became interested in studying the behavior of Brazil's jungle's big bluesilk or Morpho butterflies. These are used muchly in manufacturing the blue butterfly trinkets, such as ashtrays. We suspected that those big blue wing's flash was a sex signal. In threading the jungle trails with a

Sambo, (hybrid negro-x-Amerind netter) we were delighted to find trees completely draped in brilliant bougainvillea.*

Bougainville was a type of that precious human asset tragically decimated in the French Revolution. Bougainville ranks with Leonardo di Vinci, Gallileo, Pasteur in brilliance of imagination, also with poor Vavilov, liquidated in our generation by ruthless Soviets. Like his countryman Champolliant. Bougainville early showed signs of genius. At 25 he published a work in higher mathematics. At 27 he was made colonel because of brilliancy. He personally financed the French colonization of Falkland Islands, then became an explorer. Writer visited the Paumotos also Tahiti which he added to the French Empire. Any stamp collector knows them as "Establishments d' Oceanie". (A considerable group of South Pacific Islands bears his name.)

His manysidedness was shown in his success with scurvy. (When you stand on St. Malo's pier, remember he returned there after circumnavigating the globe with a loss of less than 4% of his crew.) His record as a naval strategist paralleled his earlier one in the army. Just as his squadron was the only one to escape Admiral Rodney, so he similarly was one of the few who outwitted the French Revolution mob and saved his neck from the guillotine. It is thus the demogogueled, moronic mob rewards its country heroes.

Another flower name reminiscent of a eugenically highpowered man was that of Dr. Leonard Fuchs. A brilliant practicing physician, his work paralleled that later of Pasteur. His illiterate neighbors came to credit him with magic powers. A Liberal in the word's best sense, he was continually in conflict with the authorities. Most of his colleagues went to the stake. He was spared, because of need of his miracle-working skill during the epidemic of that mysterious disease, the "English Sweating Sickness." He was Court Physician, also the university's professor of medicine. He found time, however, to contribute valuable books. One has some 500 outline illustrations, including one of the foxglove's part in heart ailments. . . .

FUCHS-IA

---

*One exciting use of a garden is attempting to grow exotics. Of course you do not succeed with reindeer moss on the Amazon, nor with bananas on Greenland. But even the tyro in botany can learn much by attempting to sprout, in Florida, California, seed from Java or Ecuador or Somaliland. Our excuse for pride herein is our 30-year old Bougainvillea. A half century ago we first encountered its cascades of color at Chapultepec. The cliffs around Mexico's historic castle were attractively adorned with this sharp-hooked, gorgeously-hued climber. We decided we wanted THAT glory in our home garden. Bougainvillea we afterward collected *sauvage* at about 20° South. To attempt to grow it at 37° North meant that successive failures must be encountered with continued obstinacy. Finally, by planting, with a sunny south exposure and against the chimney of one fireplace that insured some warmth thru those occasional winter nights that even Sacramento has, we have had its glory of massed color for some 31 summers. Attempting to nurse sensitive tropical or semi-tropical plants in the temperate zone can become a hobby, especially fascinating and useful in senescence.

†See Eugenics Pamphlet No. 88, in your local library, for data on this remarkable Gifted Child.

Eschscholtz escaped the fate of long-forgotten Jedediah Smith because his friend, von Chamisso, named a new genus for him. It was later to be the state flower of California, the golden poppy, or *copa d'oro* of the Spanish Californians.

ESCHSCHOLTZ-IA

Eschscholtz was the Viking type of physician. He was not only a beloved doctor, he was also an all-round naturalist. At the University of Dorpat, he was professor of anatomy. He also was director of its museum of natural history. When von Kotzebue was starting on his expedition to find a passage across the Arctic, he induced Eschscholtz to go as their doctor. They sailed from Russia around the Horn. They then went up Coast, via California and Alaska, to Kamchatka. The voyage was a highly romantic one, with a crew of less than 30. Their visits ranged from Siberia to Hawaii and the Philippines.

Eschscholtz was born in said ancient university city of Dorpat. An old map on this desk of the late 1100's shows it as the port of the snake-shaped Principality of Polotsk. This was when the Moors held Cordova and Valencia in Spain. Its university was founded by Sweden's great King Gustavus Adolphus in 1632.

RUINS OF THE CHURCH AT FORT ROSS 1906

We-2 carefully kodaked the ruins of Fort Ross immediately after the San Francisco earthquake of 1906. With our deep interest in the history of Russian California we were concerned that the valuable and resistant redwood timbers might gradually disappear.

"Scratch a Russian
And you find a Tartar"

It was the study projected out of our Garden-philosophizing of Eschscholtz and his environment of the East Baltic, (even more than of Kant) that commenced to awaken us, in the year following World War I's Armistice Day of what had happened to mankind by the Pangerman creation of the Bolshevik revolution.

More and more We-2 came to feel that above observation was pregnant with meaning. We became convinced that in Russia there had been, for centuries, a ruling class. This was drawn partly from Germany, partly from Scandinavia. The masses, particularly as one approached the Urals, (and certainly more so beyond) were "Tartars" (Asiatics). It is not accident that the unique rugs of Finland seem to have a close affinity to those of South Central Siberia.

The old Russian aristocracy was highly intelligent. It had also great charm. This, despite its contempt for its underlings, despite a ruthlessness that Anglo Saxons deplore. It was so conscious of its power it neglected to initiate reforms that might have prevented the present world situation. Improvements *were* made, such as freeing the serfs. They however did not come fast enough. The high percentage of illiteracy in Russia at the outbreak of World War I is an indication of above. Along with this was the corroding near-morons' envy of those who are of constructive minds. Few books of our time foresaw all the above as did Harvard's Dr. Lothrop Stoddard in his "Revolt Against Civilization". Is it not tragic he was silenced by U. S. A. unseen but highly efficient censorship?

Too often Americans forget the chasm between our living standards and Europe's. In Greece, this author asked for an English-speaking chauffeur. "25% higher wages." 40c daily raised to 50c. This driver had lived in California. His brother's wife there ordered food over a telephone, cooked with gas, got water thru a faucet. The wife in Greece had to haggle at a market for a quarter hour to buy a fish. Fuel came only thru picking up dead olive twigs. Water was carried by jar on head, Rebecca-like, from the village well a half mile away. Any wonder such folk break laws to enter our "Land of Gold?"

And thus, after reflection upon the garden-philosophy of plants furnishing food that there can be reproduction . . . after studying the behavior at the garden's animal visitors, from insects to birds, and their paralleling human behavior . . . after observing the biota's array of defense mechanisms, (color scent, cooperation of composites) . . . After noticing how Mother Nature works thru selection, survival, and with camouflage, likewise excessive fecundities hence population pressure stimulating radiation into ever new niches, after taking note of geography, biography, history embalmed in our garden plants, we come to the most profound "sermon" of all. It is how great teachers from Christ to Confucius resort to the garden biota for material for parables in Eugenics.

KHNUM, GOATHEADED GOD

Khnum was worshipped at the Temple of Tu-Kow. Said adoration of Khnum is an example of the tendency to revere many forms of natural phenomena. The author, when in Jamaica, was fascinated by negro terror about "Duppies". Negroes were particularly fearful of a certain ceiba or silk-cotton tree, insisting a revengeful, devilish "Duppie" lived in it.

> "To one (servant) he gave five talents, to another two, to another one, EACH ACCORDING TO HIS ABILITY." (ST. MATTHEW XXV).

"GREEN THUMB" If one's interest in the geographic origin of his garden plants stimulates him to go awanderlusting, he will commence to absorb additional ideas. He will study the actual terrain in which produced the great teachers from Confucius with his "bamboos", to Christ, with His "lilies of the field," His "grapes and thorns, figs and thistles". He will come to grasp how they aimed to give their followers, thru garden parables, codes of morals,—how they thereby also taught eugenics.

Gardening, the love of saving seeds of the best plants, of planting, of irrigating, of watching growth, flowering, fruition, is a tie that, like music, binds certain folk from within every nation. The possession of the "Green Thumb" is like the grip and password of a fraternity.

As a byproduct of contacts with gardening, Buddhist priest, Moslem *mullah*, Russian *kulak*, Confucionist peony-enthusiast comes a melting of barriers. Thus is permitted glimpses into the very souls of one's fellow horticulturists. One comes to understand folkways, folk-sayings, and to be broadened into one's attitudes toward other philosophies, other religions.

SEVERAL MANNED PUMPS FOR EVEN A SLIGHT LIFT

Be it remembered that, when Christ spoke of gathering "grapes of thorns, figs of thistles" that the home beneath the fig tree, with its grape arbor had no bath tub, no faucets. Water to irrigate the garden came from a well and was channeled into a well-side ditch. Domestic supply was transported from well to the cooking place in long earthenware jars. Even then, however, it was recognized that leadership was climbing up from the drawers of water as well as from the hewers of wood.

"De sunflowers am no daisy
 An' de melon am no rose.
 Why am you'all just crazy
 To be something else what grows.
 Yo'all stay where yo'all's planted,
 An' do de best yo' knows.
 Fo' de sunflower am no daisy
 An' de melon am no rose."   (over)

Be glad that yo' can pass de plate,
If yo' can't exhort and preach.
An' if yo am jess a pebble,
Doan yo' try to be the beach.
If yo' fin's yo's jess a tadpole,
Doan' yo' think yo' am de frog.
An' when yo knows yo' am jess de tail
Doan' yo' try to wag dat dog.
　　　　　　　(Old Plantation Song)

SUN

TREE

EAST
⟝SUN
BEHIND
TREE

DAWN
⟝SUN
ABOVE

FOG
⟝CLOUDS
AT DAWN

EXAMPLES OF CHINESE IDEOGRAPHS

Garden-philosophy teaches the value of purchasing the best seed new each year. We do this in planting calendulas. We neglect the Gifted Child. It was studying Chinese ideographs in boyhood that started Champollion toward deciphering Egyptian hieroglyphs.

On the Trail Toward Timbuctu, as well as in Cambery, Chartres, Caen, Combleux, Carcassorne, one finds, on the lintel over the door of every French government building, a narrow board lettered "LIBERTIE, EGALATIE, FRATERNITE." This slogan originally was for the illiterates of Marseilles, Lyons, Paris.

LIBERTIE
FRATERNITE
EGALATIE

Madam Roland observed, en route to the guillotine: "Libertie, Libertie, how many crimes are committed in thy name!"

As to "Fraternite", crimes in ITS name are constantly being committed in the matter of U. S. A. immigration control.

It is EGALATIE, however, upon which was based a garden incident. Dr. David Starr Jordan, pioneering President of Stanford University was an appreciated guest in our home. Once after a meal We-3 strolled in our garden. The good doctor picked a dozen leaves from an elm. These he started laying 1 atop another. They all came from one tree. Not one leaf is an exact duplicate of the next. In Nature there is no EGALATIE. Instead we have VARIATION which indeed spells PROGRESS.

Though France long has been famed for flower breeding, only too few Americans in France ever visit the Departments of Lot, of Tarn et Garrone, or of Tarn. Down there were written immortal pages of French history, as at Montauban and at Albi. One must live in said Tarn country, with its tiny 12th Century churches, to grasp how very fine-toothed was that French comb. This, not to miss the boy Champollian, when and where families of 12 to 16 were not uncommon. At 14 he was publishing original research material embodying his theory that the gods of both Hebrew and of Greek mythology were merely personification of the forces of Nature. Down there one must struggle with stubborn local chauffeurs. These obstinately refuse to motor "where no stranger ever went before." They can be convinced only by "all right, then no *pourbois*."

CHAMPOLLIAN,
GIFTED CHILD

One of the most fascinating little towns of that area is Figeac. It has quaint old houses dating back to more decades before Columbus' landing than U. S. A. has had since the Declaration of Independence. In this backwater town was born, 1790, Jean Francois Champollian, Gifted Child. So thoroughly did France comb even that backcountry for children of promise that they found this Jean Francois, made him professor of history at Grenoble WHILE STILL IN HIS TEENS.

The Garden's Eugenical Thoughts

What impressed Us-2 most, in our adventures in the Tarn area, was above democratic aspect of Champollian's career. BUNSEN DECLARED THE GREATEST DISCOVERY OF THE NINETEENTH CENTURY WAS CHAMPOLLIAN'S FINDING THE KEY TO THOSE MYSTERIOUS SYMBOLS, THE HIEROGLYPHICS OF ANCIENT EGYPT. Another critic rates him as "the founder of Egyptology." One notes he was an "appointed Government pupil".

Champollian correctly deciphered in the 1820's many of the names and titles. He formulated a grammar and a system of decipherment which has been the basis for all subsequent Egyptology. Champollian's Gallic imagination gave him the vision that Coptic, which had persisted since the early Coptic Christians was the key to Egyptian decipherment. This Gifted Frenchman became the world's foremost Coptic scholar.

In the Grenoble hinterland such an educator will recount how Young in 1817 had deciphered the name of Ptolemy, and thus gained several letters of the Egyptian alphabet. He then will expand his theme to praise the gifted Champollian: It was this youngster who found the real key when he deciphered, from Philae obelisk, the name of Cleopatra. . . .

The Egyptians grew barley, even made beer from it. They cultivated from their wild beginnings beans, peas, lentils, garlic, cucumbers, pumpkins, watermelons, also figs, dates, grapes, pomegranates. They made candies of the latter. They had beauty parlors of a kind. Their women stained fingernails, toenails with henna, rouged their cheeks, used antimony to "improve" eyebrows, eyelids. They had fans, mirrors, perfumes, enamelled jewelry.

They had theories of a kind of a Heaven. The papyrus of Anhai (B. C. 1,500) tells of the deceased in the "Other World" playing, with his wife, an ancient Egyptian game somewhat like our checkers.

The secrets of above, declared our French professor, long had been imprisoned papyrus. The Gifted Champollian found the key that unlocked them.

> "Do not throw your pearls before swine, lest they trample them underfoot and turn to attack you."
> (Matthew VII:6)

Before 1921-22-24 Quota Acts, Hyphenates fought immigration restriction. We restrictionists held frontline trenches until U. S. A.'s population reached 160,000,000 saturation. One statistician estimated we prevented a 25,000,000 immigrant deluge. This figure seems far too low. Writer, at his own expense, studied Black Sea Russian Concentration Camps, Armenian Camps in Grand Leban. Today we fight to prevent repeal of new McCarran-Walter Immigration Code. There is demand U. S. A. admit more Displaced Persons. Hindustan-Pakistan war made 20,000,000 D.P.'s. On this desk, a letter from a Colonial ancestry American:—"I believe Freedom means letting all come to share U. S. A.'s living standard." Before me is a California city's legal notice:—"Bricklayer's minimum wages, $3.25 an hour, double overtime." Writer hired Hindu coolies at 4c a day thru No. 1 boy. Latter paid 3½c a day, took ½c for "squeeze".

Once writer talked to a Gangster. He expected to make 100% annually on commercialized vice investments. Money back first year, second years equal 50% profit for 2 years. After that he said "it is velvet until Church folks wake up." Is not your job and mine to keep the "Church folks" awake?

MISTLETOE, COLORADO DESERT

Visible from our garden is a neighbor's tree with one limb snapped from mistletoe weight. The photograph above shows a mesquite. Its left half is dying from mistletoe parasitism. Its righthand branches soon may crack under mistletoe weight, now consuming more plant food than its host.

Parasitism fascinates the garden-philosopher, particularly one absorbed in the problem of U. S. A.'s immigration-control since before the 1921-22-24 Quota Acts. Many immigrants of Colonial days came for freedom of worship. There came, for example, numerous Huguenots both to New Amsterdam and to Charleston. A dramatic description of their willingness to suffer martyrdom for their faith is in Victor Hugo's "Les Miserables." He describes, (Chapter VIII, Part I) the agony of a young Huguenot mother. While nursing her child, she is seized, stripped to the waist, tied to a post. Her child is held before her. Her breasts swell with milk. The babe, famished, cries. The ruthless executioner says "Recant". Such immigrants came to U. S. A. in shiploads in Colonial Days.

Contrast with that type of devotion Displaced Person Klaus Fuchs, convicted traitor, who rewarded sanctuary with betrayal of our atomic secrets to Russia and caused billions of armament taxes.

Is it not important to select desirables from parasites?

The Garden's Eugenical Thoughts 293

EGYPT PARALLELS MEXICO AS TO WATER JARS
The *fellahin's* woman totes the family water in the good old way of B.C. 1,111 as does her Mexican sister.

At some 8 places in this year's garden this June shows blotches of coreopsis gold. One is 35 feet long. The effect is colorful-gold against green background, heightened by broom bloom skyrocketing from the greenery. This studied coloration grows out of city planning responsibility.

CRIME

To lengthen the flowering period, we clip the dead coreopsis. One day a bee seemed asleep. Poked at several times with the clippers, it still did not move. It WAS dead. The same thing with another bee. Next day .. another next ... another next. Having studied the Jack-the-Ripper murders in yesteryear's London slums here was a challenge to a gardening Sherlock Holmes. Finally the assassin was seen— a yellow crabspider lurking in a yellow coreopsis. The Zoology Professor was called as witness. (The resultant argument about camouflage was so serious he stayed away for a week, having insisted bees had no color sense, hence could not be trapped by a predator's concealing coloration). "KAM" or no "KAM", the 6-legged yellow Jack the Ripper pincered his bee, enjoyed his meal and left one more bee "asleep" on a bed of golden coverlet.

All this happened as the 1953 California legislature debated its first billion-dollar budget. One report declares our Golden State cannot build penitentiaries fast enough to hold the ever-accelerated number of convicted criminals. Some years ago the expansion problem was solved by opening road camps for the lesser offenders. Even this expedient does not levee back the flood!

A eugenist thereupon makes bold to ask whether we are not still padlocking a barn door after the equine is hours down the turnpike? The Hyphenates, hell-bent upon levelling all immigration controls, also sneer at yesteryear's research (such as the Kallikak Family) as "pseudoscientific."

ALGIERS' WATER VENDOR

Irrigation, of course, is a factor in gardening in rainless areas. It has always taken a eugenically highpowered mind to plan irrigation. This is true whether on the Nile or on the Sacramento. How many Americans who urge the scrapping of the McCarran-Walter Immigration Code, (formerly the Immigration Quota Acts of 1921, 22, 24), grasp that most of the Backward Peoples had never had the thrill of water from a faucet. The pigskin water carrier vending at veiled women's doors is still the rule over much of the world.

There actually was a "garden" in one of our Pacific Coast penitentiaries. One convict had smuggled in a bit of marijuana seed. The authorities ignored it as a weed. That "con" had quite a bit of intermural commerce, to the delight of the interned narcotic addicts.

California is having plenty of trouble just now with smokers of marijuana cigarettes, which the Arabs long have known as *"hashish"*. This is a part of the penalty we are paying for lack of immigration control on the Mexican Border. When writer was President of the Immigration Study Commission, a volunteer organization, We-2 used to go to the Border every year for field observations. The peons who were crossing then sometimes had as many as 9 children. In fact they were the basis of our 27:729 story, which became a classic.

Above mention of the Arabic word *"hashish"* recalls a story We-2 heard near the Khyber Pass. A caravan was approaching Afghanistan's side gate. 3 stragglers arrived after sunset. The gate was closed. They interrogated each other:—"How can we get thru? To stay here over night the brigands will cut our throats for just our clothing."

The Garden's Eugenical Thoughts

The man who was drunk with whiskey said:—"Let's smash down the gate." The one who had taken too much opium said:—"Let's go to sleep." The one who had indulged in *hashish* suggested:—"Let's crawl thru the keyhole."

LAUNDRY TRUCK

As this is written, the California legislature is debating a bill increasing truck speed from 40 to 50 m.p.h. The argument is "No truck driver observes the 40 m.p.h. limit." Even 40 m.p.h. is an example of the American Know How. Compare this photo your editor kodaked in Salvador. The "laundry wagon" is the negress to extreme right. Its speed was clocked at 2½ m.p.h. The ox team was 1¾ m.p.h.

> Pansies for ladies all — (I wish
> That none who wear such Brooches
> miss a jewel in the mind.)
> (A Flower in a Letter. Browning)

It is Thanksgiving Week. The leaves are falling fast. Soon the trees will be leafless. Our Neighborhood Nature Study class then will be taking its regular nest-hunt. One can find a dozen nests in December to one in May. In Spring also one disturbs avian housekeeping. Same is "shoved b'ind" (as Kipling would say), by the feathered folk. They already are in winter quarters in Guatemala or Ecuador.

But, the French say, "Let us return to our sheep!" Our sheep are those fallen leaves. We resemble McTavish. Remember when Campbell said "Why Sandy, you've lost your stutter." Came the reply "Ay, I've been a-doin' a lot of long distance telephonin' lately!" We SAVE leaves... We SAVE grasscuttings. We return to the soil almost everything except the flowers. We recall the comment of our University of Paris professor. That we might have glimpses of peasant life this scientist invited us to his rural summer cottage. In its neighborhood were gardens supplying Paris with vegetables. The folk there had a saying:—"The most valuable legacy from father to son is the compost heap."...

Mid-July, and 6 A.M. This garden-philosopher works at his "desk," a stiff cardboard on his knees. His seat, a lugbox, recently filled with asparagus from one of his river ranches. The night just ended had a heavy dew. Dewdrops on calendula and clovepink flash red, blue, violet. One recalls the old folksaying:—"All the colors of the rainbow." They truly are the spectrum's VIBGYOR. Each dewdrop is indeed the spectroscope's germ, is a natural prism. Our Sacramento-San Joaquin Valley is in Lower Sonoran Life Zone. Our garden's climate is similar to that of the Nile, the Jordan. Cheops, bossing his mounting pyramid,—Rameses, chiselling off earlier Pharoahs' cartouches to superimpose his own,—even Solomon the Wise, directing unloading of his temple's Lebanon cedar, all these great leaders must have seen color flash from dewdrops on oleander or thistle. EACH SAW THAT COLOR, YET WITH UNSEEING EYES.

"VIBGYOR" DEWDROPS

Menes, Egypt's first King, the one killed by a hippopotamus, Champollian estimated about B.C. 5,861. 7,533 years elapsed between Menes and Newton. Latter first grasped the significance of the spectrum. The sun, however, was to brighten dewdrops into color for more than three additional half-centuries before Frauenhofer was to produce, in 1817, thru his narrow slit, well-defined spectra. (We still call them "Frauenhofer's Lines") We thereupon discover helium in the sun, christen it with its sun-name. This, before we locate on our terrestial ball any of that gas.

The Garden Philosopher sits in his garden, watches dewdrops glitter their VIBGYOR, wonders why so few humans have eyes that can see! Oriental wage standards are one example. Race-suiciding unfortunately, is characteristic of Americans of creative minds. Surgeons, engineers, lawyers, research scientists, these groups all tend toward extinction. Their families only too often contain 2, 1, 0 children. Meantime morons multiply like rabbits. This spells rapid rotting of our civilization. This trend CAN be reversed because of recent research in human genetics. Action thereon depends upon intelligent public opinion. (Is it not the duty of every citizen to become informed on eugenics? Any good librarian will suggest reading.)

The Garden's Eugenical Thoughts 297

PUBLIC LETTER WRITER
More than half the world's population is illiterate. Many are of such low IQ they never can absorb an education.

SOLID WHEELED OX CART, MEXICAN CALIFORNIA
Is not the transition in less than a century from burro to airplane an impressive example of American Know-How? The ox cart, and even more often, the burro brings in what gives "hewers of wood" their tortillas, and perhaps a *vaso* of *pulque*. Bread-and-butter South of the Rio Grande for the fuel vendors is earned by gathering chaparral for fire wood. The *tortillas* are the bread—and there seldom is butter!

Eugenists are fascinated with "Public Health Service Research Grants in Biology" by Chief Allen and Director M. Endicott (A.I.B.S. Bulletin). It records "the economy of supporting OUR PRICELESS ASSET OF BRAIN-POWER WITH MONEYPOWER" now is receiving everwidening acceptance and implementation. The Increase 1946 through 1953 is: "1946, 80 projects, total funds, $780,158 . . . 1953, 2,000 projects, total funds $20,518,000." Figures from Washington indicate research, between 1946 and 1953, expanded some 2,500% in both number of projects and money invested. The comment is "at last we ARE LINKING MONEYPOWER WITH BRAINPOWER." Some of us have been hammering on this for a quarter-century. There were times when we almost lost Faith. NOW comes the Victory!

Courtesy of New Zealand World War I History

TAMARISK ON RIVER JORDAN

This Holy Land photo recalls how often gardening is mentioned in Holy Writ. Ever coming to mind is the parable "Consider the lilies." Also in eugenic selection.

"A net which was thrown into the sea . . . gathered fish of every kind. When it was full, men drew it ashore and sat down AND SORTED THE GOOD INTO VESSELS, BUT THREW AWAY THE BAD" (ST. MATTHEW XIII:47).

Our first garden was at our home facing Sutter's Fort Park. That home AND GARDEN was base for many human betterment campaigns. These included those for introducing Manual Training and

Domestic Science, likewise the Kindergarten into our native city's schools. There began California's Roadside Forestry. In its garden, our friends conspired toward creating Sacramento's playgrounds, and, later its municipal mountain camp, (Camp Sacramento). Here also was nurtured our City Planning, later, National Park's Nature Guiding.

**THE GARDEN—
BASE FOR
CIVIC REFORM**

It was the out-west bringing, from the Atlantic Coast, of the then-new City Planning Movement. This resulted in a widening of our philosophy, to include a new concept of each citizen's responsibility. It was to maintain, within his physical and financial limitations, as attractive a garden as possible. This became a matter of civic pride.

Thus came planning our second, the present Elmhurst garden. City Planning had absorbed much time. At our request Chamber of Commerce created its Committee of 150. Followed the struggle to convince Legislators as to the need of a State Capitol Planning Commission. Thus, arose above sense of responsibility to plan a colorful garden. At this writing, some 45,000 chrysanthemum blooms are this month's contribution to the annual succession of color effects. Even January has pink of Tibetan saxifrages contrasted with white of Tazettas. Some years, New Year's Day shows acacias of Dad's native Australia bursting into golden glory.

The Sweetheart's passing brought awakening as to the fact that most of creative beauty of a garden is a FORCE FROM WITHIN. IS NOT THE PROFOUND PHILOSOPHIC LESSON HEREIN, THAT COLLAPSE COMES, NOT FROM WITHOUT, BUT FROM WITHIN? IS NOT THE PARALLEL OF ABOVE IN OUR NATIONAL LIFE TREMENDOUSLY SIGNIFICANT? One ponders about the reckless national debt increase between 1932 and 1952. Have not such additions, (which, in this writer's opinion were using U. S. Treasury to buy political power toward the 4-term Presidency and dictatorship), permanently lowered the American standard of living? ...

"Throw mud. Some of it will stick"
(Cynical Continental European folksaying)

The garden teaches the value of breeding always from the best strains. U. S. A. knew nothing of Smear strategy until the 1904-1914 immigration influx. We then accepted, (despite President Theodore Roosevelt's warning about "converting U. S. A. into the world's poor house"), over a million immigrants annually.

**"PSEUDO-
ANTHROPOLOGY"**

These included a deplorable percentage of social inadequates. Certain European governments solved their armament-financing problems by the simple expedient of mass-dumping of relief-rolls folk on U. S. A. Here we were breeding humans from "weeds."

Congress then was dominated by biologically-illiterate Blundering Idealists. So powerful were these blocks politically that even Presidents bowed submissively. Study Presidential vetos of immigration control bills to grasp this.

To protect our institutions came the building up of public opinion by the American Coalition. It included representatives from nearly 100 alert organizations. These helped secure enactment of the Quota Acts of 1921-22-24. Same deserved House Chairman Albert Johnson's terse phrase: "They are our Second Declaration of Independence." ...

At a dinner was a woman we will dub "Frau Messerschmidt". During the conversation she used several technical terms from anthropology. This author asked:—"Are you an anthropologist?" "Not yet. I am studying for a degree in that science so that I can propagandize as an instructor. I'm going to eliminate from American thinking the pseudoanthropology taught today. And I am working now to have my own professor silenced!" This was her gratitude for being admitted to American citizenship!

Neither Confucius nor Lao Tze ever heard of a gene or of a chromosome. They, however, out of what we call "common sense" (and which seems none too common) philosophized eugenically. ...

> "Ten maidens took their lamps and went forth to meet the bridegroom. FIVE OF THEM WERE FOOLISH AND FIVE WERE WISE."
>
> (St. Matthew XXV)

Thus, after commencing to glimpse the meanings of the sayings of Confucius, and, later, of the parables of Christ, one comes to grasp that the great spiritual teachers were not ashamed to use the God-in-Nature concept.

The Great Creative Force, which all religions recognize, tho they may call it by different names, is the same as that of which the Psalmist was thinking when he sang:—

> "The Heavens declare the Glory of God,
> And the Firmament Showeth His handiwork."

"Learn to read a trailside like a book" (Slogan We-2 invented in launching what since has become National Parks' Interpretive Movement).

"Here is one passage which might have been written in Victorian England. The writer is describing a peculiar disease prevalent among the nomads of Southern Russia. 'The natives' he remarks 'believe that this disease is sent by God, and they reverence and worship its victims, in fear of being stricken by it themselves. I, too, am quite ready to admit that these phenomena are caused by God, but I take the same view about all phenomena and hold that no single phenomenon is more or less divine in origin than any other. All are uniform and all may be divine, but each phenomenon obeys a law and natural law knows no exceptions. (Hippocrates Opera")

"Look to the lilies how they grow!"
'Twas thus the Saviour said, that we
In even the simplest flowers that blow,
God's ever-watchful care might see.
(Moir—Lilies)

Thus comes the summary of what his garden taught one inquirer. The one dominant concept is that of God-in-Nature. One continually repeats to himself above text:

"The Heavens declare the Glory of God,
The Firmament showeth His Handiwork."

There seem to be several subheads:—

ASTRONOMY. When one from his garden adores the stars, the feeling of vast space deepens.

GEOLOGY. When one's hoe moves his garden soil, he recalls it is powdered Sierran strata. This became a vast "fan" into the Sacramento Valley. Of same, his garden is a microscopic bit. Ever more profound becomes the sense of vast time. This, because he knows that that soil must have atoms of corals, of crinoids, of brachipods from when those mountains were sea bottom.

BIOLOGY. The garden persistently dins into his ears the fact that *zeilstrebigkeit* forces infinite variety of garden insect, bird, flower.

He thus comes to accept certain facts. One is his need of humility, because of his own fleeting insignificance. Another is that, despite his having such a tiny part in this vast drama, he has a duty to speak his lines as clearly as his voice can carry.

**REACTION OF A TURKISH GARDEN-PHILOSOPHER
TO THE FALL OF A WALNUT**
"Well! Allah did know best after all!"

Like Mrs. Smith, who "learned to play golf in one lesson," humans, even the Kohja, DO learn. Many Kohja* folktales are located in Turkish gardens. The one of the walnut tree is of a garden long abandoned after the childless owner's death. All that remained was one walnut tree. One hot August noon, the Kohja, returning from Market, stopped to rest in its shade. Hungry, he cracked a few walnuts. The tree had gone long unirrigated, their shells were hard. The nuts were tiny. Their meats were scanty.

**KOHJA "IMPROVES"
ALLAH'S WORK**

As the Kohja, finding a couple of rocks, hammered nuts—and fingers, he mused:—"If Allah had asked my advice, I would have enlightened him. Then his walnuts would have been as big as pumpkins." His tummy satisfied, he leaned against the tree trunks, soon was snoring. Then a falling walnut raised a pigeon egg-sized-bump on his bald head.

Thereupon this Philosopher of Philosophers exclaimed "Well, Allah did know best after all!"

---
*Kohja-Tamerlane folktales were the backbone of the successful Young Turk Movement. This created modern Turkey, today it is our ally against the Soviets. For Turkish humor see Eugenics Pamphlet No. 76, in most libraries.

Into this melange of fact and gossip based on the musings of a Garden Philo-soph-er has crept bits of anecdote. May one more be inflicted upon the reader? The excuse for relating it is, that, in the last analysis, it is connected with the God-in-Nature concept and may be illuminating.

At a recent meeting the speaker was an Australian. This writer, whose Dad was Australian-born, was asked to introduce him. It was the custom, each session, to decorate the rostrum with a bouquet. That night it was a magnificent vase of giant flaming red blooms.

This writer understands clearly that, though chronologically he is octogenarian, his real mental age may be 1/10 thereof. In fact, some of his boyish pranks make him wonder if he is a moron. Such an impulse came without warning in that introduction. Describing the attainments of the guest from the land of kangaroos, emus, cockatoos, this yarn uncontrollably was invited:—"The Board asked me to introduce our speaker from Down Under because my Father was a countryman of his. Our family has kin there, so I cabled them to airpost me, as a special greeting for him, these gorgeous waratahs from the edge of the Never-Never." Then I pointed to the vase. . . .

The Australian's address was well received. Many, at its conclusion, pressed forward to the platform to thank him. All but two dear ladies. They personified "lavender and old lace." Their lorgnettes studied those scarlet "waratahs." I eavesdropped shamelessly. "Phoebe, I insist they are just big, red chrysanthemums". "But, Beatrice, Mr. Goethe said they were waratahs he had had flown in from Australia. He always tells the truth. If he said they are waratahs, they ARE waratahs!" (I could have hugged her.)

Since that incident there has been reflection. Miss Phoebe had the analytic, scientific, sternly fact-finding intellect. Miss Beatrice had trustful Faith. Do we, in trying with our painfully finite minds to understand God-in-Nature, not need both?

EGYPTIAN PYLON
"To Ammon-Re, the Sun God were erected vast temples on the Nile."

INCA ARCHITECTURE

It was impossible for writer to press the blade of his pocketknife between these stones, tho the wall was at least 400 years old. This engineering ability gives us a glimpse as to the remarkable leadership of their intelligentsia. As a gardener and as the owner of a string of California ranches, this author was amazed at the evidences, visible even today, of their ability in agriculture, as for example, their terracing of what we would not even think of as "marginal lands". Writer has repeatedly written of the liquidation of their leadership.*

---
*See Eugenics Pamphlets on file in most U. S. A. libraries (local, also collegiate).

>   Gold-tiled Thy temples,
>   Oh! God of the Sun!
>   Blood-red the battles
>   That for Thee we've won.
>   Here, from the Sacred Rock,
>   The Sunrise Kiss we send
>   Eastward to Thy Red-Gold Orb.
>   Rising years without end.
>   (Inca Hymn)

SUNWORSHIP In the Gardening-philosopher's desire to be more than tolerant, his wish is to respect the good there must be in any religion. For this he probes in even the nature worship of primitives. His memory therefore reverts constantly to the faith of Ancient Egypt.

It was based on Sunworship. To Ammon-Re, the Sun God, vast temples on the Nile were erected. There is plenty of evidence more than one Pharoah tickled his ego in thus exacting labor from ten-thousands of slaves. There was, however, beneath all that, (and undoubtedly based on planned religious education in his childhood), reverence for God-in-Nature. This, the Egyptian interpreted as being centered in that mighty ball of fire that daily gave warmth and light. The Pharoah, his priests, all prostrated themselves in adoration of The Sun . . .

Impressive also was the vast development of Sun-worship in Inca Land. It was indeed the accumulation of gold in the roof tiles, also the wall panelling of Inca Sun God Temples, along with their studding of emeralds, that excited the cupidity of the Conquistadores. This stimulated their strategy of "destroy all eugenical leaders." (i.e. the royal, the priestly, the warrior castes.)

With a Benjamin-Franklinese philosophy of Utilitarianism, the humble garden philosopher asks himself:—"What use can A.D. 1954 make of this concept of long before B.C. 1954? Then he asks himself the question:—Could adoration of God-in-Nature manifested in The Sun be better expressed than by the establishment of a string of Sun-therapy stations* for the children imprisoned in furnace-heated rooms of the Snow Belt? Should there not be a string of these from Texas' Pecos River to California's Palm Springs?

---
*See "Seeking to Serve" (pp 136, also 187). The book is out-of-print, but available at most public, also college libraries.

———o———

"Oh! Thou beautiful Dawn Goddess
   Clad in Thy robes of Saffron
   Thou who awakenest all luring things." (Vedic Hymn)

DAWN This is written at Dawn in our garden. Said garden was planned for Sun-worship. The dwelling was built as far as possible near the west boundary. This, because from our estate, when Elmhurst still was almost rural, we could watch the Sun God appear from Nevada's side of the Sierran Range.

This, may it be repeated, is written at Dawn in our garden. The first sun rays will not show resplendent for a half-hour. The night has been north-windy. There is much fine dust between us and the distant Tahoe peaks. Now, as when in the Punjab milleniums ago above hymn was written, the Dawn Goddess deigns to show herself. She knows it is queenly, yes, godlike to array one's self charmingly. And this morning, this north-windy morning, she has donned those Vedic "robes of saffron". One dares not look upon the awful brilliancy of a Goddess. All a mere human can see is her outer garment that prevents his being stricken sightless.

He also sees, however, that process the Vedic poet once described as "awakening all living things". Our squirrel stirs up in the elm-fork, then scamps down for his "coffee and". The sparrows commence calling. Some gulls, awakened by the growing light, wheel in the sky. A raucous crow passed, black against the saffron sky, his cawing reminding us that he, too, needs breakfast. Then, from their roost in the deodar, a pair of jays start reported "Breakfast is now being served in the dining car. The first call for breakfast."

Once more may it be repeated "This is written at Dawn in our Garden". Comes a note of sadness with the evidently joyful stirring of the wee beasties, so evidently sure breakfast will be provided by Him who cares for even the sparrows. A note of sadness because one almost an octogenarian recalls he is a remnant of the Pioneering Age. From this very garden site indeed when the home first was built, Pyramid Peak could be seen etched sharp against that Saffron Sky. Since the 1870's, increasing urbanization has come. Also the automobile. There no longer is need, as this author was taught in those 1870's, to be ready to start at the first glimmer of daybreak, that the heavy horsework should be "shoved be'ind one" before midafternoon's debilitating heat.

An evergrowing number of Americans, under increasing population-pressure, must live in apartments, in hotel rooms. What chance have they of going out into the garden at daybreak grateful that, from the deodar, said pair of jays start reporting "Breakfast is now being served in the dining car."

"Night, the Dark One,
 Impelled by impulse
  Straightway yields up her place
 Unto the Dawn"

CHILDHOOD MEMORIES (Of all the overseas geogardening experiences, none made a deeper impression than wanderlusting to Palestine. Perhaps early religious training was one factor herein. Childhood memories were of the Star of Bethlehem, of the camel-borne Three Kings, of the manger, of the Prodigal Son eating the husks of the Swine, of the animals that went, 2 by 2 into Noah's Ark, of Palm Sunday. Thus the life of an Occidental boy early was tinged with Oriental coloring.)

The membership list of an international scientific group, of which your editor is a member, is on this desk. A random sample approximately classifies names as follows: Nordic 191, South European 9, South American 3, Doubtful 5, HINDU 2. (It is one of the world's most fruitful groups in research.)

It is those 2 Hindu names, (out of 210), that fascinate this writer. This, because during much of the last 2 decades, he seemed alone in his insistence that Hindustan COULD be built into a great selfsustaining world power. He cautiously dubbed his suggestions "A 500-year Plan". This, when such articles appeared here as "India's Insoluble Hunger"—when Hindustan's own commission of native Pundits felt "absolutely hopeless"—when demagogic *babus** screamed "U.S.A., with its boundless wealth must support us."—also "must accept our 20,000,000 Displaced Persons as immigrants."

AGAIN, THE "500-YEAR PLAN"

(Writer's family has had said 3 generations' connection with Hindustan. He knows that great subcontinent from Calcutta to Lahore, from Benares to Bombay. As he discovers that precious minus-1% in the above list, his mind goes back to above experience on the Ganges. Perhaps, at last, the Dawn Goddess is sending "Heroes". Only too often it takes heroism to be a Leader.

*Why not reread Kipling's "The Head of the District" for a marvelous word picture of pompous, but cowardly Babu Chunder Dee? It will help toward a clearer insight into Hindustan's muddle of today.

VILLAGE WELL, HINDUSTAN
There probably is no world area in the world where the problem of Hewers and Drawers is more insistent than in Hindustan.

The Pah Utes of Central Nevada were the hoppickers of Sacramento Valley in the days when they rode, free, on Central Pacific passenger coach platforms. The Washoes of Lake Tahoe, also came down before snowfall to the Sierran piedmont for the acorn harvest. Both these Amerinds would yarn to an eager boy.

NATS, ALSO DUPPIES

Then, too, Dad's two years in Australia's Never-Never, with his aunt's blackfellows, brought an insight into the mental process of another group of primitives. Dad's food-getting, like that of his black-fellow companions, was confined to boomerang work. On the hunt, at the campfire, came to him glimpse of nature lore, even as to the Spirits. These he enjoyed recounting to his eldest son. Thus commenced an urge to fathom the nature-thinking of Primitives.

In the Burmese jungles was a very old teak something like our California Sequoias. By its side a little top or pagoda. A childless young wife, barefoot, with turban of pink, blouse of blue, skirt of orange steals noiselessly along the trail. She has a bit of gold leaf.

Thus came an urge that continued with negro "help", also Chinese houseboys in the closing days of the California Gold Rush. (What didn't they tell an attentive lad about devildriving, dragons, eclipses). Followed contact with West Indian negro lore about "Duppies". This seemed a probable mixture of Carib-Amerind and Congo-African.

Thus came long continued thinking about the reacting of the primitive mind about the manifestations of God-in-Nature. These were also in the garden's wind, and rain, and thunder, in its starlight, its moonlight, its sunlight.

There are so many profound facts the Garden earnestly is trying to teach us and we remain stubborn. Oh! well, in 1616 Galileo was charged with heresy because he insisted the earth revolved around the sun, when everybody knew it was the sun that daily moved across the heavens. . . .

"Eat no fig until it has donned its beggar's coat."
(Arab folksaying, based upon the fig's cracking when in full sugar).

Any native Californian's garden contains at least one figtree. Ours is doubly fortified. One is a Mission, big black fig lovingly brought into California by the Mission Fathers. (This, along with the olive, the pear, the Mission grape.

SERMON ON THE MOUNT ... ITS EUGENICAL ASPECTS

With the Padres also came "weeds" that stole rides on long woolly Franciscan robes. Same include filaree, a desirable alien. Others, such as prickly lettuce, decidedly are unwanted aliens.)

Our other fig is a white, a Kodota. This variety drips with honey. Having a tough coat, it is suitable for our home-canning. Such planning means figs, fresh or preserved, every week in the year for the true Californian. Was it not Sir Walter Scott who wrote something like this:—

Breathes there a man with soul so dead,
That never to himself hath said:
"This is my (fig-clad) native Land!"

The fig was the magnet that caused Us-2, as fig-loving Californians to make the pilgrimage to where was preached the "Sermon on the Mount". Fig enthusiasts from childhood, we have come, in mature years, to sense the eugenic aspect of "Do men gather grapes of thorns, figs of thistles?" We contacted, in Jerusalem, Biblical scholars. Their research enabled them to decide what, in the Holy Land, was authentic, what was smoke-screened for exploitation of the superstitious.

The Hillock of the Sermon was a walk of more than a mile from our auto. The way was thru lava, sharp enuf that one had to beware of cutting shoes. Its interstices, however, held enuf windblown soil to give Us-2, in full spring glory, a wild garden of unforgettable color.

"As the twig is bent, the tree will grow"

That the garden can be used to dramatize religious education was proven by the experiment of Us-2 at our church. The experiment really began with our botanizing in Palestine. We long had known the climate of the Mediterranean Basin was similar to that of our native California. It was not, however, until our contact with the group of Biblical scholars in Jerusalem that we grasped that many of the flowers and trees naturalized in our native California were originally from the Eastern Mediterranean.

RELIGIOUS EDUCATION

It was the foot journey from our automobile to the eminence where was preached the Sermon on the Mount that impressed upon us the possibilities of the use of the garden for religious education.

In our garden under the deodars, We-2 often discussed religious education strategy. One of the satisfying attempts, which seem to be growing yearly in favor, is the Vacation Bible School. One sometimes wonders, however, how well facts are absorbed. An example, a little girl had the fun of making, in the yard behind the church, a replica of a sandy desert. Asked afterwards what she had learned, she said:— "The desert is a terrible place to be in. Moses was there. Believe it or not, he could not find a place anywhere to buy ice cream or even a coke."

Watching a polar bear foraging on a Jan Mayan Land ice floe . . . or a baby wallaby peeking out of its mother's pouch in Australian's Never-Never . . . or enjoying the color feast of a half hundred flamingoes' nuptial pink, alighting against an Amazon headwaters' lake's sapphire blue, writer sometimes tries to trace back to its beginnings the urge that impelled him to go repeatedly overseas to better appreciate God-in-Nature. Did it begin in childhood's gardens?

PRIEST & SCROLL

"Consider the lilies . . . They toil not. Neither do they spin. Yet Solomon in all His glory, was not arrayed like one of these".

Intriguing it was to leave the highway toward Nazareth at Jacob's Well to visit the remnant of the Samaritans. That little group, sensed we were genuinely interested in the final extinction they were so evidently approaching. They were good enough to uncover for us the old codex or scroll they cherished so highly... That night We-2 stayed at a little inn in Nazareth. Its rooms reeked with camel-stink. Toward evening a caravan wound its way thru the narrow street. The same afternoon we had seen a young man working across the tiny lane in a carpenter shop. We easily could have thrown a stone across from our room to his feet. Seeing this carpenter at work, one sensed then the marvelous philosophy of democracy permeating Christianity.

ORPHANAGE FARM GARDEN Grandmother had been active in organizing the Protestant Orphanage. Later its 18th and K Street plant became outmoded. The Orphanage's brilliant 1907 President, Mrs. D. A. Lindley, engineered sale of the Gold Rush Days' site to the city. With the proceeds, she purchased the Orphanage Farm; built there a cottage system. Each Board member was responsible for one cottage. Ours was Rideout, gift of Dr. and Mrs. Wm. Ellery Briggs (nee Rideout). Thus began an investment of service by Us-two over most of 2 decades. We first attempted directed play. This was surprisingly successful. We-two then employed a Stanford University graduate in supervised play, to expand throughout the entire institution the work we had developed at Rideout.

One item of our successful playground work was its use as a base for Nature Study Field Excursions. In those days, the Orphanage Farm was truly rural. In Spring, native wildflowers blossomed. Summer brought butterflies, beetles, bugs. Autumn had orb-weaving spiders, turpentine weeds, tarweeds. These Mexican-originated wild flowers had their own peculiar insect visitors. The Fall yielded also seed-travelers. Winter meant search for galls, lepidoptera-cocoons, wasps' mud-jugs, other wonders beneath loose bark. The rainy months, too, included netting watertigers, whirligig beetles, backswimmers for the cottage aquarium. Winter's coolth spelt arrival of winter-visitant birds. We collected from leafless trees abandoned nests for the home museum. Winter was marked by brilliant sunsets.

The Orphanage Farm then had a clear, unbroken sweep of the Coast Range. No buildings at that time obstructed the Golden West. We educated our bairns to know that no one could rob them of the love of sunset color.

Another phase was gardens like Germany's *Kleingartenvertrieb*. Each child had its own garden. Its vegetables were peddled among the Orphanage Cottages. Pay came in colored tickets, which We-2 redeemed at intervals. Kiddies were encouraged to save 50%. We gave each gardener a $1 savings bank book toward this. Thus they learned thrift, but more so, Gardening.

Does any garden philosophizing exceed that of the strengthening of FAITH? One buys bluegrass seed for a new lawn, has FAITH it will not produce Bermuda. He plants corn, (another grass family member), with FAITH it will not produce Johnson Grass. He buys sweetpea seed for early Fall plantings, to have St. Patrick's Day flowers. He has FAITH the sproutings will not produce halogeton. In the long struggle with them one needs the FAITH of a gardener, who knows all eventually will be well.

True, there can be disillusions. Looking back over a half-century of investments, this veteran banker recalls but one instance in which he suffered loss because of FAITH. A certain bondhouse had a reputation for sterling integrity. It had built up, over three generations, a reputation for scrupulously honest dealings. One was justified in accepting their recommendations. Then a new generation preferred living in luxury on their family's accumulated profits. They sold out, shamelessly, to some aliens. These conspirators remained nameless, used the reputation of that honorable bondhouse to unload, across the nation, securities destined to final bankruptcy.

When writer is questioned: Why continue to battle vigorously for immigration restriction, he remembers those worthless securities in his safe deposit box. Because of lack of proper screening, because of politicians yielding to highly-organized alien blocks' pressure, only too many of these unscrupulous overseas characters find it easy to enter, then to milk the American cow....

It is Washington's Birthday. We have lovingly "fed" the soil where soon will appear the aspiring red shoots of our peonies. They know the sense of *"noblesse oblige"*. They grasp they must be good

ARISTOCRATIC PEONIES
guests, tho they, at heart, may be suffering from nostalgia. Some of them came to our garden a half century ago. From China, from Korea, from Japan they rickshawed to their respective transpacific steamers. One imagines his garden peonies divided into clans, so that the Chinese are politely critical of those from Japan, and vice versa. And, of course ,the Koreans, in the days of bloom to come, will gossip about both Nipponese and Celestials.

They are all as proud of their lineage as F.F.V.'s or New England's Mayflower descendants. And this rightfully, for the Japanese peonies can claim descent from Jimmo Tenno's days, and HIS is the World's oldest dynasty. The Chinese peony blooms, however, will whisper behind their leafy fans, "Upstarts".

It is the Korean peonies that stimulate fondest memories. One was a present from old Pak. He was a flowerpot-hatted noble that truly sensed *noblesse oblige*. He lived, of course, in the shadow of the Emperor's Palace at Korea. He knew Korea rested on a dragon and that recent earthquakes were caused by those American mining engineers. Latter persistently were pricking the mighty dragon's skin with their shafts and tunnels searching for gold. He saw thru the boasting of these men that in their America there were buildings 3 stories high. The astrologers had read the stars, predicted trouble from such scoffers. As he nervously fingered his amber beads, we saw we had in Pak the world's No. 1 conservative.

But we loved old Pak. We could not do otherwise. The returned missionary doctor, whose skill had saved his eldest son's life, had written of our coming. He was a Fusan Pier to properly and ceremoniously greet Us-2. We had tea together, expecting further talk on the train. "Oh! no! We would have tea together in his home in Seoul in a fortnight."

We were mystified. Later we learned from an American, then resident in Korea, he had WALKED from Seoul to Fusan to greet us! This took one fortnight, another to walk back. The Japanese militarists had taxed his old nobility with ruthless extermination strategy. If he had bought a railroad ticket, it would have cost him a half month's income. In a month, coming and going, without food, one can lose much weight. It was walk to Fusan, walk back to Seoul. But the Code required he show the proper hospitality.

So we watch the peony's red shoots appear each year thru the fertilized soil. We eagerly await unfolding of leaf, and then of gor-

God-in-Nature

geous, cerise petals. And we think of the Korea that is no more, of the grave, dignified, kindly flower-pot hatted nobles in their long togas of grasslinen, apple green or lavender.

And this year deepens our admiration of President Sygman Rhee, embodiment of the old caste's sense of honor, of *Noblesse Oblige*.

"NOBLESSE OBLIGE" AT SALZBURG

One wonders how much Mozart was aided in his compositions by the beauty of Salzburg's Civic art. This was a contribution, over the centuries, of the Prince-Bishops drawn from the aristocracy. One sees occasionally an old coat of arms whose sole device is a turnip. A peasant allegedly was appointed by the Vatican to punish the proud aristocracy of Salzburg. He chose to remind them his love of gardening was confined to that producing edibles.

"Every cloud has a silver lining"

The mid-September, our garden's sky is as clear as it has been since mid-May. In the East, however, over the Sierra Nevada's Crystal Range, the clouds bank high. Behind them, the sun is rising. The dark cloud-mass is impressively silver-lined. If there is any spiritual dividend gardening pays,—it is Peace of Mind. When one is among his **DON'T WORRY** flowers watching the insect, the bird, the color, also the perfume devices, all these that natural selection may result in evolution upward, he has a feeling of AT-ONE-MENT with God. He ceases to worry. . . . Shakespeare made Polonius counsel his son:—"To thine own self be true." This is an item the garden almost screams at one.

Those who neglect being true to their own selves sometimes occupy high places. They will do almost anything to gain a few votes.

An example of this was the face-reddening of more than one so-called statesman. These yesteryear became victims of practical joking by a group of college students. Said conspirators radiated into high places invitations to attend a celebration at their college. At same, the founder of the Republican Party, an alumnus, was to be honored. It was the centenary of his birth.

Above "failing to be true to one's own self" can lead to embarrassment. It did at that dinner to revive memories of a Forgotten Man, Hugo N. Frye. He was the founder of that long powerful elephantine Republican line of Presidents. His college now determined he should not go down in oblivion.

Invitations to this centenary dinner were forwarded nationwide to distinguished statesmen of the proper type. They were requested, if not able to accept, to send messages of goodwill. The regrets were most laudatory. More than one responded with elaborate eulogiums of the man with rare vision who saw the need of consolidating patriots into what became the Republican Party. Some reported personal experiences, to be preserved in the coming history. All this was a student prank about an imaginary "YOU-GO-AND-FRY?"

Polonius advice was not out-of-date? "To thine own self be true".

> Does gardening pay? It is difficult to define what is meant by "paying". There is a popular notion that unless a thing pays, you had better let it alone. As I look at it, you might as well ask: Does a sunset pay? ("My Summer in a Garden".) (From "Come Into My Garden" Reader's Digest 6/53.)

GARDEN DIVIDENDS On a side street in Paris is a gift shop "Au Petite Bonheurs" (To the Little Happiness). The garden philosopher sometimes wonders whether it is not the little happinesses that make life worth living. The color of a full blown pink rose on its bush . . . the smile of a baby picking a few garden flowers—the flash of orange red in a flicker's wing—the joy of a painracked patient in a hospital bed, when given a gladioli stem that can be held in the hand, but known to have been grown by the giver—a basket of persimmons from the tree in one's garden—the excitement of little Mary when she found a housefinch nest with five skyblue eggs—the "Oh-dear-me" call notes of goldencrowned sparrows beneath the escallonia shelter—the wedding dance of an Anna hummingbird—the wheeling of a flock of white pelicans against a cloudless blue sky above the garden in a Norther—the first violets peep out from their green leaves—the scent of a clove pink border under the full moon— Sirius the dogstar—(and now the knowledge it is a double)—the play-

God-in-Nature

ful dance of dried and fallen leaves along the garden path during a gale —the spectroscope color in a dewdrop on a June morning—the camouflage of newly hatched quail babies. The unwinding of the watchspring tongue of a butterfly feasting on the nectar cups of a calendula ... the love-calls of a tree cricket on a starlit summer night ... the neon-like reflection of a night moth's eyes on the screen ... the potential growth in an acorn—yes, the *Petite bonheurs* are to be had for the looking in the Gift Shop *au Jardin*. ...

The middle of April, the month of showers. Saturday, leaden skies were here, just the kind in the plantation song when
"Satan lies awaitin', creatin' skies of grey".
Followed showers. On Monday, however, the storm broke with blue skies displaying great mass of cumulus clouds in all their majesty truly. Thorean was canny when he wrote:—"We do not look up enuf at The Sky." Is this not true, materialistically and spiritually? From our garden we shall watch these cumulus clouds at sunset banked against the Sierra Nevadas. They will be pink with alpenglow. They will remind us of the Alps from Berne.

CLOUDS

"There are people all over the world eating their hearts out to travel and see wonders which are far away, yet most of them are blind to wonders near at hand. In familiar events of the familiar world about me, which I dismiss as utterly trifling, Shakespeare would find the material for a play." (W. E. Sangster. The Saturday Review/Reader's Digest 10/53.)

GARDEN-MONUMENTS IN HISTORY-EDUCATION
This old horse-and-buggy-days photograph of Berlin's Royal Museum and Lustgarten illustrates the use of the *Denkmal* or Monument as a history lesson. Do not the fountains add to what all gardening really should be? *"Lustgartens"* or PLEASURE Gardens.

MORNING GLORY MECHANICS

The 50-foot-high deodar group in our garden's northeast corner is dense. It further is flanked for 100 feet, right and left by lush escallonias. What memories these deodars recall of the real Hills, whose great forested flanks butress Himalayan passes toward Tibet. They bring recollections of gangs of saucy monkeys, of hill-wives with heavy anklets of silver, their husbands' savingsbanks, of greeneyed Chinese from the edge of Turkestan with queues of red hair. Above escallonias bring memories of botanizing for wild potatoes in Peru, of inquisitive llamas, toting loads of brick tin, of coca-chewing, ponchoed *Indios*, drunken with "tigers milk", of the first dwarf pepper trees near the timber line, like California's gnarled junipers.

In a leafy cavern of these deodars' escallonia fringe morningglory seeds have been dropped by birds. The sunrays in late October do not penetrate that "cave" until about 2 P.M. By 4 P.M., the morning glories, both magenta and violet, are in full "glory" of bloom. At noon they had shown no sign of bloom. Morning glories at our home's south facade had completed, by noon, their bloom. Their corollas then were three-fourths toward complete envelope. Is it not evident their response is to direct sunlight? The alteration of habit by the deodar-darkened morning glories stimulates memories of field studies We-2 made of Villard de Lans' sun therapy for kiddies.

> Gay circles of anemones
> Dancing on their stalks.
> The shad-bush,
> White with flowers,
> Brightened the glens.
> (Bryant—The Old Man's Counsel)

KANT'S GARDEN

The garden every day offers so much happiness ... so few take time to sip. The philosopher, Dr. Emanuel Kant, throughout his 80 years, found his home and garden all-sufficient. He left them only for occasional saunterings for a few miles in the suburbs of his native university city of Koeningsburg. An omnivorous reader, one of Kant's biographers comments: "His acquaintance with books of sciences was boundless. Did he not find communion in that garden sufficient to produce his vigorous protest against censorship in religion: *"Der Streit der Facultaeten."* How much that we owe to him is due to the fact he found his own home and garden and a few square miles surrounding it all-sufficient for his thinking. Was he not a super-philosophizing gardener, with reflections that gave us:—*"Allgemeine Natur geschicte und Theorie des Himmels.* . . ., his "Theory of the Winds" . . . his "Different Races of Men" . . . his "Volcanoes of the moon".

God-in-Nature 317

As a mere amateur garden philosopher contemplates Kant's gigantic intellect, he seems to find a parallel in classic Greece. Kant could write an essay on "Whether the Earth, in its Revolutions, has experienced some changes since the Earliest Times". Is here not something as lofty as Eratosthenes? Kant had no need to travel from Alexandria to Syene. His garden was enuf.

"My mind to me a Kingdom is"
Such present joys therein I find.

* * * * *

So, thus I triumph like a King.
With that my mind doth bring.

A distinguished scientist-philosopher, sends an arresting message. He discussed the bringing, from Europe to U.S.A., by Us-2, of what developed into National Parks Nature Guiding:—"You write of tackling the neglected problem of recreation for the Senescent. You discuss providing recreation to relieve the tragic loneliness of the aged. Are you thinking at the problem's wrong end? Were you not more canny in utilizing Europe's Nature study field excursions? Is not the real task packing youngster minds with so much about the out-of-doors, they will know the meaning of 'God gave us Memory, that we might have Roses in December' "?

RECREATION FOR SENESCENTS

Writer's own old age, forsooth, IS crammed with just such wild life memories: Auks flying under water off the Ice Barrier, with North Pole only hours away ... dignified Antarctic penguins, strutting about in their tuxedos ... blue-silk butterflies, leisurely winging thru Brazil's Golden Monkey Jungle's bougainvillea-draped trees ... A herd of wild elephants in the jungle ... Trading a can of coffee with a Lapp for shelter and a couple of meals of reindeer-blood cakes ... lyrebird's "wedding dance" in an Australian rain forest ... Somaliland negroes, hair stained green because of recent pilgrimage to Mecca ... From even one's home garden one recalls many delights, the odor of massed clovepinks in the moonlight, a little child gathering flowers for teacher ... a lizard bowing as politely as a Japanese peasant surprised on a trail in the bamboos ... a chickadee, never too busy with foraging but he makes time for gossip ... Dawn, and the contrasted shapes, against its saffron, of conifer and deciduous trees ... a meteor's flash across a moonless sky ... alpenglow on sunset clouds after yesterday's storm.

Practical ranchers are really gardeners, with city lots expanded to acres upon acres. They testify to continued indebtedness to researchists. Many acres of exceedingly fertile river bottom on one of writer's ranches was planted to grain, maturable in August. Same was choked out by radish infestation, seeding in May. Noting the menace, writer, in February, sprayed by airplane. Costing $200 per hour, a few hours work, however saved the crop. Above was only possible by COOPERATION between researchists in botany and in chemistry. Only because botanists knew difference between grasses and crucifers, could chemists work out the solution with a crucifer-killer that did not injure grain. This is "American Know How".

DEBT TO RESEARCHISTS

Our civilization, however, cannot persist if we continue race-suiciding long characteristic of Americans of creative minds. Surgeons, engineers, lawyers, research scientists, long have tended toward extinction. Many such families contain 2, 1, 0 children, whereas Patrick Henry, Virginia leader in 1776, had 16. Meantime morons multiply like rabbits. This spells rapid crumbling of our civilization. . . .

> "The years at the Spring,
> Spring's at the Morn,
> Mornings at Seven!
> The hillsides dewpearled,
> The larks on the wing,
> The snails on the thorn
> GOD'S IN HIS HEAVEN.
> ALL'S WELL WITH THE WORLD!"
> (Browning: Pippa Passes)

Just now the cherry is in blossom, while the leaves properly hesitate. The elm also is in full bloom. We clip branches of its nile green flowers to contrast the decorations of our home against the gold of forsythia. Cherry, elm, forsythia foliage all patiently await blossom-time, so as to give 100% efficiency to flowering that must precede seedmaking.

One goes up to the garage attic for a wheeled cultivator stored since last Hallowe'en. The room of the home museum is open. This always is a temptation to enter, pick up some fossil and mingle gardening with philosophizing.

COMFORT OF BEING "IN TUNE WITH THE INFINITE"

Yes, the shelf of fossil leaves from way back in the Cretaceous. One ponders:—"Did the elm-like ancestors of our moderns refrain from leafing until flowering was completed?" Probably not. Have we not something to bulwark our faith here as we lay a leafless twig of present day elm bloom beside the Cretaceous fossil. God IS in His Heaven today while the "snail's on the thorn." Evolution ever toward greater efficiency, has spaced flowering and leafing toward better seedmaking.

At this writing, debate proceeds between Fundamentalists and Evolutionists about interpretation of the Noah's Ark tale. They waste time on a theology scarce different from monkish quarrels as to those angels on the point of a needle. Meantime, the never ceasing weekend of drunken driver deaths. And the tale of a teenager who excused his series of burglaries with "a fellow gets bored with television and just has to have some real thrills!" Whose duty was it to teach him that

> "God's in His Heaven
> All's well with the World?"

> You believe in God, for your part? ay? that He who makes,
> Can make good things from ill things, best from worst,
> As men plant tulips upon dunghills when
> They wish them finest.   (E. B. Browning—Aurora Leigh)

"Happy is the man that findeth wisdom, and the man that getteth understanding: for the merchandise of it is better than the merchandise of silver, and the gain thereof than fine gold." Proverbs 3:13-14.

"We picture Buddha seated in a lotus, to remind us it could flower beautifully from the darkness of the pond's stinking muck." (This said a saffron-robed priest to this author at Temple of the Tooth, Kandy, Ceylon.)

GOD'S PROVIDENCE HOUSE, IN CHESTER

This venerable dwelling was the only one whose occupants lost no one to the Black Death. It reminds one that we Occidentals have come, through research, to enjoy much during a comparatively brief span of years.

Gardens have solaced men through the centuries that became milleniums. We Occidentals learned their value perhaps rather recently. This author keeps before him on his skyscraper office wall an etching We-2 picked up years ago in England. It is "God's Providence House", in Chester. It is a reminder that the Black Death so ravaged that city, once a Roman camp, that this one dwelling only entirely escaped. At that time what we now call "Western Europe" was submerged in biological illiteracy as today still is most of China, Hindustan, Iran, Egypt, as, indeed, was Puerto Rico until the Spanish flag was lowered, about a half century ago.

We are proud of our own national power. Is it not based on the work of our researchists, mostly of pioneer stock? They interpreted God-in-Nature, in woodland, in prairie, on mountains high. They still see Him in our gardens. We cannot hope, however, our program will continue if we persist in that race-suiciding which is characteristic of Americans to creative minds. Groups of the leadership type tend mostly toward extinction. Families of these contain 2, 1, 0 kiddies. Meantime morons multiply like rabbits. This spells rapid rotting of our civilization.

THE BLACK DEATH

INDEX

A

Acacia 206-222
Adolphus, Gustavus 285
Africa 5
Alaska 58
Albinos 174
Algae 44-118-231
Algonkian 44
Alhambra 24
Aliens 267
Allah 68
Allamanda 63
Allenby 94
Almonds 95
American Coalition 300
American Know How 128-295
Amerind 143
"Anarkali" 8
Andorra 2
Anglo-Egyptian Sudan 5
Angor-Wat 9-89
Animal, Social 169
Ant, Argentine 152
Antelope, Pronghorn 103
Anzacs 6
Appian Way 25
Apricots 10
Araucanias 16
Arizona 48
Armenian Camps 292
Artichoke 64-65
Asparagus 77
Astronomical illiteracy 282
Athens 25
Atomic secrets 243
At-one-ment 313
Attar-of-Roses 92
Australia 44-75-222-241
Avocados 50
Aztecs 80-191

B

Babylon 25
Bacon, Francis 93-177-184-279
Bacon's Essays 139
Bamboo 100
Bamboo Curtain 228
Bat clan 176
Bat, hoary 175
Bachelor Tax 128
Bees, carpenter 224
Bees, native 149
Beirut 123
Benares 33
Berbers 65
Bethlehem 254
"Bible Toter" 74-210
Big Trees 58
Bing of Singapore 185
Biological illiteracy 282
Biological-illiterates 300
Birch Woods 140

Bird Behavior 158
Bird, incredible 257
Bird Rock 163
Bird sanctuary 159
Birdsong 163-164
Birth Control 192
Birthrate 92
Birthrates, Differential 171
Bison 103
Blackfeet 191
Blackfellows 307
Black-sheep 176
Bloom, (succession of) 217
Blundering Idealists 235-300
Boerboeder 114
Botanical Garden 8
Bougainvillea 107-283
Brahmin 16
British Columbia 44
Brittany 27-67
Brontosaurus 178
Bronze Age 249
Browning 318
Bubonic Plague 185
Buitenzong 8
Bullethawk 176
Bullfighting 228
Burbank, Luther 75-117-233
Burma 8
Butterfly tongues 145

C

Calaveras, North 145
Calendula 72-124
California Church Council 230
Cambrian 44
Camels 8-62-94-130
Camouflage 172-259-265
Camp Sacramento 299
Canary Islands 168
Cannonfodder 247
Cantonese 14
Capitalism 163
Capone, Scarface Al 136-235-243
Carib-Amerind 308
Carnation Breeding 245
Caucasians 81
Cemetery 75
Censorship 286
Central Pacific Railroad 14
Ceylon 8-211
Champollian 254-290-291
"Chanticleer" 161
Chaparral Oak 271
Charles V 24
Chaucer 221
Cheney, Dr. Ralph 49
Cherry Festival 17
"Chicory Ranch" 189-190
Child Labor 124
Chin dynasty 44
China 8-12-98-129-135-244
Chinatown 198-209-281
Chinese Ideographs 289

INDEX

Chlorophyll 206
Christianity 168
Chromosome 177
Chrysanthemum 60-145-152
Cinerarias 168
City Planning 68-299
Civic Reform 299
Class Warfare 230
Clemenceau 27
Cloud Forest 278
Coal Age Plant................................42
Coast Redwoods 58
Coat of Arms 60
Cockerell, Dr. T. A........140-142-149
Code de la Famille........................128
Colombia 194
Color 205
Color charm 203
Color in foods................................172
Color variants 174
Colorado Desert 292
Coloration, Disruptive 265
Columbus 152
Communism 163
Comorants 11
Composites' cooperation 224
Condor 257
Confederate grey 173
Confucius 76-177-258-300
Conservation 101
Constantinople 181-229
Constitution 169
Cooper, Fenimore 103
Cooperation 227-228-229-231
Cooperation, Chinese 228
Coptic 291
Cosmetics 205
Courtship 161
Covered Wagon 2-180-211
Crater National Park....................58
Cress, Hoary 235
Cretaceous Trees 49
Crime 293
CroMagnon 223
Crown of Thorns............................254
Cryptomeria 47
Cuba 188
Cycads 47
Cypresses 175
Czarevitch 186
Czechoslovakia 227

D

Dachert, Papa 202
Damascus 8-122
Dandelions 223
Daphne Path 212
Darwin 89-115-139-154-158-188-249
Date Garden 214
Dawn Goddess 96
Decay 256
Declaration of Independence......169
Deforestation 252
Deglet Noors 10

Delphiniums 2
de Medici, Catherine............27-186
Demosthenes 115
Devonian 44
DeVries 233
Differential Birthrates Law......255
Dimetricon 178
Diogenes 178
Displaced Persons..........62-192-292
Domestic Science 299
Duelling Ground 225
"Duppies" 307
Dutch Flat 250
"Dutch Flat Swindle"..................14

E

Ebony 50
Ecuador 182
Edelweiss 60
Education 252
Egalatie philosophy 283
Ego 161
Egrets 170
Egypt 59-130-193
Egyptians 291
Elfin Forests 186
Empire Day 199
Eric the Red................................152
Esthonia 227
Eschscholtzia 285
Everglades 170
Everglades National Park
252-275-278
Eucalyptus 144
Eugenics 101-188-256
Eugenics Pamphlets 265
Eurasian 83
Extinction 45-50-252

F

Fairhaven 137
Faith 311
Fallen Leaf Lake............................16
Family Code 128
Family, 3-child 168
Famine 102-107
Farrolone 255
Fear 168
Feathers 171
Fecundity 103-131-185-255
Feminism 190-191
Fern seed 44
Fig milk 64
Figs 65-180
Figtree 308
Filaree 122-250
Fingernails 12
Finland 76
"500 Year Plan"..................192-307
Flavoring 212
Flickers 160-173

INDEX

Flocking 169-270
Florissant 140-142
Flottenverein 154
Flower-color 172
Flower decoration 219
Flowers, edible 65
Flowers, Language of 58
Flower-names 263
Flying fish dinners 239
Flying Foxes 114
Folktales 60
Food 215
Foodstuffs 77
Footprints 158
Forest Genetics Institute 91
Fort Ross 285
Fossil birds 157
Fox-God 11
France 5-60-78-212-247
Francis I 27
Frankfurt/a/M. 3
Fremont 180
"Fremontia" 180
French Revolution 60-284
Frontier 188
Fruit Fly, Oriental 267
Fruit Market 97
"Frye, Hugo N." 314
Fuchs, Klaus
 62-103-232-239-243-267-292
Fuchs, Dr. Leonard 284
"Fuchsia" 33-284
Fungi 88
Fuzzy-Wuzzy 6

G

Gallatin 179
Galton, Sir Francis 89
Gambling 242
Ganges 16
Gangster 292
Garden, Alhambra 24
Garden Berry 82
Garden, Botanical 155
Garden, Chinese 13
Garden City, Eugenical 202
Garden Clubs 17
Garden-Color Psychology .. 30
Garden dividends 314
Garden, Linneaus' 181
Garden of the Generalife ... 24
Garden Therapy 100
Gardenias 73
Gardening, Moslem 24
Gardening Persian 10
Gardens, French 26
Gardens, German 30
Gardens, Hanging 3-25
Gardens, Holland's 28
Gardens, Italian 25
Gardens, Japanese 20-21
Gardens, Moslem 6
Gardens, Tuilleries 27

Gardens, window 66-67
Geisha Girls 136
Geological illiteracy 282
German roadside forestation ... 31
Gifted child 233-254-290
Ginko 46
Glacier National Park 197
Goddess Fecundity 11
God-in-Nature 213-215-259
Goethe Bank 225
Goethe, J. W. von 3
Goethehaus 3-172
Gold Belt 181
Gold Rush 183-204-249
Goldfinches 168
Grand Canyon National Park ... 140
Grand Moguls 10
Grasse, Count de 212
Grasses 76
"Great American Desert" ... 73-180
Great Salt Lake 180
Greece 129
Green Church 229
Greeks 247
"Green Thumb" 287
Greenland 2-50-58
Grenoble 290
Gresham's Law 113
Guatemala 63-86-218
Gunga Din 237
Gypsy moth 216

H

Harem 68
Hasheesh 245
Hawaii National Park 58
Hayford 63
Henry, Patrick 318
Herb Gardens 78
Herbs 77
Heredity 185
Hesiod 205
Hertwig 145
Highpowers 249
Hindustan 10-60-102-107-
 113-115-135-179-192-307
Hobby 263
Holland 67-114
Hollyhocks 2
Hong Kong 245
Hopi 89
Horseradish 78
Housefinches 168
Hugo, Victor 42-196
Human Genetics 193
Hummingbird Sanctuary ... 252
Hummingbirds 92-175-252
Hungary 227
Hunger Strike 193
Hydraulic Monitors 184
"Hymn to the Dawn" 16
Hyphenate propaganda 232
Hyphenates 103

I

Iceland poppies 272
Immigration 103-232-239-276
Immigration Code 130
Immigration Quota Law 192
Immigration Study Commission
                                  294
Incas 191-304
Indo-China 258
Insects 107-140
I.Q. 84-179
Iowa Hill 183
Iridescence 265
Iris Genetics 217
Iron Curtain 228
Isis 124
Italy 2

J

Jade 219
Jaeger, Dr. E. C. 75
Jakfruit 123
Jamaica 44-185
Jardins Ungemach 109-202
Java 44-96
Jedediah Smith State Park 211
Jerusalem 94
Johnson Grass 132
Jordan, Dr. David Starr 290
"Joshua Trees" 255
Jungle 231-258-276-308
Juratrias 46-143

K

Kaffeeneons 229
Kalavala 73
Kamakatzies 176
Kanari Trees 133
Kandy 8
Kant 32-115-316
Karachi 245
Katlyn Massacre 227
Kenya 5
Kew Gardens 2-283
Khyber Pass 294
Kindergarten 299
Kings Canyon National Park 58
Kipling 58-134-170-221
Kiva 254
Klamath 132
Kleingartenvertrieb 195-311
Klondike 173
Kohja folktales 302
Koran 7
Korea 98-135-194-216-230
Kulaks 227

L

Lacquer Bridge 16
Lahore 67
Lakedwellers 245
Lao Tze 177-258-300
Lapland 83
Lassen National Park 58
Latvia 227
Laughlin, Dr. H. H. 235-244
Lavender 213
Lavoiser 186
Lebanon 195
Lepidodendron 45
"Les Miserables" 196
Letterwriter 297
Lettuce, prickly 148
Lewis and Clark 73
Lithuania 227
"Lobster Claw" 137
Locust, honey 65
Lotus 13
Louvre 27
Love 168-203-225
"Loveapple" 86
Lust-for-Power 228

M

Madagascar 212
Madam Curie 161
Madonna 124
Maeterlinck 117-151
Magna Charta 181
"Maidenhair Tree" 46
Mallophaga 161
Manchuria 11
Mandarin 198
Manhattan 103
Manual Training 298
Maori 90
Marestail 45
Marigolds 168
Marihuana 245-294
Marjoram 77
Marriage 14
Marriage Consultation Centers .. 138
Martyrs 73
Marxism 230
Massenpsychologie 183
Mating 163
McCarran-Walter Immigration
  Code 292
Mecca 9
Mediterranean 309
Merejowski 191
Metasequoia 49
Mexico 180-188-218
Midnight Sun 67
Miller, Dr. Loye 157
Millet 90
Mint 77
Moa 103
Mohammed I 24

INDEX

Mojedska Falls 179
Moon-planting 184
Morning Glory 316
Morocco 8-90
Moron 92
Moslems 7-94
Mother 191
Mother, Heroic 168
Mother Nature 230-246-265-286
Museum 155
Museum, Home 62
Mushrooms 56
Mussolini-complex 178
Mutants, Human 233
Mycologist 56

N

Names, bird 281
Narcotics 245
National Forests 31-223
National Parks 58
National Parks' Interpretive
  Movement 300
Nats 186-307
Nature's Laws 214
Nature Study 69
Nature Study Class 171
Nature Study Field Excursions .. 310
Neanderthaloids 245
Nebuchadnezzar 3
Negro drums 6
Negro, Jamaica 242
Neighborliness 95
Nepalese 242
Nest making 163
Netherlands 114
Never-Never 272-307-309
New England 171
New South Wales 75
New Zealand 149
Nicaragua 194
Niche 145-204-266-269-271-
  273-275-278
Nikko 16-129
Nile 94-237
Nineveh 3
Noblesse oblige 312
Nordics 306
North China 252
Norway 67
Nuremberg 33

O

Oak "apples" 151
Ocotillo 204
Oleanders 63-92
Olympic Games 123
Opium 244-245
Oranges 10-93-211
Orchids 70-161
Ordivician 44
Organgrinder 228

Oriental Rug Motifs 7
Orinoco Jungles 143
Orphanage Farm, Sacramento
  137-311
Orveito 78
Osborne 193
Overpopulation
  127-131-185-192-194
Overurbanization 194
Oxford 73

P

Pah Utes 307
Painted Desert 47-48-89
Paleobotany 58
Palestine 5-84
Palm Springs Museum 149
Pamphlet 133
Panama 140-170
Panhandle 3
Pansy-breeding 26
Parachuting 275
Paraguay 194
Parasitism 144-292
Parks 98
Parks (River) 69
Parmentier 60
Pasteur 161-186
"Patent Office" 230
Peacemakers 169
Peach 93
Peacock, California 157
Pecans 95
Pecos 3
Pelicans 314
Penicillum 186
Peonies 12-61-100-312
Perfumery 212
Peridenya 8
Permafrost 83
Peru 86-219
Pest Resisters 216
Petrified Forest 16-48
Pharoahs 80
Philippines 124
Philosophy of Rest 199
Phoenix 177
"Pidgin" English 14
Pilostyles 75
Pinchot, Governor 101
Pine Hybrids 91
Pines, Stone 25
Plato 178
Playground 123
Point Lobos Park 163
Polyandry 256
Pomegranate 68-73-93
"Pomegranate Blossom" 8
Potato 60
Poverty, Reduction of 177-186
Propaganda 182
Protestantism 169
"Pseudo-Anthropology" 299
Ptolemy 291

INDEX

Public opinion 198
Publicity 207
Pueblo 90
Puenemuende 72
Puerto Ricans 242
Pumpernickel 90
Pumps 288
Punjab 8
Pyrenees 2

Q

Quail 163-169
Quota Acts 103-232-291-300

R

Rabbit 241
Radish, wild 132
Ranches 203
Rattan 276
Redwoods League 210
Regimentation 2
Registration of Aliens 232
Reindeer 83
Reproduction 115
Researchists 318
"Revolt" 63
Rhodesia 129
Rice 90
Rice growing 197
Ricepaper tree 50
River Jordan 298
Roadside Forestry 299
Rosales 269
Rosegardens 199
Rosemary 77
Roses 61
Rosettes 250
Rothenburg 74
Roumania 227
Russia 243
Russian Concentration Camps 292
Russo-Japanese War 46

S

Sabertooth 157
Sacramento 73
Sacramento Church Council 230
Sacramento-San Joaquin Valley
.... 180
Sagas 73
Sahara 65
Sahara Desert 81
St. Francis 155-174
St. Joachimsthal 161
Samaritans 310
San Domingo 283
Sand dunes 272
Sassafras 50
Saturation 241

Scotland 2
Scurvy 284
Selection 237-286
Selection, Artificial 86
Selection, Natural 86-249
Selection, Research 243
Selection, Sexual 118
Sequoia National Park 58
Sermon on the Mount 309
Sex 215
Shade-lovers 268
Shading, Obliterative 265
Siberia 58
Siderophyll 206
Sierra Nevadas 180
Silurian 44
Sitka Spruce 16
Slavery 13
Slums 110
Smear strategy 299
Smith, Jedediah 32-74-179-180-210
Somaliland 8-9-207
Sociology 221
Sociology, avian 169
Solutre 76
Spain 2-10
Spiders 154
Spitzbergen 58
Spy 232
"Squaw Men" 84
Stalin 102
Star Thistle 239
State Capitol Planning
  Commission 299
Stegosaurus 178
Sterculiaceae 180
Stoddard, Dr. Lothrop 63-283-286
Stork, Asphalt 157
Strassburg 56-232
Stratford-on-Avon 2
Strawberry 99
Submarine 176
Succotash 89
Sugar beets 77
Sun-energy 237
Sun-lover 268
Sunflowers 201-231
Sunworship 304
Superstition 184-186
Suttee 135
Sutter's Fort Park 298
Survival
  131-230-231-250-256-270-286
Survival Mechanisms 215
Switzerland 58-67-78
Sweden 56-179
"Sylvan Islands" 58

T

Talented, the 269
Tanagers 151
Tamarisk 298
Teagarden 80
Teak 308

INDEX

Telegraph Pole "beauty"............21
Temple of the Tooth.................319
Terman, Dr. Lewis....................233
Thayer 173-264-266
Thistle 65-243
Thrift 230
Tibet 80-88-241-256
Timbuctu 7-92-290
Tomatoes 77
Tomato, wild 85-86
Trial-and-Error 179
Triassic 47
Tricerotops 178
Trilobites 141-142
Turkey, California 157
Turkey-in-Asia 129
Tulip 29
Tundraberries 83
Tyrannosaurus 178

U

Underpopulation 126

V

Vavilov 186
Vedic hymns 73
Vegetable seeds 77
Vegetables, green 181
Vegetarians 76
Vice, Commercialized 154
Viking 2-242-259
Violet 185-212
Virginia 171
Visigoths 246
Vitamins 181
Vladivostok 12
Volga Pears 181
von Goethe, J. W........................3
von Siebold 12
von Tirpitz 264
Vosges 56
Vulcanism 209

W

Wages 292
Wallflowers 233
Wanderlusting seeds 122
War 154-227
Waratah 60-303
Washington 212
Wasps 151
Water Jars 293
Water Vendor 294
Waxwings 159
Weather prediction 71
Wedding 190
Weed Stalks 101
Weeds 132
Weeds, human 241-245
Weimar 172
Western Front 233
Weyang-Weyang 96
Whitechapel 110
Will-to-Survive 102
Wisteria 61
Woman's Council 68
Woman's Suffrage
189-191-193-195
Women 188
World War II..............266-270

X

Xanthophyll 206

Y

"Yellow Peril" 208
Yellow ribbon 205
Yellow Therapy 208
"Yellowhammers" 173
Yellowstone National Park......58
Yorkshire 72
Yosemite National Park..........58
Young Turk Movement.........302
Yuccas 271

Z

Zeilstrebigkeit 102-123-232